TRUE WEST

TRUE
WEST

Authenticity and the American West

Edited by
William R. Handley and Nathaniel Lewis

UNIVERSITY OF NEBRASKA PRESS • LINCOLN AND LONDON

Publication of this volume was assisted by
The Virginia Faulkner Fund,
established in memory of Virginia Faulkner,
editor-in-chief of the University of Nebraska Press.

A portion of chapter 1
was previously published in
Unsettling the Literary West: Authenticity, Authorship, and Western American Literature,
by Nathaniel Lewis
(University of Nebraska Press, 2003).
Reprinted with permission of University of Nebraska Press.

A portion of chapter 4
was previously published in
Marriage, Violence, and the Nation in the American Literary West,
by William R. Handley
(Cambridge University Press, 2002).
Reprinted with permission of Cambridge University Press.

Library of Congress Cataloging-in-Publication Data
True West : authenticity and the American West / edited by William R. Handley
and Nathaniel Lewis.
p.   cm. — (Postwestern horizons)
Includes bibliographical references (p.   ) and index.
ISBN 0-8032-2410-9 (hardcover : alk. paper)
1. American literature—West (U.S.)—History and criticism.   2. West (U.S.)—
Historiography.   3. West (U.S.)—In literature.   4. Realism in literature.
I. Handley, William R., 1963–   II. Lewis, Nathaniel, 1962–   III. Series.
PS561.T78   2004
810.9′3278—dc22   2003019518

CONTENTS

ILLUSTRATIONS

ix

ACKNOWLEDGMENTS

We gratefully acknowledge financial support for this book project from St. Michael's College and the University of Southern California. We would like to thank the readers of the University of Nebraska Press for their very helpful and encouraging comments and Ladette Randolph for her energetic support throughout. Bill thanks Lynn Wardley and Harvard University's (formerly named) Center for Literary and Cultural Studies for providing a forum for the germination of his essay on Willa Cather. For realizing that we really should start an intellectual conversation, given our shared interests, Larry Buell has our gratitude. Not just a book but a valued friendship developed from that first lunch at Bartley's burger joint—one of the few remaining "authentic" businesses left in Harvard Square. Conferences of the Western Literature Association and the American Literature Association have been productive workshops for the development of many of this volume's essays. Finally, we express our deep appreciation to our contributors for their patience and commitment throughout this project.

INTRODUCTION

William R. Handley and Nathaniel Lewis

True West explores the multifaceted meanings, uses, and critiques of "the authentic" in western American literary and cultural history. There are few terms at play in the history of this vast region that have as wide a reach and relevance, and there is no other region in America that is as haunted by the elusive appeal, legitimating power, and nostalgic pull of authenticity, whether with regard to ethnicity, cultural artifacts, or settings. For more than two centuries, western history and western landscapes have overwhelmed much of America's literary and artistic expression. Readers and critics have consistently evaluated western literature and other forms of representation against what historian Patricia Nelson Limerick calls, with some amusement, "the Real West." Familiar critical terms like "mythological," "antimythological," "realistic," and "nostalgic" abound, and often their users make unexamined assumptions about what is authentic, what is real, what is true. We feel the need for this volume because, in the fields of western American literary and cultural studies, rhetorics and critiques of authenticity circulate with the ubiquity of oxygen in the atmosphere—and are often invisible to both marketers and scholars of the West who nevertheless depend upon them. Examining the conceit of western authenticity is, to contemporary critics, the revisionary equivalent of historians' reevaluation of Frederick Jackson Turner's frontier thesis. It challenges many assumptions we make about western writing and opens the door to an important new chapter in western literary history and cultural criticism— while returning us to some old, recalcitrant problems in the history and culture of the American West.

The essays in this volume examine how the concept of authenticity is used to invent, test, advertise, and read the West. Lately, Limerick writes in *The Real West*, "the search to distinguish 'the Real West' from 'the Fake West'" has become a nearly impossible quest, a game with ever-changing rules and no winner. She concludes that "the Real West and the Fake West end up tied together, virtually Siamese twins sharing the same circulatory system." The doctors trying to separate those twins, performing what she calls "intellectual surgery," are historians; the "system," however, is cultural, produced by "creative, literary, artistic, and commercial energy."[1] Historians have traditionally served as proprietors of the authentic, examining history's influence on the West's literary and artistic cultures. Yet to literary critics, as Forrest G. Robinson and others have demonstrated, the relationship between history and representation in the American West is dramatically complicated and the distinction between them far less easy to maintain—not simply because our postmodern age places notions of "truth" in quotation marks.[2]

Our imitative use of the phrase "True West," the title of Sam Shepard's well-known play, neither denigrates nor celebrates the notion of an authentic, real West. Just as Shepard's play refuses to take sides between the West of smog and freeways or the West of cowboys and horses, we recognize that the very indeterminacy of the terms *West, history, literature,* and *reality* is a central component of the region's unfolding cultural legacy. As Neil Campbell writes, "The American West has always been, by the very nature of its mythic representations . . . a simulation reproducing images conforming to some already defined, but possibly non-existent, sense of Westness."[3] The most continuous story of the West, then, is neither the (Old) clash of civilization and savagery nor the (New) legacy of conquest, but competing claims of cultural authenticity, even of belonging—in the sense both of an original "at home-ness" and of possession. Seen in this light, even the claims of Manifest Destiny relied upon a rhetoric of authenticity in that divine predestination is itself an ontological claim to a sacred sense of origin as much as it is a claim on a future. By replacing that sense of authenticity with one associated with a more true account of the past, contemporary historians and cultural critics continue and broaden, but do not dispel, the associative meanings of western authenticity.

Indeed, the association of the term authenticity with "truth" is a misleading one, because authenticity so often refers to the capacity of any author, whether novelist or historian, and any artifact, whether artistic or archaeological, to bespeak originality. And originality has little authority or meaning without being copied. While the trope of the "hyperreal"—one that European critics largely generated in western American contexts—refers to a copy without an original, the authentic is an original that has many copies. Indeed, the "authentic" gains authority the more it is copied. The New Western History, for example, claims originality at the same time that it creates a following: influence is the paradoxical (and often desired) result of originality. Yet influence is also a burden that Americans have for so long sought to shake culturally from their shoulders (usually by abjuring European models) and a burden within any marketplace of new ideas and products under capitalism. The revolution Turner caused in American historiography was propelled by his notion that American institutions and ways of life were not derivative of European "germs." Historians ever since have sought to break away from Turner's influence, and yet the "new" becomes perpetually old the more it is imitated. More than "truth," authenticity is associated with authority and originality, and it is under those latter terms that history and representation in the American West so often meet in vexed ways, not only in the academy but in popular culture and national memory.

At the barest level of representation, whether in the writing of history or fiction, the *word* is the shared medium that, as Theodor Adorno argues in *The Jargon of Authenticity*, blocks us from historical reality even as it implies access to that reality: "History does intrude on every word and withholds each word from the recovery of some alleged original meaning, that meaning which the jargon [of authenticity] is always trying to track down."[4] In this sense, Patricia Limerick is right to argue that "the Real West and the Fake West end up tied together, virtually Siamese twins sharing the same circulatory system." By this logic, that circulatory system is representation itself, the origins of which are untrackable, its progeny legion.

One might ask, however: What does Adorno have to do with it? How "inauthentic" a theorist for understanding the American West! Even though he lived in Los Angeles for a period, he's not "native." (How few, indeed, are— such is the legacy of conquest, and such is the necessary fiction of our continuity with any ancestral past.) Adorno was writing against a strain of German existentialism that, while seeking the freedom and autonomy of the self in an inauthentic and regimented world, helped to obscure the real social relations from which it sought to emancipate people. In the literature of the American West, the first-person authorial voice is back—as if it were the most natural form of writing. Even the historians have returned to representations of their own "authentic" experience as a kind of original claim on their version of history. They have also, as in Limerick's image of the Siamese twins, become both literary artists and literary critics, as if tacitly acknowledging that historiographical authority is increased rather than threatened by incorporating the lessons of literary and historiographical theories of representation.

The relation between history and representation, which includes the relation between history and its representations, is the most crucial subject for critics of the American West to engage. Mark Twain became a writer in *Roughing It* by making that relationship his theme, by examining, in a much less naïvely subjective fashion than many writers today, his experience in relationship to everything he had read. He gained his authority as a writer by consistently undermining it, self-conscious about the fact that he was adding to the literary stew by creating himself as a literary figure. He became a western original by declaring himself a fabricator who cared little for facts—those nuggets of the "real" West that eastern readers longed for. In contemporary political battles over cultural representation, a very different relation between author and text emerges, one that presumes that the text is the authentic reflection of the authentic author. The disparagement by some of any Indian writer who does not live close to the reservation is a symptom of this imagined relation among author, text, and the social sphere. But then who is authentic or original: the writer who speaks for the group and/or history, or the writer who refuses to do so? Within the competing answers to such a question lies the value of this volume. "The interested parties who use the jargon [of authenticity] as a means of power," Adorno wrote of the Germans, "or depend upon their public image for the jargon's social-psychological effect, will never wean themselves from it. There are others who will be embarrassed by the jargon. Even followers who believe in authority will shy away from ridiculousness, as soon as they feel the fragile nature of that authority to which they look for support." [5]

Of course, much is at stake politically in both the use and the critique of authenticity, especially with regard to identity and the struggle to correct ongoing structural inequities in society. When the Chicano movement invokes the myth of Aztlán, for example, one would have to put on historical blinders to see no important political and ethical distinctions between its romanticized invocation of origins and the myth of American exceptionalism. Indeed, much of the history of conquest and dispossession on this continent has involved the clash of competing narratives that give peoples and nations a sense of legitimacy; in the ensuing struggles for power, new narratives emerge to justify and energize both conquest and resistance. In these ongoing political and social debates, it is important, we believe, to subject even the most cherished narratives to critical reflection, recognizing without cynicism that while we use and need narratives that lend meaning and purpose to social life, narratives can tend to use us if we do not reflect upon them. When James Joyce argued that "paternity is a fiction," for example, he did not make the general problem of paternity—one's cultural, national, and religious inheritance or legacy—simply vanish; but he did denaturalize it in a way that allows one to understand, for example, how a notion such as America's "Founding Fathers," while not real, is no less forceful as a way in which Americans tell stories about themselves.

Most of this volume's essays refuse to judge a text's or author's authenticity but rather study how the idea of authenticity is deployed. What kinds of claims do authors and artists make about their work? How has the notion of authenticity haunted, hindered, or benefited Native American cultural production? What kinds of interpretive strategies are necessary to read history through aesthetically complicated, fictionalizing texts that stand in for "the real West"? And how does the reliance on and celebration of western landscape inform or intimidate the writer's imagination? Similar, related questions about textual and cultural authenticity are being asked in humanities departments across the country with regard to a range of texts, canons, and identities. This collection demonstrates how such questions constitute not only the central discourse of contemporary western studies but of much of the West's cultural history as well, burdened as the West has been by the popular and imperialist notion that it made Americans American.

As laden with meaning as it is difficult to define, authenticity is, like the American West itself, a hotly contested and widely deployable concept in American culture. While the definition and meaning both of authenticity and of the American West are debatable and shifting, they bear an informing relationship to each other. The "New" Western History, for example, assumes in its appellation the sense not of "recent" or "different" but of "real" or "accurate"—old western history is, by contrast, distorting and one-sided. Yet many Americans would say that the "old" West is the real, authentic West—the West of ghost towns and tepees, cacti and covered wagons, as opposed to the "new" West of freeways and urban sprawl. The ways in which words like "old" and "new" can, depending on their context, contradictorily evoke both the authentic and the inauthentic suggest the very malleability and arbitrariness of the concept of authenticity, a concept that itself assumes not arbitrariness but a time-tested hierarchy of value, not change but durability. Given that the West has undergone such immense and constant change in its history and seen the clash of so many conflicting values, the cultural fascination with notions of western authenticity represents, if not a reactionary response to history, then an almost willed form of historical amnesia or denial.

Indeed, long before white Americans located in the process of western settlement the source of a purportedly universal American character and the significant difference of American history in relation to that of the Old World, they sought to create an authentic national identity that would justify what was new about their experience and historical significance. The notion of American exceptionalism has long carried with it the ideological assumption that America's original difference is grounded in historical truth, the "truth" that America is not a bastard copy of Europe, even that it marks the highest stage in the history of civilization. Like the phrase "Manifest Destiny," authenticity may only seem to have a transparent, manifest meaning because it was or is widely embraced; as such it has social force even if it lacks legitimacy or clarity. And for popular interpreters of American experience in the West, the West has often been the legitimating source and sanctifying ground of American authenticity. With the grandeur of its landscapes seeming to point for many in the nineteenth century to providential design, and with the "rugged individualism" and democratic strength of character needed, according to Turner, to settle the wilderness, "westering" in the vast spaces of the American West came to stand in for white Americans' notion about what essentially defined their authentic difference. Such images were as rhetorically and politically useful to Ronald Reagan as they continue to be for the selling of tobacco and automobiles.

If it is Nature or the natural landscape that serves as the sanctifying or authenticating stage of American western experience, then human cultural "artifacts" in the West are already one step removed from their authentic source and influence: the wilderness. When we preserve the wilderness, we are preserving something more authentic than civilization or progress; as Thoreau wrote in "Walking," equating the West with wildness, "in Wildness is the preservation of the world." Native American cultures, whose indigenous histories often suggest a more authentic "connection" than the pasts of recent transplants, may also locate spiritual meaning and value in nature and perhaps for this reason serve the "imperialist nostalgia" (to borrow Renato Rosaldo's term) for that which imperialism has irrevocably altered if not destroyed.[6] ("Come to where spirits are real," says promotional literature for a video collection about Native American spiritual beliefs.) Whether it be past ways of life, distant landscapes, untainted but always corruptible nature, or the promise of spiritual fulfillment or material wealth, the horizons of authenticity—that which limits and thereby enables the desire for it—are always somewhere else in space or time, like F. Scott Fitzgerald's famous dream of the New World at the end of *The Great Gatsby* that "year by year recedes before us" as we are "borne back ceaselessly into the past." That dream, which seems at once to authenticate Jay Gatsby's significance even as it shows him up to be a fake, is by nature elusive, always occurring somewhere else: "He did not know," Nick Carraway says, "that it was already behind him, in that vast obscurity beyond the city, where the dark fields of the republic rolled on under the night." That Nick prefaces this vision by saying, "I see now that this has been a story of the West, after all" suggests that not only is the significance of American history located in the West, the West itself is always moving somewhere else and stands as the very dislocation at the heart of the American dream of progress in the wilderness. As Turner described "American life" in his frontier thesis, so might one describe the notion of authenticity: "movement" is its "dominant fact." [7]

A national culture's sense of its historical distinction—its sense of its origin and of its future, of its place in space and time—determines or limits the meaning of authenticity. Yet the authentic is always, like an asymptotic line, approaching but never meeting the limit it nears. Such is the case with those values or character traits at the heart of America's more popular images of experience in the West: it is far easier to imagine where our values are missing than where they exist. Indeed, cultural values are easily defined, often in order to advertise something else, by their absence. The image of the Marlboro man seems to suggest individualism and freedom, but this is not the case with regard to what it means in reality to work as a cowboy in a difficult environment or what it means in reality to smoke and to acquire an addiction. By virtue of its distance from reality, this "authentic" Western image takes on a life of its own, preserved in a static realm beyond experience, beckoning us and leading us in circles that feed and thwart desire, into tautologies of identity and difference, as in the title of Harold Wright Bell's 1916 western, *When a Man's a Man*.

It would be meaningful to say that something is inauthentic only if authenticity is presumed to exist; but if "authenticity" is examined as a rhetorical figure or concept that works in and works on culture and society, then its "existence" is a kind of effect of desire, an effect of loss, or an effect of displacement. Concerning Walter Benjamin's notion of the "aura"—that mystic sense of originality possessed by the work of art before the age of mechanical reproduction—Adorno argued that "it is hardly an accident that Benjamin introduced the term at the same moment when, according to his own theory, what he understood by 'aura' became impossible to experience." [8] The "hyperreal," according to Umberto Eco and Jean Baudrillard, is presumed to be more real than the (nonexistent) real thing, the paradox inherent in the phrase "authentic reproduction." The ongoing frenzy for authenticity in American life and culture, from the authentic (smaller scale) reproductions of Venice and Paris in Las Vegas to the Mormons' 1997 sesquicentennial replication of the pioneer trek to Salt Lake City, does not indicate the profundity of Americans' connection to the past or to other places. Rather, it reveals how little has been represented in mass culture regarding the profound transformation of the West by America and its ramifications for the world, and how little of that transformation has been absorbed in the consciousness of the majority of Americans. Before the "frontier" had ceased to exist, Buffalo Bill's Wild West show was already touring the world, satisfying a desire for what General George Custer's wife described as a "most realistic and faithful representation of a Western life that has ceased to be." That we may judge Buffalo Bill's touring show as involving more artifice than authenticity is an index for how unstable our own notions of authenticity may one day seem to later generations.

True West offers both theoretical perspectives and specific literary and cultural analyses that have geographical and historical breadth. This collection is divided into four sections that investigate the cultural work of authenticity with regard to western American literary history, Native American cultures, visual culture, and the imagining of place. The essays range geographically from the Old Northwest of the Ohio Valley to the Canadian Prairies, Montana Rockies, and Buena Park's Entertainment Corridor in Southern California; and chronologically from early tourist narratives to the art of World War II Japanese-American internment camps to current environmental writing. The contributors display a considerable diversity of approaches and perspectives, including cultural anthropology and cultural geography, Native American studies, ecocriticism, art history, and gender studies. Once the force of authenticity is recognized as an omnipresent influence, suddenly every text, every topic, and every critical treatment is open to question. But realizing that authenticity is the oxygen of our critical environment does not necessarily give us more breathing room. That is, by emphasizing certain themes in this collection, we are not merely reproducing topics of current and ongoing interest to western critics, but risking as well a kind of authenticating act. We can only hope that this volume might serve to precipitate a far broader discussion of the role of authenticity in the western cultural and critical imagination.

8

This volume's first section opens our exploration of the construction of authenticity in western literary history. The very concept of a "western literary history" is almost unspeakably burdened, in large part by the occluded tension between the terms "literary" and "history." With implications for the subsequent development of western criticism and historiography, this tension is always already in play in western representation, informing the idea of "tradition" while erasing itself as it goes. At the very least, the force of authenticity has worked to obscure its own past: critics have tended to evaluate the historical realism of a work rather than examine the idea of historical realism itself. Don D. Walker, whose investigations into the fallacy of authenticity in the early 1970s now seem prophetic, wrote that "western literary criticism has for a long time been dominated by the historian's way of judgment." [9] Or, to put it differently, "history" overwhelms "literature" with the effect that the inevitable fissures and fractures, inherent in any literary tradition, seem to disappear behind a simple question: is the work true? If authenticity is recognized as a textual and cultural construction, however, then that question is itself a register of the work's context and effect. That "history" becomes contingent is only one result; more to the point, new narratives are opened up, revealing how authors and artists employ the idea of authenticity, and how in turn they are limited by it.

Simply put, discourses of authenticity have contributed to the constructions of canonicity, ethnicity, cultural nationalism, regional ideology, and gendered identities. The first two essays of this section implicitly examine divisions in literary history, often identified along the lines of East and West. Nathaniel Lewis traces the claim of authenticity back to an early wave of self-consciously western writing and criticism in the 1830s. Western authors such as James Hall and Timothy Flint used the claim of textual authenticity to legitimize their own work. In fact, they refused to acknowledge imaginative or stylistic authority, eastern attributes that might suggest inauthenticity, and thus they initiated a dependence on regional realism that set the stage for the troubled reception history of western writing that followed. Moreover, as Lisa MacFarlane suggests, in the nineteenth century the idea of "western literature" was inevitably a relative one: "The making of a 'true' West was inextricably intertwined with eastern representations, eastern expectations, and eastern desire." MacFarlane pursues this point by studying Henry Adams—a writer generally seen as quintessentially eastern—and his novel *Esther*. MacFarlane argues that Adams "tried to write a national allegory in *Esther*, and instead wrote an eastern narrative of western

cultural confrontation." In this way the novel is, surprisingly, a Western—
"that is, a meditation on relations between the East and the West."

MacFarlane emphasizes the role of gender in understanding the region-
alized tensions within literary history, and this approach is extended in the
section's final two essays. Alison Calder and William R. Handley consider
gender as a primary category for rethinking region, and in turn suggest that
the relation between regionalism and representation informs (if not determines) how we think of gender. In her essay on the demand for authenticity
in western Canadian writing, Calder repositions the geographical boundaries of the discussion. Calder argues that "the general demand for authenticity in 'regional' writings intersects with, and is increased by, the demand
for authenticity in 'Canadian' writings" to produce complex literary and
cultural results, including a critical distinction between Canadian and
American Wests. Ultimately, she argues, the preoccupation with landscape
as authentic icon has produced a myopia, relying on a reductive environmental determinism, ignoring other influences such as gender, race, class,
or ethnicity, and producing "an artificial tradition." Finally, William R.
Handley demonstrates in "'The West Authentic,' the West Divided" how
Willa Cather begins with a different set of assumptions about romance and
realism and the cultural value of the West from those she evolves after the
"discovery" of the Southwest and her subsequent determination to make
Nebraska not only a fit subject for her fiction but the authenticating ground
of her authorial self. At the same time, she writes against the fraudulent assumptions of a masculinist American West and its cultural authority. Her
authentic difference in portraying life on the plains carries with it a veiled
critique of the distortions of retrospective narratives of national identity in
their attempt to be true to authentic, lived experience.

Section 1 treats contested claims of cultural authority: how a country's
political and literary histories are shaped in part by the constant redefinition of such terms as margin and center, East and West, male and female,
nature and culture. The investigation of these misleading binaries is further
developed in section 2, in large part through a critique of ethnic "nativeness." Perhaps no dimension of western literary and cultural representation is so vexed, for in the popular imagination American Indians seem to
embody the authentic, even in their apparent remoteness (or "foreign-
ness") from quotidian Anglo experience. Euro-Americans "play Indian" (as
Philip J. Deloria and others argue) in an effort to access some sense of original America; the vision-quest and powwow have become widely favored

means of crossing cultural lines and embracing the real. Even if Indian "memory" (standing in for tribe, ancestry, nature, spirituality, and history) is "in the blood," it can be simulated through imitation, a Lamarckian adaptation to a postmodern erasure of identity. There is no escaping simulation; as Gerald Vizenor writes in *Manifest Manners*, "The most secure simulations are unreal sensations, and become the real without a referent to an actual tribal remembrance"—a simulacrum. "Tribal realities," he continues, "are superseded by simulations of the unreal." [10] Native Americans may themselves end up playing Indian, living in a hyperreal world where identity is always constructed in relation to a dominant culture. By this logic, the Indian becomes a hybridized figure "naturalized" only by a repeated "song and dance," a kind of performance of ethnicity. Yet still the figure is marginalized, made liminal by this interplay of authenticity and reproduction. Louis Owens writes that "it is at this disjunction between myth and reality that American Indian novelists most often take aim," and we might say that it is at this disjunction (between copy and original, history and narrative, illusion and reality) that the essays of this section take aim. [11] Each writer investigates the interstices of cultural and literary projection, the metaphorized space (as Christine Edwards Allred points out in her essay) between the Deep Woods and Civilization.

Thus, Drucilla Mims Wall writes that, in the heart of "the market-driven consumer," she finds "an unexamined acknowledgment of something needed, something lost that forms an intense longing for meaning, for connection to the authentic sacred in landscape," a connection problematically linked throughout American literary history to Native American cultures. Using a style that is itself a hybrid of scholarly and personal voices, Wall sets out to study "how mainstream Euro-American culture performs its continuing ambivalence about the land and its native people." In her essay on Charles Eastman, Christine Edwards Allred turns her attention to similar complexities: the political and social problems of defining "Real Indian Art." Allred shows how Eastman's developing understanding of Indian assimilation, progressivism, cultural relativism, and Sioux "purity" informed his autobiographical writings: "In the presence of competing culture concepts—evolutionary, relativistic—that disallowed Eastman's own 'real Indian' experience, his search for an authenticating culture concept necessarily occurred within, and defended, that ill-defined realm of cultural contact *between* the 'Deep Woods' and 'Civilization' that his autobiography's title seems to suggest he only traversed." Next, Nancy Cook studies the unstable public identity of Long Lance, widely known in the 1920s as a "Blackfoot Indian Chief" (in large part through his autobiography) and respected as a spokesman for Plains Indian culture, but who in fact was, by various accounts, an African American, mixed blood, or descendant of Indian slaves. Cook argues that in a world where the only "real" Indians were western ones, where "noble savages" looked like Plains Indians, Long's experience may be emblematic rather than merely eccentric. Finally, Susan Bernardin argues that such writers as Sherman Alexie, Gerald Vizenor, and Louis Owens "enter the authenticity game," suggesting how "discourses of authenticity might both empower and entrap, subvert and confirm, readers and readings of Native American literature." Bernardin remarks that "despite the recognition and publication of increasingly diverse Native American literary texts, Euro-America's fixation with selective indices of Indian authenticity delimits the kinds of texts circulating in national markets."

The third section approaches pictorial and photographic representations through which historical memory is negotiated. If Hollywood film has sought to "capture" the West as a place of movement or as an idea that can be relived, the very stillness of the visual image in painting and photography seems to call up the authentic pastness of the past.[12] Yet its historicity is both on display and hidden by what the frame delimits and excludes. Reading the visual past involves challenging questions about the artifice of the frame and the historicity of the visual. Gerald Vizenor, in his essay on Edward Curtis and the photographic record of Indian cultures, asks: "Why would natives pose to create a portrait simulation, a pictorial image not their own, for photographic adventurists who later nominate their pictures as the *real*, and the ethnographic documents of a vanishing race?" Vizenor goes on to consider this complex of presence and absence in Curtis's photography, remarking that "the absence of the natives is the simulated presence of the other in the narratives of cultural dominance." Of course, the attempt to shape a world through visual representation is always an act of interpreting that world as well. Thus Stephen Tatum, in his reading of Frederic Remington's 1905 painting *Coming to the Call*, is primarily concerned with teasing out the larger aesthetic operations of an artistic consciousness striving to realize an imaginative vision within the constraints posed by his own abilities and personality, by his culture's way of making sense of the world, and by the demands of the commercial marketplace. Tatum's essay argues that the painting expresses a strategic response to a dominant culture's class and gender anxieties about the definition and viability of masculine authority in the face of modernization's supposed betrayal of authentic experience. Melody Graulich examines a dramatically different kind of historical witnessing: the written and visual representation of World War II Japanese-American internment camps. The familiar big-sky western images (ranch fences, powerful cowboys, spatial expanses) are here altered by the fact of imprisonment: camp fences suggest spatial limitations, camp guards suggest a revised form of law-bringing. We are in a West defamiliarized by enclosure and captivity. Graulich argues that Nikkei writers and visual artists "provide, in effect, new captions and frames for old photographs, raising questions about the historical uses to which photographs have been put and about what photographs can help us to understand." Graulich shows how these representations reveal a contested West, and how regional and nationalist ideologies impose (once again) on western landscapes and peoples.

Section 4, finally, treats the construction of *place* in contemporary western nature writing, reconsidering ways in which landscape and environment inform writing, identity, and canonicity. (As Wallace Stegner wrote, "Western writing turns out, not surprisingly, to be largely about things that happen outdoors.") Indeed, the reception history of western writing suggests that landscape is the original source of the authentic: it shapes experience, produces the rugged western character, and ultimately directs representation. Of course, this conceit is not uniquely western; ecologists, ecopsychologists, and geographers have long considered the influence of the natural environment on individual and social identity, just as cultural critics have pondered in turn the degree to which nature itself is an ideological construction. Still, for a nation insistent on locating the authentic, the natural West was and is the manifestation of America, from the mountains to the prairies, spacious skies and amber waves of grain. The National Park system was conceived not for conservation of public lands but for tourists to behold the myth of America. As Alfred Runte has argued, Yellowstone in 1872, like Yosemite before it, "appealed to the nation as a cultural repository." [13] Throughout the twentieth century and into the twenty-first, western nature writers (such as John Muir, Mary Austin, John C. Van Dyck, Aldo Leopold, Edward Abbey, Terry Tempest Williams, and Gary Snyder) have investigated the relationships among culture, representation, and nature. And, over the past two decades or so, ecocriticism, the study of literature and the environment, has emerged (largely from within the folds of western literary criticism) to explore writing about place.

Ecocriticism is beginning to revolutionize scholarly reading practices, not only emphasizing the role of "nature" in American literature but also implicitly demanding social change through environmental awareness. These goals are not without risks, however, for to celebrate a deep ecological connection to place without careful deliberation and mindful action can produce, paradoxically, a naïve erasure of the complexities of biodiversity, regional diversity, cultural diversity, and literary representation. In short, we risk asserting an authenticity that essentializes place. Scott Slovic's essay, "Authenticity, Occupancy, and Credibility: Rick Bass and the Rhetoric of Protecting Place," frames these issues by rethinking the central questions of this collection. What does it mean to be a western writer or artist? What does it mean to be western? What does it mean to be *native*? What does it mean to "live in place"? Slovic writes, "I'd like to begin developing . . . an idea about the pervasive uncertainty in western environmental writing regarding sense of place and attachment to place and what I see as a parallel uncertainty about the 'place' of literature in our culture, about the potential social ramifications of environmental literature." Through a reading of Rick Bass's writings, Slovic proposes the idea of "literary occupancy," a way of writing and living in place, but argues that "authentic occupancy in the American West requires accepting our geography and our language as zones of tension."

In her essay "Authoring an Authentic Place: Environmental and Literary Stewardship in Stegner and Kittredge," Bonney MacDonald follows up on this spatialized idea of cultural and regional "zones of tension" by addressing the complex relationship between authorship and ecosystems. Where many ecocritics tend to challenge the hegemony of anthropocentrism, claiming that we must overcome our humanness in the name of biophilial interconnectedness, MacDonald investigates the idea of a "responsible anthropocentrism" through a reading of works by Wallace Stegner, William Kittredge, and Wendell Berry. Arguing that, at least for Stegner and Berry, "if you cannot acknowledge your own human needs and position, you cannot know how to regulate your living and your (responsible) use of your surroundings," MacDonald clears a space, at least metaphorically, for the role of rhetoric, "naming," and authorship in environmental practices. "The labor of authoring," she concludes, "opens up a dwelling place and helps us move into belonging." This crucial theme of "belonging" is central as well to Joanna Brooks's essay on authority and Mormon identity politics in Terry Tempest Williams's *Refuge*. Brooks's focus is the tension between authority

14

and genealogy in *Refuge*, considering ways in which Williams uses ideas of gender, "blood," and "nativism" (including Native American, Mormon, and western claims) to legitimize her development of a naturalist activism. Again, we return to some of this volume's central theoretical questions: do we construct our own sense of "belonging" through language, through institutions, or through genes, for example? Is one's "connection" to the genealogical past and to place "natural" or fictive? Do ancestral and regional origins "authenticate" the self or displace it?

The vital notion of place in western literature—a complex notion, as this section's essays reveal—tends to imply some shared conception of *natural* place: Oregon's Warner Valley, the Colorado Plateau, the Grand Canyon, the Yaak Valley. Indeed, the West is often symbolized in popular iconography from Bierstadt to beer commercials as big sky, big mountains, and big animals. Hsuan L. Hsu examines a radically different—but equally definitive—kind of place, Buena Park's Entertainment Corridor near Los Angeles, a series of tourist attractions, such as Knott's Berry Farm, Wild Bill's Western Diner Extravaganza, and the Covered Wagon Motel, that recreate western landscapes and histories as both reproducible commodity and as experientially authentic. Using theories of contemporary cultural studies and cultural geography, Hsu considers the Entertainment Corridor's advertised "exact replicas" and "authentic representations," noting the endless ironies of crowded ghost towns and alcohol-free "family saloons." Finally, then, authenticity itself becomes a kind of display, the main attraction of the funhouse. As Baudrillard wrote, "The impossibility of rediscovering an absolute level of the real is of the same order as the impossibility of staging an illusion. Illusion is no longer possible, because the real is no longer possible."[14]

Since the inception of this project, we have enjoyed conversations together about our own personal relationships to notions of authentic experience, including our experiences out West. While one of us was born in the West and both have traveled extensively throughout the region, neither of us really lives there. One lives on the wooded shores of a lake in Vermont; the other in the concrete megalopolis of Los Angeles, which, along with much of western California is not, according to the editors of the *Atlas of the New West*, part of the American West. When we have attended conferences of the Western Literature Association, we have tried to have our own "authentic" adventures in the often stunning surroundings. So it was with a touch of chagrin that we embarked on this critique of authenticity.

As it is with notions of authenticity, so it is with the cultural marketplace: even as a critic, one can never presume to stand entirely outside of the object of criticism—in our case to be exempted from what Susan Bernardin calls "the authenticity game." Cultural criticism, we believe, needs to be its own strongest critic as something both within and without the marketplace of commodities. Otherwise, it can be its own worst enemy in pretending to exceed the inherent limitations of its authority and cultural power. As the title of the volume suggests, both drawing upon a phrase made famous by Sam Shepard and returning authority to it, criticism's ironic stance can only give us distance, but never entirely free us, from the mediating power of representation. We hope this volume will engender greater dialogue about not only the competing and intertwined claims of western experience and representation but also criticism's own claims and roles as cultural product, mediator, and maker in a western cultural landscape as hallucinatory as it is human and historical.

Notes

1. Patricia Nelson Limerick, "The Real West," in *The Real West*, commentary by Patricia Nelson Limerick, intro. Andrew E. Masich (Denver: Civic Center Cultural Complex, 1996), 13.
2. See "Clio Bereft of Calliope Literature and the New Western History," in Robinson, ed., *The New Western History: The Territory Ahead* (Tucson: University of Arizona Press, 1997), 61–98. See also Krista Comer, *Landscapes of the New West: Gender and Geography in Contemporary Women's Writing* (Chapel Hill: University of North Carolina Press, 1999); the afterword to William R. Handley, *Marriage, Violence, and the Nation in the American Literary West* (Cambridge: Cambridge University Press, 2002); and Nathaniel Lewis, *Unsettling the Literary West: Authenticity, Authorship, and Western American Literature* (Lincoln: University of Nebraska Press, 2003).
3. Neil Campbell, *The Cultures of the New American West* (Edinburgh: Edinburgh University Press, 2000), 103.
4. Theodor Adorno, *The Jargon of Authenticity*, trans. Knut Tarnowski and Frederic Will (Evanston: Northwestern University Press, 1973), 8.
5. Adorno, *Jargon of Authenticity*, xxii.
6. Renato Rosaldo, *Culture and Truth: The Remaking of Social Analysis* (Boston: Beacon Press, 1989).

7. *Rereading Frederick Jackson Turner: "The Significance of the Frontier in American History" and Other Essays*, commentary by John Mack Faragher (New York: Henry Holt, 1994), 59.

8. Adorno, *Jargon of Authenticity*, 9.

9. Don. D. Walker, "Can the Western Tell What Happens?" in *Interpretive Approaches to Western American Literature*, ed. Daniel Alkofer et al. (Pocatello: Idaho State University Press, 1972), 35.

10. Gerald Vizenor, *Manifest Manners: Narratives on Postindian Survivance* (Lincoln: University of Nebraska Press, 1999), 8.

11. Louis Owens, *Other Destinies: Understanding the American Indian Novel* (Norman: University of Oklahoma Press, 1992), 4.

12. Hollywood film has, in the past century, dominated the iconographic West and shaped, as Lee Mitchell has demonstrated in *Westerns*, the construction of western masculinity (the West's putatively authentic and authenticating gender in popular culture). We have chosen to de-emphasize film in this volume precisely because its dominance occludes other histories of visual representation that give context to the western's film history.

13. Alfred Runte, *National Parks: The American Experience* (Lincoln: University of Nebraska Press, 1997), 34.

14. Jean Baudrillard, *Simulacra and Simulation*, trans. Sheila Faria Glaser (Ann Arbor: University of Michigan Press, 1994), 19.

1. RHETORICS OF AUTHENTICITY

1. TRUTH OR CONSEQUENCES

Projecting Authenticity in the 1830s

Nathaniel Lewis

In his introduction to *Sketches of History, Life, and Manners in the West* (1834), James Hall reflected at length on the troubled condition of writing in the American West.[1] Hall, an influential Cincinnati lawyer, editor, and author, remarked that "few of the writers who have treated of the western country, rank above mediocrity; and little of all that has been written on this subject is interesting or true. Books we have had in abundance; travels, gazetteers, and geographies inundate the land; but few of them are distinguished by literary merit or accurate information."[2] The complaint is typical of Hall's thinking, for he had long worried that western writing was a series of "failures"—the available books, he wrote, "are the hasty productions of incompetent writers, whose opinions are generally wrong."[3] And literary history has largely agreed: of the seemingly limitless contingent of authors who wrote on the West in the first half of the nineteenth century, only one, James Fenimore Cooper, is canonically remembered for his western writings, even though, strictly speaking, little of Cooper's prose took place in the West, and he himself never went west. History has forgotten scores of others, including Timothy Flint, Henry Marie Brackenridge, Charles Fenno Hoffman, and Hall himself. But during the 1830s the West was quite literally "cultural capital" for enterprising writers, a topic of enormous commercial appeal to both eastern and western authors—and the site of considerable writerly competition.

Although contemporary literary scholars have aggressively studied the formation of an American canon and the development of authorship that occurred in the East during the first half of the nineteenth century, few have considered the parallel struggle taking place in the West. In fact, western writers such as Hall and Flint were energetically voicing the need for a recognized literature of the West, trying to corral a proliferating market of writings about the West into a more profitable situation for the region's authors. And just as the debates over authorship—and copyright and nationalism—taking place in the major eastern cities helped determine the course of a recognized national literature, so too the early debates in the West contributed to the condition of western authorship for years to come. The difference, of course, is that no effective regional or national literature emerged from the struggle, no Hawthorne or Longfellow or Sedgwick or Poe around whom to build a powerful tradition. This essay attempts to establish the condition of authorship in the 1830s for those writers "treating of the Western country" (in Hall's language)—that is, for authors writing in the West and about the West. The struggle to incorporate (give recognizable body to) western authorship finally points to a historical absence and to a set of troubled expectations and conditions that predict the broader nineteenth-century failure of a recognized western canon.

In many ways, the tangle of the western marketplace in the 1830s serves as a model in American literary history of how authors and cultures interact. Importantly, the terms of the western literary debates were often exactly the same as those heard in the East. Words such as *romance, imagination, originality, fancy, genius*, and *truth* were heatedly discussed in deploying the emerging literature. Moreover, the challenges to western authors were largely the same challenges being faced by Poe, Emerson, Sedgwick, and Sigourney: although the explosive proliferation of writings may have produced an optimism for authorship, it also caused significant problems for aspiring authors, raising questions applicable to any burgeoning literary moment. How do authors assert themselves in a crowded market? What claims do they make about their work and themselves? And how do those claims influence a developing tradition? The answers to these questions help explain how culture works to determine authorship and how, in response, authors assert themselves against cultural pressures in the struggle for self-invention.

If, however, the inchoate western market echoed the same terms and concerns as that of the East, it also developed in significantly different ways. That is, if the early development of western literature can serve as an American model, it also precipitated a regionally unique condition. In fact, authorship was developing along dramatically different paths, and the very different shades cast by those literary terms (such as "romance") suggest the uneasy dialectic between West and East. If, as others have argued, authorship for eastern writers increasingly emphasized the individualized authorial personality and imaginative genius, authorship in the West revolved first around the perceived *authenticity* of the work and *authority* of the writer, and second around any internal "interest" of the text. James Hall signals these two related points when he laments the lack of "interesting or true" writing in the West. Authenticity (often coded in the words "fidelity," "accuracy," and "truth") implied factual representation of landscape, population, and historical record. For western writers, experience preceded authentic writing, whereas genius and imagination were the purported foundation for eastern writing. The "interest" of the western text—what set it apart from other authentic works—was far more nebulous, and usually suggested not imaginative originality but the stunning and even original presence of western landscapes and people. The two concepts were central to the discourse on authorship at the time and contributed to the problematic construction of authorship and authority, one that precipitated the subsequent nineteenth-century canonical failures of western literature.

Virtually every author in every western genre from novel to tourist manifesto claimed that his or her work was "true," an accurate representation of the western landscape and its people. In fact, the claim of authenticity was often the primary raison d'être for the presented work. Amos Parker began his *Trip to the West and Texas* (1835) by noting that "the author . . . has not attempted the regions of fancy and fiction; but has told his own story. . . . He hopes it may be found to contain information sufficient to repay a perusal." Likewise, Samuel Parker opened his popular *Journal of an Exploring Tour* (1838) by remarking that "it is believed that no defects exist in the work, irreconcilable with a strict adherence to facts. The principal merit which is claimed for this volume is, a scrupulous adherence to truth." Charles Augustus Murray, an English author, makes the same advertisement in *Travels in North America* (1839): his book "pretends to no other merit than that of truth." Some writers were less emphatic: William Keating explained that his *Narrative of an Expedition to the Sources of the St. Peter's River* (1824) sought "to present a faithful description of the country." Still others considered their reliability in extravagant terms: James Hildreth began his *Dragoon Campaigns to the Rocky Mountains* (1836) by explaining that many writers "overstep the limits of their circumscribed boundary of truth, and soar away upon the wings of imagination, into the boundless and inviting realms of fiction"; he suggests that his book, on the other hand, would be accurate.[4]

That authors would assert authenticity may hardly seem surprising; textual reliability was essential to many forms of western writing, for very obvious reasons. Exploration and survey expeditions were often designed to produce scientific and geographic data—and the purpose of the narrative write-ups was to report the findings accurately. Other works were written specifically for prospective visitors or armchair travelers. For example, Calvin Colton, an American minister who moved to London, concisely summarized his intentions in *Tour of the American Lakes, and among the Indians*

(1833) with a simple question-and-answer: "Why should this book be written? To give information."[5] And, as easterners saw increasing opportunity for investment in the West, they demanded accurate reporting, not jingoistic dogma. Furthermore, it must be understood that the claim of textual realism was by no means limited to western writing; eastern authors energetically employed the discourse of authenticity as well. Even fictional forms such as the novel, as Nina Baym has shown, were often judged by their "fidelity to nature," the catchy, often-heard criterion.[6]

The difference between eastern and western conceptions of representational fidelity was based on the presumption that eastern reality conveyed a familiar and visible set of cultural codes, character types, landscapes, and social values; hence "nature" in the East was eminently knowable. But western life, on the other hand, was thought to be remote, exotic, "other." Beyond the experience of eastern readers, western life required other methods of representation. "Fidelity to nature" in the West had nothing to do with "a perfect transcript . . . of ordinary life" (to borrow from a *New York Mirror* review) but, rather, a mimetic representation of an extraordinary world. Indeed, the ubiquity and assertiveness of the claim in all forms of early western writing—including fiction, sketches, and "entertainments" —suggest more than a simple desire for veracity. Because the West was represented as an emphatically different and alien environment, one beyond the imaginative vision of eastern essayists, historians, and novelists, the claim of authenticity seemed to situate power in the author. Authenticity therefore referred to both the work and the author: textual authenticity meant mimetic "fidelity," while authorial authenticity suggested individual authority and credibility. And if "fidelity to nature" was often unprovable, authorial integrity could be determined, almost legalistically. The claim became an assertion of writerly authority and a marker for the author's presence, both in the West and in the text. As such, it became a form of authorial self-identification, a way for authors to describe and even invent themselves. With eastern readers increasingly fascinated by all things western, writers who spoke with credibility and insight about the West could take great advantage of the flowering market.

The claim of authenticity, however, also produced troublesome results. First, it obscured the considerable liberties that authors took with their writing. Calvin Colton, for example, does much more than "give information"—his *Tour* is often a provocative polemic on Indian rights, slavery, and English and American federal policy. More familiarly, Hall's own contention of accuracy thinly veiled his myopic and romantic representations. Predictably, as western writing leaned harder on exaggerated romance, it also affirmed its reliability more vociferously. The claim of authenticity thus produced a problematic condition of authorship that seemed to pull in two directions: on the one hand it centralized authority in the figure of the reliable author; on the other hand it obviated the author's stylistic or imaginative power by emphasizing the process of regional translation: what was being conveyed was the landscape and people, not the author's creative vision. If authenticity became the discourse of legitimation, it also proved to be an implosive and crippling foundation for western literature.

In keeping with the autogenetic power of authority on which western authorship was based, many leading western writers held positions of public trust, converting their professional authority into literary authority: Hall, Flint, Daniel Drake, and Lewis Cass were, respectively, a judge, a minister, a doctor, and a state governor. The authorial reliability of less renowned writers could also be established through the testimony of editors and publishers—themselves authorities who could attest to the author's integrity. For example, the publisher of Tilly Buttrick's *Voyages, Travels, and Discoveries* (1831) combined respect for Buttrick's factuality with sympathy for his condition: "In preparing this little work . . . the Editor had not only in view the interest with which an enlightened people seize upon facts not previously in their possession; but sympathy for this unfortunate traveler," who by then had lost his property and eyesight.[7] Timothy Flint himself, in "editing" James O. Pattie's *Personal Narrative* (1831), vouched for "the literal truth of the facts, incredible as some of them may appear," with a long list of evidence supporting Pattie's virtuous credibility, including Flint's own "acquaintance with the Author . . . the respectability of his relations, the standing which his father sustained, the confidence reposed in him by the Hon. J. S. Johnston, . . . the concurrent testimony of persons now in this city," and so on.[8] And D. W. Moore, the publisher of Zenas Leonard's *Narrative* (1839), explained that the truth of the text could not be permanently verified because a part of the original journal "was stolen from [Leonard] by hostile Indians"; nevertheless, Moore wrote that Leonard's "character for candor and truth, among his acquaintances, we have never heard suspected; and, indeed, among the many who heard the narrative from his own lips, we have yet to hear the first one say they disbelieve it. At all events, in its perusal, the reader will encounter no *improbabilities*, much less *impossibilities*."[9]

25

Authors pressed their own claims of textual authenticity in a number of ways, most of which located credibility in the site of the author. The three principal methods were through the memory of firsthand experience, through the notes and letters they wrote on the spot, and through references to other recognized authorities. The most frequent and perhaps convincing claim was that of authorial experience—that the author spoke as witness. James Hall inevitably recalled as evidence his "long residence in the Western States" and his "opportunities for personal observation." Likewise, Samuel Parker noted that "most of what is narrated in this work came under the author's personal observation." [10] Yet as powerful as firsthand experience was, memory was also susceptible to challenge; consequently, many authors explained that they relied on their own notes, journals, and letters written soon after, or even during, the related experience. Such notes and letters revealed textual immediacy, an unvarnished relationship with the land and the people. Caleb Atwater, in the preface to *Remarks Made on a Tour to Prairie du Chien* (1831), suggests both the bustling activity of his travels and the original foundation of his book: "Employed as I was, on my Tour, I had only leisure to reduce to writing a few leading facts, at the time, the remarks were made. From my original remarks, I have selected only a part of them, for the public eye." [11]

After tour narratives, collections of letters may well have been the most popular form for writing about the West, and they served as a self-authenticating genre. Newspapers and publishers would often commission a traveler to send letters east for publication, and these letters would later be collected, perhaps rewritten, and then offered in book form. Edmund Flagg explained at the beginning of his memoir, *The Far West* (1838), that the *Louisville Journal* had requested that he "contribute to the columns of that periodical whatever, in the course of his pilgrimage, might be deemed of sufficient interest." [12] Other examples of the genre include George W. Ogden's *Letters from the West* (1822), Timothy Flint's *Recollection of the Last Ten Years* (1826), James Hall's *Letters from the West* (1828), Mary Austin Holley's *Texas: Observations, Historical, Geographical and Descriptive, in a Series of Letters* (1833), Charles Fenno Hoffman's *Winter in the West* (1835), James Hildreth's *Dragoon Campaigns* (1836), Caroline Kirkland's *A New Home, Who'll Follow?* (1839), and Frederick Hall's *Letters from the East and from the West* (1840). [13]

The reliance on other authorities was perhaps the most complicated play of authorial assertion, for it ran the risk of belying the author's own authority. The employment of sources could result in stale reproductions or, at worst, approach plagiarism. For these reasons many authors opted to deny that they had been influenced by other writings; Flint wrote in *Recollections*: "I have striven to depart from the common fashion of emptying the contents of one book into another, and serving them up to you in new form. . . . I can assert, with perfect confidence, that I have not consulted a book on my subject." More often authors were eager to enlist the authority of others as support for their own truthfulness. Edmund Flagg gave credit "to [John M.] Peck, Hall, Flint, [Alphonso] Wetmore, and to others"; Hoffman pointed to "the eloquent writings of Mr. Flint, the graphic sketches of Judge Hall, and the valuable scientific researches" of Henry Rowe Schoolcraft, William Keating, and Thomas Say; and Washington Irving acknowledged the "collateral lights" such as Lewis and Clark that helped produce *Astoria*.[14] By referring to other authorities, writers could establish or augment the accuracy of their own work while simultaneously reinscribing the accuracy of the chosen authority. The continual circulation of certain names—notably Flint and Hall—maintained the value of their currency and allowed derivative authors to borrow against them.

Moreover, it is essential to recognize that the claim of authenticity was by no means limited to nonfiction. Indeed, the necessity of realistic representation in fiction was arguably more important than in nonfiction. Daniel Drake, the influential orator, doctor, and scholar, criticized Cooper and novelist James Kirke Paulding for their illegitimate creations. Drake argued that "the failure of Mr. Cooper in his *Prairie*, and Mr. Paulding in his *Westward Ho*, is conclusive evidence, that in delineating the West, no power of genius, can supply the want of opportunities for personal observation on our natural and social aspects. No western man can read those works with interest; because of their want of conformity to the circumstances and character of the country."[15] Drake's use of the word "failure," like James Hall's, does not signal a lack of commercial success (both Cooper and Paulding were enormously popular) but, rather, the failure of imaginative and historical fiction to produce authentic western material. Because these works were being judged on their accuracy and not their "genius," no brilliance could substitute for authentic experience. Such criticism echoes the advertisements of western nonfiction: it was authorial experience, not bookish learning or inventive vision, that counted; the West had to be *seen* to be textually represented.

To enforce their claims of representational authenticity, fiction writers who wrote about the West made elaborate assertions for the truth of their work, even while acknowledging a certain inventiveness. Timothy Flint, in dedicating his novel *Francis Berrian* (1826) to his friend Henry A. Bullard, remarked that Bullard, a surveyor of the Southwest, would "well know, that no inconsiderable portion of these adventures is any thing, rather than fiction." Likewise, James Kirke Paulding, the prolific New York author and intimate friend of Irving, at first claims that his novel *Westward Ho!* (1832) "professes no connexion with history, and aspires to no special chronological accuracy"; but Paulding (who was later rebuked by Drake) next stakes his claim to authenticity as well: "It is believed that sufficient regard has been had to truth in this respect to give it the interest of something like reality." And in the preface to his historical romance *Elkswatawa* (1836), James S. French explained that "the main incidents detailed in this work are strictly historical, and drawn from authentic sources." Most emphatic is James Hall, who in introducing his *Souvenir* sketch-collection (1829) vouched for its validity by remarking that "it is written and published in the Western country, by Western men, and is chiefly confined to subjects connected with the history and character of the country. . . . Most of the tales are founded upon fact, and though given as fiction, some of them are entitled to the credit of historical accuracy." Hall's language is even stronger three years later in the preface to his popular collection of sketches *Legends of the West* (1832), neatly epitomizing the claim. He acknowledges that "the legends now presented . . . are entirely fictitious," but by no means does he suggest that they are not authentic representations: "The sole intention of the tales comprised in the following pages is to convey the accurate descriptions of the scenery and population of the country in which the author resides. The only merit he claims for them is fidelity." Hall can claim that "fidelity" because the legends "are founded upon incidents which have been witnessed by the author during a long residence in the western states, or upon traditions preserved by the people, and have received but little artificial embellishment."[16]

The willingness to eschew the "embellishment of style," in Hall's words, for the authenticity of fact had a startling effect on the implicit advertising of the writings: the claim of authenticity often displaced and even erased any claim of aesthetic quality or imaginative power.[17] By suggesting that the "only merit" he claims is "fidelity," Hall subordinates any "literary merit" (to return to his complaint in *Sketches of History*) and concentrates that desired fidelity in both his own experience and in the authorities of the region's "traditions." Such a strategy appears even more emphatic in nonfiction: as early as 1807, when Patrick Gass (an officer in the Lewis and Clark expedition) put out his *Journal*, the publisher admitted to "difficulty" in "determining the form": he could "preserve the form of a daily journal" or, "assuming less of the journal form and style, [could] describe and clothe the principal parts of it as his fancy might suggest." In choosing the former, the publisher considered that "the climate and face of the country will be more satisfactorily described." In 1810 Fortescue Cuming suggested in *Sketches of a Tour to the Western Country* that "as the intention of the author was the increase of information, he makes no apology for the plainness of his style, and he expects, on that account, to be spared any criticism." Edwin James compiled his *Account of an Expedition from Pittsburgh to the Rocky Mountains* (1823) from "a large mass of notes and journals," including the notes of the leader Major Stephen Long and Major Thomas Say; Edwards remarks that "it was not deemed necessary to preserve uniformity of style, at the expense of substituting the language of a compiler for that of an original observer."[18]

These writers were acutely conscious of both literary form and style, as were eastern writers, but in the West the desire for authenticity often meant the emphatic avoidance of "high" literary delivery.[19] Imagination, style, fancy, and genius were avoided, and any polished regularity of form or sophistication of style became suspect, for they suggested the authorial manipulation of material rather than the faithful recording of region. Presentational roughness—and the claim thereof—became signs of authenticity. Charles Murray explained that "the careless arrangement of materials . . . will furnish . . . more than abundant evidence of the fact, that the manuscript has been untouched" since his return from the West.[20] Similarly, in editing *Pattie's Personal Narrative*, Flint decided to "leave the narrative as [he] found it," despite the fact that Pattie "thinks more of action than literature, and is more competent to perform exploits, than blazon them in eloquent periods." Flint corrected spelling and punctuation, he admits, but "to alter [the narrative], to attempt to embellish it . . . would be to take from it its keeping, the charm of its simplicity, and its internal marks of truth."[21] Perhaps most revealing is James Hildreth, who notes that books based on letters such as his may "wear the appearance of roughness" because of the "sometimes disconnected manner in which they are thrown together"; Hildreth claims that "this should . . . be construed as a commendation," for it avoids the "inviting realms of fiction." Indeed, he had given "serious consideration" to "the manner in which to lay the incidents . . . before the public." The continuous narrative of a journal might be more rhetorically fluid but, as Hildreth puts it, "letters themselves would be better calculated to carry with them the impress of the truth, than if the story had been told in the smoother style of romantic narrative." [22]

Yet if stylistic or imaginative quality was so rarely foregrounded, and if any author who traveled in the region could claim authenticity, how then could an author make an impression in that crowded marketplace? Could one author be "more authentic" than another? Broadly, how does a western work, limited to authentic representation, become "of interest," become "interesting" (to use the deceptively mundane keywords of Flint and Hall)? On rare occasions authors would call attention to themselves as the explicit point of interest in their narratives, but for the most part, western authors refused to celebrate themselves: at exactly the period that the United States was beginning to recognize literary personalities such as Irving and Sedgwick and Cooper, western authors were playing a dangerous game. Just as the "merit" of the work lay in its representational fidelity, similarly the central point of textual "interest" became the West itself, not the authorial persona or the power of rhetorical expression. While writers in the East increasingly marketed their own reputations and reveled in the genius or power of their imagination, western writers avoided such self-identification. If style for eastern writers was the de facto "objectification of a personality," in Mark Rose's terms, exotic landscapes and peoples became the "personality" in western works. [23] For western authors, their writerly identity was dependent on the power of western place; more authentic meant closer to actual experience and meant somehow closer to the physical sense of place. Accuracy could be interesting or thrilling or seductive exactly because the West exhibited those marketable features.

Similarly, "originality" was an especially elusive concept, implying in many writers a desire for imaginative capacity. The works themselves were rarely described as original; quite the opposite, writers increasingly relied on rigid generic forms and rhetorical conventions. Originality could be traced to an original experience—perhaps a first contact or wilderness journey—but, conveniently, this again situated originality in the place, not in the text. Often, originality was expressly avoided: James Hall displaced any originality of his *Sketches of History* by explicitly relying on "facts" (a word repeated eight times in four pages) and on the research of other authorities: his book "has no claim to originality, but is properly a compilation." Hall's prose, however, often belied his claim, as James Freeman Clarke argued in the *North American Review*: "On this subject of originality, Judge Hall will do well to revise his conclusions. The very vice of his historical works is, that they are too original. He confounds too much the departments of history and romance. Let him give to the incidents of his histories less originality, and to those of his romances more, and he will find that both will profit."[24] Clarke neatly conflates two shades of originality: on the one hand, Hall's histories, while hardly rhetorically imaginative, were unreliable and mythologized (hence too original); on the other hand, his romances—his fiction—were unoriginal and stilted.

In Clarke's charge we glimpse the unfortunate result: accuracy was often compromised by romance, and the tension between the two poles was frequently vague and self-perpetuating. Constrained by their claims of "fidelity," western writers reverted to romance, which they claimed to be more authentic and interesting. As novelist James S. French put it, "The nature of his [historical] materials . . . make truth appear stranger than the wildest fiction."[25] Calvin Colton epitomizes the rhetorical self-justification and inevitable perpetuation: he wonders whether his book should be *"properly fiction, or sober history"* (the descriptive choice itself a tip-off), and then determines that "the facts were abundantly sufficient to demand [history], and that no fictitious dress could equal the interest of the exact truth." Yet the "interest of the exact truth" became increasingly problematic. Colton lays it bare in discussing American Indian culture and the nature of that "exact truth":

> The maxim of Byron: "Truth is strange, stranger than fiction"—
> was perhaps never more applicable, than to the principal subject of
> these pages. The history of the American Indians is the *Romance of
> Fact.* It needs not a single dash of the pencil—not a single ingredi-
> ent of the sentimentality of poetry, to give it life and power over the
> feelings. The naked truth has in it more of poetry and a more ener-
> getic challenge to the affections, than any possible embellishment,
> or fictitious garniture, that could be thrown around it—more than
> any creations of fancy, with which it could be charged.

Thus Colton imbues a factual and truthful representation of the West with a sentimental "poetry" and "power over the feelings."[26]

That a popular but unreliable form of writing emerged from the Romance of Fact is by now critically established. Hall, Hoffman, and others were hardly realists, and were not reliable historians or cultural commenta-

31

tors, but for this essay's purposes we must also appreciate the result for the western author, who becomes an authority—and potentially a romantic one—dwarfed by his or her subject. Even if authors such as Hall "invented" the West in their own ideologically partisan terms, their self-conception is the opposite: that the author is not an active constructor of the region but, rather, that place dictates text. Thus, the claim of authenticity produced an uneasily doubled result, a condition of simultaneous power and authorial invisibility. On the one hand, the claim of authenticity situated a forceful presence in the author, ultimately reflecting on his or her literary integrity. Western authors identified themselves as truthful witnesses, strong figures who were attempting to codify history in a manner fair to the region's population. On the other hand, the claim to factual authenticity risked reducing the author's position to one of mere translator or observer: he or she became the vehicle for reproducing the contours of landscape or articulating local traditions—but not a creative visionary. The lack of authorial individualism spelled monstrous trouble for future writers. Here were authors invested with an obvious romanticism, filled with imaginative abilities, but who opted to claim the opposite. Quite simply, they lost their chance at becoming individualized romantic authors, imbued with power and imagination.

Authorship in the 1830s West existed in a bizarre conflation of preromantic and early romantic conditions: it was both an identifiable professional position that empowered itself and an insecure position of derivative invisibility. Michael J. Colacurcio is just one of many critics to argue that, in the East, Emerson and other writers of the 1830s and 1840s were working "to free the American Mind, including the fledgling Imagination, from its peculiar problem of imitation," imitation meaning both debt to other writers and narrow mimetic reproduction of "specific conditions of local culture."[27] Even so, at the same time western authors were advertising a mimetic ability and a reliance on other authorities.

Because western authorship was established through this unstable condition of simultaneous power and invisibility, it was particularly susceptible to challenge and subversion. Indeed, from the beginning the position was weakened and subject to attack. In this way we can say that western authorship was easily deconstructed, by which I mean simply that strong western authorship depended on difference (author and place, power and invisibility, West and East) and that epistemological, rhetorical, and cultural forces all acted to put these dualities in flux, forever undoing any established stability. In the West, authority itself was negated; yet it was also, in certain historically traceable patterns, successful. That a writer like James Hall can be simultaneously ignored as a minor figure in literary history and also held up as a prime mover in the institutionalization of the patriarchal, prejudiced "Wild West" myth is a sure sign that Hall and other authors had a curiously powerful *and* impotent reach. Western authorship deconstructed itself because it had effect *and* was also erased. Rather than writing themselves into canonical celebrity, they wrote themselves out of literary history. Further, that Cooper and not Hall survived canonically emblematizes the eastern subversion of western literary authority; that Cooper's western contemporaries did not survive argues for the displacement of authorial authenticity.

In fact, the claim of authenticity carried an inherent susceptibility to implosion, a frailty that helped produce those historical consequences. Western authorship did itself in from the beginning. For those works of the Far West that claimed to reveal an original experience (such as a first contact) or travel in unmapped territory, there was an insurmountable gap of logic: authenticity was inherently unverifiable and thus epistemologically meaningless. How could one "prove" a unique and remote experience? What evidence could convince a skeptical audience of the author's veracity? What established language could convey a legitimately "new" landscape, animal, or people? James Hall, responding to an early showing of George Catlin's landscape paintings, commented that the pictures would "communicate valuable information—to all who have never had the good fortune to see a prairie, they will convey some idea of the appearance of those vast meadows, so boundless, so beautiful, so rich in scenic attraction. The shores of the Missouri have a peculiar and strongly marked character. They are like nothing else in nature but themselves." [28] Yet being like "nothing else in nature" made comparison at best a type of metaphor. Rather than enforcing a strict adherence to fact, the claim of authenticity was, conversely, poetic license, in the truest sense; there were almost no limits on authors, and they could write whatever they wanted.

Further, as the 1830s wore on, the claim of authenticity necessarily became an implicit criticism of other works; each text that purported to tell the "real truth" about the West cast doubt on the veracity of others. If every text claimed authenticity, authenticity itself was demeaned. That is, the success of the market itself spelled trouble—as did the success of western expansion. The migrations of the 1840s made authorial authenticity largely obsolete, for there were suddenly thousands of authorities, witnesses to the land

and the people of the West. The exotic became familiarized, accessible, and even mundane. Western writing risked becoming dull. The most obvious remaining options were to turn inward, toward ludicrous extremes, or backward to past, pre-settlement events. Thus the claim of authenticity developed a kind of rigidity that approached self-parody, and resulted in static formulaic genres, emerging almost immediately as nostalgic romance and later as dime-novel adventure, both genres that conspicuously obviated authorship. Moreover, the claim solidified a pattern of reception, a way of reading. Following the instructions of James Hall and others, readers do not treat western literature as an aesthetically complex or imaginative body of writing. Rather, western literature is advertised, reviewed, read, and studied for its representations of historical conditions and natural landscapes. The range of reading room is extraordinarily narrow.

How do we begin to reclaim the creative, artistic dimensions of western writing? For openers, let us imagine Oscar Wilde during his 1882 tour of the country, proselytizing his aesthetic theories and offering his own gestures and poses as examples. (Vladimir Nabokov once speculated on scenes he would like to have filmed, including Poe wedding his cousin Virginia and Melville "feeding a sardine to his cat." My list would include Wilde lecturing to a largely Mormon audience in Salt Lake City, or descending by bucket into the Matchless Mine in Leadville, Colorado.)[29] Wilde's tour of the West is often remembered as the meeting point of civilization and savagery, the dandy wit addressing the gregarious roughs. But this meeting is far more complex, a reworking of the dynamic axes of region and representation. Wilde did more than parody or dismiss authenticity; he offered performances of gender, language, and desire that at first may have seemed out of place in Denver or Houston, but ultimately demonstrated the unfolding performance of place and the wonderful indeterminacy of the West.

Reviewers at the time didn't quite know what to make of Wilde and his popularity, but I think Wilde's West show gives us hope by encouraging us to rethink the claims of realism in western literature. Wilde wrote that "all bad art comes from returning to Life and Nature, and elevating them into ideals." As if critiquing western writing, he remarked that "the moment Art surrenders its imaginative medium it surrenders everything." What then of western literature, which seems to surrender—indeed, to foist and unload—its imaginative qualities? Is western literature simply bad art? On the contrary, the very constructedness of the claim of realism, starting in the 1830s, suggests that western literature displays anything but the "decay of lying"; it suggests that western literature is joyfully deceptive. The obvious fact that we rely on literature to be authentic proves that "Life imitates Art." And if, as Wilde said, "the only history that [art] preserves for us is the history of its own progress," then we have before us a history of the literary imagination that is alive, elusive, and beckoning.[30]

Notes

1. This essay considers *western authors*—a term that requires some definition. First, critics and historians inevitably struggle to define the geographical boundaries of the West. I take the West to be self-determined by its authors; thus it does not begin at a specific longitudinal line, but rather as authorial consciousness. James Hall and other Ohio Valley writers of the 1830s saw themselves as western writers, and advocated for the recognition of western writing. Second, I am bound to put some constraints on the idea of "authorship." This essay will consider those texts that (1) appeared in print during the period and (2) appealed to a relatively catholic audience. Thus, I am not treating unpublished diaries, religious sermons, oral legends, and so on. That the writers/ speakers of such texts considered themselves authors I have no doubt— but they did not generally consider themselves professional authors in relation to a literary marketplace.

2. James Hall, *Sketches of History, Life, and Manners in the West; Containing Accurate Descriptions of the Country and Modes of Life, in the Western States and Territories of North American* (Cincinnati: Hubbard and Edmands, 1834), 9. The first volume of *Sketches* appeared in 1834, but it was not until the following year that both volumes were published together; the 1835 edition is identical to the 1834, with a preface. Most reviewers were responding to the 1835 edition.

3. Hall, *Sketches* (Philadelphia: H. Hall, 1835), no page (see preface), 12.

4. Amos A. Parker, *Trip to the West and Texas, Comprising a Journey of Eight Thousand Miles, Through New-York, Michigan, Illinois, Missouri, Louisiana and Texas, in the Autumn and Winter of 1834–5: Interspersed with Anecdotes, Incidents, and Observations* (Concord NH: White and Fisher, 1835), 3; Samuel Parker, *Journal of an Exploring Tour Beyond the Rocky Mountains* (Ithaca NY: Self-published, 1838), iii; Charles Augustus Murray, *Travels in North America during the Years 1834, 1835, and 1836. Including a Summer Residence with the Pawnee Tribe of Indians, in the Remote Prairies of the Missouri, and a Visit to Cuba and the Azore Islands*, 2 vols. (New York: Harper and Brothers,

1839), dedication page; William H. Keating, *Narrative of an Expedition to the Source of St. Peter's River, Lake Winnepeek, Lake of the Woods, &c. &c. Performed in the Year 1823* (Philadelphia: H. C. Carey & I. Lea, 1824), vii; James Hildreth, *Dragoon Campaigns to the Rocky Mountains* (New York: Wiley and Long, 1836), 5.

5. Calvin Colton, *Tour of the American Lakes, and among the Indians of the North-West Territory* (London: Frederick Westley & A. H. Davis, 1833), 1:xi.

6. See Baym, *Novels, Readers, and Reviewers*, 160–72.

7. Tilly Buttrick Jr., *Voyages, Travels and Discoveries of Tilly Buttrick, Jr.* (Cleveland: Arthur H. Clark, 1904), 19.

8. Timothy Flint, editor's preface to James O. Pattie's *The Personal Narrative of James O. Pattie of Kentucky During an Expedition from St. Louis, through the Vast Regions between That Place and the Pacific Ocean, and Thence Back through the City of Mexico to Vera Cruz, during Journeying of Six Years, etc.*, ed. Timothy Flint (1833; reprint, ed. Reuben Gold Thwaites, Cleveland: Arthur H. Clark, 1905), 25.

9. Zenas Leonard, *Narrative of the Adventures of Zenas Leonard, a Native of Clearfield County* PA, *Who Spent Five Years Trapping for Furs, Trading with the Indians, &c., &c., of the Rocky Mountains: Written by himself* (Clearfield PA: D. W. Moore, 1839), iv.

10. Hall, *Legends of the West* (Cincinnati: Robert Clarke, 1885), no page (see preface); Parker, *Journal of an Exploring Tour*, iii.

11. Caleb Atwater, *Remarks Made on a Tour to Prairie du Chien; thence to Washington City, in 1829* (Columbus OH: Isaac N. Whiting, 1831), v.

12. Edmund Flagg, *The Far West; or, A Tour Beyond the Rockies* (New York: Harper and Brothers, 1838), 1:vi.

13. British travelers often used the same format, such as Morris Birbeck's *Letters from Illinois* (1818) and James Flint's *Letters from America* (1822).

14. Flint, *Recollections*, 4; Flagg, *The Far West*, vii; Charles Fenno Hoffman, *A Winter in the West*, (New York: Harper and Brothers, 1835), no page (see preface).

15. Quoted in Rusk, *The Literature of the Middle Western Frontier*, 1:272.

16. Timothy Flint, *Francis Berrian, or The Mexican Patriot* (Boston: Cummings, Hilliard, and Co., 1826), 1:iii; James Kirke Paulding, *Westward Ho! A Tale* (New York: J. & J. Harper, 1832), 4; James S. French, *Elkswatawa; or, The Prophet of the West* (New York: Harper and Brothers, 1836), 1:ix; James Hall, *The Western Souvenir, a Christmas and New Year's Gift for 1829* (Cincinnati: N. and G. Guilford, 1829), iii; Hall, *Legends*, no page (see preface).

17. Hall, *Sketches* (1834), vii.

18. Patrick Gass, *A Journal of the Voyages and Travels of a Corps of Discovery, under the Command of Capt. Lewis and Capt. Clarke* (Pittsburgh: David M'Keehan, 1807), viii; Fortescue Cuming, *Sketches of a Tour to the Western Country, through the States of Ohio and Kentucky; a Voyage down the Ohio and Mississippi Rivers and a Trip through the Mississippi Territory and Part of West Florida* (Cleveland: Arthur H. Clark, 1904), 24; Edwin James, *Account of an Expedition from Pittsburgh to the Rocky Mountains*, 3 vols. (London: Longman, Hurst, Rees, Orme, and Brown, 1823), 1:1.

19. The suspicion of rhetorical sophistication goes far beyond any culture-wide resistance to "polish." William Charvat points out that many writers of the time "assumed that much finishing reduced strength." By "finishing" he means "fine effects" and detailed rhetorical flourishes, as opposed to "broad" effects. See William Charvat, *The Profession of Authorship in America, 1800–1870*, ed. Matthew J. Bruccoli (Columbia: Ohio State University Press, 1968), 72.

20. Murray, *Travels in North America*, v–vi.

21. Flint, preface to *Personal Narrative of James O. Pattie*, 26–27.

22. Hildreth, *Dragoon Campaigns*, 5, 6–7.

23. Mark Rose, "The Author as Proprietor: Donaldson v. Becket and the Genealogy of Modern Authorship," *Representations* 23 (summer 1998): 75.

24. Hall, *Sketches* (1835), 8; James Freeman Clarke, *North American Review* (July 1837): 235.

25. French, *Elkswatawa*, 1:ix.

26. Colton, *Tour of the American Lakes*, 1:xii–xiii; William Handley, responding to my reading, has suggested that in the phrase "naked truth" Colton may be implicitly playing on the representation of Indians as "naked" savages; clothes suggest culture here, a falseness, inauthenticity.

27. Michael J. Colacurcio, "Idealism and Independence," in *Columbia Literary History of the United States*, ed. Emory Elliott (New York: Columbia University Press, 1988), 215.

28. Hall (unsigned), "Literary Notices: Mr. Catlin's Exhibition of Indian Portraits," *Western Monthly Magazine*, November 1833, 537.

29. Vladimir Nabokov, *Strong Opinions* (New York: Vintage, 1990), 61.

30. Oscar Wilde, "The Decay of Lying," in *Aesthetics*, ed. Susan Faegin and Patrick Maynard (New York: Oxford University Press, 1997), 40–45.

2. COWGIRLS AND SAGE HENS

Henry Adams's Western Fantasy

Lisa MacFarlane

What's a Harvard trained, Eurocentric, Boston Brahmin, establishment historian like Henry Adams got to do with the West? Plenty, in fact: among his intimates were geologist Clarence King and western émigré Elizabeth Cameron; his cousin was Francis Parkman; he founded the Cosmos Club with John Wesley Powell in 1878; in 1871 he had ridden west to follow the trail of King's U.S. geological survey of the fortieth parallel; in 1886, after his wife's death, he repeated the trip with his friend the painter John La Farge. And in his little-read 1884 novel, Esther, he makes the central narrative force a young orphan who arrives in New York from Denver to "be finished," as her mentor Aunt Sarah Murray ominously puts it.[1] This is a significant literary event for scholars of the American West, as it reveals how eastern intellectuals struggled to control the representations of a capacious and diverse landscape: the making of a "true" West was inextricably intertwined with eastern representations, eastern expectations, and eastern desire. Esther highlights the West's role in disrupting the culturally authoritative narratives that structured the American national imaginary.[2] Adams's effort to incorporate the West into his exploration of American identity laid bare the disjunctures of regional identity.

Claiming Henry Adams as a writer of the American West is probably a hard sell. Few American intellectuals have been as quintessentially northeastern. His training, his political connections, his tastes, his personal fortune, his instincts all derived from and reinforced his position as a member of a northeastern elite, one posited as central to political, social, and cultural power. Moreover, Adams wrote in a period when enormous energy was directed toward turning groups of local elites like his into a national ruling class. This energy found its outlet in cultural products and in institutions, in political organizations and in economic intersections and transactions. Adams of course participated in all these activities: he served as his father's personal secretary during the latter's tenure as ambassador to Great Britain during the Civil War; he taught at Harvard; he edited the North American Review; he and his wife Clover hosted some of the most important political and cultural soirees in Washington; he advised presidents and diplomats; and he wrote culturally authoritative histories and biographies that made their subjects—easterners all, like John Adams, Thomas Jefferson, and Albert Gallatin—signature figures in United States history. Indeed, his lineage by definition was a metaphor of nineteenth-century nation-building. As an Adams, he was from birth, he well knew, multiply invested in a process by which the Quincy Adamses (a rural political elite) and the Boston Brookses (an urban financial elite) merged to produce New England presidents and public servants who distinctly identified their civic-religious calling as founding and stewarding American national interests.

Historically informed readers, moreover, are quickly drawn to the novel as a roman à clef with an eastern perspective that follows from the novel's location in New York City. The central action takes place in and around St. John's Cathedral, a thinly disguised Trinity Church of Boston's Copley Square; the main characters are paleontologist George Strong (modeled on Clarence King); Stephen Hazard, a minister (cousin Phillips Brooks); Wharton, a painter (longtime friend John La Farge); and the title character, Esther Dudley (fans of that other frontier writer, Nathaniel Hawthorne, will recognize her literary foremother). Esther was closely modeled on Clover Adams; Edward Chalfant argues that the novel was in many ways Clover's, written for and with her.[3] For most critics, the novel's central interest lies in its explicit debates about the relationships among science, religion, and aesthetics as historical "forces"; discussions that follow from these approaches usually ignore the western accents in the text.

Scholars of the West similarly feel justified in giving scant attention to Adams, only using him, as Wallace Stegner does, as a foil by which to celebrate "real" westerners like Powell.[4] When we speak of "selling the West," as Christine Bold succinctly puts it, we tend to think of dime novels and Wild West shows, of "playing Indian," in Philip Deloria's phrase, or of rough riding. A self-consciously intellectual novel set in New York would hardly seem to qualify. Nevertheless, I want to consider Adams's novel, with its New York setting and East Coast cultural elitism, as part of a western literary tradition. Drafting the novel in 1879, revising it in 1883, Adams wrote Esther at a formative moment for the western territories. The latter part of the nineteenth century marked a systematic and violent expansion of the cultural and social dimensions of U.S. imperial activity, when its military was systematically engaged in subduing Indians: press coverage of the Modoc Wars of 1872 and 1873, for example, called national attention to native resistance to U.S. occupation. American geological science matured alongside American anthropology, as ethnographers from Albert Gallatin to Henry Schoolcraft to Lewis Morgan cross-fertilized their studies of North American Indians with theories adapted from the scientists who accompanied the King, Powell, Wheeler, and Hayden surveys of the late 1860s and 1870s. Adams of course knew many of these men, understood the political implications of their work, marked their appropriations battles, and actively followed government policy toward the West, for example, famously calling the funding of the U.S. geological surveys in 1869 "the first modern piece of legislation."[5] And cities from Denver to Seattle to San Francisco were rapidly expanding into prominent centers for both national and international commerce, yoked in symbiotic economic union with New York, Boston, and Chicago.

In these contexts, Adams's national interests were indeed regional ones, and his career-long concern with the nature of political and moral authority in the United States was intimately bound up with representing, literally and figuratively, the West. Far from being peripheral to his interests, the West was central to how he imagined the East and, by extension, America itself. As Adams and the other members of his caste and class struggled to define and control what they saw as the increasingly chaotic—to use Adams's word—forces that would govern the public sphere, they were crucially shaped by half-conscious beliefs about an inescapable West. Acting on those beliefs, they authenticated the West they imagined into being.

Yet this easterner's West was a fractured place, and in *Esther*, Adams struggled to reconcile divergent nineteenth-century visions of the American West. On the one hand, the West was a resource-rich region available for his elite friends and relatives to survey, catalog, mine, and market to private industry and public expansion; on the other, the mythologized West of the receding frontier was essential in maintaining the national fantasy of righteous Manifest Destiny. These competing visions, often complicit with one another, coexist uneasily in *Esther*. Moreover, the unapologetically elitist *Esther* is distant kin to the popular genre of the Western. Their relation is not structural, through action or language, but thematic: they share a deep concern with representing the liminal space in which East and West meet; they elaborate that concern through characters who transgress closely monitored boundaries of gender and race; and they affirm the reciprocity of East and West in any formulation of American identities. Adams tried to write a national allegory in *Esther*, and instead wrote an eastern narrative of western cultural confrontation. Think of *Esther*, then, as a Western: that is, as a meditation on relations between the East and the West, embodied not by a male

Virginian who heads west to Medicine Bow, but by a female Coloradan who heads east to New York City. What does it mean that Henry Adams placed at the elusive center of what he called his "most precious" work a western woman?[6]

That center is Catherine Brooke, who holds together both the competing narratives of the American West and the novel itself. To her eastern friends, Catherine is a fascinating resource to be examined, painted, educated, even dressed. But she also embodies mythic narratives that should remain, as one of them puts it, "unspoiled." Both as Woman and as the West itself, she catalyzes the novel's underlying and unacknowledged debate about how the East was to represent, manage, and incorporate the West. As an eastward-bound westerner who mocks received beliefs about her region, she invokes ironically the conventions of more recognizable Westerns. Yet if narratives of American literary history have often failed to notice the West as a deter-mining and foundational place, so too has Catherine slipped through the critical discourse relatively unnoticed. Far from being a peripheral charac-ter in an unprepossessing novel, Catherine Brooke is the central character in a revealing text that struggles to but cannot fully repress the West. More-over, the repressed West in the novel mirrors the repressed West in Adams's construction of America; Catherine illuminates his class's and his region's difficulties in controlling and representing the region and its resources.

Catherine has a real-life counterpart: she was modeled on Henry and Clover's close friend, Wyoming native Elizabeth Sherman Cameron, the wife of Donald James Cameron, a senator from Pennsylvania. Adams ad-mired and trusted Elizabeth Cameron; after Clover's death, he came in-creasingly to confide in her.[7] Adams's decision to have Catherine Brooke re-tain Elizabeth Cameron's western origins is important. Cameron was both a native-born westerner and an unimpeachable member of the eastern po-litical establishment, representing both the myth of rugged western indi-vidualism and the political reality of western integration into national pol-icy, and Adams extended those paradoxes onto Catherine Brooke. Like the region she represents, at various moments Catherine is scientific specimen, aesthetic raw material, and ground for religious and cultural expansion. Yet always Catherine seeks to be a character in her own right, writing her own story in defiance of the narratives other characters choose to assign her. Catherine can be read, then, as a symbol of the larger struggle over the West and western autonomy and identity in the latter decades of the nineteenth century.

Let's reverse the usual reading of the novel, then, to focus on the elusive character of Catherine, the absent landscape of the West, and the novel's unspoken assumptions about region, race, and gender. Catherine Brooke comes to New York to escape her stepmother's repressive Presbyterian household in Denver and to inherit an "independence" from her well-connected mother. Catherine's geographical movement, then, also reverses the traditional narratives associated with westward mobility: she is a young, financially independent, western woman who heads east in search of new experiences, a salutary cultural frontier, and increased autonomy. She shadows Esther formally and thematically; both her representation in the text and her strategies for self-representation highlight Esther's inability to affirm her own autonomy. The other characters in the novel strenuously seek to reconcile Catherine to what they see as the contradictory categories of woman and West; they initially view her as "natural and sweet as a flower" and about as proactive (208). Catherine's complexion, however, with "the transparency of a Colorado sunrise," diverts them from the "mutinous" expression in her eyes. She emerges unscathed from her studies, slipping on a New York overcoat without ditching the "raft of things in her [Colorado] trunk." As Esther notes, "Catherine hates driving unless she drives herself" (209, 323, 208, 283).

As she learns to navigate her new surroundings, Catherine cheerfully engages the roles the others assign to her, of country cousin, Indian "squaw," gunslinging frontierswoman, "practical young savage" (230, 326). Yet, as daughter to easterners, reared in repressive Presbyterian domesticity, enjoying the returns of an inheritance safely nurtured by Wall Street, she is from the beginning yoked in harness with the East, its values and worldview, arriving, Aunt Sarah is relieved to note, in a modest dark-blue woolen dress instead of the "linen duster and waterwaves" she had feared (208). In this, Catherine resembles the city she calls home. As William Wyckoff reminds us, "What had begun as a brawling frontier outpost was rapidly evolving into a dominant center of regional trade, and more important, into a community increasingly self-conscious of its own potential." By 1885 Denver was one of the twenty-five largest cities in the United States, with an expanding economic base that benefited from the discovery of gold and silver, technological advances in smelting operations, and the expansion of the Denver and Pacific Railroad. The 1880s, Wyckoff points out, saw "the development of increasingly elaborate residential architecture" in a city whose skyline owed almost as much to European architectural influences as it did to sublime mountain views. By 1873 gas-powered streetlights illuminated the city's downtown; the first poles and wires of a new telephone exchange went up in 1879; and by 1881 much of central Denver had electricity. In 1890 the city boasted over thirty millionaires, safely ensconced on more desirable suburban lots and far from ethnic ghettoes populated by African Americans and Chinese, Italian, German, Polish, and Serbian immigrants. Catherine's Denver was a bustling, diverse, polyglot urban landscape—indeed, in some ways, like New York.[8] Catherine herself is also a vehicle for the intercourse Adams well knew existed between western resources and eastern ambitions, and for the symbiosis between rapidly developing western industries and eastern financial institutions. Culturally heterogeneous, she is indebted to eastern money and intellectual traditions and eager for New York experience; yet her identity was also predicated on an emotional and cultural investment in the western landscape, economy, and cultural heterogeneity.

Catherine is implicitly aware of this: she enjoys sparring with the others about her western trappings, reinforcing, then dismantling, their expectations for their "authentic" western visitor. Like his more popular counterparts—Owen Wister, Frederic Remington, and other popular authors of more conventional Westerns—Adams struggles with some of the contradictions Catherine suggests. As a western woman, Catherine reveals how uncomfortable Adams is with cultural narratives about gender and race. Her relationship with Esther is erotically charged, and although she is clearly Anglo-American, the other characters persist in referring to her as "Sioux." Catherine's figurative cross-dressing and the other characters' construction of her as "passing" for Indian bring together two of Adams's long-standing concerns: his romantic idealization of female power, and his concern with racial identity and ethnic descent as key components of the American character. Understanding how Adams represents Catherine, then, helps us sketch how gender and race intersect in the cultural work of constructing western—and American—identities.

The relationship between the "West" and "America" is highlighted by the relationship between Catherine and the eponymous Esther, her foil, who represents the New American Woman and, by extension, America herself. "Miss Dudley," Wharton proclaims, "is one of the most marked American types I ever saw" (199): educated, attractive, well-off, a resolute freethinker—and, like her creator, chronically ambivalent about her own beliefs and desires. She is the object of a complicated homosocial romance involving Strong, Hazard, and Wharton, Esther's painting teacher who is charged with decorating Hazard's newly constructed St. John's Cathedral. Longtime friends, with divergent temperaments, values, professions, and intellectual allegiances, they are both highly competitive and deeply intimate, and they transfer their conflicted desire for each other onto their equally conflicted desire to influence Esther's sensibilities.[9] William Dudley urges his daughter to maintain an ironic, skeptical distance, to accept multiplicity as the only certainty, to engage all with humor and courage: "Laugh, Esther, when you're in trouble! Say something droll! Then you're safe" (283). Yet after his death, Esther craves certainty and accepts Hazard's proposal, if not the totalizing and authoritative vision of the world he preaches. The engagement is disastrous, however; nor can Esther accept Strong's proposal. The last line of the novel reveals her paralysis: she cannot accept Hazard, and yet she despairingly tells Strong, "I love him" (335). The novel, a critique of the social constraints placed upon talented, intelligent women, thus begins and ends with Esther, talented, intelligent, and aimless, paralyzed professionally and personally, able neither to marry nor to claim, as Catherine has done literally, her independence. If she represents not only the American woman but also America herself, Adams is not sanguine about the nation's prospects.

In contrast to Esther, Catherine is relentlessly practical, comfortable with intellectual contradictions and the messy disorder of everyday life. Esther's charitable work, for example, consists of spinning fanciful stories for hospitalized children while her aunt cautions that "one of these days you will have to be useful whether you like it or not" (202). Catherine meanwhile matter-of-factly recounts that she "made friends on the [train east]. I have been taking care of a sick lady and her three children" (208). Ostensibly artless, natural, and unselfconscious, she nonetheless executes plans with dispatch: she carries out Esther's escape from New York to Niagara and plans a trip for them both to Europe. Far from languishing for love, Catherine is in no danger of making a hasty or imprudent match. While Esther cannot even imagine a future, Catherine cheerfully projects for herself one in which she becomes a cattle rancher, an independent businesswoman. In spite of Wharton's claim that Esther represents the American type, Adams implicitly concedes that the future belongs to the shifting, enigmatic western energy that is Catherine.

Adams's struggle to represent that energy is recapitulated in the central conceit of the novel: everyone takes a turn at "capturing" Catherine's likeness, through a series of sketches, studio portraits, and murals. Throughout, the characters maintain they understand Catherine as original and "authentically" western; in practice, they know her only through eastern and European conventions. Catherine's likeness is cast and recast, as St. Cecilia, as Petrarch's Laura, as a "large Colorado beetle, with wings extended" (225). The men argue over how Catherine is to be represented; they collaborate to critique devastatingly Esther's renditions of her. Esther accepts their criticisms: she paints, revises, repaints, and rejects her own work. Just as in her courtship, she cannot find her own voice; here she cannot trust her own eyes. However, Catherine resists both her fellow fictional characters and her creator: she rejects being interpreted by these multiplying images of herself.

While Esther tries to paint Catherine as a "new Madonna of the prairies, over the high altar," Wharton and Hazard seek to accommodate Catherine to the gothic revival conventions of the cathedral. Catherine "would hardly have been surprised to find herself turned into an Italian peasant-girl" (222). And so she is: Wharton engages Esther to represent Catherine as a St. Cecilia. Hazard too invents Catherine as a representative cultural figure: for him, she becomes Petrarch's idealized, golden-haired, sweet-lipped, graceful-gaited Laura, and Esther's St. Cecilia becomes grafted onto Laura, "a beautiful girl with golden hair and a green dress whom Petrarch first saw in a church in Avignon" (238). As Nancy Vickers points out, Petrarch's sonnets create Laura as a dismembered rather than whole woman. Vickers argues that Petrarch's Laura embodies a romantic ideal that turns out to be a fragmented woman, represented in pieces, in language.[10] The ideal is a collection of body parts—each lovely, each disconnected from any whole person who might actually use those sweet lips to talk back.

If Laura is a model of an ideal woman, however, Catherine isn't. "She had no mind to be treated as if she were an early Christian lay-figure," refusing Wharton's instructions to paint her as "lean and dingy, in a faded brown blanket" (224). And instead of passively allowing herself to be painted as Laura, Catherine wants to translate Petrarch, and challenges Hazard to participate in making Laura. The ensuing negotiation of identity is appropriately complex: Catherine and Esther will translate Petrarch, while Catherine models Laura for Esther on Hazard's behalf. In return, Hazard will paint Petrarch, with Wharton as model, facing Catherine as St. Cecilia on the walls of a gothic New York cathedral. The others are skeptical: "It is one of her Colorado jokes," asserts Esther; "she does not know what a sonnet is. She thinks it is some kind of cattle punching" (240). Yet Catherine's verse is "quite good enough for Hazard," and as recompense, Wharton gives Catherine his sketch of her as the aged saint: a narrowed face with "deepened lines . . . eyes much stronger and darker . . . and at least ten years [added] to Catherine's age" (242, 224–25). She had wanted, and now owns, Wharton's image of her. Instead of being sanctified by either Wharton's hagiographic representation or Hazard's romantic one, Catherine unceremoniously asserts her humanity over the traditions in which they have invested her meaning. Rather than be the object of visual and literary arts, Catherine claims the right to represent the artist, be it Petrarch or Wharton.

Catherine is no more manageable in the narratives that Strong assigns to her that invoke romantic idealizations of the West. Inspired by the image of the beetle, he "declared that as they were all bent on taking likenesses of Catherine, he would like to try his own hand at it, and show them how an American Saint ought to look when seen by the light of science." He paints Catherine under the figure of a large Colorado beetle, with wings extended. "When it was done, he pinned it against the wall" (225–26). "Sta. Catarina 10-Lineata (Colorado)" is surely a species indigenous to the Rocky Mountain West, which Strong himself has made a career of, in his own word, "taking": identifying and cataloging, fixing to cardboard and repackaging for eastern naturalists seeking to understand the essence of the West through its camphorated, pinned, and decontextualized insect life. "For some time," Adams tells us, Catherine "was called the beetle." Strong's beetle casts Catherine as entomological specimen; she is ready for dissection, just as Laura was for Petrarch. "No one dared carry the joke far enough to ask Mr. Hazard's consent to canonize this American saint," however, "and . . . Strong gave [his sketch] to Catherine as companion to Wharton's." As did Wharton with his St. Cecilia, Strong gives up his beetle to Catherine. While they struggle to contain her likeness, Catherine confounds rigorous taxonomies and claims the right of the westerner, of the western woman, to represent herself.

In other ways, too, Catherine refuses to make a good "native" specimen. Before her arrival, the others call her a rattlesnake; Mrs. Murray's first impressions of her "Colorado orphan" are that she is "fresh as a summer morning . . . as natural and as sweet as a flower . . . with a complexion like the petals of a sweetbrier rose, and the transparency of a Colorado sunrise" (208). Catherine is by turns a sage hen, a prairie creature, a prairie sunrise, a fawn, an innocent, a mustang. Embedded in these stock phrases are the familiar litany of the many and contradictory constructions of the West.[11] Adams's descriptions of Catherine reveal long-cherished myths about Nature and the West, and woman: that they imply both wilderness and garden, unspoiled nature and potential cultivation, the salutary effects of the natural on the civilized, the potential danger that lies beneath too calm surfaces.

Nowhere are these contradictions more freighted than when Adams imagines Catherine as Indian. In addition to—and aligned with—the botanical and zoological classifications are Catherine's association with the Indian: for the other characters, her Colorado antecedents render her a "full-blooded Indian squaw" (230). Her relationship to the wilderness, to nature, is confirmed for the easterners by their appropriating on her behalf Indian identity. Strong teases her about an Indian name: "'What is your name in Sioux, Catherine?' he would ask; 'Laughing Strawberry, I suppose, or Jumping Turtle?' 'No! She answered. 'I have a very pretty name in Sioux. They call me the Sage Hen, because I am so quiet. I like it much better than my own name'" (210). Strong is never sure she's serious, but he claims to tell a colleague that "I have a young Sioux in the city. . . . He asked me what genus you belonged to. I told him I guessed it was the grouse gens [sic]. He said he was not aware such a totem existed among the Sioux. I replied that . . . you were the only surviving member of your family. . . . Have you an Indian grandmother?" Catherine claims to be able to "lariat an old aunt . . . [but] a professor with spectacles is worth more than a Sioux warrior. I will go to him" (220). These exchanges are light and witty; the characters play carelessly with languages and customs not their own. Yet Adams endows these conversations with the sense that vital and serious issues quiver beneath the frivolous surface: "My colleague will only want your head to dry and stuff for his collection," warns Strong. Indeed, as Adams well knew, Strong's anthropologist would have been complicit in policies that asserted military as well as epistemological control over native populations.[12]

In his representation of Catherine, Adams, like his other characters, invokes but cannot confront the racial and gendered implications of his narrative. As Gail Bederman reminds us, gender and race are mutually constitutive. In late-nineteenth-century America, to be a man was to be white, and to be white was to be civilized. And if to be white and male is to be civilized, that is, if race and gender are pretexts for the values associated with "civilization," then Catherine, as female and a "Little Sioux," must be uncivilized. According to Bederman, this formulation went further: her subjects created a hierarchy in which gender differentiation increased the more "civilized," the more "white," a society became. Conversely, she notes, white explorers claimed to notice that in more primitive societies, men and women tended to behave and even physically resemble one another. As the boundaries between savagery and civilization blur, so too do boundaries between genders and races. Keeping gender roles "straight," identifying and classifying Indian and white, maintaining the lines between the primitive and the civilized: these are all related cultural imperatives. If any of these oppositions collapses, so go the others.[13] Certainly, this is what Aunt Sarah had feared. She is much relieved to have Catherine arrive with only a few western accents: "She asks haow and says aout; but so do half the girls in New York, and I will break her of it in a week so that you will never know that she was not educated in Boston and finished in Europe" (208).

As Philip Deloria has traced, white Americans have historically used "Indian" to "find an ideal sense of national Self"; "national definitions," he argues, "have engaged racialized and gendered Indians in curious and contradictory ways." This has special resonance for those invested in imagining America as a place where whites "naturally" replace Indians. For Adams, as for fellow historian Frederick Jackson Turner, Catherine's "Indian-ness" serves as both a sign of her inherent "American-ness" and her inexplicable difference; it is both central to developing what Turner called a "composite national character" and yet, literally in Turner's essay, a footnote.[14] Adams's characters display this familiar cultural schizophrenia through their obsession with Catherine's assumed racial identity. They exhibit both a sense of racist superiority toward Native Americans and an unconscious recognition of how central Native American culture and history are to any conception of national identity. Their discomfort at this paradox is supposed to be safely displaced onto the Virgin Land of Catherine, but Catherine mocks the appropriation of a faux Indian identity: "I have a very pretty name in Sioux. They call me the Sage Hen, because I am so quiet. I like it much better than my own name" (210). Claiming the identity of Sage Hen, she appropriates Native American culture and history to release her from fixed gender roles dictated by her class and ethnic heritage; she lays claim to nature and the native to be able to act freely, even as the others mobilize art, theology, and science to label, define, and take her likeness.

In resisting their efforts to aestheticize her, Catherine explicitly scorns the idea that the West is "natural," without self-consciousness. With cosmopolitan condescension, Wharton laments the encroachments of civilization:

"You have the charm of the Colorado hills, and plains . . . but you won't keep it here. You will become self-conscious, and self-consciousness is worse than ugliness."

"Nonsense," said Catherine boldly. "I know more art than you if that is your notion. Do you suppose girls are so savage in Denver as not to know when they are pretty? Why, the birds are self-conscious! So are horses! So are antelopes! I have seen them showing off their beauties like New York women, and they are never so pretty as then." (227)

For Wharton, beauty lies solely in the eyes of the beholder; for Catherine, beauty is a conscious attribute of a self-aware subject, whose self-awareness, far from spoiling the view, enhances it. Catherine implicitly critiques the idea that there can be an "authentic" or original West: "natural" beauty, "unspoiled" landscape, "primitive" people, even the idea of the West itself, are all conventions more or less successfully rendered, as even the "natives" know.

Indeed, Catherine mocks all the stereotypes of the West the others place on her, not just conventions of Indianness or untamed nature. She is not domesticated easily, as we have seen in her experiences as a model: "I'm not strong enough to use heavy shooting irons. . . . One night I took one of our herders for a thief and shot at him, but missed and got laughed at for a week. That was before we moved to Denver, where we don't use pistols much" (209). After her theologically conservative training, she declares that her idea of heaven is reading novels in church, which she does—the capacious and middle-brow Dickens.[15] When Esther struggles to break with Hazard, suggesting that she and Catherine elope—"anywhere but to Colorado," replies Catherine—Catherine agrees, but pragmatically suggests that the girls "go to bed just now, and elope in the morning" (299). And Catherine plots her and Esther's escape to Europe: "We want excitement. . . . When we come home from Europe, I am going to buy a cattle ranch in Colorado and run it myself. . . . I mean to have ten thousand head, and when you see them, you will say that they are better worth painting than all the saints and naiads round the Mediterranean" (323–24).

Sage Hen, Little Sioux, and beetle alternate with Laura and St. Cecilia, as Catherine blurs the ostensibly clear lines between genders, between races, and between the cultures of East and West, Europe and America. One final portrait of Catherine suggests how fully Adams, and his characters, fail to

49

understand Catherine and all she represents. Esther paints Catherine too as the Sage Hen, complete with "sage brush . . . a stuffed sage hen, and photographs of sage plains, to give . . . the local color for her picture," all props that Strong has sent from the West (211). Hazard offers an opinion: "Give to Miss Brooke the soul of the Colorado plains!" So Catherine and Esther retreat to Esther's penthouse studio: "Here Catherine Brooke was now enthroned as the light of the prairie" (216–17). Esther considers the painting a failure, however: "Esther was surprised to find what a difficult model [Catherine] was, with liquid reflections of eyes, hair and skin that would have puzzled Correggio" (211). "Do what she would, Catherine's features and complexion defied modeling and made the artificial colors seem hard and coarse. The best she could paint was not far from down-right failure. . . . It would not have been with impunity that Tintoret himself had tried to paint the soul of the prairie" (218).

It is significant that neither Esther nor anyone else in the book can paint a decent picture of Catherine. Nor can Adams himself, if his critics are to be believed. After all, Catherine's key feature is her ability to defy immutable categories. Consider her many positions as the plot progresses: exiled daughter of eastern migrants; irrepressible child of repressed Presbyterian domesticity; fresh, pure, ignorant girl receiving an education in art, philosophy, and social arrangements; the artist's model; the object of desire; the faithful female friend. Each of these is a conventional plot for a woman character, but Catherine refuses to provide any endings. Moreover, as we've seen, she disrupts even the plots Esther is meant to fulfill. Strong offers Esther marriage as a reward for having "fought your battle like a heroine" (335); Catherine reverses the conventions of the romance, proposing instead that she and Esther "elope" to Europe because "America is too tame" (323). While Hazard sneers that Esther only parrots ideas given her by Strong, Catherine extravagantly asserts her authority over them both, claiming that when she has her ranch, "You will want me to take you on wages as cowboys" (324). Both on her own behalf and on Esther's, Catherine challenges the underlying assumptions of the romance plot: "Men are always making themselves into ideals and expecting women to follow them. . . . You are all selfish" (324). Positioned between a series of readily apparent and commonly constructed oppositions—male and female, Europe and America, East and West, white and Indian, civilized and savage—Catherine forces the implied hierarchies uncomfortably into play and undercuts each of them by not seeming to take any of them seriously. Indeed, she rather than Esther follows William Dudley's deathbed advice: she laughs, and makes her way to Europe.

Catherine's presence, then, continually interrupts the central story-line, both in plot and in theme. If the portrayal of Catherine is slight, as many critics claim, it is precisely because of her slightness, her suggestive-ness, that Catherine is so important to understanding how eastern elites struggled to plot the region they were so eagerly surveying, mapping, min-ing, and slicing with railway lines—all the while romanticizing it and its population as unspoiled. As a representative westerner, as the representa-tive of the West itself, Catherine is unrepresentable in the standard narra-tives—romantic, scientific, theological—available to other characters. She is indeed resistantly self-conscious; that is to say, she understands her own complicated positioning in their schemes and seeks to engage them on her own terms. In Wharton's eyes, this will spoil her, but for Catherine it is an assertion of autonomy and self determination, a recognition that if western identity must always be made, rather than simply be, then she must control the making.

In creating Catherine as the central energizing force in the novel, Adams allowed her to disrupt both his own understanding of U.S. history and his effort to construct fiction. Adams had hoped to engage a wide audience with the philosophical concerns articulated by the men, packaged in a ro-mance about Esther; he hoped to bring the intellectual vigor of his nonfiction to the wide readership of a popular novel. Yet Esther appeared un-der the pseudonym Frances Snow Compton to a deafening critical and com-mercial silence. With his insistence on the marketing conditions for the novel, Adams begged such a reaction. He kept the secret of the novel's au-thorship from all but his publisher, Henry Holt, and his most intimate circle of friends. He refused to allow Holt to promote the book: he wanted "au-thorship without advertisement," reminding the nervous Holt that "au-thors, if not publishers, have to look many years ahead and yet sometimes miss their mark." Apparently, Esther did. Adams experienced a dishearten-ing failure: "So far as I know, not a man, woman or child has ever read or heard of Esther. . . . My inference is that America reads nothing—advertised or not—except magazines." [16]

Adams's problem with Esther was not that "America reads nothing," however. Esther baffled readers, and baffles them still. Adams's "most pre-cious work" inhabited a no-man's land between an American, and national, imagined community, built on the idea that America was somehow more "authentic" in its western origins, and the regional materiality of national policies involving land rights, farming, mining interests, railroad development, tourism, and the military and social policies for Indian removal, with their attendant legal complexities, cultural contradictions, and moral travesties. Within a decade of *Esther*'s publication, that interstitial space would be built into the landscape (to take the most dramatic example) of the 1893 Chicago World's Fair, in anthropological exhibits, Midway attractions, synecdochal structures like the "frontier cabin," speeches, and Wild West shows (Annie Oakley as an untamed Catherine). Adams had no ready answers for these pressing intraregional and international concerns, nor indeed did the ruling national class of which he was a charter member.

If Catherine represented Adams's West, then he was torn between believing her to be authentic and representing her regional identity as performance. Adams knew that the West was not an unmediated space, that it had always been invested, implicated, and constructed by national economy, national policy, and national mythology, but he could not escape the trap Catherine sets for the men in the novel: his own romantic investment in the myth of the West as a vehicle for American identity. Adams implicitly recognized what Patricia Limerick and other western scholars explicitly argue, that the West was susceptible to capricious and constantly relative representations. But which of Catherine's qualities were embedded in her western experience—which were "authentic"? And which were projections of eastern desire, repressed and refigured? Adams couldn't answer. He ultimately abandoned writing about the West and sought a historical explanation for the United States and an epistemological compass for the twentieth century at Chartres and Mont St. Michel, and even in the Fiji Islands. Ironically, he chose to work with conventional representations over uncertain realities, and to focus on European intellectual theory rather than empirical western data.[17]

Adams's difficulties will hardly be surprising to readers of The Education of Henry Adams. As a historian, Adams recognized the power and the failures of representation and of narrative. Just as in The Education, where the discourses of Virgin and Dynamo cannot fully explain the trajectories of history, here too Adams must have realized that the discourses—scientific, religious, aesthetic—available to control and represent the West would also fail. Most troubling to Adams must surely have been the threat to American authority itself. The United States, he believed, was a nation constructed out of language and imagery, justified in its belief in its own exceptionalism by the presence of an authentic and original space, the West. Yet like the West she represents, Catherine mocks her creator: the vital force at the center of the national romance, she offers an unrepresentable multiplicity of meanings, a return to language and representation. To those who want their "true West" etherized, sterilized, and categorized, she asks George Strong: "Are all professors as foolish as you?" (220).

Notes

1. Henry Adams, *Selections: Democracy, Esther, Mont Saint Michel and Chartres, The Education of Henry Adams*, ed. Ernest Samuels and Jayne N. Samuels, Library of America ed. (New York: Literary Classics of the United States, 1983), 202. Subsequent citations from this edition of the novel will be given parenthetically in the text.

2. For a discussion of the national imaginary, see Lauren Gail Berlant, *The Anatomy of National Fantasy: Hawthorne, Utopia, and Everyday Life* (Chicago: University of Chicago Press, 1991); see also Benedict Anderson, *Imagined Communities: Reflections on the Origin and Spread of Nationalism* (London: Verso, 1983).

3. See Edward Chalfant's monumental three-volume biography: *Both Sides of the Ocean: A Biography of Henry Adams, His First Life, 1838–1862* (Hamden CT: Archon Books, 1982); *Better in Darkness: A Biography of Henry Adams, His Second Life, 1862–1891* (Hamden CT: Archon Books, 1994); and *Improvement of the World: A Biography of Henry Adams, His Last Life, 1891–1918* (North Haven CT: Archon Books, 2001). See also Ernst Scheyer, *The Circle of Henry Adams: Art and Artists* (Detroit: Wayne State University Press, 1970).

4. Wallace Stegner uses Adams as a foil for Powell, whose informal, field-based education better fits him for modern American life than Adams's bookish one. See Stegner, *Beyond the Hundredth Meridian: John Wesley Powell and the Second Opening of the West* (New York: Viking Penguin, 1992), 1954.

5. Christine Bold, *Selling the Wild West: Popular Western Fiction, 1860 to 1960* (Bloomington: Indiana University Press, 1987); Philip J. Deloria, *Playing Indian* (New Haven: Yale University Press, 1998); Amy Kaplan and Donald Pease, eds. *Cultures of U.S. Imperialisms* (Durham: Duke University Press, 1993); Adams, *Selections*, 312.

6. See Bold, *Selling the Wild West*; and Lee Clark Mitchell, *Westerns: Making the Man in Fiction and Film* (Chicago: University of Chicago Press, 1996); Jane

Tompkins, *West of Everything: The Inner Life of Westerns* (New York: Oxford University Press, 1992); and of course John G. Cawelti, *The Six-Gun Mystique* (Bowling Green: Bowling Green University Press, 1971); J. C. Levenson et al., eds., *The Letters of Henry Adams* (Cambridge: Harvard University Press, 1982–88), 3:34.

7. For a discussion of Adams's relationship with Elizabeth Cameron, see Samuels and Chalfant; also Arline Boucher Tehan, *Henry Adams in Love: The Pursuit of Elizabeth Sherman Cameron* (New York: Universe Books, 1983).

8. William Wyckoff, *Creating Colorado: The Making of a Western American Landscape, 1860–1940* (New Haven: Yale University Press, 1999), 110, 108. See especially chapter 4.

9. For more on how homosocial desire between men is triangulated through women, see Eve Kosofsky Sedgwick, *Between Men: English Literature and Male Homosocial Desire* (New York: Columbia University Press, 1985); also David Leverenz, *Manhood and the American Renaissance* (Ithaca NY: Cornell University Press, 1989); and Christopher Newfield, "The Politics of Male Suffering: Masochism and Hegemony in the American Renaissance," *Differences* 1.3 (1989): 55–87.

10. Nancy J. Vickers, "Diana Described: Scattered Women and Scattered Rhyme," *Critical Inquiry* 8 (1981): 265–79.

11. Glenda Riley, *Women and Nature: Saving the "Wild" West* (Lincoln: University of Nebraska Press, 1999); Annette Kolodny, *The Land Before Her: Fantasy and Experience of the American Frontiers, 1630–1860* (Chapel Hill: University of North Carolina Press, 1984).

12. For more on the role anthropology played in "taming" the West and recording the "vanishing" Indian, see Laura Wexler, *Tender Violence: Domestic Visions in an Age of U.S. Imperialism* (Chapel Hill: University of North Carolina Press, 2000); for a comprehensive collection dealing with the intersection between colonialism, representation, and anthropology, see Elizabeth Edwards, *Anthropology and Photography, 1860–1920* (New Haven: Yale University Press, 1992).

13. Gail Bederman, *Manliness and Civilization: A Cultural History of Gender and Race in the United States, 1880–1917* (Chicago: University of Chicago Press, 1995).

14. Deloria, *Playing Indian*, 5, 9; Frederick Jackson Turner, *The Significance of the Frontier in American History*, ed. Harold P. Simonson (New York: Ungar, 1963).

15. Patricia Nelson Limerick refers to the plots of western history as Dickensian in their complexity; Catherine presumably likes them for their occasional low-brow humor. See *Legacy of Conquest: The Unbroken Past of the American West* (New York: Norton, 1987).

16. Levenson et al., *Letters of Henry Adams*, 2:527, 568, 543, 567.

17. See Limerick, *Legacy of Conquest*; see also Patricia Nelson Limerick, *Something in the Soil: Legacies and Reckonings in the New West* (New York: W. W. Norton, 2000); Clyde Milner, ed., *A New Significance: Re-Envisioning the History of the American West* (New York: Oxford University Press, 1996); *Under an Open Sky: Rethinking America's Western Past*, ed. William Cronon et al. (New York: W. W. Norton, 1992). On Adams and women, see Eugenia Kaledin, *The Education of Mrs. Henry Adams* (Philadelphia: Temple University Press, 1981), in which she begins to sketch Adams's concerns with gender; see also Chalfant's discussion of Adams's interest in Polynesian women in *Both Sides of the Ocean*.

3. GETTING THE REAL STORY

Implications of the Demand for Authenticity
in Writings from the Canadian West

Alison Calder

Canadian literary criticism has always been caught up i4n questions of imaginative citizenship: What is a Canadian? What is Canadian literature? And what is the difference between what Margaret Atwood describes in *Survival* (1972) as *"Canadian* literature" and "just literature that happened to be written in Canada"? This search for an authentic literature repeats itself on regional levels. Edward McCourt's 1949 statement that "if [writing] does not illustrate the influence of a limited and peculiar environment it is not true regional literature" (55) remains paradigmatic of much regional theorization.[1] The relation of literature to environment is perceived as particularly intimate in the Canadian West, which has led to the construction of a narrow category of landscape-based "prairie" writing; writing that deals with something other than the human relation to the environment is given another designation. This cause-and-effect relation of land to literature is linked to the idea of an autochthonous regional identity, an identity that comes from the land. More disturbingly, the linking of "authentic" prairie writing with exposure to the environment has led to attempts to separate the "real" regional writers from those without the right to claim regional citizenship. The critical belief that representation of the West must be somehow *true* has also led some critics to present shockingly negative views of prairie reality in their attempts to make that reality match the critical paradigms they advocate. The combined result of such demands for authenticity has led to the creation of a "prairie" writing that bears little resemblance to the Canadian West it ostensibly represents. Deborah Keahey stresses the necessity of revising this distorted vision of prairie writing in *Making It Home* (1998), arguing that "the motive of the ideal must be balanced against the practice of the real" if literary criticism is to be at all meaningful.[2] More crudely put, it may be time for a critical reality check: seeking an artificial regional unity through landscape or through the imposition of an exclusionary critical politics will not address the very real divisions within the Canadian West and will do little to understand the complicated representations of an equally complicated region.

The development of a distinctly Canadian literature has always been seen as necessary to national survival. Thomas D'Arcy McGee's 1857 assertion that "every country, every nationality, every people, must create and foster a National Literature, if it is their wish to preserve a distinct individuality from other nations" (43) is echoed in Margaret Atwood's 1972 assertion that "for the members of a country or culture, shared knowledge of their place, their here, is not a luxury but a necessity. Without that knowledge we will not survive" (19).[3] Early boosters of Canadian literature argued that the nation's unique geography provided both the base and the inspiration for a unique race. Both national identity and national literature would spring from a distinctly Canadian spirit of place, as in D'Arcy McGee's prescription for a native literature: "It must assume the gorgeous colouring and gloomy grandeur of the forest. It must partake of the grave mysticism of the red man, and the wild vivacity of the hunter of the western Prairies. Its lyrics must possess the ringing cadence of the waterfall, and its epics be as solemn and beautiful as our great rivers" (44). Such prescriptions, later described by Northrop Frye as "the harnessing of Niagara Falls" school of Canadian criticism, demonstrate an obvious dependence on a romanticized landscape capable of shaping literature into a genuine expression of Canada.[4] Such a literature would then be in some senses autochthonous, springing from the soil, and thus truly "in place."

One of the reasons the development of an authentic national literature has been seen as particularly important in Canada is because of our uneasy relations with our much more powerful neighbor to the south. After all, Canada achieved confederation in 1867 largely through the exploitation of well-founded fears about American expansion. A national railway system was developed in the 1880s primarily to ensure that what is now British Columbia would not be seduced away to join the United States. Efforts to initiate the development of a distinctly Canadian literature can be read as strategies of containment, as attempts to defend the forty-ninth parallel and to assert Canadian difference from a threatening American culture. Edward Hartley Dewart's 1864 remark that a national literature is "not merely the record of a country's mental progress: it is the expression of its intellectual life, the bond of national unity, and the guide of national energy" makes explicit the links perceived between national political and cultural unity.[5] Thus, nationalist attempts to create or recuperate a genuine Canadian literature have emphasized Canadian difference from America. While continually present, this emphasis on national difference is particularly explicit in criticism from the late 1960s and early 1970s, as Canadian writers and academics responded negatively to American imperialist activity in Asia: Dennis Lee's 1973 essay "Cadence, Country, Silence: Writing in Colonial Space" eloquently describes his feeling that Canada was becoming an American colony. Similarly, Margaret Atwood's highly popular survey of Canadian literature, Survival, sought to differentiate Canadian writing from that of Britain and the United States and argued for the importance of empowering the "reader as citizen" through providing a literature that mirrored a distinctly Canadian reality: "If a country or culture lacks such mirrors it has no way of knowing what it looks like; it must travel blind. If, as has long been the case in this country, the viewer is given a mirror that reflects not him but someone else, and told at the same time that the reflection he sees is himself, he will get a very distorted idea of what he is really like" (15–16).[6]

Canadian literature thus became a vehicle for national identity, and, as Atwood's words suggest, that identity must be genuine. If, as Frye asserts in his 1965 conclusion to the Literary History of Canada, "the Canadian cultural public" has "the obvious and unquenchable desire . . . to identify itself through its literature," then that literature must accurately reflect what Canadian identity actually is.[7] It must be true at some level; it must reflect what it is to be Canadian.

The concerns Atwood expressed about authenticity are echoed in later, much different criticism, as in Linda Hutcheon's The Canadian Postmodern (1988). Like Atwood, Hutcheon seeks to identify a national literary unity, which she paradoxically locates in a disparate and diverse postmodernism. Although the postmodern, she writes, is not a uniquely Canadian phenomenon, it is especially appropriate to Canada because "Canadian writers . . . may be primed for the paradoxes of postmodernism by their history . . . and also by their split sense of identity, both regional and national." Thus, the Canadian condition is distinguished from a generalized American ethos, as Hutcheon remarks: "Canada has never really been in synch with the U.S. in terms of cultural history, so it is perhaps unwise to look for [literary] parallels today." Hutcheon's location of Canadian unity in diversity, recalling the traditional cultural metaphors of the Canadian mosaic and the American melting pot, posits a postmodernism that is appropriate to Canada because Canada is "primed for the paradoxes of the postmodern."[8] Postmodernism therefore provides an authentic expression of Canadian culture and reality. At the same time, the potentially fragmentary power of diversity is contained—since all Canadians are split between national and regional identities, everyone is the same, and so we all belong together.

Hutcheon writes that "Canada can in some ways be defined as a country whose articulation of its national identity has sprung from regionalist impulses: the ex-centric forces of Quebec, the Maritimes, the west" (4), and it is in the context of how Canadian critics have constructed regional writing that I want to situate my discussion of the treatment of writings from the Canadian West. As with writings from the American West, writings from the Canadian West are most commonly treated under the rubric of the regional, a classification that carries its own criteria and assumptions. To be labeled "regional," a work has to be perceived as a carrier of a kind of truth: it must provide an example of real life within that region and be based on genuine regional experience. The author must also be seen as someone who has inside knowledge of the region, someone who is familiar with the ins and outs of that regional experience and who can serve as the reader's guide or native speaker. The most basic way of determining regional citizenship is birthplace or childhood home—Frye writes, for example, that an artist who moves from one region to another may "live with its people and become accepted as one of them, but if he paints or writes about it he will paint or write as an imaginative foreigner."[9] Other critics may discard such an extreme belief in the determinative power of the genius loci, while still conserving the idea that the influence of the genius loci is necessary. Even critics explicitly concerned with redefining the regional label preserve an author's lived experience in the region as a criteria for inclusion in that category. David Jordan, writing in New World Regionalism (1994), cites Mary Austin's much earlier assertion that a region is defined "not as a catalogue of quantifiable entities, but as experience itself." This regional experience, he clarifies in Regionalism Reconsidered (1994), "is born of a sense of identity and belonging that is shared by a region's inhabitants; this sense of community springs from an intimate relation to the natural environment."[10] The demand for authenticity, for the authorial experience enabling an insider's view, thus also conserves a reliance on the genius loci: it is exposure to the "natural environment" that confers both authenticity and authority.

The authority of the insider, or native speaker, is derived from the reader's faith in the insider's capacity to function as a regional representative, to speak for the region and in some way to embody what are perceived to be distinct regional characteristics. This capacity is closely linked to the text's perceived truth-value: readers trust the author to provide them with a true, insider's view of regional life. An early example of such insistence on regional authenticity occurs in E. K. Brown's *On Canadian Poetry* (1943): "Regionalist art may be expected to possess certain admirable virtues. One of these is accuracy, not merely of fact, but accuracy of tone; and throughout our literature there has been a tendency to force the note, to make life appear nobler or gayer or more intense than life really is in its typical expressions. It would help us towards cultural maturity if we had a set of novels, or sketches, or memoirs, that described the life of Canadian towns and cities as it really is, works in which nothing would be presented that the author had not encountered in his own experience."[11]

Here we see the insistence on the truth-value of regional writing and the related belief in the authority of the native speaker. However, the emphasis Brown places on actual life experience is troubled by his remark that Canadian writers tend "to force the note." Since all life experience is necessarily personal and subjective, Brown's assessment appears as an attempt to standardize the representation of reality, to modify the ways in which regional writers articulate their experiences. While he feels it important that a record be made of Canadian life "as it really is," for that record to be valid it must match Brown's own perceptions. And in order for the native speaker to speak authoritatively, the region in question must also be perceived and represented as largely homogeneous. As McCourt writes, "The creation of a native regional literature is dependent in part upon the existence of a relatively populous and stable society" (4). In other words, a regional culture must become fixed to the extent that it is both recognizably and representably different from other cultures. If there is change in the region, such as increasing urbanization or differing immigration patterns, then the regional model (here the "native regional literature") is threatened. As Gerald Haslam points out in *Western Writing* (1974), "regionalism is nurtured by homogeneity."[12]

The critical demand for authenticity in writings from the Canadian West is amplified because the general demand for authenticity in "regional" writings intersects with, and is increased by, the demand for authenticity in "Canadian" writings. If writings considered "regional" are seen as accounts of genuine regional experience, and an expectation of truth-value is inherent in the regional label, then it becomes necessary to examine exactly what the cultural implications of this expectation are. Probably the best-known essay on western Canadian writing is Henry Kreisel's 1968 "The Prairie: A State of

Mind," in which he argues that "all discussion of the literature produced in the Canadian west must of necessity begin with the impact of the landscape upon the human mind" (6). Here treatment of land and its effect on the individual are posited as the criteria of authenticity: it is assumed that all writings from the Canadian West must in some way reflect that effect.[13] Writing then grows out of place, from exposure to the prairie genius loci—the distinct impact of a distinct landscape produces a distinct literature. Articulation of this distinction results in a truly western writing, and western writings not only depict the impact of landscape, they also result from it. Consider, for example, Kreisel's remarks on the frequency of melodramatic scenes in prairie realist fiction:

> It can be argued that in order to tame the land and begin the building . . . of something approaching a civilization, the men and women who settled on the prairie had to tame themselves, had to curb their passions and contain them within a tight neo-Calvinist framework. But it is not surprising that there should be sudden eruptions and that the passions, long suppressed, should burst violently into the open . . . though this sudden eruption of violence sometimes seems contrived for the sake of a novel's plot, it is also clearly inherent in the life the novelists observed. (13–14)

Melodrama becomes realism, as events that may seem "contrived" are attributed to the effects of landscape and thus extended beyond the borders of fiction and applied to the prairie population at large. Plot becomes, in a sense, unplotted, as these writings become documentary rather than imaginative.

Until the publication of Deborah Keahey's *Making It Home* in 1998, there were only two exclusively Canadian book-length studies of Canadian prairie fiction: Laurie Ricou's *Vertical Man/Horizontal World* (1973) and Dick Harrison's *Unnamed Country: The Struggle for a Canadian Prairie Fiction* (1977).[14] These books are very much of their time, but they remain influential, continually turning up in current arguments, reading lists, and critics' endnotes. Together, Ricou and Harrison defined prairie writing as a unique and valuable field and laid the groundwork for contemporary work in the area. Examining their criticism reveals the extent to which ideas of authenticity govern their views of both prairie and literature. Like many other Canadian critics, Ricou saw the human relation to landscape as the underlying theme of all Canadian literature: the prairie writer just asked "a regional form of the question" (2). To support his argument that there is an obvious opposition between human beings and landscape which is apparent in prairie fiction and which relates directly to "the totality of the vacuum in the modern age" (xi), Ricou must build a prairie canon that bolsters his view. Thus, prairie realism is "mature fiction" (64), and works like popular romances, which view the prairie more positively, are "slight, lacking in seriousness, insipid" and "minor" (65, 64). Robert Stead's novel *Grain* is rejected for its "pervasive nostalgia and its neglect of the harsher aspects of prairie life" (21), and Martha Ostenso's novel *Wild Geese* is praised as "the most important prairie novel to be published between the wars" because "Ostenso is conscious of the inherent cruelty of the prairie and of the great emptiness which encircles man in the landscape" (74).

Ricou evaluates writing in terms of what he sees as a realistic portrayal of landscape. This idea of authenticity is important because, for Ricou as well as for other Canadian critics of the time, prairie writing must reveal both a national and a universal condition to be seen to have value. The model of regional literature as sociological or anthropological in nature is thus preserved: like E. K. Brown earlier, Ricou wants prairie writing to reflect us so that we may know ourselves. And as with Brown, the critic appears as the authority legislating what the reality of that reflection actually is. Early romantic prairie writers are dismissed because "they leave the actual prairie quite invisible," and Laura Goodman Salverson's novel *The Viking Heart* is rated "inauthentic" because in it, as in other "minor" works, "the landscape does not seem essential to the story; the reader does not have a strong sense of its distinctive features or influences" (70). The critic's valorization of one version of prairie truth is demonstrated in Ricou's assessment that Wallace Stegner's *Wolf Willow* provides "the right verbalization of the prairie experience" (111). The critic can then evaluate texts in relation to this ideal.

Because this kind of argument depends so heavily upon the perceived truth-value of the texts the critic discusses, Ricou depicts a prairie that supports his contentions. Thus, he writes, "in attempting to depict the universal meaninglessness posited by existentialism, the Western Canadian writer found an obvious metaphor in the prairie landscape," and that as "an image for the stubborn resistance of nature, the unchanging prairie was an obvious choice" (120, 43). Metaphor slips from literary device to "obvious" description. Similar slippage occurs in Ricou's assertion that he discusses a constructed prairie, not a real one: it "may in many instances not be as flat as it is described, but it is precisely this prairie—that seen by the artist and conceived to be necessary in his design—which is significant" (5). Real and imagined prairie immediately become confused and conflated, however, as he describes "the myth of the land" as a "collective consciousness, or unconsciousness" which "is imaginatively valid, by virtue of its being shared, often almost intuitively, by a people trying to express their sense of themselves in time and place" (5). Prairie writers' depictions of landscape then arise not from individual creativity but from some intuition governed by landscape. The introduction of mythology gestures toward the idea of landscape imagery being a cultural production, but the environmental determinism underlying the analysis obscures the recognition of that construction. The "myth" of the hostile prairie is naturalized through the idea of autochthonous production: because it springs from the landscape, it is therefore "true" or "imaginatively valid."

Like *Vertical Man/Horizontal World*, Harrison's *Unnamed Country* participates in a larger context of Canadian criticism that sees Canadian literature as the expression of a battle between the creative writer and the landscape he or she seeks to articulate. *The Struggle for a Canadian Prairie Fiction*, the subtitle of Harrison's book, is located in "the encounter between the civilized imagination and an unnamed country" (xii). The result is estrangement and alienation. Harrison sees much prairie writing as a record of the failure to deal adequately with the environment, beginning with settler accounts and the struggles they record. Yet for Harrison to maintain his theory, like Ricou he must construct a timeless prairie to which the imaginative response is always the same. It therefore "remains particularly tough to humanize, particularly intractable to the imagination," because "the austere face of the prairie has not changed that much since Henry Kelsey first saw it" and "the incongruities of that first response to the plains have never been overcome" (134, 28).[15] Here the prairie appears impossible to "humanize," as even those born there cannot make it a home. To reinforce his case, Harrison must locate any sources of alienation in the landscape itself, rather than in any historically specific ways of dealing with it: "As the settlers fortified their separate farms with fences and windbreaks they were shutting themselves in, aggravating the loneliness and isolation which were among the most threatening aspects of the prairie landscape" (22). Loneliness and isolation are not intrinsic to any landscape, however; they are abstract projections. As Harrison points out, the Mennonite settlers who farmed communally had a far different experience of the prairie, a difference which suggests that the tradition of "Canadian Prairie Fiction" he identifies is at least as much informed by cultural expectations and practices as it is by geographical immanence. Though both Ricou and Harrison strove to establish prairie fiction as a respectable area of study, in their constructions of valuable prairie writing as environmentally determined and authentic to a landscape that is itself a construct, they reified images of regional powerlessness through their depiction of a prairie population alienated from, yet dependent on, the land.

Self-consciously postmodern writers and critics also predicate their criticism in ideas of authenticity. In "Writing West" (1977), Eli Mandel describes the western writer as "a man not so much in place, as out of place and so one endlessly trying to get back, to find his way home, to return, to write himself into existence, writing west." The western writer's search is thus a search for origins, a search for the home place. This search also marks the writings of one of Canada's best-known creative writers and critics, Robert Kroetsch. In "The Moment of Discovery of America Continues," Kroetsch asserts that his own writing was motivated by the recognition of a disjunction between the Canadian history he was being taught and the western Canadian life he was living.[16] Such a recognition provoked alienation: he writes that "the authorized history, the official history, was betraying us on those prairies" (2). Underlying this betrayal is the official failure to recognize regional difference, the failure to understand that a central Canadian experience cannot be transplanted meaningfully into the Canadian West. "Our inherited literature, the literature of our European past and of eastern North America," Kroetsch explains, "is emphatically the literature of a people who have not lived on the prairies. We had, and still have, difficulty finding names for the elements and characteristics of this landscape. The human response to this landscape is so new and ill-defined and complex that our writers come back, uneasily but compulsively, to landscape writing" (5). Kroetsch argues that the inadequacy of "Canadian" literature and history to prairie reality is grounded in the experience of place. Like Harrison, he locates the nexus of prairie writing in the clash between an inherited literary tradition and a new land. Yet where Harrison emphasizes the settler's struggle with the land, Kroetsch foregrounds the writer's struggle with language. The writer's task is now not to "settle" the frontier, but to "unsettle" the language; hence, Kroetsch's well-documented insistence on the writer as archaeologist, "unhiding" words buried beneath other cultural contexts. For Kroetsch, as for Mandel earlier, western Canadian writing must become process-oriented, drawing attention to its own attempts at articulation, and so avoiding the falseness he identifies in "the literature of a people who have not lived on the prairies." At the same time, his return to the landscape, coupled with his insistence on the search for origins, can be read as indicating a desire for an autochthonous prairie literature, one that rises naturally from the soil. Or, as Kroetsch asks in *Seed Catalogue*, how do you grow a poet? [17]

Kroetsch characterizes his initial reading of Sinclair Ross's novel *As for Me and My House* as "an enabling moment" that, through "a system of contraries . . . released [him] into a memory of the politics and the poverty, of the card parties and the funerals and the wedding dances and the sports days and the auction sales, the silences and the stories of the thirties" ("On Being" 5). This sense of community, he argues, is the true hallmark of prairie culture, and is most prominently displayed in oral, not written, literature; it is in tall tales and bunkhouse stories that he first locates "the archaeological sites of [his] own childhood" (4). "The great subtext of prairie literature is our oral culture," he elaborates. "In the face of books, magazines, films, and TV programs that are so often someone else, we talk to each other by, literally, talking" (4). The subversive nature of this orality is clear in Kroetsch's declaration that "the bastards can't keep us from talking" (18). Further, he constructs this subversive orality as a means of authentic regional expression in his statement that "the oral tradition, become a literary tradition, points us back to our own landscape, our recent ancestors, and the characteristic expressions and modes of our speech" (7). [18] This orality is therefore autochthonous. It is located in, and directs us back to, the landscape.

Some troubling implications of the desire to "authenticate" literature by predicating it on place can be seen in Dennis Cooley's 1987 study of Canadian prairie poetry, *The Vernacular Muse*. [19] Cooley builds on Kroetsch's theories to develop the argument that what he calls a popular, vernacular, and vigorous "ear" poetry has historically been devalued and suppressed, while a lyrical, romantic, and solitary "eye" poetry continues to be widely published and taught. Ear poetry becomes a political medium, the production of which works to subvert what Cooley sees as a European or central Canadian cultural hegemony. He argues that the vernacular is a tool for political empowerment: "Literature becomes vigorously rooted—in *our* time and in *our* places, subject to *our* values, *our* sense of what is real. It also becomes, for many, vernacularly based, speaking from or for minority groups who have become marginalized (women, the Third World, the poor, the 'under-educated,' natives, working people, ethnics, those in 'the hinterland'), in short, central to my argument, the disenfranchised" (182).

Cooley's vernacular is thus figured as inclusive, accessible, and above all authentic, responsive to "*our sense of what is real.*" But the italicized *our*, instead of operating as an inclusive gesture, participates in a rhetoric of exclusion, dividing readers into "us" and "them," into insiders and outsiders. "It seems to me," he writes, "that what I am calling 'eye' poetry tends to be written by women, and 'ear' poems tend to be written by men" (14). Furthermore, while ear poetry is written by young, prairie-born poets, eye poetry continues to be written primarily by the old, and by immigrants (14).[20]

What is going on here? If ear poetry is the only true prairie tradition, then the critic must construct eye poetry as other to the prairie, with the corresponding caveats against women and immigrant writers. The effect of this view is shown in his description of the selection criteria he used in compiling *Inscriptions: A Prairie Poetry Anthology* in 1992: "One consideration has been residence—imaginative residency. I didn't want to include those who had simply passed through, and I didn't want to feature those who had just arrived, nor did I want to bring in those who physically lived in the prairies but wrote as if they were somewhere else entirely. The writing in some way had to show signs that it came out of the prairie or that it engaged with the place."[21] Cooley's dismissal of prairie writers who "wrote as if they were somewhere else entirely" recalls Margaret Atwood's earlier concentration on "*Canadian* literature—not just literature that happened to be written in Canada." The insistence on writing that "came out of the prairie" reflects a desire for an autochthonous poetry, a poetry that rises from the land and that is therefore seen to provide authentic regional expression. His introduction demonstrates the ways in which critical reliance on environmental determinism shapes the publication, distribution, and evaluation of writing from the prairies. Like Ricou's evaluation of Wallace Stegner as producing "the right verbalization of the prairie experience," Cooley too has in mind a "right verbalization"—ear poetry rather than eye poetry—writing that must come out of the prairie *in a certain way*. The result of this demand for "authenticity" is the legislation of a particular kind of expression to the exclusion of others, and a self-perpetuating category of "Canadian prairie poetry."

The construction of Canadian prairie writers as distinctly Canadian and emphatically not-American points to one of the fundamental contradictions underlying attempts to criticize and theorize writings from the Canadian West. Criticism of prairie writing is overwhelmingly based on a belief in the precedence of the environment, which is seen to shape a distinct regional character and thus an authentic regional writing. Critics with vastly different perspectives base their interpretations of writing from the prairies on what they feel is the impact of the landscape on the human mind.[22] The problem with this approach is that Canadian critics then use this theory to construct what they see as a distinctly Canadian prairie identity, which would perhaps not be such a problem if the prairie stopped at the forty-ninth parallel. The critical acrobatics necessary to consider the Canadian prairies in isolation from a general North American Great Plains community are highlighted in Ricou's assertions that the American Wallace Stegner provides the "right" articulation of the Canadian prairie.[23] If critics are going to argue that there is an authentically Canadian writing being produced in the prairie provinces, then they cannot base that authenticity in an essentializing and reductive environmental determinism.

The refusal to recognize complications and contradictions in what we call authentic "national" or "regional" writing leaves us with only an artificial tradition. This difficulty may lie in the problematic idea of "authentic" literature. Ought we to insist that literature, inherently implicated in the conventions of genre and representation, be true? Perhaps only by discarding such notions can we develop a theory of writing from the Canadian West that responds to the complexity within the region, to the literary and cultural connections to other regions, and to the need to develop an understanding of a West that is politically present and meaningful.

Notes

1. Margaret Atwood, *Survival: A Thematic Guide to Canadian Literature* (Toronto: Anansi, 1972), 13; Edward McCourt, *The Canadian West in Fiction* (Toronto: Ryerson Press, 1970), 55. This limited model of literary regionalism is currently undergoing reevaluation, primarily from critics writing from the regions. See particularly *Marketing Place*, by Ursula Kelly (Halifax: Fernwood, 1993); *A Sense of Place*, ed. Christian Riegel and Herb Wyile (Edmonton: University of Alberta Press, 1997); and *Defining the Prairies*, ed. Robert Wardhaugh (Winnipeg: University of Manitoba Press, 2001); as well as Lisa Chalykoff's article "Overcoming the Two

Solitudes of Canadian Literary Regionalism" (*Studies in Canadian Literature* 23.1 [1998]: 160–77) and Herb Wyile's article "Regionalism, Post-colonialism, and (Canadian) Writing: A Comparative Approach for Postnational Times" (*Essays on Canadian Writing* 63 [1998]: 139–61).

2. See Alison Calder, " 'The Nearest Approach to a Desert': Implications of Environmental Determinism in the Criticism of Canadian Prairie Writing," *Prairie Forum* 23 (1998): 171–82; and Deborah Keahey, *Making It Home: Place in Canadian Prairie Literature* (Winnipeg: Turnstone, 1998), 161.

3. One indication of the continuing desire for a specifically national literary culture is shown in Canada's growing number of national annual literary awards: the $10,000 Governor-General's Literary Awards, Canada's most prestigious literary honor, were joined by the $25,000 Giller Prize for fiction in 1994; by the $10,000 Drainie-Taylor Literary Prize for biography, autobiography, and personal memoir in 1998; and by the $40,000 Griffin Poetry Prize in 2000. This nation-building desire is also being replicated on a smaller scale at regional levels, with a proliferation of provincial and civic book awards.

4. Northrop Frye, "Criticism and Environment," in *The Eternal Act of Creation: Essays 1979–1990*, ed. Robert P. Denham (Bloomington: Indiana University Press, 1993), 146.

5. James Polk's 1844 presidential election slogan, "Fifty-Four Forty or Fight," which referred to American hopes of expanding their boundary from the forty-ninth parallel to the fifty-fourth, is indicative of the political relations between the two nations in the years prior to Canada's confederation. See *The Penguin History of Canada*, by Kenneth McNaught (London: Penguin, 1988), on how fears of American annexation contributed to the Canadian political process; see also J. L. Granatstein's *Yankee Go Home?* (Toronto: HarperCollins, 1996) on how anti-Americanism was used then, and is still used, as a tool to achieve distinct national political ends. Concerns about the "seduction" of Canada, or parts of it, surface explicitly in works like William Henry Fuller's 1880 operetta *H.M.S. Parliament* (*Canada's Lost Plays*, ed. Anton Wagner and Richard Plant, 2 vols. [Toronto: CTR Publications, 1978], 158–93). E. J. Pratt's long poem "Towards the Last Spike" similarly tropes the relationship between British Columbia and central Canada (*Poets Between the Wars*, ed. Milton Wilson [Toronto: McClelland & Stewart, 1966]); Edward Hartley Dewart, "Introductory Essay to Selections from Canadian Poets," in *To-*

wards a Canadian Literature, ed. Douglas Daymond and Leslie Monkman (Ottawa: Tecumseh, 1985), 50.

6. Dennis Lee, "Cadence, Country, Silence: Writing in Colonial Space," in Towards a Canadian Literature, 497–520. The identity of the "someone else" that Atwood mentions becomes clear in the following paragraph, where she cites examples of Canadian characters found in Henry David Thoreau's Walden, Malcolm Lowry's Under the Volcano, William Faulkner's Absalom, Absalom, and Radclyffe Hall's The Well of Loneliness (16).

7. Northrop Frye, conclusion to Literary History of Canada, ed. Carl F. Klinck et al. (Toronto: University of Toronto Press, 1965), 463.

8. Linda Hutcheon, The Canadian Postmodern (Toronto: Oxford University Press, 1988), 4, 3.

9. Northrop Frye, The Bush Garden (Toronto: Anansi, 1971), ii.

10. David Jordan, New World Regionalism (Toronto: University of Toronto Press, 1994), 8; David Jordan, ed., Regionalism Reconsidered (New York: Garland, 1994), xv.

11. E. K. Brown, On Canadian Poetry (Toronto: Ryerson Press, 1943), 23–24.

12. Gerald Haslam, "Introduction: Western Writers and the National Fantasy," in Western Writing, ed. Haslam (Albuquerque: University of New Mexico Press, 1974), 4.

13. Henry Kreisel, "The Prairie: A State of Mind," in Essays on Saskatchewan Writing, ed. E. F. Dyck (Regina: Saskatchewan Writers Guild, 1986), 6; Canada has no term equivalent to the American "Midwest"—in Canada, the West consists of both plains and ranchland, and might be thought of as including the provinces of Manitoba, Saskatchewan, Alberta, and British Columbia. However, definitions of "West" vary by region.

14. Laurie Ricou, Vertical Man/Horizontal World (Vancouver: University of British Columbia Press, 1973); Dick Harrison, Unnamed Country (Edmonton, University of Alberta Press, 1977). There have, however, also been two comparative studies of Midwestern American and Canadian Prairie fiction: Robert Thacker's The Great Prairie Fact and Literary Imagination (Albuquerque: University of New Mexico Press, 1989) and Diane Dufva Quantic's The Nature of the Place: A Study of Great Plains Fiction (Lincoln: University of Nebraska Press, 1995). These studies provide a provocative recontextualizing of prairie writing that reads regional commonality rather than national difference. The danger here, of course, is in going too far the other way and negating the importance of the border. The forty-ninth parallel might be invisible from the ground, but you can see

the dividing line made by different histories of land use even in photographs taken from outer space.

15. It bears repeating that the Canadian prairie represents one of the most drastically altered ecosystems in the world. Human habitation and cultivation have changed the prairie since the disappearance of the buffalo, and continue to change it with newly available technology. Barry Potyondi makes clear the extent of environmental change in *In Palliser's Triangle* (Saskatoon: Purich, 1995), writing that 90 percent of the fescue grassland extant in the 1850s has been cultivated and that, as a result, "almost the entire tallgrass prairie is gone. Only one-fifth to one-quarter of the once-abundant short-grass prairie, the mixed-grass prairie, and the aspen parkland remains in what we, too optimistically, call a native state" (7).

16. Eli Mandel, "Writing West: On the Road to Wood Mountain," in *Trace: Prairie Writers on Writing*, ed. Birk Sproxton (Winnipeg: Turnstone, 1986), 40–41; Robert Kroetsch, "The Moment of Discovery of America Continues," in *The Lovely Treachery of Words* (Toronto: Oxford University Press, 1989).

17. See particularly Kroetsch's essays in *The Lovely Treachery of Words*; Kroetsch, *Seed Catalogue* (Winnipeg: Turnstone, 1986).

18. Kroetsch's admission of only "our recent ancestors" suggests one of the difficulties with his theory—since all non-Native prairie dwellers are immigrants, the genealogy of prairie culture must of necessity reach far beyond the prairie itself. In contrast, First Nations people have been in the Canadian West for thousands of years. The recognition of only recent ancestors thus works in some ways to erase this difference and to grant non-Natives native status: immigrants have equal connection and claim to the land.

19. Dennis Cooley, *The Vernacular Muse* (Winnipeg: Turnstone, 1987).

20. See Frank Davey, "A Young Boy's Eden: Notes on Recent Canadian 'Prairie' Poetry," in *Reading Canadian Reading* (Winnipeg: Turnstone, 1988), for a discussion of how Cooley's vernacular can be itself read as a strategy of colonization.

21. Dennis Cooley, ed., *Inscriptions: A Prairie Poetry Anthology* (Winnipeg: Turnstone, 1992), xv.

22. See McCourt, Jordan, Quantic, Thacker, and Cooley; also Rudy Wiebe, "Passage by Land," in *The Narrative Voice*, ed. John Metcalf (Toronto: McGraw-Hill Ryerson, 1972), 257–60; D. M. R. Bentley, *The Gay]Grey Moose*

(Ottawa: Tecumseh, 1992); Sharon Butala, "The Reality of the Flesh," in *Writing Saskatchewan: Twenty Critical Essays*, ed. Kenneth G. Probert (Regina: Canadian Plains Research Centre/University of Regina, 1989), 96–99; in addition to Ricou and Harrison. For arguments that the importance of the environment to prairie writing has been overstated, see Aritha van Herk, *A Gentle Circumcision in "A Frozen Tongue"* (Sydney: Dangaroo, 1992), 90–99; and Deborah Keahey, *Making It Home* (Winnipeg: University of Manitoba Press, 1998).

23. For a recent discussion of Canadian critics' responses to cross-border literary criticism, see Robert Thacker, "Erasing the Forty-Ninth Parallel: Nationalism, Prairie Criticism, and the Case of Wallace Stegner" (*Essays on Canadian Writing* 61 [1997]: 179–202).

4. WILLA CATHER

"The West Authentic," the West Divided

William R. Handley

We are born, so to speak, provisionally, it doesn't matter where. It is only gradually that we compose within ourselves our true place of origin so that we may be born there retrospectively and each day more definitely.

RAINER MARIA RILKE

To a contemporary ear, "the real West" and "the romance of the West" may or may not be synonymous. At the beginning of the twentieth century, however, with the transformation of frontier settlements into communities and cities that increasingly resembled those in the East, the romantic West was also the real West—the old West untouched by the rapid transformations of an industrialized, immigrant society, and for that reason compelling to many readers in its nostalgic appeal. Willa Cather's fiction satisfies this nostalgia yet also upsets any formulaic expectations about heroism and the "real" West that her setting might initially instill in readers familiar with literature of the American West. From our contemporary revisionist viewpoint, Cather seems to have captured an authentic West—with her unassimilated immigrants and harsh environments—more accurately than some of her male contemporaries did in their romanticized renderings of it. Yet for a writer of such ironic detachment, it is ironic that she too should have depended on the West's ability, as literary setting, to authenticate and legitimate her own authorship. This essay examines Cather's "authentic" difference in some of her early western fiction: in developing her "home style," she simultaneously provided a critique of the nationalizing distortions of prevailing retrospective narratives of the West in their attempt to be true to lived experience. What makes Cather original for her time and her work seem authentically "real" was her refusal of a romantic, synthesizing telos so often applied by writers such as Frederick Jackson Turner, Owen Wister, and Theodore Roosevelt to representations of western experience. Cather gives her readers a romantic tone, but irreconcilably divides it against a heavy dose of realism in a manner that undercuts rather than supports prevailing national myths about the West and the homogenizing effects of Americanization that those myths often shaped. ("This passion for Americanizing everything and everybody is a deadly disease with us," she commented in 1924.)[1]

Rilke's observation that individuals compose retrospective narratives of "true" personal origin, as opposed to the accident of their geographical origin, is also true of nations. This cultural back-formation is reflected in the personal narratives of many of the most nationally important writers of the West. Prominent among them were Wister, Cather, and Roosevelt, all of whom were born in the East and lived there most of their lives, yet who all located in their experiences out west the sentimentalized source of their true identity and their authority and authenticity whether as writer, politician, or polemicist. They used romantic language to convey the authenticity of their identities and origins: "I am myself at heart as much a Westerner as an Easterner," wrote Roosevelt; in the West, "the Romance of my life began." Inserting women into this American romance with the West, Cather wrote in *O Pioneers!*, "The history of every country begins in the heart of a man or a woman." Toward the end of her life, Cather wrote to Zoe Akins that the most real and interesting part of her life had been spent in the West with her brother.[2]

Whether personal or national, these narratives of origin were written as historical even if they followed literary convention more than chronology; they could not convince the imagination without a patina of historicity. The oft-observed vanishing of the Old West gave writers the license to fill in the picture of "history." In his preface to *The Virginian* (1902), Wister writes, for example, "Any narrative which presents faithfully a day and a generation is of necessity historical; and this one presents Wyoming between 1874 and 1890." Wister's seemingly ingenuous comments to the reader respond to a predominantly white readership's interest in authentic writing about the West. Since frontier life was not only geographically but, after the turn of the century, also temporally distant, eastern readers of the time wanted to know what it was *really* like. The contradiction that Wister's influential romance presents itself as historically faithful bothered neither the author nor most of his numerous readers. A decade later, Zane Grey also presented his dramatic novel of southern Utah in the early 1870s, *Riders of the Purple Sage*, as an authentic rendering of a particular historical time, place, and people. One key to the success of these early popular Westerns was their rudimentary historical anchoring: if the author provided dates and state names and drew on a known political controversy (whether, in Wister's case, Wyoming's Johnson County War of 1892 or, in Zane Grey's, Mormon polygamy), he had recovered literarily what had been presumably lost in fact: the true West, uncorrupted by industrialism and holding social change at bay. It is difficult to imagine early-twentieth-century Westerns with settings contemporary and hence most familiar to their readers. The claim to authenticity often depended for its success upon a historical and not just geographical distance between the reader and the novel's setting, the divided sense that the author's literary landscape is real but gone. "Had you left New York or San Francisco at ten o'clock this morning," continues Wister with the air of empiricism, "by noon the day after to-morrow you could step out at Cheyenne. There you would stand at the heart of the world that is the subject of my picture, yet you would look around you in vain for the reality. It is a vanished world."[3] By invoking the certainties of space, federal naming, and railroad time, Wister connected his readers to the "reality" of his West. Wister's rhetoric likely dissuaded many readers from considering whether his picture had in fact ever existed at all—especially since discourse about the West for decades nostalgically described it as vanishing, a belief as true as its meaning and significance were contestable.[4]

In the context of Westerns by Wister and Grey, an often overlooked literary context in which Cather needs to be read, her early Nebraska novels *O Pioneers!* (1913) and *My Ántonia* (1918) stand out as not only aesthetically more complex but as more authentically historical portraits. An artist must possess "two things, strong enough to mate," Cather claimed, "without either killing the other—technique and a birthright to write." If we read "birthright" as experience, Cather's birthright—though not birthplace— is among the reasons for her noted authenticity. Unlike Wister and Grey, who visited Wyoming and Utah after their youth, Cather grew up in the state she wrote about and based many of the characters in *O Pioneers!* and *My Ántonia* on people she knew, such as Annie Pavelka, the Bohemian girl upon whom she modeled Ántonia Shimerda. In explaining why she chose not to tell Ántonia's story from the perspective of Annie Pavelka's lover, Cather argued, "my Ántonia deserved something better than the *Saturday Evening Post* sort of stuff," suggesting an intentional divergence from the clouds of popular romance—and from some of her early stories.[5] Cather criticism and biography abound in the unearthing of the real people and places that by proxy fill her fictional worlds. Whereas Wister's Wyoming is, in a sense, not to be found on any map, one can still go see the physical testaments of Cather's Red Cloud, and each year thousands do so. (One of the curiosities of visiting Red Cloud is that tour guides refer to characters from *My Ántonia* and not the real people who inspired them when describing who lived in what houses: "This is where the Harlings lived," one guide told me.) Wallace Stegner's appellation for Cather's work, "the West Authentic,"[6] is echoed in Sharon O'Brien's title for the last chapter of her study of Cather's early years: "The Road Home," which the Cather scholar John Murphy also used as the title for his study of *My Ántonia*. O'Brien observes that in Cather's essay "My First Novels (There Were Two)," Cather uses the word "home" several times to describe her discovery and return to her own "authentic" material. O'Brien argues that *O Pioneers!* marked the beginning of Cather's repeated arrival at that destination, "so while all the novels she would write after *O Pioneers!* are not set in the West . . . it is safe to say that after *O Pioneers!*, Cather never wrote an inauthentic or 'external' novel."[7]

This school of Cather criticism—like the tourism it helps to inspire— seeks to authenticate historically what feels authentic artistically, as if the critic's role is to honor the second narrator's assertion in the preface to *My Ántonia* that she and Jim Burden "agreed that no one who had not grown up in a little prairie town could know anything about it."[8] Written after the immense popularity of Wister and Grey, whose work invited its readers to inhabit a vanished West, Cather's preface reads in part as a criticism of (men's) imaginative colonialism and sham history. Yet if the second narrator's statement in *My Ántonia* about experience and knowledge is true, then logically no reader who had not grown up in Nebraska can claim to "know *anything* about" Nebraska after finishing Cather's novel—and thus cannot but accept that the portrait is authentic without the experience to discount it. Even so, many of Cather's contemporary readers claimed to recognize its authenticity without such experience. Ferris Greenslet, Cather's editor at Houghton Mifflin in New York, experienced "the most thrilling shock of recognition of the real thing of any manuscript" he ever received, while H. L. Mencken, who praised it as the most romantic novel of its time, wrote that "its people are unquestionably real." Randolph Bourne, whom Cather thought the best reviewer in the business, wrote, "You picked up *My Ántonia* to read a novel . . . and find yourself enthralled by autobiography."[9]

Such an effect was clearly Cather's intention. Strongly lending to it is the novel's introductory frame, a device she borrowed from French and Russian novels, in which a narrator comes into possession of a manuscript. With this introduction, Cather establishes a double narrative structure: a first narrator, identified only as a childhood friend of Jim Burden's and as a woman (in the 1918 introduction) is given the manuscript by Jim Burden.[10] The act of creation of this manuscript is fictionally represented, paradoxically lending the subsequent text the sense of a real, historical origin, as if the narrator briefly introduces herself in order to authenticate the manuscript and then disappears to let an old friend speak. Given the way in which Jim's adult career and his wife's political causes, as described by the first narrator, are contemporaneous for the novel's first readers, the introduction serves as a window that opens onto a historical past connected to the reader's present in 1918. Yet while the introduction serves this authenticating function, it also calls it into question by means of the gendered difference between Jim and the extranarrative voice, who never writes *her* version of Ántonia. Only with both versions, the narrator states, "we *might* . . . get a picture of her" (xii). In referring to this "necessary duality," Cather gives us, writes Janis P. Stout, "the key that helps us see the deficiency of Jim's view, and uses his omissions to convey more than his self-consciously romanticized narrative can accommodate."[11] Though her version remains unwritten, the narrator claims it is Jim's version she is most interested in because "he had had opportunities that I, as a girl . . . had not" (xii–xiii). Lending the novel a sense of historical authenticity, then, the introduction also points to the enabling limits of men's narratives of western experience. While their opportunities, like Jim's, provide them the power to raise capital, develop the railroad, and write the story of the West, we *might not* have an accurate or authentic picture of Ántonia and the "country" that she "*seemed* to mean" (xii, xi–xii).

The novel's reality effect thus simultaneously foregrounds the romanticizing act of male possession—this is Jim's Ántonia—and introduces us to Cather's duplicitous literary terrain.[12] By claiming the literary territory of Nebraska for herself and by authorizing her own experience, Cather competed with the prominent men of her time who claimed the West as both personal and national ground. By asserting that no one who had not grown up there could know anything about it, Cather made manifest her literary authority to write about her West, against the wests of Roosevelt and Wister, who arguably exemplify the kind of masculine acquisitiveness she found sterile and adolescent and that she made a subtle critical subject of her art. Aware and fiercely protective of her artistic image, Cather would not, of course, describe her aesthetic choices as professional jockeying, but rather as a matter of almost unconscious discovery. The authenticity she claimed to feel after writing *O Pioneers!* was similar to the feelings of her reviewers: "In this one I hit the home pasture and found that I was Yance Sorgeson and not Henry James." To distinguish her literary style and regional allegiance, Cather makes a fabulous claim: "I am a Swedish immigrant farmer, not a Henry James." (Though he wholly admired *A Lost Lady*, F. Scott Fitzgerald would later joke about Cather's "History of the Simple Inarticulate Farmer Turned Swede.") Cather's new—and, she liked to claim, unique—literary territory, her sense of home in Nebraska, and her personal identity were imaginatively bound together, forming a self-generated myth of the artist sprung organically from her native soil.[13] Employing images of pastoral journeys and creation sui generis, she claimed in 1931 that her Nebraska novels virtually wrote themselves. "Here there was no arranging or 'inventing'; everything was spontaneous and took its own place, right or wrong. This was like taking a ride through a familiar country on a horse that knew the way," Cather wrote of *O Pioneers!*. "When the next book, *My Ántonia*, came along, quite of itself and with no direction from me, it took the road of *O Pioneers!*"[14] Cather is literally saying that horses can know intuitively where the rider wants to go and that a book can write itself with no help from an author, but she is effectively making a more believable assertion: "I am the Real Thing." Yet as her anthropomorphizing diction suggests, and as her novels demonstrate, the "real thing" is produced through literary craft, as in her imagery above: she naturalizes the act of writing ("taking a ride through a familiar country on a horse"), erases the author ("with no direction from me"), and anthropomorphizes the novel ("it took the road"). Cather wants her readers to believe that her writing is as natural as an unadulterated landscape. By metaphorizing artistic production with pastoral and arguably frontier images, Cather succeeded in getting the western landscape to authenticate her writing, given that the West was so often imagined as the source of authentic American character even by urban readers who had never lived there.

As with Wister's, Cather's work encourages the reader consensually to grant its historical authenticity, to confirm that the author knows of what she speaks. And Cather scholars have written a great deal in corroborating that point. The first narrative voice in *My Ántonia*, for example, often has been read unproblematically as Cather's, as Jim Burden's has been also.[15] The first sentence of *O Pioneers!* situates her contemporary reader temporally in relation to the novel's setting, suggesting a past as real as, and connected to, the present: "One January day, thirty years ago, the little town of Hanover, anchored on a windy Nebraska tableland, was trying not to be blown away." In relation to the novel's first readers, "thirty years ago" would have meant 1883—the year Cather moved with her family to Nebraska from Virginia and also, curiously enough, the year the railroads across the nation agreed on daily standard, uniform time.[16] Yet how does this opening sentence situate later readers? Just as the town is ambiguously anchored on the plain, the novel is ambiguously anchored in time. At points during the novel, as the novel's present passes into the twentieth century but not up to the first readers' present, Cather uses the present tense to give a sense of immediacy, as when she describes Alexandra Bergson's brothers: "Lou now looks the older of the two" (93). As the novel's first sentence suggests, what seems anchored historically by dates and names is as tenuous and ephemeral, because literary, as life on the harsh prairie itself—and yet, paradoxically, authentic *because* ephemeral, a relation Wister relied on in asserting his Wyoming's historical reality in the same breath that he proclaimed it nonexistent. Wister's vanished West would prove more reproducible and hence seen in film versions and in the films and television shows they inspired. Cather sold film rights only for *A Lost Lady*; her West thus remained mostly unseen in this image-oriented century when many Americans have remained nostalgic for the authentic living West they cannot experience but always like to go see, whether at the movies or in a recreational vehicle.

No matter how successfully Cather steered her readers toward authenticating her version of the West, and no matter how often her critics have fulfilled her wishes, biographical verisimilitude may be the least of the reasons Cather's work has historical and aesthetic value. Hermione Lee argues that although Cather

> draws intensely on her personal experience, her fiction is not satisfactorily accounted for in biographical terms. . . . Her apparent simplicity, her authenticity and authority, her deep connection to places . . . make her look straightforward and available. But she is no public monument, no laureate of rural America. The journey for Cather must be through her language, her obsessions, and her evasions. . . . The memorial signposts helpfully put up all over "Catherland" by the State of Nebraska are misleading markers.[17]

The significance of Cather's work lies not in her personal history, her historical accuracy, or in Catherland, but in how she questioned and reshaped the literary materials and cultural presumptions that surrounded her: the alignment of masculinity with pioneering; the nationalist (and seemingly manifest) significance of the frontier; the belief that Americanization was possible, necessary, and valuable;[18] and naturalism's belief that nature and culture are more powerful than the individual.

That her early Nebraska novels are implicit and sometimes quite ironic commentaries on so many American beliefs yet as seemingly plain and flowingly woven as the Great Prairie is perhaps her most significant and broadest contribution to writing about the West, a body of literature that over the last century has ranged widely between dishonest romance and the cynicism frequently born of even the most honest historical revisionism. Cather's "authenticity," the sense that her characters seem so real, needs to be understood within the cultural context in which a few young men from the East—chief among them, Harvard-educated Owen Wister and Theodore Roosevelt—came to claim authority to represent the West as it "really" was for reasons that had less to do with either art or disinterested history than the public might have believed they did. Despite some of the conservatively nostalgic leanings Cather shared with the men who also most notably represented the West for the American public, her work is singular for the fiction of her time about the West: it tells the truth not so much about real places and people, but the more telling truth about the need for fictions of them—and about the real social consequences and blind spots of synthetic, synthesizing narratives.

Discovering the West

Cather's short story "Eric Hermannson's Soul," published in *Cosmopolitan* in 1900, reveals her early awareness of, and even subjection to, the romantic fantasy about the West for which *The Virginian* became famous.[19] It is also a subtle critique of that fantasy's limits and failures. Cather's story certainly leans more in the direction of popular romance fiction, with regard to tone if not plot, than any of her later Nebraska novels, but the story is also about the untranslatability of experience and the uncrossable divides among differing cultural experiences. Where Wister makes humorous the Virginian's and Molly's cultural differences and brings his characters to the altar, Cather conveys the poignant impossibility of a life shared by her story's romantic protagonists, Eric and Margaret: "She was a girl of other manners and conditions, and there were greater distances between her life and Eric's than all the miles which separated Rattlesnake Creek from New York city." Cather engages the materials of popular romances but alters the happy convenience of their conventional plots. She clearly believes the romantic impulse merits description, yet she thematizes not romance itself but the gap between experience and the (often romantic) representation of experience, what one Cather critic has called "the gap between the actuality of things, the lived event, and its subsequent narration." [20] Narratives of the West so often participate in, yet deny, this gap, but Cather, along with Stephen Crane, is one of the first major writers about the West after Mark Twain to make it her theme.

The historical distinctiveness of Cather's attitude about the West as a literary subject is clarified when situated against Owen Wister's and Theodore Roosevelt's experiences out west and the fact of their subsequently influential writing about it. Roosevelt graduated from Harvard in 1880, got married, and began a career in law; but in the winter of 1884 he suffered a double tragedy with the deaths of his mother one day and his wife the next, after which he famously wrote that "the light had gone out of my life." [21] This suffering was quickly followed by a political setback, and Roosevelt decided in the summer of 1884 to renounce politics, make ranching his business, and center his life around Dakota, where he went in August on an extended hunting trip. That he associated the wild outdoors with its restorative effects on his childhood asthma added to the reasons Roosevelt looked back on this experience as a saving and defining one. Wister had an experience similar to the man's to whom he later dedicated *The Virginian*: after graduating from Harvard in 1882, Wister considered pursuing his love of music in Europe, which brought him into conflict with his father; though his father eventually consented, Wister vengefully determined to follow his father's original suggestion and work for the investment firm of Henry Lee Higginson. In the spring of 1885 his health broke down—possibly a nervous breakdown—and Dr. S. Weir Mitchell, who had delivered Wister as a baby, recommended a trip to a ranch in the West as a cure. From that point on, although Wister practiced law until his father's death in 1896, his true career was settled: he would write about the West.

These experiences have echoes—and interesting divergences—in both Cather's fiction and in her life. In "Eric Hermannson's Soul," Wyllis Elliot, who "had spent a year of his youth" in Nebraska, revisits the area in order to buy cheap land. "When he had graduated from Harvard," Cather writes, "it was still customary for moneyed gentlemen to send their scapegrace sons to rough it on ranches in the wilds of Nebraska *or* Dakota" (26, emphasis added). When Roosevelt ventured his first trip to Dakota in 1883, he took his brother, Elliott. In 1884 he made his second trip (like Wyllis Elliot) in search of good investments, and became a part owner of a Wyoming cattle ranch run by a Harvard classmate. In 1885 Roosevelt published his first book on the West, *Hunting Trips of a Ranchman*, which he dedicated to Elliott, his brother. That Cather names her character Wyllis Elliot is probably no co-incidence, if one also considers the fact that Cather published "Eric Her-mannson's Soul" fours years after Roosevelt's popular, multivolume The Winning of the West was completed and two years after Roosevelt had become famous at San Juan Hill in 1898. Cather also inserts her boyish nickname as a youth in her character's name: Wyllis ("Will is") Elliot—suggestively identifying herself with this young rancher and relating herself familially to the most famous living American and writer of the West. It also suggests the beginning of Cather's own distinct significance in the literary West.

Such identification serves revision, not simply reinforcement, of Roo-sevelt's ethos and significance. Cather's story is about the struggle over the soul of the rural immigrant whose name "Her-mannson" androgynously rewrites the kind of masculinist ventures for the (western) country's soul that made Roosevelt famous. In this and other early western stories, one witnesses the beginning of Cather's professional struggle over the literary terrain seized for both private and public mythology in the decade after the frontier's passing by the period's most celebrated man. That terrain for Cather was never male-dominated or -defined, except in the male imagina-tion. Cather's revision is a blunt and ironic reminder of the privilege that en-ables both the purchase of land and the power to narrate history, and it un-dercuts the eastern establishment's sense of its own importance. By not choosing solely regional influences and institutions for her characters, she also illustrates the complex and symbiotic relationship—both in her cul-ture and in her own life—of the mutual validation of both eastern and west-ern origins and authority.

Cather's 1900 story portrays its male characters against western type, a type constructed for an eastern audience. "These young men," continues the narrator, "did not always return to the ways of civilized life," but, like Roosevelt, Wister, and the narrator of The Virginian, Wyllis Elliot "had not married a half-breed, nor been shot in a cow-puncher's brawl, nor wrecked by bad whisky, nor appropriated by a smirched adventuress" (26)—in other words, he did not live out the popular literary convention for masculine ad-venture. Instead, he "had been saved by his sister," Margaret, the story's heroine, "who had been very near to his life ever since the days when they read fairy tales together and dreamed the dreams that never come true" (26). During their visit, Margaret meets and comes to love Eric Hermann-son, who was "handsome as young Siegfried, a giant in stature, with a skin singularly pure and delicate, like a Swede's . . . and eyes of a fierce, burning blue, whose flash was most dangerous to women. He had in those days a certain pride of bearing, a certain confidence of approach, that usually accompanies physical perfection" (33).

Dividing her characterization between romance and naturalism, she adds, "but the sad history of those Norwegian exiles, transplanted in an arid soil and under a scorching sun, had repeated itself in his case. Toil and isolation had sobered him, and he grew more and more like the clods among which he labored. . . . It is a painful thing to watch the light die out of the eyes of those Norsemen, leaving an expression of impenetrable sadness, quite passive, quite hopeless, a shadow that is never lifted" (33). In her work, Cather shares with Frederick Jackson Turner an environmentalist interpretation of culture and character, but rewrites his view of the frontier's progressive evolution and its socially homogenizing effects. Whereas the light went out of Roosevelt's life back east, propelling him to seek rejuvenation in Dakota, the harsh Dakotan existence takes the life out of Cather's Swedish immigrant. Whereas the Virginian rubs the taint of eastern civilization out of his bride, in Cather's early manner it is the awkward, rough immigrant who yearns for but falls short of what the East represents. "You are the only beautiful thing that has ever come close to me," Eric says to Margaret. "You are like all that I wanted once and never had, you are all that they have killed in me" (37).

A story that often reads as if it anticipates the sappiness of romantic Westerns ("the strength of the man was like an all-pervading fluid, stealing through her veins" [40]) fulfills its deeper naturalist impulse: "All her life she had searched the faces of men for the look that lay in his eyes. She knew that that look had never shone for her before, would never shine for her on earth again, that such love comes to one only in dreams or in impossible places like this, unattainable always. . . . All that she was to know of love she had left upon his lips" (43, 44). Though Cather's novels would never be as purple in their prose as this story in *Cosmopolitan*, the double impulse to represent the most romantic version of experience with the most brutal recognition of the hard soil upon which it most often falls never leaves her work.

Between the publication of "Eric Hermannson's Soul" in 1900 and the publication of *O Pioneers!* in 1913, a change occurs in Cather's view of the West: it is not the East but the West that comes to represent rich, authentic life, the life that has "light" in it. It is as if Cather turns against the language of popular romance employed in her early work only to romanticize the West in a manner she had previously reserved for eastern and European culture. In effect, she begins to find in the West a rejuvenating source of life and the pull of found identity that Roosevelt and Wister experienced and wrote about. Curiously enough, this turn seems to have come about primarily through an experience similar to theirs.[22] The Nebraska writer "discovered" the West's restorative powers when she took a trip to the Southwest—her first—in 1912. As if imitating her story of a decade before, Cather went to Winslow, Arizona, and explored "a new country" with her brother Douglass, who was working on the Santa Fe railroad. Cather envisioned the trip "as a restorative vacation." It became more than that, however: having long suffered, in her friend Elizabeth Sergeant's words, a "truly gruelling inner pull" between eastern literary culture and her western background, she found a new "integration and tranquillity" and seemed to "be all of a piece" during this trip, after which she began to write *O Pioneers!*.[23]

It was the beginning of her subsequent identity as an artist. "Cather believed she had discovered her authentic, essential identity in the Southwest in 1912 and then expressed that identity honestly and openly in *O Pioneers!*," writes Sharon O'Brien.[24] Elizabeth Sergeant cites the fact that Cather composed the poem she was later to use as the epigraph to *O Pioneers!*, entitled "Prairie Spring," after her stay in the Southwest. "The vast solitude of the Southwest, its bald magnificence, brilliant light and physical impact," Sergeant writes, toned up her spirit and suggested to her that "a new artistic method could evolve from familiar Nebraska subject matter."[25] While Cather's western youth provided the authentic materials for her art, the impulse to employ them came from the release that only an easterner, and not a westerner, is capable of feeling in the "new" country of the Southwest.

If Cather's transformative experience seems to share much with the experiences and stories of some of her male contemporaries, the experience gave birth to a more complex and distinctive literature. Whatever one might say today about Cather's conservatism, she made bold choices aesthetically and professionally, as she continued ironically to undercut masculinity's alignment with nation-building and to criticize the most homogeneous forms of Americanization, setting all this against a naturalist's landscape that revealed people to be small, distinct, transient, and yet heroically enduring. Unlike such writers of Westerns as Grey and Wister, Cather does not treat the individuals of her story and the story itself as a telling instance of a larger national or moral allegory. Even though she personifies the land and seems to spiritualize human interaction with it, nowhere can one locate the kind of political or social debates that male writers engaged in their literary wests; nor does Cather directly engage herself with contemporary debates about women. Like the landscapes in her fiction, her nonpolemical reticence creates a leveling effect. In contrast to the homogeneous leveling of an assimilationist culture and the economic inequities created by capital, Cather's naturalist leveling was both egalitarian and, by her culture's standards, unrecognizably "American." Her writing implicitly but bluntly acknowledges that the continent cannot—any more than our stories about it—be mastered or honestly put to the service of American beliefs in progress or in capitalism. The land and the human interaction with it may be shaped by such material and symbolic forces in Cather's work, but her work suggests that much that was lived remains unassimilated by culture, narrative, or nation.

Obscure Destiny

In 1896 Cather wrote an essay in the *Nebraska State Journal* on Walt Whitman: "A man without the finer discriminations, enjoying everything with the unreasoning enthusiasm *of a boy* . . . he accepted the world just as it is and glorified it, the seemly and unseemly, the good and the bad. He had no conception of a difference in people or in things" (emphasis added). His literary ethics, she wrote, were no more than nature's, with its level playing field. By the time she took her title from Whitman and wrote *O Pioneers!*, that which Cather found in Whitman to be both charming and yet alien to her own aesthetic sense became the "home" style by which she rendered life on the Great Divide. More harshly than in her judgment of Whitman, Cather decried Mark Twain in 1897 as "neither a scholar, a reader or a man of letters and very little of a gentleman . . . nor a man who loves art of any kind." She compared Twain's laugh to that of "the backwoodsman" and described him as a "rough, awkward, good-natured *boy*." [26] Even though their carefree attitude resembles that of her boyish youth, in her early assessments of Whitman and Twain both their subject matter and style are attacked for boyishly making no distinctions, including that between East and West. Early in her career, Cather looks over—and down—from the eastern side of their aesthetic divide at Whitman and Twain.

By the time she sets her second novel in Nebraska, however, such undiscriminating boys become subjects for her sympathizing art and are joined to a balancing strength in figures like Alexandra Bergson and Ántonia Shimerda. *O Pioneers!* begins, as perhaps no novel of the West ever had, with the image of a male "crying bitterly" and a female coming to the rescue:

Emil Bergson's kitten is atop a telegraph pole, and his tears are soothed by "a ray of hope: his sister was coming," walking, like a cowboy hero, though in less melodramatic circumstances, "as if she knew exactly where she was going and what she was going to do next" (12, 13). Although Alexandra will not ultimately be able to rescue Emil from boyish passions, in *My Ántonia*, Jim Burden's undiscriminating younger self grows up to recognize gratefully Ántonia's powerful, continuing influence on his adult sensibility.

Despite her seeming personal desire to reconcile her divided sensibility, Cather departed both from what she perceived to be the romantic excesses of women novelists and from what she judged the boyish predilections of male American literary writers. In the divide between them, she situated romance against reality, pitted youthful passion against sacrifice, and joined femininity with independence. Like Grey's *Riders of the Purple Sage*, which appeared one year before, *O Pioneers!* represents a woman whose father bequeaths her land and who has to struggle to keep it. Unlike Jane Withersteen, however, who gains her freedom from Mormon tyranny only by losing her land, Alexandra Bergson keeps both her independence and her land and prospers on it. "I'll do exactly as I please with the rest of my land, boys," Alexandra says to her brothers (151), and she does so without a shoot-out, without a man. "The authority you can exert by law is the only influence you will ever have over me again," Alexandra says to her brothers (155). Her fate is not beholden to marriage, her land is not wedded to Empire: more influential than the men in her life is the land itself, the problem of aridity, and her own courage. Sentiment surrounds this woman and her land in Cather's novel, but such affect is divorced from domesticity and nation. For all of her noted mythic qualities, Alexandra is particular, distinctive, even flawed—at times uninteresting, at others blind. And the reality of the masculine world in which she must live is acknowledged sympathetically by her future, self-deprecating husband, Carl, who says to her, "It is your fate to be always surrounded by little men. And I am no better than the rest" (163).

Despite Cather's reversal of female subordination, her work nevertheless portrays the frontier as less socially egalitarian than Frederick Jackson Turner, for one, liked to believe it was. In their misogynist denunciation of women in business, for example, Alexandra's brothers seem impervious to family feeling: "You can't do business with women," Oscar complains after trying to convince Alexandra that only the men of the family can be responsible for the land (155). Whereas Turner argued that the frontier produced composite Americans, Cather's composite picture of immigrants in Nebraska stresses not their Americanness but their ethnic, cultural, physical, and linguistic distinctiveness. Cather neither dramatizes their sense of belonging to America nor downplays the barriers and tensions among immigrant groups. At the same time that she conveys a sense of her characters' quiet but epic heroism, she is unsparing in her portrayal of their unaccountable failures and despair. Cather's description of Emil scything, for example, invokes Alexandra's happy destiny without making its justification any more manifest than the tragedies that outnumber it: "He was not thinking about the tired pioneers over whom his blade glittered. The old wild country, the struggle in which his sister was *destined* to succeed while so many *men* broke their hearts and died, he can scarcely remember" (75–76, emphasis added). Emil embodies the pioneer's optimism as the narrative questions destiny as manifest. He also embodies the kind of leveling Cather saw in Whitman; Emil cannot remember the pioneers' exhausted, broken lives any more than he can foretell how his life and passion will be cut down suddenly, like the leaves of grass he scythes.

With an equal sense of unaccountability, the unconventional heroine nevertheless forgives Frank Shabata for murdering his adulterous wife and Alexandra's brother Emil, telling him in prison, "I understand how you did it. I don't feel hard toward you. They were more to blame than you" (260). Yet the novel's epigraphic poem seems to celebrate the Whitmanian youthful passion that brought the slain couple together. Cather revises Whitman by irreconcilably but accurately invoking the unaccountable. Cather's contrasts and contradictions do not synthesize teleologically into a sense of national destiny, and her equanimity does not imply an escape from history or a social prescription. Despite Cather's constantly metaphoric images, such as the scythe, they do not suggest the kind of larger allegorical design of progress installed in "manifest destiny," only an allegory of unaccountably unequal fates. The narrative voice that describes Emil scything, for example, suggests no explanation of or moral accounting for the disparate fates it recounts, even though the scene seems allegorically loaded. Cather associates Alexandra with the soil and also privileges her as perhaps the first "human face" to look on the land with "yearning and love" in a kind of double erasure of Indian presence. Yet when the narrative voice adds, "The history of every country begins in the heart of a man or a woman" (64), the romance here is with the land more than with a nation; the word "country" in the novel is always ambiguous. Does this sentence mean American history is beginning in Alexandra's heart? Or is this a regional statement? Although there are many nations and cultures referred to in the novel (Mexico, Bohemia, France, Sweden, Norway, Russia, among them), the word "America" never appears; "American" appears suggestively only once in the phrase "American law" and twice in the phrase "American boys" (59, 108, 137), to distinguish Emil from them. While Alexandra thinks Emil is the one Bergson "who was fit to cope with the world" (191), suggesting the promise of assimilation, his murder and the likelihood of Alexandra's continued childlessness call into question the promise of the future: what kind of history is beginning in Alexandra's heart and what are the signs of its posterity or continued prosperity? Though Emil's death is often read as representing the loss of innocent youth, it also represents the loss of an explicitly non-American boy. Emil is survived by his legalistic older brothers, who resemble Americans more than he: this is the price, Cather suggests, of the assimilation sometimes necessary for economic survival.

Cather romanticizes the immigrant experience in O Pioneers!, not by linking it to national narratives of progress or to the racialized rhetoric of Manifest Destiny—though its omissions do encourage the erasure of native peoples' dispossession—nor even by linking it to the vague promise of Americanization. Instead, she romanticizes immigrant experience by anthropomorphizing the land and establishing analogues between people and natural objects. In one example, Cather writes that the field "yields itself eagerly to the plow . . . with a soft, deep sigh of happiness. . . . There is something frank and joyous and young in the open *face* of the country" (emphasis added). In contrast, Emil "was a splendid figure of a boy, tall and straight as a young pine tree" (74, 75). As a result of such naturalizing metaphors, Cather implies that our more essential "nature" is in relation to nature itself and its cycles of growth and death. Farmer immigrants, by implication, are potentially more "authentic" people than urbanites: they choose their environment as opposed to being chosen by the accident of their birth. Their national origins are not the determinants of authenticity, even if they are in part determinants of their memory and their struggle.

Cather's resistance to the more invidious forms of Americanization and her celebration of immigrant farmers is also the result of her distaste for her culture's alignment of masculinity with racialized nationalism. The "country" of the plains offers not only an authentic literary terrain to make her own but stands as a feminized agrarian alternative to masculine "America." Her naturalism suggests not only her belief that Nature will have the last word but also her desire that women, less invested in masculine myths and denied civil rights, would have the last word on narrating the West's history. When Cather ends the novel by imagining a "fortunate country, that is one day to receive hearts like Alexandra's into its bosom," the personified "country" is more land than nation, more nature than culture—yet also a country more of the future than the present. The natural, cyclical economy of the "fortunate" country that will profit from its past has nothing to do in the text with capitalism or national progress. Behind the exuberant prose lies a naturalist's fatalism that no patriot or booster would countenance, but it is one that many women of her time might have identified with.

To label this interpretation as a sign of Cather's feminism is to be anachronistic, however, given her later, strong ambivalence about women's politics. At her most explicitly political Cather is merely appalled by the "mediocrity and vulgarity" of industrial civilization, and turns to nature and region for alternatives. The politics of her art derive primarily from, or at the least exhibit, her understanding that point of view conditions everything and that something always escapes in the divide between historical experience and retrospectively told stories about it. That loss is what nation-building, with its requisite optimism and unifying symbolism, cannot heuristically incorporate.

The epigraphic poem in *O Pioneers!* thematizes the (American) optimism that escapes even the harshest reality, just as the somber land escapes human will. Divided into two sets of images, the poem begins with descriptions of the "flat," "sombre," "silent," "heavy," and "black" land, the "tired men," the "long empty roads," the sunset "fading," the sky "unresponsive." "Against all this," the poem then situates "Youth, / Flaming . . . Singing . . . Flashing" with its "fierce necessity, / Its sharp desire." Cather's gerunds provide a sense of movement and life that the land's blunt characteristics do not. While Youth knows an "insupportable sweetness," the poem implies that the silent land, the empty roads, and the heavy soil are insupportable without that sweetness and the Whitmanian "Singing and singing." There is no unifying synthesis in Cather's poem to compare with Whitman's, however, or to Turner's synthesis of opposite forces on the frontier. There is no reconciliation or even accounting of the sharply poignant contrast between agriculture and desire or between silence and song. Although Youth receives one more poetic line than the land's gradual cycles and silence, the novel introduced by this poem silences Emil's and Marie's passion and soils the ground with their blood, sacrificing their narratives to Alexandra's larger, more lasting story of survival and sacrifice. Cather disavows the purposes to which poetry is put in the American original she borrowed from: she refuses to synthesize harmoniously what she perceives to be the unaccountable, unconquerable, and brutally exacting contest between ideals and reality, between nature and culture, and between art and experience. It is perhaps because of this refusal that many readers find O Pioneers! oddly unsatisfying and that some critics have found it lacking solid arrangement.

Among common readerly dissatisfactions is the character, situation, and fate of the heroine herself. Neither backwoodsman nor cowboy, neither sweetheart nor suffragette, neither rough immigrant nor composite American, Alexandra is a study in nonassimilation to cultural and gendered types. As much as Cather seems to paint her heroism—for standing up to her brothers, for prospering, for being independent—she pointedly denies her character and plot the formulaic expectations of her time. As a locus of cultural assumptions, Alexandra is suited to the Great Divide, which is neither the Wild West nor the East, a region of cultural discontinuity and cultural transplant, a land both barren and fecund. As David Laird has observed, Alexandra saves her family only to have to fight for her own independence against her family.[27] Alexandra breaks the constraints of gender in order to help her family survive but suffers the constraints of gender with her prosperity. Whereas the popular, Turnerian rendering of the frontier saw a linear progress for world civilization through its rapidly recurring cycles of social evolution, the cyclical life on Cather's frontier follows the logic of a zero-sum game between culture and nature or of the cultural contest between an individual woman and her demanding social and natural environment. When Emil and Marie are killed, the reader is left doubting the good of sweet youth and the social point of Alexandra's forgiveness of their murderer. When the novel ends with the suggestion that nature's victory is far greater than Alexandra's, the reader is left to wonder what progress, civilization, and even survival either mean or make. Despite the novel's nostalgic sentiment, a reader would be hard-pressed to say precisely what the nostalgia is for: harsh conditions? loneliness? the murder of innocents? sibling conflict? In Cather's "country" nothing is morally unambiguous, there is no progress without a high cost, and the landscape takes as much as it gives from the people whose stories it dwarfs and swallows up. No destiny is manifest in Cather's country, except with hindsight, and even then its significance is unclear.

If Cather seems to offer a wolf in sheepskin, such duplicity is the key not only to the novel's critical success when it was first published but also to its importance in contemporary American classrooms, given the country's present interest in a reconceived "real" and "authentic" West. Today, we now see with hindsight, in the real West nothing is won without a real loss, and the stories of ordinary people are more moving than narratives of mastery and conquest. In *O Pioneers!* Cather conjoins two irreconcilable stories, one of a woman's nondramatic, hard-won survival and independence and the other of murdered innocents. The stories seem so mythically familiar that one wants to assume their import is transparent, but it is not. Emil thinks of Alexandra testing her seed-corn in the spring and of how "from two ears that had grown side by side, the grains of one shot up joyfully into the light, projecting themselves into the future, and the grains from the other lay still in the earth and rotted; and *nobody knew why*" (148, emphasis added). Many of Cather's urban, white readers *would* have thought they knew why, if those two ears of corn stood for differently racialized people. Her dominant culture believed that anything in society could be explained, improved, reformed, or assimilated through conventional categories of social identity and moral behavior—categories that valued whiteness, Christianity, and masculinity. Emil's modest assertion of wonder and ignorance about survival and causality pits two of the same species against each other; there is no categorical distinction that can account for the difference in their fates.

By relying heavily on such presumed distinctions to make their plots matter, formula Westerns in Cather's time offered starkly contrasting versions of her revisionist parable about a frontier landscape that defied the expectations that most often led people there. In that ironic gap between representation and experience, or between romance and realism, Cather's art achieves at once a sense of historical authenticity and aesthetic duplicity. To paraphrase the extranarrative voice in the introduction to *My Ántonia*, a book romantic in tone yet littered with horrible acts of violence, we "might get a picture" of the country of Cather's youth when we read her work; or we might not: we might instead get an imagined world that feels authoritative yet both satisfies and thwarts a desire for a western past whose truth is unavailable to either romance or realism alone. Jim Burden's romantic tone at the end of *My Ántonia* is also ironic: sensing that he has "come home to [himself]" and found "what a little circle man's experience is" (360)—leaving undescribed his professional life as a lawyer for one of the great railways that transformed the West—Jim composes a fictive, circumscribing origin that retrospectively substitutes for all the human reality that he, in the trajectory of his life, has not been able to assimilate or possess. "Man's experience" gains its inflated, universal meaning only because Jim fails to make greater interpretive sense of the many other fates and destinies that his rhetorical figure leaves out, including Ántonia's. Nostalgia for authentic origins, Cather reminds us, fictionally distorts and diminishes a past whose truth is far more complex than any one man's experience.

Notes

1. Quoted in L. Brent Bohlke, ed., *Willa Cather in Person: Interviews, Speeches, and Letters* (Lincoln: University of Nebraska Press, 1986), 71–72.

2. Geoffrey C. Ward, *The West* (Boston: Little, Brown, 1996), 358; Willa Cather, *O Pioneers!*, ed. Susan Rosowski and Charles Mignon, Willa Cather Scholarly Edition (Lincoln: University of Nebraska Press, 1992), 64; Letter to Zoe Akins, January 3, 1946, Huntington Library. Further references to *O Pioneers!* will be cited parenthetically in the text.

3. Owen Wister, *The Virginian: A Horseman of the Plains* (1902; reprint, New York: Macmillan, 1955), ix.

4. For a study of this discourse in the nineteenth century, see Lee Clark Mitchell, *Witnesses to a Vanishing America: The Nineteenth-Century Response* (Princeton: Princeton University Press, 1981).

5. Sharon O'Brien, *Willa Cather: The Emerging Voice* (New York: Oxford University Press, 1987), 422; James Woodress, *Willa Cather: A Literary Life* (Lincoln: University of Nebraska Press, 1987), 289.

6. Wallace Stegner, "The West Authentic: Willa Cather," in *The Sound of Mountain Water* (1969; reprint, Lincoln: University of Nebraska Press, 1985), 237–49.

7. O'Brien, *Willa Cather*, 424–25.

8. Willa Cather, *My Ántonia*, ed. Charles Mignon, Willa Cather Scholarly Edition (1918; reprint, Lincoln: University of Nebraska Press, 1994), ix–x. Further references to this novel will be cited parenthetically in the text. O'Brien cautions, however, against presuming that the overt texts always conceal covert biographical texts that are the "real" stories. As John Murphy also warns about interpreting *My Ántonia*, "sifting through Jim's memoir merely to understand Cather discredits her accomplishment and reduces the novel to psychoallegory" (*My Ántonia: The Road Home* [Boston: Twayne, 1989], 98).

9. Woodress, *Willa Cather*, 300–301.

10. For a discussion of the 1918 and 1926 versions of the introduction that explores the implications of the indeterminate gender of the first narrator in the latter version, see Karen A. Hoffmann, "Identity Crossings and the Autobiographical Act in Willa Cather's *My Ántonia*," *Arizona Quarterly* 58, no. 4 (winter 2002): 25–50. For a more extended discussion of the two introductions and Jim's narrative than the one in this essay, see William R. Handley, *Marriage, Violence, and the Nation in the American Literary West* (Cambridge: Cambridge University Press, 2002), 141–51.

11. Janis P. Stout, *Strategies of Reticence: Silence and Meaning in the Works of Jane Austen, Willa Cather, Katherine Anne Porter, and Joan Didion* (Charlottesville: University Press of Virginia, 1990), 71.

12. In her chapter "The Duplicitous Art of Willa Cather," Stout quotes *The Song of the Lark*: "You must tell it in such a way that they don't know you're telling it, and that they don't know they're hearing it."

13. Mildred R. Bennett, *The World of Willa Cather*, rev. ed. (Lincoln: University of Nebraska Press, 1961), 200; Hermione Lee, *Willa Cather: Double Lives* (New York: Vintage, 1991), 4. Responding to a New York critic's complaint that "I simply don't care a damn what happens in Nebraska, no matter who writes about it," Cather explained his shock by saying that her second novel "was not only about Nebraska farmers, the farmers were Swedes! At that time, 1912, the Swede had never appeared on the printed page in this country except in broadly humorous sketches" ("My First Novels (There Were Two)," in *Willa Cather: Stories, Poems, and Other Writings* [Library of America, Viking Press, 1992], 964). Like many authors' statements about their originality, however, this one is untrue, and it is unlikely that Cather did not know this. She certainly knew two people who would have known: a Miss Larsen, one of the editors of the *Scandinavian Review*, and Anna Erika Fries, a Swedish writer and a lecturer on Scandinavian literature, both of whom suggested to Cather the possibility of Swedish translations of *O Pioneers!* and *The Song of the Lark* (letter to Ferris Greenslet, December 16, 1916, Houghton Library, bms Am 1925 [341]: 46). Swedes had been appearing on the printed page in the United States for more than a decade—albeit most often in Swedish. For a comprehensive survey of Swedish and other Scandinavian immigrant literature in the United States, see Dorothy Burton Skårdal, *The Divided Heart: Scandinavian Immigrant Experience through Literary Sources* (Lincoln: University of Nebraska Press, 1974).

14. Cather, *Stories*, 963, 965.

15. James Woodress writes, for example, that Jim Burden's "age, experience, and personal history closely parallel [Cather's] own" and that the novel is structured by Jim's memories, "which, of course, were her memories" (289, 290); Cather, *O Pioneers!*, 11.

16. It was the railroad companies, not governments, that first instituted standard time, because the confusion between departure and arrival time zones—two hundred changes between Washington and San Francisco, for example—had complicated railroad companies' functioning and cut into their profits. In 1870 there were about eighty different railroad time zones in the United States alone. The day the railroads imposed a uniform time, November 18, 1883, was called "the day of two noons," because at midday clocks had to be set back in the eastern part of each zone. See Stephen Kern, *The Culture of Time and Space, 1880–1918* (London: Weidenfeld & Nicolson, 1983), 11–13.

17. Lee, *Willa Cather*, 3–4.

18. Guy Reynolds reads Cather's work as fundamentally not about escapism and nostalgia but about racial diversity and the fall of empires. *My Ántonia*, he argues, is a "radical commentary" for its time "on what it is to be 'American'" (*Willa Cather in Context: Progress, Race, and Empire* [New York: St. Martin's, 1996], 83).

19. For a discussion of this and other early western stories by Cather, see Susan Rosowski, *Birthing a Nation: Gender, Creativity, and the West in American Literature* (Lincoln: University of Nebraska Press, 1999), 67–78. Rosowski argues that while "acknowledging the romance traditions of prose narrative, [Cather] neither revolted against nor broke with these traditions; rather she passed beyond them, reinventing the idea of the heroic and revisioning creativity as desire" (67).

20. Cather, *Stories*, 26 (further citations from this story will be given parenthetically in the text); David Laird, "Willa Cather's Women: Gender, Place, and Narrativity in *O Pioneers!* and *My Ántonia*," *Great Plains Quarterly* 12 (fall 1992): 243.

21. G. Edward White, *The Eastern Establishment and the Western Experience: The West of Frederic Remington, Theodore Roosevelt, and Owen Wister* (New Haven: Yale University Press, 1968), 65. See "The East and Adolescence" in this important study for a lengthier description of the motives each man had to go west (52–74). For an account of Roosevelt's and Wister's western experiences and their relation to ideas about masculinity, see the final chapter, entitled "Smile When You Carry a Big Stick," of Kim Towns-

end's *Manhood at Harvard: William James and Others* (New York: Norton, 1996), 256–86.

22. One experience that differed from Roosevelt's, at least, was Cather's infatuation with a young man named Julio, about whom she wrote rapturous letters (see Handley, *Marriage, Violence, and the Nation*, 132–33).

23. O'Brien, *Willa Cather*, 403.

24. O'Brien, *Willa Cather*, 7.

25. Elizabeth Shepley Sergeant, *Willa Cather: A Memoir* (1953; reprint, Athens: Ohio University Press, 1992), 95.

26. Cather, *Stories*, 889, 890, emphasis added.

27. Laird, "Willa Cather's Women," 246.

2. AUTHENTICITY AND NATIVE AMERICAN CULTURES

5. SIMULATIONS OF AUTHENTICITY

Imagined Indians and Sacred Landscape
from New Age to Nature Writing

Drucilla Mims Wall

I have found it a rare experience to speak with people in the United States who feel they are truly living in their home place, who live not on the land but of the land. In the United States, the question "Where are you from?" appears as frequently in ordinary conversation as comments on the weather. So many of us are from somewhere else within our own lifetimes that the ubiquitous, and more important, subsequent question can be predicted as well: "Where is your family from originally?" Such narratives of personal immigration or migration history allow us to define ourselves as we would like others to understand us, as if we could carry a smidgen of the land of our origin with us.

From an indigenous perspective, it can be tempting to interpret this nostalgia for European roots as yet another piece of evidence for the settlement culture, which has become the mainstream, as being dangerously disconnected from the actual American landscape. The Euro-American consumer society so bent on devouring land and resources certainly fits such a profile. However, I will not focus on the hunger and thirst of the market-driven consumer for material things but rather on what I have noticed lying in the consumer's heart—an unexamined acknowledgment of something needed, something lost that forms an intense longing for meaning, for connection to the authentic sacred in landscape that is simultaneously revered and degraded on an ongoing basis. I have further noticed the curious form this longing often takes. Europeans and Euro-Americans have of late intensified their long-established predilection for representing American Indians as the human embodiment of the sacred in "Mother Earth." This phenomenon is as old as first contact but is receiving increased contemporary currency through nature writing, eco-tourism, alternative religious pursuits, and environmentalism generally. The non-Indian seeking imagined Indian connections to authentic truth and sacred wisdom strikes me as a phenomenon that can provide important insight into how mainstream Euro-American culture performs its continuing ambivalence about the land and its native people. Not so long ago, white settlers wanted to Christianize Indians to save them from what whites saw as ignorance and savagery. Now

97

the counterstrain in white culture (that was always there to a lesser extent) seems to have become dominant, and Europeans and Euro-Americans want the Indians to save them. But save them from what?

What is really happening here? In examining these processes of seeking and claiming authentic connection to a sacredness of place, I believe that my particular vantage point on Indian-white crosscultural interaction can be of use because I come from both traditions. Through my father's side of the family, I belong to the Southeastern Creek (Muscogee) Indians of what is now south-central Alabama. The indigenous members of my family never left during removal times, when most southeastern Native people traveled the Trails of Tears to Indian Territory (present-day Oklahoma). For generations those relations have intermarried with fellow mixed-bloods, full-bloods, and whites. Our Indian identity was known to us and our neighbors, but not considered something to be shared casually with government officials or other outsiders. We had survived the bloody Creek Red Stick Civil War, which eroded trust among some of our bands. We survived the subsequent harsh removal policies pushed by Andrew Jackson, and the continuing pressures of rural disenfranchisement and poverty. Even up to the time of the Civil Rights movement and after, Indian identity in the South could be a very private matter, complicated by racist laws such as the "one drop" rule, which stated that any person with one drop of Indian or African blood was to be classified as "colored" and treated accordingly. Violence and betrayal have remained a lingering possibility, but the home land base has remained alive and enduring. The old farm that housed my great-great-grandmother down to my father is now paved under Ruckers Air Force Base. Some of us live near the old stomp grounds, and some are scattered from Arizona to Philadelphia. We don't know the old language, but we still tell the stories that bind us to the place of origin, only in English now.

Of the seven state-recognized bands of Creeks/Muscogees, only one—the Poarch band—is federally recognized. The Southeastern Creeks have no reservation lands, are struggling to recover much of our Indian culture, and often find our authenticity as Indian people questioned by other Indian groups who experienced white contact hundreds of years after we did. Yet we have always known who we are, however embattled and compromised that knowledge may have become.[1]

As a Southeastern Creek of mixed heritage, I have learned to be comfortable being uncomfortable in both traditional Indian and mainstream white culture. Neither an insider nor an outsider in either group, I am an intensely interested observer of both. I also understand what it is to experience longing for recovery of what has been lost culturally and spiritually.

I began looking into the representation of Indians as symbolic of sacred landscape in an unlikely place—among the misty mountains and deep lakes of County Sligo in the West of Ireland. I can attest to the powerful presence of the sacred in that landscape. In July 1999 I was descending from the cloud-softened crest and neolithic tombsite of Knocknarea, ancient mountain whereon stands the stone cairn of Queen Mebhdh (pronounced *maeve*). My sister-in-law Susan Frasier, whose family has lived in the area for generations, chatted with me as we trod grassy turf that cushioned us from black granite and stepped over rushing rivulets shed by the rain-saturated ground. She had explained one of the site's many powers, that of making people feel stronger and more energetic after spending just a short time on that low peak. I agreed. I felt charged with life and ready for a big dinner at her house. I asked about the odd bunch of skinny wooden poles we had found near the tomb. Someone had set poles into the frame of a tepee about five feet high—no covering, just long twigs, really, that couldn't have served as broom handles, let alone a tepee structure. I felt deeply unsettled seeing that phony tepee frame set on a sacred site of ancient Ireland, as if someone had tried to exploit imagined trappings of spirituality mixed up in some kind of New Age stew.

Susan had lived in Germany for several years before returning to her home area in Ireland, and she explained to me that in many countries on the continent, especially Germany, people pursued their version of American Indian traditional spirituality. She figured that a tourist of this type had set up the tepee shape to celebrate the special earth powers believed to emanate from sacred places such as Knocknarea. She further told me that you can have special Indian ceremonies performed in Europe to cleanse your spirit and restore your body. You could have a sweat lodge, a water lodge, an air lodge, a pipe lodge, a leather lodge; there seemed to be no end of lodges. For a minute I wondered if I had missed something I ought to know about in actual American Indian cultures. What was a leather lodge, for instance, and what kind of faded-out fake Indian was I for never having heard of it? Susan elaborated that you could have ceremonies in real tepees and everything. She wondered if any Indians back in America still lived in tepees. Although she doubted it, Susan said many Europeans believed that Indians did prefer tepees. I explained that even historically, many Indians had never lived in them. The tepee was a Plains Indian invention. As we neared the bottom of the trail, I imagined all these recent European simulations of Indian spirituality might well be the legacies of earlier simulations performed by touring Wild West shows and dime novels. The Noble Savage was alive and well in the trappings of the Shaman.

I forgot about the phony tepee until shopping in Enniscorthy, far southeast of Sligo, in the rich Irish farmland of County Wexford. Among aromatherapy candles, greeting cards, pottery, Celtic design jewelry, and gift-packaged gourmet condiments, I was surprised to find a large, locked glass case full of American Indian–style items. Medicine bags, pipes, arrows, tomahawks, porcelain dolls, kachina figures, jewelry, each item dripping beadwork and feathers, shimmered artfully on small fur pelts of what looked like rabbit. Rabbit is the trickster figure in Creek oral tradition. His presence felt appropriate. This was the only case in the shop secured with a lock.

In a related incident, a Lakota friend had told me about a visit to her reservation by a German "Indian Club" group. After three or four days of pow-wow, including traditional dancing and the ubiquitous fry bread, one of the German guests confided to a Lakota man, "This visit has been wonderful, but I must tell you that we are really better Indians than you are." The Lakota man smiled and replied, "Yes, that is true. But give us a year, and we'll be better Indians than you."

European fascination with their perception of authentic American Indian connection to the sacred earth reflects, among other more dubious things, what I believe is a well-intentioned, increasing awareness of ecological concerns that are, by their nature, intrinsically tied to issues of the sacred in landscape. At the heart of the environmental crisis of exterior landscape is an analogous crisis of internal, spiritual landscape centering on the longing for meaning and authenticity—true immersion in and communion with the thing in itself that can be described as the divine power at the heart of the living world. Surely this is a worthy spiritual pursuit, but not at the expense of Native people.

Perhaps actual Indian approaches to land conservation and respect for sacred presence will help redeem people of the European tradition. There is evidence of scientific interest in the environmental-management potential of Native American approaches to nature.[2] However, what I have seen of European and Euro-American engagement with Indianness remains a representation or simulation—to use Gerald Vizenor's term—of Indianness, not anything to do with actual Native Americans.

Euro-Americans, more so than Europeans, have been engaged in Indian tropes, both in literature and popular culture, since colonial times, and commonalities between popular-culture and high-culture simulations of Indianness abound. Although those representations found in the high culture of nature writing, which is the type of writing that concerns me here, are more subtle and sophisticated than those of mass culture, they function in the same way. There is something about the idea of the Indian so deeply embedded in the non-Indian American psyche that it remains largely unacknowledged, seemingly a "normal" part of the way nature gets written about. One can trace the cultural legacy from earlier writers such as William Bartram, Henry David Thoreau, and Mark Twain, up through modernists such as William Carlos Williams, culminating with Gary Snyder and Annie Dillard, among others. Before delving into how the links between Indianness and sacred landscape function literarily, let's consider the context for both high- and mass-cultural expressions through Indian eyes.

Consider for a moment how movies and television have treasured the figure of the Indian for dramatic, often contradictory, purposes. We all know well the violent savage, tragic half-breed, and beautiful princess. Interestingly, Spokane/Coeur d'Alene Indian writer Sherman Alexie's film Smoke Signals plays with the romantic construction of Indianness as presented in Dances with Wolves, setting it at odds with the actual life of two Indian boys becoming men as they search for a father who disappeared. Alexie's characters are more complex and alive than the Kevin Costner creation, but box-office sales have not competed with Dances. The moviegoing public has hung out its sign: No Realistic Indians Need Apply.

Not surprisingly, the appropriation of Native American cultural and religious material has long been a sore point for Indians. Recent writings on this phenomenon include Wendy Rose's eloquent indictment of white-shamanism and Jimmie Durham's polemic on representations of Indianness in American art, literature, and culture in The State of Native America. Philip Deloria's book Playing Indian explores the exploitation of imagined Indianness by white American males in particular. Ward Churchill discusses the emotionally charged issue of literal threat of extinction for Native people in his article "A Little Matter of Genocide: Native American Spirituality and New Age Hucksterism." The anger underlying the irony of that title alone speaks volumes for the depth of controversy surrounding this topic. One of the more curious written replies to Indian protests about religious appropriation appears in *Woman of the Dawn: A Spiritual Odyssey* by "Wabun Wind" (Marlise James), a white ex-New Yorker and New Age follower of the man Wendy Rose describes as "the notorious 'Sun Bear' (Vincent LaDuke), Chippewa by blood, who admitted to members of Colorado AIM that he never participated in or attended bona fide native activities." Wabun Wind portrays herself, "Sun Bear," and a large gathering of their white followers as victims of a "disruption" of their "sacred gathering" by an Indian activist who shouted at them about cultural imperialism. She claims to have silenced and dismissed the disrupter by refusing to engage in his argument and that everyone joined her at the "Medicine Wheel" for such procedures as the "Rainbow Crystal Healing Ceremony." There must be hundreds of books mapping similar spiritual quests by non-Indians, not to mention what appears to be an industry involving the various types of healing attempted by whites through "channeling" supposed Indian spiritual guides.[3]

Those appropriating authors who are Native American draw equal fire from Indian critics. Ed McGaa (Eagle Man), Oglala Sioux, is one. His 1990 book published by mainstream publisher HarperCollins, *Mother Earth Spirituality: Native American Paths to Healing Ourselves and Our World*, expertly targets readers longing for meaning and authentic spiritual communion with the sacred in landscape. In short, easy-to-read chapters, McGaa lays out a spiritual all-you-can-eat buffet of ceremonies, including "Receiving Your Earth Name and Finding Your Wotai Stone," "Healing Mother Earth in Your Own Community," and my personal favorite, "Sweat Lodge Checklist."

It is tempting to dismiss such goings-on as just the latest permutation of a nut fringe, but we shouldn't. These instances I have mentioned are just a few in a multimillion-dollar industry. I wonder how many industry dollars go to actual Indian nations. More important than the unethical profiting involved is the deflection of serious inquiry away from the functioning of the figure of the Indian deeply embedded in the Euro-American and European psyches. It may well be that increased desire among non-Indians for a respectful and meaningful relationship with the earth reflects something very sane. The Green Party movement in Europe shows promising advances in environmental policy at the most practical level. Even the mayor of Dublin, Ireland, is a greenie who prefers a bicycle to a limo. But before we can explore just what it is that non-Indians believe the mythic Indian can save them from, we must face clearly the illusions, simulations, and representations of Indianness that obfuscate real spiritual and ecological issues. Such removals of actual Indians in favor of simulated ones, in nature writing as well as popular culture, works to erase Indians, reducing them to controllable, sanitized, virtual Indians. When spiritual/ecological issues are contained by this method, they become just as easily manipulated and dismissed as the phantom Indian figure used to represent them.

Anishinaabe writer Gerald Vizenor offers a complex and playful examination of simulated Indianness in *Fugitive Poses: Native American Indian Scenes of Absence and Presence*. He explains how the representation of Indianness as something mysterious, tragic, nostalgic, wise, and in the past tense effectively constructs the absence rather than the presence of any distinct Native culture. Dominant culture wishes the difficult and complex Native to disappear so that the constructed, controlled, and purely simulated Indian can conceal Indian people rather than reveal them. Vizenor calls for Indian people to turn to what he calls Native transmotion—a creative transforming force at the heart of Native world views—to overturn entrenched notions of the dominant culture. The increasing interest in Native American writing and performance offers many opportunities to accomplish this, but the old constructions die hard.

They die hard because they are treasured images of something more true of Euro-American selfhood than anything truly Indian. A careful look at patterns of representation in American nature writing provides some fruitful insights. The romantic, modernist, and postmodernist notions that permeate American nature writing have so permeated mass culture that they crop up in the exported American pop culture that fuels European fascination with Indian sacred wisdom. The simulated Indianness I encountered in Ireland is not that different from the consumption of American rock music, blue jeans, or movies. We must look at American culture to find what the Europeans are mirroring back at us now.

One of the foundational influences on European concepts of Indianness can be traced to the 1792 book by Quaker Philadelphian William Bartram, *Travels Through North and South Carolina, Georgia, East and West Florida*. Greatly admired by Thoreau, this volume did much to establish the representation of the Indian as the human aspect of the wild American paradise of flora and fauna. Having been commissioned and published first in England by John Fathergill, *Travels* received much wider circulation and more popular reception in Europe than in America. In his introduction to the 1928 Dover edition, Mark Van Doren notes in his introduction that poet Samuel Taylor Coleridge read *Travels* avidly, and that significant influence can be seen in the nearly parallel descriptions of landscape in *Travels* and "Kubla Khan." [4] Perhaps Bartram's and others' reports of Indians hunting and taking their leisure as only nobility could do in Europe also influenced Coleridge's construction of the figure of Kubla Khan, as well as his landscape. Such reports almost certainly contributed to the formation of the Noble Savage stereotype still active in Euro-American nature writing. [5]

Bartram worked to present conscientious observations, with scientific standards of inquiry foremost in his mind. Even though we now regard such attempts at objectivity to be just more phantasms of colonialism, Bartram used these limited techniques much better than many of his contemporaries. The Creeks and Cherokees, among others, were portrayed forthrightly as unpredictable or threatening at times, but Bartram took pains to present them as people, not savage beasts in the way many of his contemporaries did. He strove to be accurate in his writings and drawings of people as well as plants and animals. So Bartram's general depiction of Indians living in close harmony with nature and as knowledgeable about local plants and animals is not surprising.

The 1980 facsimile edition offers an important new introduction by Gordon DeWolf that contextualizes Bartram in both his British and American milieu. DeWolf sees Bartram's text as "the most important and beautiful description of the southeastern United States of the eighteenth century," as not merely a "technical work" of natural history but also "an intensely poetic one." [6] In many ways Bartram serves as a touchstone for European and Euro-American conceptualizations of wild American landscape, with Indian people as integral parts of that landscape. This idea continues to permeate the nature-writing drama—a drama I see as a European or Euro-American search for the authentic and sacred as manifest in aboriginal American land.

However, Bartram's rhetorical stance is one of interested observer rather than one who seeks spiritual answers from Indians. He offers a window on the Southeast of my own ancestors (Creek Indians, Spanish, and English settlers) in the important sense that he tried to observe closely and accurately but with little of the troubled moralizing of later missionary or land-hungry types. He embraces a joy and tolerance in his observations. Perhaps this can be attributed to his Quaker background from his native Philadelphia. Interestingly, some of his opening lines reflect a view of divine creation not unlike the Indian view as I generally know it from my own father's stories. "This world, as a glorious apartment of the boundless palace of the sovereign Creator," Bartram writes, "is furnished with an infinite variety of animated scenes, inexpressively beautiful and pleasing, equally free to the inspection and enjoyment of all his creatures." [7] The bitter wilderness of the Puritans is absent; Bartram wrote against the grain of the growing settler hostility toward Indians and wilderness. For example, he reports that Indian women, who were described by other whites as dirty savages used as beasts of burden by their men, appeared to Bartram to be no more or less happy than their white counterparts in Europe or Euro-America.

Annette Kolodny comments that the negative depiction of Indian women began to be more and more prevalent "after the seventeenth century . . . [when] the excitement that greeted John Rolfe's marriage to Pocahontas, in April of 1614, [ended] due to the fact that it had failed to serve, in some symbolic sense, as a kind of objective correlative for the possibility of Europeans actually possessing the charms inherent in the virgin continent." [8] Bartram writes against this possessive strain as well, showing no interest in converting Indians to Christianity. Thoreau would later provide an updated—and romanticized—variation on this theme.

The nature writer can be reasonably positioned as the essential American writer. After all, many critics have argued that the encounter with wilderness (read nature in its least familiar form), and the individual's struggle to "tame" it, defines American writing generally. And although in this sense nearly every American writer can be read as a nature writer, the master narrative was shaped by Henry David Thoreau, whose influence is pervasive. Bartram may have shaped Thoreau, but it is Thoreau most people think of when they think of the founder of Euro-American nature writing.

In one of many evocations of the Indian, Thoreau expresses admiration for the simplicity with which Penobscot Indians build their homes in the "Shelter" chapter of *Walden*: "Consider first how slight a shelter is absolutely necessary. I have seen Penobscot Indians in this town living in tents of thin cotton cloth, while the snow was nearly a foot deep around them, and I thought that they would be glad to have it deeper to keep out the wind." He saw their shelter as a reflection of Indian ability to be happy simply, rather than any reflection of having to do without. This is to his credit, but he neglects to ask any Indians for their thoughts on shelter; Thoreau leaves them silent, their voices unnecessary to his conclusions about their lives. In continuing his argument for inexpensive housing for all people, especially poor whites, Thoreau explains: "Though the birds of the air have their nests, and the foxes their holes, and the savages their wigwams, in modern civilized society not more than one half of the families own a shelter. In the large towns and cities, where civilization especially prevails, the number of those who own a shelter is a very small fraction of the whole. The rest pay an annual tax . . . which would buy a village of Indian wigwams. . . . It is evident that the savage owns his shelter because it costs so little."[9] An opposition between the problems of "civilized" and "savage" shelters develops further, as Thoreau makes his somewhat confused point that although civilized ways are superior generally, savage wigwams are cheaper and possibly set a good example for poor white people of how to live more independently and simply. The problem of who owns the land on which the shelter is pitched is not broached. Land ownership is the problem for both Indians and poorer whites, not shelters built on land, as the Penobscot Indians could have no doubt explained if they had been asked.

Earlier in *Walden*, Thoreau imagines that he is stepping in the footprints of Indians who are now gone. He walks along the pond and praises the beauty of nature, imagined to be almost as lovely as when the vanished Indians walked there. Treading "like" an imagined Indian, Thoreau imbues himself with an authenticity of appreciation for the place. His tone combines the wistful romantic with the didactic preacher, with an effect approaching moral nostalgia for those people who really knew how to live in harmony with nature.

In *The Maine Woods* Thoreau flavors much of this kind of appreciation for Maine's semi-wilderness with the reported perceptions and behavior of his Penobscot Indian guide. Although he has a name—Joe—Thoreau mostly refers to his guide as "the Indian." When the guide sings one evening, Thoreau writes: "His singing carried me back to the period of the discovery of America . . . when Europeans first encountered the simple faith of the Indian. There was, indeed, a beautiful simplicity about it; nothing of the dark and savage, only mild and infantile. The sentiments of humility and reverence chiefly were expressed." In response to the guide's explanation of what a will-o'-the-wisp is, Thoreau adds: "They [Indians] are abroad at all hours and seasons in scenes so unfrequented by white men. Nature must have made a thousand revelations to them which are still secrets to us."[10] Here is Thoreau representing Indian secret wisdom complete with wonder and nostalgia. Again, his fancy of bonding with the footsteps and perceptions of Indians helps Thoreau claim an authenticity as interpreter of nature that he would otherwise lack.

During the time both Bartram and Thoreau were writing, Indian people were losing more and more land, and their population continued to suffer brutal decimations through disease and war. The forced removal of the five Southern tribes (sometimes referred to as the Five Civilized tribes) under the Indian Removal Act of 1830 happened about sixteen years before Thoreau first visited the Maine woods, for example. Euro-American sentiment was overwhelmingly unsympathetic to Native peoples. Indian women, a group that had been romanticized in the figure of Pocahontas and other aristocratic types of "princesses," were being portrayed as dirty, sullen, and sexually promiscuous.[11] Indian wars were fought regularly in an east-to-west progression throughout the nineteenth century and would have been a familiar piece of background context for Thoreau, and even more so for Mark Twain—another writer who wrote against the grain. Unlike Bartram, who wrote against Puritan attitudes, or Thoreau, who wrote as promoter of Noble Savage romanticism, Twain wrote with an antiromantic stance in creating the character of Injun Joe.

The figure of the noble savage fading into a western sunset, the consummate vanishing American, served well as a safe emblem for the romantic spirit of nature. The Indian could be comfortably written about as an ancient, a possessor of sacred wisdom, victim to the regrettable but inevitable march of progress in the new Euro-American nation. Mark Twain chose to write another type of simulated Indian—the figure of Injun Joe in *The Adventures of Tom Sawyer*. There is no doubt that Injun Joe is associated with nature. He lives as a shadowy, animal-like criminal in caves or woods removed from "civilized" society. I have reason to believe that Injun Joe represented an exaggeration of real Southeastern woodland Indian people, such as my own Creek relations, who refused removal from their ancestral homes to Indian Territory. These Indian communities did live isolated rural lives on land considered undesirable by whites.[12] I know also from my own family's oral histories that such Indians would have been tough fighters, survivors resistant to the laws of a society that had treated them so badly, and frightening figures in the imaginations of white land-takers—perfect material for Injun Joe. He, like the actual Indian refusers, embodies the dark threat of justice or vengeance—the repressed, violent truth about whites' enforcement of Indian removal.

Mark Twain's depictions of human nature often struck close to the bone, and Injun Joe is no exception. The Disney film based on *Tom Sawyer* removed Injun Joe completely, replacing him with an outrageously drunken, dirty, white man. I am not sure what that says about continuing stereotypes about Indians, but I am sure that once again the Indian disappears. That film was sanitized to rid it of a racist stereotype, but, in the process, any Indian presence was removed as well. No "bad" Indians need apply. We see a variation on Vizenor's idea of absence again.

Thoreau's and Twain's opposing uses of Indian constructions point to the enduring tension and ambivalence toward the Indian in Euro-American literature and culture. Often the writer's method for dealing with the tension is to translate it into something else, most often a struggle to discover an authentic identity as an American writer as opposed to a European or Euro-American writer.

Hart Crane concludes the "Quaker Hill" segment of *The Bridge* by evoking the "tribal morn" where we may find Pocahontas—before she meets any white men—or take part in an Indian corn dance. Here, the longing for some meaningful connection to the land is clearly evident. Later, William Carlos Williams would continue the search for what defines American writing. In *In the American Grain* he insists, "The land! Don't you feel it? Doesn't it make you want to go out and lift dead Indians tenderly from their graves, to steal from them as if it must be clinging even to their corpses some authenticity?"[13]

Many may like to think this phenomenon is passing. In answer to this, I offer an example of how digging authenticity from the American land continues to be a common expression of this longing. Nature essayist Lisa Knopp, in her contemplative 1996 collection, *Field of Vision*, includes a section in which a naturalist whom she admires pursues a hobby of finding Indian arrowheads embedded in the Iowa soil. The arrowheads speak of a magical connection to a sacred past when the land was unspoiled by overcultivation. Knopp seems compelled to establish her authorial voice, unconsciously perhaps, and to claim her part in the nature-writing tradition by—at least once in her first published book—getting down in the dirt and digging for Indian cultural remains. How emblematic the Indian arrow is—weapon of defeated and removed enemy no longer a threat, link to the unmediated hunt for animals as food source, evidence of life and work unalienated by a market-driven, urban economy. Still, what happened to the memories of all the arrows that must have been shot for centuries in Europe? I suspect that those arrows are tainted by memories of class inequalities, land lost, people subjugated; but those are European sufferings remembered, unconsciously perhaps and certainly unacknowledged, and not Indian sufferings remembered as Indians remember them. It is a luxury of the colonizing group to play with imagined memories of the subjugated Other. Even when that colonizing group has the best intentions, as ecologically and politically sensitive nature writers do, they still enjoy the benefits, advantages, and casual use of power that allows for such imagined evocations of Indian-arrow symbolism.

Annie Dillard, an established and respected nature writer with a deep Christian spiritual bent, describes herself in great detail as an Indian arrow that will carry her words to the reader in *Pilgrim at Tinker Creek*. The shaft of this arrow is carved by "certain Indians" with grooves resembling lightning. Dillard claims a shamanlike power from this arrow symbol, elaborating that "if the arrow fails to kill the game," the lightning marks will "channel" blood to "spatter to the ground, laying a trail . . . that the barefoot and trembling archer can follow. . . . I am the arrow shaft . . . and this book is the straying trail of blood." [14] Does that make the archer the reader, or the author, or some invoked Indian of the "certain Indians"? Logic dictates that the one following the trail is the Indian archer. So are we made into Indian hunters as we read the trail of blood that is the book? There is no doubt that *Pilgrim* deals with matters sacredly intertwined with nature. Is part of the appeal that the reader can become conjoined with the mythic Indian, holder of authentic sacred knowledge of the native land? Is another part of the appeal that the author can imagine herself as the instrument of the mythic Indian hunter, since she describes herself as the arrow shaft? Is this a variation on serving as an instrument of the Christian God? Such questions are thorny indeed, especially when considering the logical next step, which would join the mythic Indian and the Christian God.

Gary Snyder, eco-poet of substantial white following, has encountered his share of criticism from Indian people for his extensive use of Indian "symbolic" material. *Turtle Island*, his 1975 Pulitzer Prize–winning collection, serves as the most widely read example of his work. Snyder directly embraces his idea of Indianness right from his introductory note: "Turtle Island [is] the old/new name for the continent, based on many creation myths of the people who have been living here for millennia." He adds his ecological focus, explaining that the title should help us "see ourselves more accurately on this continent of watersheds and life-communities. . . .

The poems speak of place, and the energy pathways that sustain life." He concludes by encouraging all people "beached up on these shores" to "see our ancient solidarity." Yet even though Native people have inspired his title, Snyder does not include them in the list of peoples. They are the invisible ones who inspire but do not participate in the life celebrated in the poems. I am sure this was not Snyder's intention, but the limitations of good intentions are exactly the point. All the representations of imagined Indianness I have included so far, as well as hundreds of others, are created with the best intentions. But they nevertheless leave the Indian as nothing but a series of Vizenoresque "fugitive poses," absent from the heart of the matter.

Snyder invokes the old ones in his opening poem, "Anasazi." He links them beautifully to the desert landscape, but with the same free-floating nostalgia he will touch upon again and again. Indians offer pathways to the sacred in the landscape, but only in the past tense. The speaker operates as one who wishes to call up the past and connect with its mystery. The technique is simple and elegant. "Anasazi, / Anasazi," the speaker calls in invocation of the spirits. The next and longest stanza places the speaker in the Anasazi world:

> tucked up in clefts in the cliffs
> growing strict fields of corn and beans
> sinking deeper and deeper in earth
> up to your hips in Gods
> your head all turned to eagle-down
> & lightning for knees and elbows.[15]

Imaginative quality is clearly evoked by the crisp, lean lines. The romanticism of the description is so beguiling that it is easy to forget that the ghostly Anasazi figure is purely a figure and not something based on reality. The connection between the Indian and the land is also packed into the poem. After reading the curious lines "women / birthing / at the foot of ladders in the dark," one wonders: Really? Giving birth at the foot of ladders, and in the dark no less? This is Snyder's imagined female Anasazi? Snyder drops in "trickling streams in hidden canyons / under the cold rolling desert." The word "hidden" captures much of the thrust. These Indians are literally hidden under the desert in the form of bones. They are hidden by time, hidden by the inaccessibility of their dwellings, hidden by cultural distance also. And that is the attraction, the magic that resides in imagining the long-gone Indian (and Snyder does use the singular, not the plural) who can be the object of poetic play in any way the poet pleases.

Such ghostly Indians can be controlled. "Control Burn" and "Prayer for the Great Family" show the poet's control in action. In "Control Burn," no specific Indians are named, as though all Indians were the same, instead of the multicultural beings Indians have always been. Snyder tells how "the Indians" used to "burn out the brush every year in the woods up the gorges" in order to prevent the kind of wildfires that even now devastate large areas of the western United States every year. His ecological point is well taken, but why does Snyder choose anonymous Indians from the past?

"Prayer for the Great Family" ends with the aside, "after a Mohawk prayer." Gratitude is repeatedly expressed to all aspects of the natural world, each stanza devoted to a different element. The poet's concept of unity between Native American spirituality and nature couldn't be clearer. This is the same idea dispensed by Wabun Wind and many other pop-culture New Agers. Why is it palatable from Snyder but poison from Wabun Wind? Where do we locate aesthetic accomplishment in the complex phenomena of imagined Indianness? How do we protect artistic freedom and also protect the actuality—the real existence—of Indian people, none of whom want to be absented from the world in which real issues of sovereignty and land use are matters of life and death? I wonder if some recent developments in tourism, of all things, point toward positive change.

For all the simulations, appropriations, and exploitations of Indianness—well-intentioned or not—a major change is also becoming evident. Indians themselves are making their own presence felt—taking back control of representations and experiences of the spiritual on their own lands. The front-page headline of the *New York Times* from September 21, 1998, reads, "Indian Reservations Bank on Authenticity to Draw Tourists." [16] German and Dutch visitors (American visitors are also present, but Europeans were focused on) who pay to sleep on a dirt floor in a real tepee express such sentiments as, "When I sleep in the Tepee, I feel a lot of connection to the earth"; "I have had a fire every night and I have been able to walk over the prairie. It has a very special energy"; and "It is so interesting to see how these people live today." Photographs show tepees on the Blackfeet Reservation in Montana at the "high drama nexus of the Great Plains and the Rocky Mountains." At last a specific Indian nation gets mention. These are not theme parks built around the fantasies of non-Indians. Authenticity may be an actual possibility in this context. Visitors are just that, welcomed guests in another country, an Indian country, and control of cultural representations is in the hands of Native people.

In addition to tours of Indian lands, Egan notes that record numbers of people (more than six hundred thousand) have visited the National Museum of the American Indian. Other such museums report the same trend. In addition, the Museum of the Plains Indians in Montana notes that, typically, half their visitors are from Europe. Although the Blackfeet Nation expresses concern over holding the line between sharing culture and exploitation, the issue is under Indian control.

N. Scott Momaday addresses this phenomenon in *The Man Made of Words*. He presents himself as a cosmopolitan world traveler and spiritual pilgrim in search of sacred experience at sites in Europe and elsewhere. His Indianness informs his experience just as the identities of non-Indians informs theirs. In the chapter "Sacred Places," Momaday and an Indian friend take a wrong turn on their way to the Medicine Wheel sacred site in the Big Horn Mountains. The layering of history and irony become particularly enjoyable when the two friends encounter another pilgrim who has taken the same wrong turn on his way to the same site. Momaday tells us that this man, Jurg, is from Switzerland. The three continue together and later part after sharing a deep spiritual communion with the divine power of place at Medicine Wheel. Indian and European travel as equals, part as equals. Momaday emphasizes his positive feeling about the adventure. Again we see an Indian in control of the means of representation.

In the storyteller section of the book, Momaday offers a humorously illustrative narrative about knowing one's true place: "The Indian Dog." He tells of buying an Indian dog, which, in spite of being tied and locked in a shed, nonetheless escapes to return to follow his original master's wagon: "The Indian dog had done what it had to do, had behaved exactly as it must, had been true to itself and the sun and moon. It knew its place in the scheme of things . . . in the tracks of the wagon. . . . *Caveat emptor*. But from that experience I learned something about the heart's longing." What of the longing in the human heart? Have we lost sight of our path behind the master's wagon? "To encounter the sacred is to be alive at the deepest center of human existence," Momaday writes. "Sacred places are the truest definitions of the earth. . . . If you would know the earth for what it really is, learn it through its sacred places." [17]

The answer to the longing for authenticity resides in the sacredness of place, not in imagined Indians, nor in any purchased piece of imagined authenticity. No one can buy or borrow the rightness of being in the sacred by grabbing a piece of "Indianness." Both Native and non-Native traditions hold that certain places retain a special share of that deep, divine power. I would expand that idea to include all places as imbued with the sacred; that is part of the important work of the environmental movement, to help us all realize this and act to celebrate and preserve the integrity and authenticity of all the earth. The purely scientific approach to land that has dominated the ecology movement of mainstream European and Euro-American cultures is inadequate.

Perhaps non-Indians' obsession with how simulated Indianness can save them asks the wrong question. It is not what Indians can save non-Indians from, but rather by what process and for what reasons we all experience the heart's longing for the sacred in landscape. It is only in pursuing this question's implications that we can honestly and authentically locate ourselves in our sacred place—here, now, and within our own cultures.

One of the strengths of Momaday's book is that it offers a reversal of the non-Indian view of what is imagined to be Indian, which is so common in the popular culture and nature writing I have discussed. He accomplishes this reversal with a grace and humor that makes clear how the encounter with the sacred otherness of place and other people can happen anywhere. Indians have no more special connection to the earth in, say, Bavaria, than any other non-Bavarian.

Sometimes, if we allow ourselves to be open and respectful to the possibility, sacred places will reveal themselves. Sometimes the human spirit of the place is someone familiar rather than imagined. That is what the sacred in landscape can do, make the familiar new, strange, and just beyond the edges of language. I remember a night when, as an outsider, an American, an Indian, and a relative of local natives, I became a Momadayan pilgrim visiting Lough Arrow, one of the deep island-dotted lakes in the hills of County Sligo in the west of Ireland. I didn't go looking for the sacred; it found me.

Even at ten o'clock at night the lake, under the still-bright sky, flicked small waves like silver conchas upon its illuminated body. Strong, diffuse twilight endured until nearly midnight. It felt like early evening light would feel back in Nebraska. Trout broke the surface here and there, and a plentitude of frogs sang along the banks before plunking under water at my footfalls. This would have been a good time for fishing, but that was not our reason for boating. My husband, two children, and I had returned to my husband's native Ireland for the summer and were visiting his youngest brother, Michael, his wife, Susan, and their two children, who live beside the lake. Michael and Susan use water directly from the lake in their home; that's how clean it is.

Knocknarea Mountain, where Susan and I had wondered about the "tepee" sticks the day before, shadowed the horizon to the north. Oak, ash, and whitethorn gathered shadows beside me in the whisper of field grasses, as the stiff reeds used for centuries to weave St. Brigit's crosses waved from their advance into the lake's edge. Behind me sounded heavy Wellington boots across the bog meadow. Surely my husband and Michael, never trained to be light on their feet, had brought the old outboard motor for the boat. Our children ran over from the road where they had been arguing over naming a cat that had taken an interest in their shoelaces. We tumbled into the boat, Michael set the motor down and took the oars, speeding us out toward the largest island perhaps a mile away or more.

He smiled, saying, "Now you'll really see something," and we did. We saw Michael rowing, his strength in perfect balance, his smile, his health, his love for the lake combined in perfect balance, propelling us over the silver glow of deep cold smoothness that splashed us as the wind increased on open water. We slipped into silence, unable to articulate our excitement. My husband managed to say, "The distances are longer than you'd think." I offered something like, "The light is so beautiful," and fell silent again under the inadequacy of our words. The children let their hands plow the water over the sides. Michael rowed. His oars curled waves of black unbroken by froth—the only sounds the steady wind and voluminous water. The island moved nearer. A little silver fish jumped close to our daughter's hand, and we all exclaimed at such an amazing event. Twilight deepened. The low mountains that cradled us in the lake darkened to pine greens and black. Silhouetted against the still-bright western sky atop Knocknarea Mountain we saw the ancient stone cairn of Queen Medhbh's tomb. No cars stirred on the distant roads. Few lights winked from houses on hillsides. Michael swung the boat toward the island and pulled the oars again. His motion flowed into the yielding lake water itself, into the darkening shore, the air wet and chill with spray, the grassy turf blanketing the granite of Knocknarea, the neolithic tombs as common as farmhouses all over Sligo. Under the silent oncoming stars, my husband's little brother had become the na-

SIMULATIONS OF AUTHENTICITY

tive spirit of the place, the human conduit for the sublime and sacred land of Ireland's "wild West."

Notes

1. For an informative overview of the current situation, see Frank W. Porter, *Strategies for Survival: American Indians in the Eastern United States* (New York: Greenwood, 1986).
2. Annie L. Booth and Harvey M. Jacobs, eds., *Environmental Consciousness—Native American Worldviews and Sustainable Natural Resource Management: An Annotated Bibliography* (Chicago: Council of Planning Librarians, 1988).
3. Wabun Wind, *Woman of the Dawn: A Spiritual Odyssey* (New York: Prentice Hall, 1989), xi–xiii; see also Michael F. Brown, *The Channeling Zone: American Spirituality in an Anxious Age* (Cambridge: Harvard University Press, 1997).
4. See Helen Carr, *Inventing the American Primitive: Politics, Gender and the Representation of Native American Literary Traditions, 1789–1936* (New York: New York University Press, 1996), 53; Mark Van Doren, ed., *Travels of William Bartram* (New York: Dover, 1928).
5. John F. Moffitt and Santiago Sebastian, *O Brave New People: The European Invention of the American Indian* (Albuquerque: University of New Mexico Press, 1996), 133.
6. William Bartram, *Travels Through North and South Carolina, Georgia, East and West Florida*, intro. Gordon DeWolf (Charlottesville: University Press of Virginia, 1980), 3.
7. Bartram, *Travels*, 28.
8. Annette Kolodny, "Unearthing Herstory: An Introduction," in *The Ecocriticism Reader*, ed. Cheryll Glotfelty and Harold Fromm (Athens: University of Georgia Press, 1996), 172.
9. Henry David Thoreau, *Walden; or, Life in the Woods* (New York: Library of America, 1985), 345, 346–47.
10. Thoreau, *The Maine Woods* (New York: Library of America, 1985), 730, 731.
11. Robert S. Tilton, *Pocahontas: The Evolution of an American Narrative* (New York: Cambridge University Press, 1994), 22.
12. Porter, *Strategies for Survival*, 54.
13. William Carlos Williams, *In the American Grain* (Norfolk CT: New Directions, 1940), 57.
14. Annie Dillard, *Pilgrim at Tinker Creek* (New York: Harper & Row, 1974), 12.

15. Gary Snyder, *Turtle Island* (New York: New Directions, 1974), 3.
16. Timothy Egan, "Indian Reservations Bank on Authenticity to Draw Tourists," *New York Times*, Sept. 21, 1998.
17. N. Scott Momaday, *The Man Made of Words: Essays, Stories, Passages* (New York: St. Martin's, 1997), 173, 114.

6. "REAL INDIAN ART"

Charles Eastman's Search for an Authenticating Culture Concept

Christine Edwards Allred

No observer would have been surprised by Charles Eastman's attendance at the first conference of the Society of American Indians in 1911. The individual Indians who gathered to articulate the society's aims "believed," Hazel Hertzberg has argued, "in adapting their attitudes, values, and habits of life to those of the larger American society." Indeed, the society's primary objective was to "help in all progressive movements of the North American Indians."[1] Such an objective only echoed Eastman's own. His history was a history of progressive adaptation. Eastman's great-grandfather was among the first Santee Sioux to embrace white American civilization. Eastman's maternal grandfather, Seth Eastman, a white man, further exposed Eastman's family to the "habits of life" of the "larger American society" in the 1830s. Although the Sioux Uprising of 1862 divided Eastman's family, driving Eastman and others of his tribe into Manitoba, his father, imprisoned in the conflict's aftermath, became assimilated. And in the early 1870s, when Jacob Eastman sought out his son, Charles Eastman followed his father's course. As one of the best-known Indian authors and lecturers of the early twentieth century, Eastman subsequently advocated such adaptation for all American Indians.[2]

The society's intent to ground its defense of progress—cultural adaptation—in scientific theory also resonates with Eastman's earliest autobiographical writings. "The advancement of the Indian," the official report of the society's proceedings insisted, would occur as the Indian was made "free . . . to develop according to the natural laws of social evolution." H. David Brumble's reading of Eastman's *Indian Boyhood* (1902) suggests just how influential such evolutionary thought was in Eastman's early writings. Brumble argues that an analysis of Eastman's initial epigraphic commentary on the American Indian in *Indian Boyhood*—"The North American Indian was the highest type of pagan and uncivilized man"—reveals Eastman's familiarity with the tenets of social-evolutionist thought that sought to classify human societies into stages of development. Juxtaposing Eastman's self-pronounced status as the "highest type of pagan and uncivilized man" and Lewis Henry Morgan's division of Indian societies into stages of savagery, barbarism, and civilization in *Ancient Society* (1877), Brumble suggests that even though Eastman resists the modest "bow-and-arrow Upper Savagery" categorization that Morgan's work implied for the Santee Sioux, he "did assume . . . that societies could be ranked in terms of their stage of evolution." The very "evolutionary thinking" that Brumble identifies in the earliest of Eastman's prose was, Hertzberg argues, "evident" throughout the society's 1911 meetings.[3]

For at least a moment, however, during those meetings, Eastman challenged the general faith in cultural adaptation through a vehement defense of "real Indian art." Responding to Angel DeCora Deitz's address on "The Preservation of Native Indian Art," Eastman's argument was striking, in part, because it relied upon the vocabulary of social evolutionism even as it argued that civilization couldn't hope to realize all that barbarism once offered:

> We have been drifting away from our old distinctive art. . . . I hope that in this gathering we will come to some realization of these things in the proper sense; that we may take a backward step, if you please, in art, not in the sense of lowering our standard, but returning to the old ideas that are really uplifting . . . and that we may conserve and preserve some of these beautiful principles which were the very inspiration of the North American Indian. . . . Sometimes when we see things in this way and have gone back to the old order, our teachers have said that we have gone back to barbarism, and many times I believe it would be well if we had.

Eastman's awkward injunction of moving "back to barbarism" signaled a redefinition of his understanding of Indian cultures. Morgan's division of human societies into stages of savagery, barbarism, and civilization didn't admit the possibility of "real Indian art." Art was evidence of culture, and culture, social evolutionists claimed, was the distinguishing mark of civilization, not the province of the barbaric. Although Eastman had once relegated his own tribe to the "highest type of pagan and uncivilized man" and recommended, without hesitation, its adaptation to American society, in 1911 he rebelled against such evolutionary theory in order to authenticate his interest in a "real Indian art" and the "true Indian" who produced it.[4]

Eastman's defense, though constrained by an evolutionary vocabulary, suggests his awareness of the cultural relativism even then appearing in American anthropology. In the very year that Eastman protested Morgan's evolutionary thought, Franz Boas published The Mind of Primitive Man, a monograph that achieved the subtle shift in vocabulary that would allow for Eastman's embrace of "real Indian art." Redefining culture from its singular, progressive meaning to a plural, relativistic concept, Boas defended the reality of American Indian arts and cultures. Eastman's own anthropological endeavors had undoubtedly exposed him to this emerging redefinition. Between 1903 and 1909, he worked to clarify and alter the names on Sioux allotment rolls. In 1910 he accepted a commission from George Heye of the university museum of the University of Philadelphia to collect ethnographic objects among the Ojibwes of northern Minnesota. In 1911 participation in the society ensured his interaction with anthropologist Arthur C. Parker, whose own uneasy negotiation of the word "culture" at the first conference meetings suggests a definition that hovered between evolutionary and relativistic significance.[5]

It is upon the publication of his later autobiography, *From the Deep Woods to Civilization* (1916), that the extent and meaning of Charles Eastman's own redefinition of the culture concept becomes apparent. Eastman, who published his first essay, "Recollections of the Wild Life," in 1893 and his last book, *Indian Heroes and Great Chieftains*, in 1918, thought and wrote about Indian cultures during the very years that American anthropologists redefined their own understanding. While his defense of "real Indian art" in 1911 marked his early questioning of Morgan's evolutionary vision, Eastman's 1916 autobiography offers, through its reliance upon metaphor, a thorough critique of social evolutionists' intent to dismiss Indian cultures as early and inadequate expressions of white American civilization. Although Eastman abandoned social evolutionism, he did not fully embrace anthropologists' alternative vision. Even as Eastman's effort to define his own writings as authentic records of Indian culture rather than inroads into mainstream American civilization affirmed his commitment to cultural relativism, he recognized, I would argue, that the very existence of these texts alienated him from the then-emerging Boasian ethnography.[6] Eastman's literary texts complicate his redefinition of culture by suggesting his own distance from the untouched culture of the Santee Sioux. Of course, his writings merely confirm what Eastman's history had long suggested: Eastman had never known an untouched Indian culture. In the presence of competing culture concepts—evolutionary, relativistic—that disallowed Eastman's own "real Indian" experience, his search for an authenticating culture concept necessarily occurred within, and defended, that ill-defined realm of cultural contact between the "Deep Woods" and "Civilization" that his autobiography's title seems to suggest he only traversed, then abandoned.

In his 1916 autobiography, Eastman offers the narrative of his assimilation through simile and metaphor. These figures—the most striking literary flourishes in Eastman's entire narrative—persist through the first four chapters of his text, then abruptly disappear. In her analysis of Eastman's use of metaphor, Hertha Dawn Wong suggests that Eastman invokes "metaphors of wild nature" to emphasize the feeling that he is "out of place in this new world." [7] Eastman's metaphors, Wong suggests, are intended to emphasize difference. Certainly, they do. However, I would argue that this difference is far more problematic than Wong's reading of Eastman's figurative language suggests. It is problematic because the trajectory of Eastman's narrative initially suggests that he intended these similes and metaphors to serve as the literary equivalents of assimilation. Through metaphorical equations, Eastman thought to write the "new world" in terms of his own world until, through assimilation, he transcended this gesture of translation. As such, Eastman's similes and metaphors were to underscore similarity, not difference. Only to the extent that Eastman's metaphors allowed for a meaningful equation of his own culture with the larger American society could he begin to envision himself as a member of that society. Such a reading accounts for the absence of Eastman's similes and metaphors following the fourth chapter. In the moment that his assimilation is completed, he discontinues the process of translation.

However, in From the Deep Woods to Civilization, Eastman's similes and metaphors insist upon difference. In doing so, they offer, I would argue, a critique of social evolutionism. Social evolutionism, like metaphor, depended upon the meaningful equation of its terms. Evolutionism's "practical impact," George Stocking has argued, "was to confirm Western man in a belief that every aspect of his own civilization provided a standard against which all primitive cultures could be judged and found inferior." This "comparative method" assumed the existence not of a plurality of cultures, which might resist a common "standard," but of a plurality of stages within a progression toward the cultured state of civilization. While the former could allow for difference, the latter guaranteed similarity. Thus, Lewis Henry Morgan's evolutionary thought envisioned the "Upper Savagery" of Eastman's Santee Sioux, marked by its "invention of the Bow and Arrow," as a preparatory pause on the course to "Civilization," which would itself depend on the "use of writing." Civilization, in Morgan's system, promised the realization of the imperfect, inadequate impulses of Sioux society through its full flowering into Western culture. The sustained metaphorical equation of books to bow and arrows throughout Eastman's writings suggests his intimate awareness of Morgan's thought.[8]

Assuming the reality of social evolutionism, Eastman's metaphors could never elucidate true difference—only distance—between Indians' ways and Western civilization's high culture. Eastman's 1917 sketch, "The Language of Footprints," published in St. Nicholas: An Illustrated Magazine for Young Folks, most clearly suggests the way in which an evolutionary system might hold Indian cultures to the standard of mainstream American society. In Eastman's sketch, the "language" of literacy guides the young St. Nicholas reader through an imaginary hunt. The animal's "footprint" becomes the "wood-dweller's autograph." These "autographs" tell "a bit of history," a history easily "read" where the tracks are "clear and plain," but difficult to decipher where they are "illegible." By translating the hunting of an animal into the act of reading, Eastman assures his readers—young, white, middle-class individuals already engaged, presumably, in the act of reading—of the accessibility of Indian culture. He achieves accessibility, however, at the cost of cultural difference. Although Eastman's sketch insists that "actions speak louder than words," his own metaphor of reading reduces the action of an Indian hunt into the words of an American literary magazine. His invitation to young readers—"I will now ask you to enter the forest with me"—is an invitation into a text that effectively eliminates the possibility of real action. As the act of hunting is translated into the act of reading, the significance it achieves in the minds of Eastman's readers is utterly distinct from the significance it had among Eastman's Santee Sioux. This is, Max Black suggests, the problematic reality of metaphor generally. To insert Eastman's metaphor into Black's analysis: "The enforced choice of the [reading] vocabulary will lead some aspects of the [hunt] to be emphasized, others to be neglected. . . . The [reading] vocabulary filters and transforms: it not only selects, it brings forward aspects of the [hunt] that might not be seen at all through another medium." While Eastman's metaphor of reading emphasizes the Indian's "insight" and "powers of observation," it elides the hunt's physical demands and its dramatic life-and-death relevance to the cultures dependent upon its success.[9]

Eastman's adoption of this very metaphor through the first four chapters of his autobiography facilitates his critique of the "filtering" and "transformation" implicit in evolutionary thinking. In From the Deep Woods to Civilization, Eastman learns the metaphor from his father, an assimilated Sioux clearly versed in evolutionary stages: "He was now anxious to have his boys learn the English language and something about books, for he could see that these were the 'bow and arrows' of the white man." Equating books to bow and arrows, Eastman's father assures his son that an education is the equivalent to the path of hunting and war: "Remember, my boy, it is the same as if I sent you on your first war-path. I shall expect you to conquer." Eastman's entrance into an American education, however, reveals differences from the war-path rather than its promised equivalency. Reading fails to realize the "interest" of the hunt as the teacher's "curious signs upon a blackboard" can't "compare in interest" with Eastman's "bird's-track and fish-fin studies on the sands." Reading also fails to achieve the war-path's objectives. Eastman, wondering whether attending school will "make a man brave and strong," recognizes that it will not. Eastman's frustrations with this metaphorical war-path ultimately prompt his vision of a literal alternative. Tired of fighting words, he imagines fighting enemies instead, and predicts a victory for himself and his schoolmates: "Imagine the same fellows turned loose against Custer or Harney with anything like equal numbers and weapons, and those tried generals would feel like boys!" Similarity is dissolved in difference as stages of culture suddenly threaten to become conflicting cultures.[10]

For Eastman, cultural conflict is, at least momentarily, preferable to an assimilation that implies not the perfection but the elimination of Indian cultures within mainstream American society. Metaphor, Ted Cohen has suggested, has the "capacity to form or acknowledge a . . . community and thereby establish an intimacy between the teller and the hearer." To establish intimacy is Eastman's intent in his St. Nicholas sketch. His translation of the hunt into the language of literacy fosters a community between himself and his young readers. In From the Deep Woods to Civilization, however, Eastman acknowledges the cultural cost of establishing such a community. Social evolutionism, Eastman realizes, demands that he write his way into civilization through the metaphorical murder of the Indian. Such metaphors, "hostile" metaphors, as Cohen calls them, become "all the more painful because the victim has been made a complicitor in his own demise." If, for a moment, Eastman's shift from the metaphorical to the literal reverses this gesture, threatening not Indian culture but the larger American civilization through the actualization of the war-path, his autobiography nevertheless remains a record of assimilation. The meaning of this assimilation, however, is altered as Eastman's acknowledgment that the cultural difference elucidated by his own similes and metaphors is a difference lost, not perfected, in the entrance of the Santee Sioux into civilization. This realization strikes Eastman as powerfully as it does his readers: "I was now a stranger in a strange country, and deep in a strange life from which I could not retreat. . . . I discovered that my anticipations of this new life were nearly all wrong." Assimilation, Eastman realizes, effectively eliminates the Indian: "I renounced finally my bow and arrows for the . . . pen. . . . Every day of my life I put into use every English word that I knew, and for the first time permitted myself to think and act as a white man." To assimilate is to experience the absence of the authentic Indian self in the presence of a "stranger," a "reconstructed" or "artificial" Indian, the "imitation" of a "white man." [11]

For Eastman, this strangeness is grounded largely in literacy. His equation of the acquisition of literacy and the loss of the authentic Indian self is an equation for which not only Morgan's evolutionary system, but Arnold Krupat's analysis of autobiography offers an explanation. In his study of white American autobiography, Krupat argues that "literacy" is "precisely" the trope that "distinguished the European 'man of culture' from 'nature's child,' the Indian—who did not write." In "self-consciously literary" autobiography, Krupat argues, "scenes of writing (and reading)" suggest "culture." Such scenes certainly communicate the cultural inheritance of Elaine Goodale Eastman, Eastman's wife and editor, in her autobiography, Sister to the Sioux. Elaine Goodale Eastman, a white woman who intended, as a government teacher among the Sioux, to "create a little center of 'sweetness and light' . . . in a squalid camp of savages," considered herself to be a bearer of an Arnoldian high culture communicated through literacy. Her own autobiography chronicles her precocious entrance into print, and is marked throughout by self-conscious references to her own previously published writings. I find it suggestive—perhaps of Eastman's understanding of the woman he met and married during his doctoring among the Sioux, perhaps of her own editorial influence—that her literacy is similarly emphasized in From the Deep Woods to Civilization. In her husband's autobiography, Elaine Goodale Eastman exists as a text. At the moment of their meeting at the Pine Ridge Indian agency, "Miss Elaine Goodale" is "not entirely a stranger" to Eastman because he "had read her 'Apple Blossoms' in Boston, and . . . her later articles on Indian education." His own lecture-circuit travels, following their marriage, confirm her cultural status when Eastman discovers, at a Cherokee seminary, the students "in the act of reading an essay on my wife." The only photograph of Elaine Goodale Eastman in her husband's text—a photograph that shows her reading—is a display of her cultural inheritance.[12]

Although Elaine Goodale Eastman's literacy exists as the mark of her culture, Eastman's entrance into such scenes of reading and writing mark the transformation of the authentic Indian self into the object of high culture. Attending a school where, he has been promised, the "white men have everything in their books," Eastman realizes that he is, suddenly, an "object of curiosity." Exiting his own culture is to enter, repeatedly, into civilization's books as white authors—including his wife—publish their own accounts of his experience. Although Eastman finds many of these writings to be "innocent enough," most are inaccurate, and the resulting objectification of the Indian self marks the real Indian's textual demise. Less innocent inaccuracies threaten not only the textual death of the real Indian through Eastman's failure to recognize an authentic self in the white-authored text, but the real Indian's literal death as well. Entering college only months after "Custer's gallant command was annihilated by the hostile Sioux," Eastman's life is endangered when a journalist wrongly identifies him as the "nephew of Sitting Bull" come to "study the white man's arts" in order to enhance Indian warfare. In his recounting of the Wounded Knee massacre, Eastman argues that journalists' textual inaccuracies led not only to the dehumanizing objectification of the Sioux, but to a disastrous escalation of anxiety. "Of course," Eastman recalls, "the press seized upon the opportunity to enlarge upon the strained situation and predict an 'Indian uprising.' The reporters were among us, and managed to secure much 'news' that no one else ever heard of. Border towns were fortified and cowboys and militia gathered in readiness to protect them against the 'red devils.'" Such accounts, in which white authors recreated a Sioux gathering as an "Indian uprising" and Sioux individuals as "red devils," led to not only the textual but also the literal deaths of real Indians.[13]

The fact that the literary texts of high culture dictated the death—metaphorical, literal—of the Indian suggests the extent to which ideas of author and Indian were opposed within evolutionary thought. In the very address that elicits Eastman's defense of "real Indian art" in 1911, Angel DeCora Deitz, herself a Winnebago artist, mourns this opposition: "The Indian in his natural state was a source of inspiration to the artist. Painter, poet and sculptor have immortalized him on canvas, in marble and in verse. They have realized that he was akin to the arts, but it was the general effect of the Indian in buckskin and feathers that the artist took for art, never dreaming there was a cause for effect." Taking the Indian as its inspiration or its object, white American culture, Deitz argues, denies the Indian a distinctive artistry. Although Deitz attempts to defend such artistry—"The Indian," she insists, "is an artist"—her own society members resist her defense. "Nobody," Horton G. Elm, an Oneida, responds, "appreciates more than I do that this matter of Indian art is important, yet at the same time, we as a race cannot all be artists." It is as if Elm insists that not all Indians can afford to be Indians. In his view, the Indianness of Indian art must be abandoned in order to secure an entrance into American civilization. Even Charles Doxon's intent to moderate between Elm and Deitz reveals his own inability to imagine an Indian artist whose Indianness exists as a cultural subjectivity rather than as the object of his art: "I have known a man, an artist, who draws Indian characters entirely,—Indian figures and Indian faces. . . . I have known him for a good many years, and he has been spending all his time in painting Indian faces, and his dress, and Indian characters,—devoting all his time to just that one subject." Doxon, an Onondaga, progressively envisions the Indian artist as simply "a man, an artist," but regrettably eliminates the possibility of an artistry grounded in the perspectives of Indian culture.[14]

Of course, Elaine Goodale Eastman intended to assist in the transformation of her husband into the author, not the object, of such literary texts. However, her own evolutionary vision made authorship—or the entrance into literary culture—dependent upon the renunciation of Indianness. If, as Krupat argues, the literary text is the indication of high culture, then it is, simultaneously, the indication of not being Indian. In Elaine Goodale Eastman's 1911 novel, *Yellow Star*, the young Indian heroine, Stella—child survivor of the Wounded Knee massacre—initially wields a cultural authority to critique inaccurate images of Indians. When her fellow students read lessons on "cruel and treacherous savages," Stella challenges the trusted history book with her own narrative of Wounded Knee and envisions justice through the possibility of an Indian-authored history: "Maybe, if we wrote the history books, there wouldn't be so much in them about the 'treacherous Indians!'" Stella's literacy establishes an authoritative voice through which she critiques the errors of a literate culture. In a note, self-consciously published in the text of the novel, Stella writes to her guardian that "the book was wrong and I was right." Literacy allows Stella to redefine the Indian within American culture as she herself shifts from being an object of New England ethnocentrism to an individual of authority.[15]

However, Stella's literary authority—the sign of high culture—necessarily dictates her own distance from the very Indian culture she attempts to redefine. At a Wild West performance, Stella's speech separates her from the Sioux performers. Her protest—"I never saw anything like this before"—confirms that while the Indians are admittedly Sioux, they are, culturally, "not Sioux at all." Once Stella's own people, these Sioux performers are reduced to silent, inauthentic spectacle. It is a spectacle in which Stella can choose to participate—"unconsciously" making a "picture which was thoroughly appreciated by several of the bystanders"—but which she can circumvent with an authority that allows her to step "behind the scenes" and wield her influence. Although Stella speaks in sympathy with the silenced Sioux, her literate authority is most powerfully a mark of her difference from them. Constantly contrasting Stella's "expressive" features with the "stolid," "unnaturally quiet," "expressionless," and "sulky" Indians, Elaine Goodale Eastman naturalizes the manner in which Stella's authoritative voice not only aids but also dominates those who were once her people. "Docile" Indians "yield" to Stella's "peremptory orders," her "command of the situation," and her "final instructions" as she wields a cultural literacy they do not comprehend. Although her authority defends Indian culture, it is, most clearly, the mark of her own departure from that culture. Powerfully literate, Stella is no longer Sioux. Highly cultured, she is no longer a participant in Sioux culture.[16]

Although fictional characters could not, Eastman, in his search for an authenticating culture concept, resisted his wife's evolutionary thought. Differing attitudes toward culture necessarily dictated differing attitudes toward the literary text. Nowhere is this more apparent than in the narrative that Eastman and Elaine Goodale Eastman offered of Eastman's own entrance into authorship. In *From the Deep Woods to Civilization*, Eastman depicts his earliest literary effort as an attempt to record Santee Sioux culture:

> While I had plenty of leisure, I began to put upon paper some of my earliest recollections, with the thought that our children might some day like to read of that wilderness life. When my wife discovered what I had written, she insisted upon sending it to St. Nicholas. Much to my surprise, the sketches were immediately accepted and appeared during the following year. This was the beginning of my

first book, *Indian Boyhood*, which was not completed until several years later.

Elaine Goodale Eastman's narrative of her husband's authorship is substantially different: "In an hour of comparative leisure I had urged him to write down his recollections of the wild life, which I carefully edited and placed with St. Nicholas. From this small beginning grew *Indian Boyhood* and eight other books of Indian lore, upon all of which I collaborated more or less." Eastman and Elaine Goodale Eastman disputed not only the authorial impulse but also the meaning of the text.[17] While Eastman thought of his earliest literary effort as a private record of his Indianness, Elaine Goodale Eastman envisioned her husband's writings as documents that achieved their primary purpose upon publication in national literary magazines and, later, as books. Eastman invoked his literacy as proof of his cultural origins—his Santee Sioux origins. In Elaine Goodale Eastman's analysis, however, Eastman's writings existed as inroads into American literary culture, the high culture that social evolutionists located exclusively in civilization. Elaine Goodale Eastman's account even suggests that she knowingly ushered her husband into high culture along the very path she herself had followed as a girl. His literary career, like her own, began with publication in St. Nicholas. Eastman's narrative of his wife's "discovery" and "insistence," however, marks his resistance to her intent, a resistance confirmed by Eastman's biographer, Raymond Wilson, who suggests that Eastman "despised" his wife's editorial influence.[18]

Eastman's intent to authenticate Indian culture through his literary efforts—to defend Santee Sioux culture against an encroaching high culture—suggests an adherence to Boasian cultural relativism rather than to Elaine Goodale Eastman's controlling vision. However, if Elaine Goodale Eastman's commitment to high culture dictated the impossibility of Indian art, Boasian ethnography increasingly assumed the absence of the real Indian. Contact with mainstream American society, Boas feared, corrupted authentic Indian cultures. His salvage ethnography sought to establish a record of real cultures before their disappearance into American civilization. While Boas's anxiety resulted in elaborate monographs, it dictated the dismissal of Eastman's literary efforts. In a posthumously published paper, "Recent Anthropology II" (1943), Boas discouraged anthropologists' reliance upon Indian autobiography as an ethnographic tool. He warned against the "doubtful" reliability of Indian autobiographies that, he wrote, contained "not facts but memories." These memories, he argued, were "distorted by the wishes and thoughts of the moment," so that "interests of the present determine[d] . . . the interpretation of the past." Boas cautioned ethnographers "particularly" against the accounts of "North American Indians" whose "fundamental changes of life . . . make it likely that customs that were at one time highly significant have lost or changed their meanings and are now reinterpreted according to the present state of mind of the informant." Boas's dismissal of Indian autobiography as an ethnographic tool underscored his interest in obtaining a record of Indian cultures untouched by American civilization, a record of "real" Indians offered by "real" Indians, an authentic record.[19]

According to such criteria, Eastman's From the Deep Woods to Civilization, a narrative of assimilation into American civilization, falls well beyond the Boasian ethnographer's realm, while the fact of Eastman's literacy—proof of cultural contact—ensures the failure of even his less obviously autobiographical writings about Santee Sioux culture to satisfy Boas's demands. Admittedly, Eastman was not engaged in writing formal ethnography. As Frances Karttunen has argued, Eastman's writings were so "self-conscious" as to cast suspicion on the accuracy of his record, while his idea of the Indian was "a construct" of his "experience and imagination." Similarly, Philip Deloria has argued that although Eastman's advocacy of Indian cultures reconnected him to "his Dakota roots," his participation in the various expressions of these cultures within mainstream American society was, nevertheless, "more compellingly" an "imitation" of "non-Indian imitations of Indians."[20] However, even as Eastman departs from a Boasian ethnographer's standards for recording authentic Indian cultures, he offers a critique of those standards that the ethnographers themselves would ultimately echo.

It was within Boasian anthropology, ironically, that the proliferation of the Indian autobiography as an ethnographic tool occurred. In his foreword to Walter Dyk's Son of Old Man Hat: A Navaho Autobiography (1938), Edward Sapir suggests that the failure of ethnographers' objectivity to achieve the very vision of authentic Indian culture it sought prompted anthropologists' attention to Indian autobiography: "The truth of the matter is that in their efforts to be precise, detailed, objective, and impersonal, the ethnologists have inevitably been drawn away from the recognition of universal modes of behavior, of universal feelings, of inescapable human necessities." Only Indian "biography or autobiography," Sapir suggests, "partly under cover of orthodox ethnology, partly in unconcern of it," could offer the "meanings" of Indian cultures that scientific ethnographies failed to divulge.[21] Although Sapir's defense of Indian autobiography occurred on the margins of Boasian anthropology, Eastman, in his foreword to The Soul of the Indian (1911), rejected a scientific vision altogether in his effort to communicate the "universal quality" of Indian cultures in an argument that portends Sapir's own: "My little book does not pretend to be a scientific treatise. It is as true as I can make it to my childhood teaching and ancestral ideals, but from the human, not the ethnological standpoint." In 1913 Paul Radin similarly turned to Indian autobiography to avoid the objectification implicit in ethnographic objectivity: "Ethnological memoirs . . . represented but the skeleton and bones of the culture they sought to portray." His commentary recalls Eastman's dissatisfaction of 1911: "I have not cared to pile up more dry bones, but to clothe them with flesh and blood."[22] Eastman, as well as Boas's students, rejected the objectification, implicit in an ethnographic objectivity, that prohibited the communication of authentic Indian cultures.

Eastman's privileging of his Indian autobiography, written from the "human standpoint," over ethnographic monographs ultimately critiques the very possibility of a scientific objectivity.[23] Boas's confidence in an authentic ethnography depended upon the ethnographer's objectivity—the ability to "divest" the self of cultural "influences" in order to experience the "perspectives" of a different culture. In From the Deep Woods to Civilization, Eastman challenges the possibility of such divesting by assuming the ethnographer's role. In a gesture that thwarts the critique of Indian autobiography that Boas advanced, Eastman's autobiography knowingly satisfies ethnography's demands. His chapter "Back to the Woods" portrays his return to Indian lands, but not through memory's aid. Hired by George Heye to obtain "genuine" Indian artifacts for "one of the most important collections in the country," Eastman acts as ethnographer to the northern Ojibwes of Minnesota and Ontario.[24] Armed with an ethnographic authority, Eastman nevertheless produces a text that challenges such authority.

This challenge begins, I would suggest, as his own method of collection —a method that depends upon his uneasy negotiation of Indian and ethnographic customs—reveals the objectification of Indian cultures implicit in salvage ethnography:

> My method was one of indirection. I would visit for several days in
> a camp where I knew, or had reason to believe, that some of the cov-

eted articles were to be found. After I had talked much with the leading men, feasted them, and made them presents, a slight hint would often result in the chief or medicine man "presenting" me with some object of historic or ceremonial interest, which etiquette would not permit to be "sold," and which a white man would probably not have been allowed to see at all.

Eastman's method relies on his ability to wield "old-time Indian etiquette" and "the good old customs" in a manner he considers impossible for a white man. It relies as well, however, on a willingness to enact monetary exchanges for objects that that very etiquette forbids being sold. As the collector of Indian objects, Eastman approaches the exchange of presents for cultural mythologies he had once critiqued in The Soul of the Indian. And in reviving Indian customs for the purpose of obtaining Indian objects—objects he removed from an Indian culture to place in a museum—he risks the "piling up of more dry bones" that he himself found so troubling. In his venture "Back to the Woods," Eastman's Indian knowledge threatens "to revive indigenous history and culture as archeology," which, Mary Louise Pratt has argued, is "to revive them as dead." [25]

However, in "reviving" his own customs for the purpose of collecting, he seems to renew in himself the life of which those customs were a part. Eastman's entrance among the Ojibwes, "once the fiercest of [Sioux] enemies," is as problematic as his entrance into American civilization in that it elicits the memory, if not the reality, of cultural conflict: "It appeared that some of the older warriors, recalling hand-to-hand scrimmages with my forbears, were somewhat embarrassed by the presence of a Sioux visitor." However, Eastman's ability to display "customs relating to intertribal meetings" leads to acceptance and the communication of information about his own people. Although ancestral antagonisms may compromise the objectivity of his ethnography, they prompt his identification with the "old, wild life." Declaring himself an Indian once more—"I am a Sioux"—Eastman revives the life those customs recall: "The sweet roving instinct of the wild took forcible hold upon me once more. I was eager to realize for a few perfect days the old, wild life as I knew it in my boyhood." His intent to collect the objects of an Indian culture ultimately results in the realization of his own Indianness, even to the exclusion of objects of American civilization: "I set out with an Ojibway guide in his birch canoe, taking with me little that belonged to the white man, except his guns, fishing tackle, knives and tobacco." Having once revived his Indian life, it is a life that Eastman finds difficult to abandon: "Every day it became harder for me to leave the woods." [26] The meaning of Eastman's ethnography—an ethnography that threatens to objectify the Ojibwes but still relies upon Eastman's own Indianness—is difficult to decipher. As ethnographer, does Eastman intend to revive his own Indian identity or to revive the Ojibwes as dead for Heye's museum? Do his collections insist, as he would insist at the Society of American Indian's organizational meetings of the same year, upon the perpetuation of "real Indian art" by "true Indians" or upon the preservation of the objects of an inevitably disappearing Ojibwe culture?

The very ambiguity of Eastman's ethnography exists as a critique of Boasian participant observation. Whereas Boas insisted upon the ethnographer's "intimate" knowledge of Indian culture and the disavowal of one's own cultural influences, Eastman's prose discovers the impossibility of such demands. Eastman concludes *From the Deep Woods to Civilization* with a chapter titled "The Soul of the White Man," in which he enumerates his ethnographic ventures. This final commentary on his own soul is, in part, a commentary on the inevitable departures from, and returns to, the native point of view implicit in his ethnographic practice. While Eastman insists that he "fully appreciat[es] the Indian's viewpoint," he nevertheless writes in order "to convince him [the Indian] of the sincerity of his white friends" (emphasis mine). Such third-person references—references that occur with striking regularity throughout Eastman's autobiography—only suggest his distance from an authentic Indian self. However, Eastman qualifies this reference, like many, by insisting that "[my success] has encouraged me to attempt a fuller expression of *our* people's life from the inside" (emphasis mine). Eastman's narrative calls into question the very possibility of reliably writing "from the inside." [27]

It is a question he raises through photographs as well as text. Although Hertha Wong, who seeks to understand Eastman's work in terms of traditional Sioux and white autobiographical forms, hesitates to call Eastman's photographs "narrative pictographs," I would argue that his photographs sustain a complex reading or insist, visually, upon the complexity that Eastman's narrative sustains. In each of the five photographs of himself to appear in *From the Deep Woods to Civilization*, Eastman, who frequently allowed himself to be photographed in traditional Sioux clothing, wears mainstream American dress. In the first four photographs, this appearance arguably resists the narrative of social evolution in which his autobiography

131

initially seems to engage. Two of these portraits, "Eastman at Knox College, 1880" and "Eastman in 1890," appear on a single page. Here, the very sameness of Eastman's personal appearance through time—dark suit, white collar, and thoughtful, confident gaze—thwarts the impulse of readers familiar with the before-and-after photographs of assimilating Indians to imagine him from one cultural stage, Savagery, to a later one, Civilization. Whereas Morgan's adherents insisted upon the "evolution of culture," Eastman's photographs insist, instead, on the education of the individual.[28]

His appearance in mainstream American dress in the final photograph, however, invites the reader to question the boundaries across which his ethnographic endeavor plays. This last photograph displays a moment in Eastman's efforts to "realize . . . the old, wild life" in the midst of his ethnographic venture "back to the woods." Having declared his renunciation of the "things" of American civilization, Eastman still stands before the reader in the dress—hat, shirt, and tie—of that civilization. The photograph, which marks the moment when Eastman may turn into a "real" Indian once again, simultaneously challenges his ability, as an ethnographer, to assume a native point of view. Is Eastman, his own photograph demands, an imitation or a real white man, an artificial or a real Indian? At one moment or another, he has claimed for himself most of these identities. At one moment or another, Boasian ethnographers would have confirmed or denied just such claims. The photograph insists on the complexity of an ethnographer's objectivity that must be lodged, paradoxically, in a native subjectivity. Ira Jacknis suggests that Boas's own writings reveal his discomfort with the fragmentary vision that a photograph necessarily offered: "He was uncomfortable with [the photograph's] privileging of a particular moment of inscription" and considered it "suspect" as "an object produced by the observer rather than a native." Boas did not, Jacknis writes, "seem to have realized the possibilities of native photography in conveying a native world of thought and meaning."[29]

In its own particular moment, Eastman's final photograph intentionally alerts the reader to the suspect quality of his—and every—ethnographic narrative through questioning the possibility of communicating "a native world of thought and meaning." It is a question Eastman complicates by the narration of his last hours in the "deep woods." Finding it "every day . . . harder" to leave the "old, wild life," he is, nevertheless, caught in that life when a storm of wind and rain forces him and his companions to abandon their boat: "There was nothing to do but jump and swim for it, and it seems almost a miracle that we all landed safely. There were just four of us playing Robinson Crusoe on a lovely little isle. . . . The boat was gone with all its freight, except a few things that drifted ashore. Here we remained for two nights and a day before we were discovered." Realizing the "old, wild life" turns, in crisis, not into "being" Indian but into "playing" a figure of literary high culture.[30]

I have suggested that although Boas cautioned ethnographers against the "perversion of truth" in Indian autobiographies, Charles Eastman turned a similar critique against ethnographers' writings. Eastman offers *The Soul of the Indian* as a corrective to the "ethnological standpoint": "My little book does not pretend to be a scientific treatise. It is as true as I can make it to my childhood teaching and ancestral ideals, but from the human, not the ethnological standpoint." While Eastman carefully qualifies a claim to truth in his own writing—"It is as true as I can make it"—he dismisses the very possibility of truth in an ethnography that intends to offer a record of Indian religion untouched by American civilization. Such documents, Eastman insists, simply don't exist: "Practically all existing studies on this subject have been made during the transition period, when the original beliefs and philosophy of the native American were already undergoing rapid disintegration." The remainder, Eastman argues, are "superficial accounts" or even Indian "inventions": "Give a reservation Indian a present, and he will possibly provide you with sacred songs, a mythology, and folk-lore to order!" "The Indian," Charles Eastman believed, "does not speak of those deep matters so long as he believes in them."[31]

In offering the texts themselves as proof of the impossibility of their truth, Eastman must be aware that he implicates himself in his own critique. He is himself speaking of "those deep matters" that silence once defended. Yet even as *The Soul of the Indian* celebrates the silence that marked the real Indian—"silent, because all speech is of necessity feeble and imperfect"—it is this very speech through which Eastman paradoxically seeks to authenticate Indian identity. If it is the act of writing that ensures Eastman's estrangement from his own culture, it is this very act that serves as his culture's primary defense. It is, ironically, within his autobiographical chapter, "Soul of the White Man," that Eastman celebrates his success: "My chief object has been, not to entertain, but to present the American Indian in his true character before Americans. . . . Again and again I have been told by recognized thinkers, 'You present an entirely new viewpoint. We can never again think of the Indian as we have done before.'" Embracing literacy, Eastman becomes a stranger to his culture, but only through literacy's influence can he become an Indian once again: "It was not until I felt that I had to a degree established these claims, that I consented to appear on the platform in our ancestral garb of honor. I feel that I was a pioneer in this new line of defense of the native American. . . . I am glad that the drift is now toward a better understanding, and that he is become the acknowledged hero of the Boy Scouts and Camp Fire Girls, as well as of many artists, sculptors, and sincere writers." Through his literacy, Eastman embraces that "shifting space in which two cultures encounter one another," that "frontier" space of which, Krupat argues, Indian autobiography is the representative genre.[32]

While Elaine Goodale Eastman's commitment to high culture dictated the impossibility of Indian art, and Boas's salvage ethnography foresaw the disappearance of the real Indian, Eastman's embrace of the complicated realm of cultural encounters offers the only possibility of the pursuit of that "real Indian art" he envisioned and defended during the initial meetings of the Society of American Indians. It is, admittedly, a vision that cultural relativism facilitated. Elaine Goodale Eastman's idea of high culture was grounded in a social evolutionism that advocated, in the words of its staunch supporter, Richard Henry Pratt, the initiation of the Indian into "our best civilization." Eastman's continuing opposition to such a vision is suggested by the publication of his 1914 article, " 'My People': The Indians' Contribution to the Art of America" in Carlisle's The Red Man. Made possible only by Pratt's departure from Carlisle, this monthly magazine, published first in 1909 as The Indian Craftsman, proclaimed itself a forum for the investigation of Native American interests through a distinctly Native American perspective. As its masthead insisted, The Indian Craftsman was "A magazine not only about Indians, but mainly by Indians." In its descendant, The Red Man—written "by Red Men"—Eastman celebrated the continuation of Indian artistry through his attention to the forum in which he published: "When we recall that, as recently as twenty years ago, all native art was severely discountenanced and discouraged, if not actually forbidden in Government schools and often by missionaries as well, the present awakening is matter for mutual congratulations." Eastman echoed not the evolutionary-minded Pratt but Indian commissioner Francis Leupp, who defined himself against Pratt's intent to eradicate Indian cultures: "I like the Indian for what is Indian in him. . . . Let us not make the mistake, in the process of absorbing them, of washing out whatever is distinctly Indian."[33]

Eastman's authenticating culture concept defined itself, however, just as vehemently against Boasian cultural relativism and in embrace of a distinctly Arnoldian ideal. Eastman's only departure from that ideal—admittedly a significant one—was his celebration of the "best that has been thought and known" within Indian cultures rather than in the confines of mainstream American civilization. This celebration led, naturally, to an Indian artistry and authority that Elaine Goodale Eastman's vision of high culture had denied. Such authority is audible in Eastman's essay "My People," as his efforts to "impress" Sioux chiefs with "the wonderful achievements of civilization" elicit their critique of American high culture. Eastman's sympathy with the Indians' critique of the "strange philosophy of the white man"—"He ruthlessly disfigures God's own pictures and monuments, and then daubs a flat surface with many colors, and praises his work as a masterpiece!"—elevates the excellence of Indian culture above that of the "civilized world." It transforms the "red man's failure to approach even distantly the artistic standard of the civilized world" into success through the celebration of a difference in "point of view." "In his sense of the aesthetic," Eastman writes, "the American Indian stands alone." It is a sentiment that Eastman furthers in *From the Deep Woods to Civilization* as he suggests that it is among Indians that "the best that has been thought and known" actually resides: "The philosophy of the original American was demonstrably on a high plane, his gift of eloquence, wit, humor and poetry is well established; his democracy and community life was much nearer the ideal than ours today; his standard of honor and friendship unsurpassed, and all his faults are the faults of generous youth."[34]

It is near the conclusion of *From the Deep Woods to Civilization* that Eastman imports a last metaphor of literacy to suggest his ideal of Indian culture. In the chapter "Civilization as Preached and Practiced," Eastman "reopen[s] the book" of Indian culture. It is Eastman's first reference to a written text that does not result in the objectification of Indian culture. In fact, his metaphorical equation of the exploration of Indian culture and reading, while suggesting the distance he has traveled from his own cultural origins, empowers real Indian speakers. Indeed, Eastman, the authority on "the white man's ideals," is silenced by Indians' critical comparison of American society's highest cultural values and Indian philosophy. One "old battle-scarred warrior" insists that the cultural ideals that Eastman defends as white are, in reality, the simplest standards of Indian culture: "These are not the principles upon which the white man has founded his civilization. It is strange that he could not rise to these simple principles which were commonly observed among our people." As the speaker's words "put the spell of an uncomfortable silence upon [Eastman's] company," Eastman and his readers experience a moment of reversal. In their mutual silence, they confront the speaker's demand that civilization must rise to the standards of Indian culture. Social evolutionism is once again confounded, cultural relativism not entirely embraced, as Eastman's speakers urge him to a reconsideration of Indian cultures. Throughout From the Deep Woods to Civilization, Eastman's efforts to articulate white ideals are silenced by Indian speech, until this repeated reversal of authority accomplishes its inevitable end in the confirmation of his continuing presence in the complicated place of cultural contact: "I am an Indian. . . . Nevertheless, so long as I live, I am an American." [35]

Notes

1. Hazel Hertzberg, The Search for an American Indian Identity: Modern Pan-Indian Movements (Syracuse: Syracuse University Press, 1971), 31; Society of American Indians, Report of the Executive Council on the Proceedings of the First Annual Conference of the Society of American Indians (Washington DC, 1912), 7 [hereafter SAI, Report].

2. For a history of Eastman's grandfather, Seth Eastman, see John Francis McDermott, Seth Eastman: Pictorial Historian of the Indian (Norman: University of Oklahoma Press, 1961).

3. SAI, Report, 7; Eastman, Indian Boyhood (Lincoln: University of Nebraska Press, 1991); H. David Brumble, American Indian Autobiography (Berkeley: University of California Press, 1988), 157; Hertzberg, American Indian Identity, 73.

4. SAI, Report, 88–89.

5. Franz Boas, The Mind of Primitive Man (New York: Macmillan, 1911). For an account of Eastman's involvement in Hamlin Garland's renaming project, designed in consultation with anthropologists George Bird Grinnell and W. J. McGee, see Raymond Wilson, "Renaming the Sioux, 1903–1909," in Ohiyesa: Charles Eastman, Santee Sioux (Urbana: University of Illinois Press, 1983); and Daniel F. Littlefield Jr. and Lonnie E. Underhill, "Renaming the American Indian: 1890–1913," American Studies 12 (fall 1971): 33–45. A brief account of Eastman's expedition for George Heye is offered in "American Section: The Heye Collection," University of Pennsylvania: The Museum Journal 1 (June 1910): 11–12. For Arthur C.

Parker's commentary on Indian culture(s), see "The Philosophy of Indian Education," in SAI, Report, 68–76.

6. Eastman, From the Deep Woods to Civilization: Chapters in the Autobiography of an Indian (Lincoln: University of Nebraska Press, 1977). At the conclusion of his essay "Charles Alexander Eastman's Indian Boyhood: Romance, Nostalgia, and Social Darwinism," H. David Brumble advocates, although he does not pursue, a consideration of Eastman's later writings within the moment of Boasian anthropology (American Indian Autobiography, 163). Hertha Wong investigates the ethnographic overtones of Eastman's early autobiography in "Oral and Written Collaborative Autobiography: Nicholas Black Elk and Charles Alexander Eastman," in Sending My Heart Back Across the Years (New York: Oxford University Press, 1992). Erik Peterson investigates Eastman's idea of ethnicity in "An Indian, an American: Ethnicity, Assimilation and Balance in Charles Eastman's From the Deep Woods to Civilization," Studies in American Literatures 4 (1992): 145–60. Most recently, Gerald Vizenor explores Eastman's creation of a native self between cultures in Fugitive Poses: Native American Indian Scenes of Absence and Presence (Lincoln: University of Nebraska Press, 1998), 17–22.

7. Wong, Sending My Heart Back Across the Years, 146.

8. George Stocking, Race, Culture and Evolution: Essays in the History of Anthropology (New York: Free Press, 1968), 129; see also Stocking's discussion of competing definitions of culture in "Matthew Arnold, E. B. Tylor, and the Uses of Invention," in Race, Culture and Evolution, 69–90. Lewis Henry Morgan, Ancient Society (Cambridge MA: Belknap Press, 1964), 18.

9. Eastman, "Language of Footprints," St. Nicholas: An Illustrated Magazine for Young Folks, January 1917, 267; Max Black, Models and Metaphors: Studies in Language and Philosophy (Ithaca: Cornell University Press, 1962), 42; Eastman, "Language of Footprints," 269.

10. Eastman, Deep Woods, 16, 32, 23–24, 46.

11. Cohen, "Metaphor and the Cultivation of Intimacy," in On Metaphor, ed. Sheldon Sacks (Chicago: University of Chicago Press, 1978), 9, 10; Eastman, Deep Woods, 54, 58; Eastman, The Soul of the Indian: An Interpretation (Lincoln: University of Nebraska Press, 1980), 88, 18.

12. Arnold Krupat, For Those Who Come After: A Study of Native American Autobiography (Berkeley: University of California Press, 1985), 41; Elaine Goodale Eastman, Sister to the Sioux, 30; Eastman, Deep Woods, 86, 146, 126.

13. Eastman, *Deep Woods*, 21, 73, 53, 102–3.

14. SAI, *Report*, 82, 91, 89.

15. Elaine Goodale Eastman, *Yellow Star: A Story of East and West* (Boston: Little, Brown, 1911), 41, 44–45.

16. Eastman, *Yellow Star*, 79–82, 88, 82, 88–91. Elaine Goodale Eastman's Stella was modeled on a child, Zintkala Nuni, discovered on the Wounded Knee battlefield during Charles Eastman's rescue effort. See Eastman, *Deep Woods*, 113, and Renee Sansom Flood, *Lost Bird of Wounded Knee: Spirit of the Lakota* (New York: Scribner, 1995), 270.

17. Eastman, *Deep Woods*, 139; Elaine Goodale Eastman, *Sister*, 173; see also Elaine Goodale Eastman, *The Voice at Eve* (Chicago: Bookfellows, 1930), 30. Scholars' accounts of Eastman's authorship recreate the inconsistencies that exist in the Eastmans' own writings; see Wilson, *Ohiyesa*, 131, and Ruth Ann Alexander, "Elaine Goodale Eastman and the Failure of the Feminist Protestant Ethic," *Great Plains Quarterly* 8 (1988): 93.

18. The early *St. Nicholas* sketches include Dora Goodale and Elaine Goodale, "Poems by Two Little American Girls," *St Nicholas*, December 1877, 109–10, and Charles Eastman, "Recollections of the Wild Life," *St. Nicholas*, December 1893–May 1894, 129–31, 226–28, 306–8, 437–40, 513–15, 607–11; Wilson, *Ohiyesa*, 191.

19. Franz Boas, "Recent Anthropology II," *Science*, 15 October 1943, 334–37.

20. Frances Karttunen, *Between Worlds: Interpreters, Guides, and Survivors* (New Brunswick: Rutgers University Press, 1994), 164, 149; Philip J. Deloria, *Playing Indian* (New Haven: Yale University Press, 1998), 123.

21. On the use of Indian autobiography in anthropology see L. L. Langness, *The Life History in Anthropological Science* (New York: Holt, Rinehart and Winston, 1965), and Clyde Kluckhohn, "The Personal Document in Anthropological Science," in Louis Gottschalk, Clyde Kluckhohn, and Robert Angell, *The Use of Personal Documents in History, Anthropology, and Sociology* (New York: Social Science Research Council, 1945), 79–173; Edward Sapir, foreword to *Son of Old Man Hat* (New York: Harcourt, Brace, 1938), vi.

22. Eastman, *Soul*, xii; Paul Radin, "Personal Reminiscences of a Winnebago Indian," *Journal of American Folklore* 26 (1913): 293; Eastman, *Soul*, xii.

23. This critique has now been thoroughly investigated, most notably, perhaps, in *Writing Culture: The Poetics and Politics of Ethnography*, ed. James Clifford and George E. Marcus (Berkeley: University of California Press,

1986), and *Anthropology as Cultural Critique: An Experimental Moment in the Human Sciences*, ed. George E. Marcus and Michael M. J. Fischer (Chicago: University of Chicago Press, 1986), as well as in James Clifford's *The Predicament of Culture: Twentieth-Century Ethnography, Literature, and Art* (Boston: Harvard University Press, 1988).

24. Franz Boas, "The Aims of Ethnology," in *A Franz Boas Reader: The Shaping of American Anthropology, 1883–1911*, ed. George Stocking (Chicago: University of Chicago Press, 1982), 71; Eastman, *Deep Woods*, 166.

25. Eastman, *Deep Woods*, 166–67, 171–72; Eastman, *Soul*, xii; Mary Louise Pratt, *Imperial Eyes: Travel Writing and Transculturation* (New York: Routledge, 1992), 134.

26. Eastman, *Deep Woods*, 170, 172, 170, 175, 175, 178.

27. Boas, "Recent Anthropology," 334; Boas, "Aims of Ethnology," 71; Eastman, *Deep Woods*, 183, 185.

28. Wong, *Sending My Heart Back*, 150; Eastman, *Deep Woods*, 76. I borrow the phrase "evolution of culture" from the title of A. Lane-Fox Pitt-Rivers's 1875 essay in which he defends the arrangement of ethnographic objects in museum displays that suggests the reality of social evolutionism; see A. Lane-Fox Pitt-Rivers, *The Evolution of Culture and Other Essays* (Oxford: Clarendon Press, 1906).

29. Eastman, *Deep Woods*, 58; Eastman, *Soul*, 88; Ira Jacknis, "The Ethnographic Object and the Object of Ethnology in the Early Career of Franz Boas," in *Volkgeist as Method and Ethic: Essays on Boasian Ethnography and the German Anthropological Tradition* (Madison: University of Wisconsin Press, 1996), 204.

30. Eastman, *Deep Woods*, 179.

31. Boas, "Recent Anthropology," 335; Eastman, *Soul*, x–xii.

32. Eastman, *Soul*, 4, 187, 189; Arnold Krupat, *Ethnocriticism: Ethnography, History, Literature* (Berkeley: University of California Press, 1991), 5.

33. Richard Henry Pratt, "The Advantages of Mingling Indians with Whites," in *Americanizing the American Indians*, ed. Francis Prucha (Cambridge: Harvard University Press, 1973), 261; Charles Eastman, "'My People': The Indians' Contribution to the Art of America," *The Red Man* 7 (December 1914): 138; Office of Indian Affairs, *Annual Report of the Commissioner of Indian Affairs* (Washington DC: GPO, 1905), 12.

34. Eastman, "My People," 133–34; Eastman, *Deep Woods*, 188.

35. Eastman, *Deep Woods*, 141–43, 195.

7. THE ONLY REAL INDIANS
ARE WESTERN ONES
Authenticity, Regionalism, and
Chief Buffalo Child Long Lance, or Sylvester Long

Nancy Cook

When first published in 1928, *Long Lance: The Autobiography of a Blackfoot Indian Chief* received lavish praise. For example, the *New Statesman* claimed: "This book rings true; no outsider could explain so clearly how the Indians felt." [1] Yet it *was* written by an outsider. Long Lance was born Sylvester Long on December 1, 1890, in Winston-Salem, North Carolina. By varying accounts, he was the son of either blacks, mixed-bloods, or descendants of Indian slaves. In his teens Long decided to trade labels, from one persecuted minority to another, and attended Carlisle Indian School as an unenrolled Eastern Cherokee. Throughout his life, Long continued to realign himself with increasingly western Indian tribes and to fabricate a more glorious personal past.

This essay examines Long Lance's published work, including a 1927 article in *McClure's* and *Long Lance: The Autobiography of a Blackfoot Indian Chief*, in conjunction with Donald B. Smith's 1982 biography, *Long Lance: The True Story of an Imposter*, revealing the ways in which, although "fictive," the autobiography allows Long a space to critique racial relations, establish a personal mythos, and connect with an empowering and distinctly *western* history. I want to suggest, along the way, some problems with the continued deployment of authenticity as a category of evaluation in contemporary writing about the West.

In examining Long Lance's writing and his story, I want to question what "authentic" Indian identity was, and is, as well as the way questions of identity are bound to questions of location. The "West" gave Long Lance opportunities to fabricate a more or less enabling identity, and that identity relied on popular images of tribal people of the nineteenth-century American West.

Although Long Lance's family asserted that they were of Indian and white but not African heritage, some of Long Lance's contemporaries read him, and several scholars since have read him, as "colored" or "black." [2] Mixed blood of some sort had condemned Long Lance's family first to slavery, then to segregation in the South, where they were arbitrarily attached to a black community, which quite possibly they themselves disdained. As long as he lived in Winston-Salem, Long Lance could never claim legitimacy through his Indian heritage. In Winston-Salem, there was no legal distinction for his lineage, no cultural distinction, and certainly no enabling mythology connected with that lineage. Like most Americans, Long Lance connected with Indian culture through images and texts, and those told of a grander past, with remnants left only in the West. Long Lance spent most of his life trying to connect himself with that mythic past, and part of that included the myth of racial purity. As Long shifted his identity to Long Lance, then to Chief Buffalo Child Long Lance, he erased his mixed-blood heritage and ultimately identified himself as a full-blood member of the Blood band of the Blackfeet nation.

The Long Lance autobiography, now generally considered to be "inauthentic," foregrounds the process of invention and revision that occurs to a lesser extent in all autobiography. Long Lance continually revised his past, seeking to render it both more distinguished and more immediate than he felt it really was. And yet, without embellishment, Long Lance was an extraordinarily accomplished man. He aggressively sought a good education and earned a presidential appointment to West Point (where he never matriculated). He joined the Canadian army to get into World War I and mustered out to western Canada with a distinguished record. He was a fine athlete, a successful journalist, and a well-liked fellow with a reputation as a ladies' man. He was a riveting actor and a talented aviator. Even with the powerful anti-Indian sentiment expressed during the early twentieth century, as Chief Buffalo Child Long Lance he had far more opportunities and consequently accomplished a good deal more than would have been possible as Sylvester Long.

Long Lance's appropriation of history and lore from various western tribes allowed him, as a fine specimen of the "noble savage," to be desirably exotic in Jazz Age America. Moreover, it allowed him an altered relation to white society as well as a more immediate relation to an honorable past. As Long Lance, Sylvester Long could outrace many aspects of his past, but he never outran the myth of racial purity. And geography, as much as genealogy, constituted one's racial classification. I want to suggest here that in analyzing the work of Long Lance, the issue is as much one of regional identity as it is of race.

In his critical study *Mixedblood Messages: Literature, Film, Family, Place,* Louis Owens discusses the problem of authenticity as it marks who and who is not an Indian writer. Owens, a non-enrolled man of Native American heritage, writes: "In order to be recognized, to claim authenticity in the world—*in order to be seen at all*—the Indian must conform to an identity imposed from the outside. Native American writers are unavoidably conscious of this predicament, knowing that in order to be readily recognized (and thus sold) as authentically 'Indian' their art must be figuratively dressed in braids, beads, and buckskin."[3] Owens adds that this problem is not new. Not only are Native American authors subject to a pedigree check when most non-ethnic identified authors are not, but such essentialism, if carried to its logical conclusion, would require that Native American writers write *only* of their own tribal experience.

Critics may find themselves in all sorts of ideological trouble when they ascribe, whether consciously or not, to the "blood quantum" theory of ethnic or racial identification. What then, is Indian identity, and why has Long Lance failed most critics' and historians' tests? Why is Sylvester Long a fraud, and his book generally dismissed as "inauthentic"?

Long Lance's story can tell us something about constructions of the West and western identities and their apparent dependency on legitimation via authenticity. Owens is helpful here, too: he wants to foreground contested spaces within discourse, spaces where Indian identity and authenticity have been identified. "Communication between cultures," he says,

> takes place within what Mary Louise Pratt calls those 'social spaces where disparate cultures meet, clash, and grapple with each other.' Such seams constitute what I prefer to call 'frontier' space, wherein discourse is multidirectional and hybridized. . . . Because the term 'frontier' carries with it such a heavy burden of colonial discourse, it can only be conceived of as a space of extreme contestation. Frontier, I would suggest, is the zone of trickster, a shimmering, always changing zone of multifaceted contact within which every utterance is challenged and interrogated, all referents put into question.[4]

I, too, want to use "frontier" in my discussion of Long Lance, for I hope its deployment here will show how authenticity, race, and region become inextricably bound together in the circumstances of Long Lance's life and writing. In Mary Louise Pratt's terms, and in Owens's usage, I want to see Long Lance, not as a faux Blood Indian, but rather as the producer of a hybrid "autoethnography." Owens claims, "Native American novels are such

autoethnographic texts, though we must qualify this distinction by point-
ing out that, inhabiting both sides of the frontier plus the middle, the
mixedblood text also writes back to itself." [5] While this both-sides-against-
the-middle construction may make for many contradictions, I hope it will
allow for a complexity within which we can see Long Lance as other than an
imposter.

The urge to claim authenticity, within this context, may be one strategy
to limit, or even ward off, the ways in which "disparate cultures meet, clash,
and grapple with each other" and to delimit the contradictions inherent in
the fixation of identity within so much autobiographical writing. That is, it
may be easier to construct a singular, albeit fictitious, identity than it is to
write the complexity of identity as we currently configure it within the multiple matrices of race(s), class(es), gender(s), and sexual orientation(s).
Some critics point out that "passing," "ethnic impersonation," or "playing
Indian" was not an uncommon practice in twentieth-century America.[6] For
the American and Canadian wests, where contact between cultures dominates the historical narrative from at least the sixteenth century forward, authenticity continues to be claimed to assert "insider" status for "outsiders"
and to keep newer "outsiders" at bay or powerless.

For Long Lance, especially after his oftentimes unpleasant experience at
Carlisle (where he was taunted by fellow students, who called him "black"),
"authentic Indian" increasingly became associated with "full-blood" and
with "western," for it was most often the image of the Plains Indian that be-
spoke authenticity to North Americans in the late nineteenth—and early
twentieth—centuries. And for many North Americans, and for Long Lance
in particular, the tribes of western Canada looked to be the least assimilated, and therefore the most "authentic," of these Plains tribes.

In 1922 Long Lance began his connection with the Blood Indian Reserve,
south of Calgary. He developed a friendship with an Anglican missionary
on the reserve, who was fluent in Blackfoot, and with his help Long Lance
was adopted into the tribe in 1922. As early as 1920, Long Lance met Mike
Eagle Speaker, who became Long Lance's blood brother in 1924, and who
was the unacknowledged "native informant" for much of *Long Lance*.[7] Long
Lance dropped his Cherokee ancestry almost immediately after the adoption ceremony, and his byline became Chief Buffalo Child Long Lance, a
leader of the Blood tribe. While some Blood elders objected to the use of
adoption for commercial advantage, Long Lance continued to identify him-

self as a Blood Indian, born and bred. He seemed to have found his identity in western Alberta.

Occasionally, Long Lance had misgivings about his exploitation of this identity and the eagerness with which newspapers, magazines, and companies marketed his identity as a "full-blood chief of the Blood Indians." Often Long Lance offered his services as a journalist, only to be sold to the public as a "native informant." In the 1920s the Canadian Pacific Railroad hired Long Lance to greet guests and host tourists at its Banff Springs Hotel in the Canadian Rockies. Long Lance sometimes dressed in the ceremonial garb of a Blackfoot warrior and leader, sometimes in tux and tails. Tourists adored the surprise of Long Lance's boundary crossing and often commented on their thwarted expectations when they met the "Chief" dressed for the ballroom, not the war dance.

In an article published in McClure's in 1927, titled "Princes Go West, but What of the Young Man without Money?", Long Lance asserts that the Canadian West remains a frontier of opportunity.[8] He announces that the Canadian West is a land of opportunity for average young white men, as it is for European royalty and full-blood Indian alike. The Canadian frontier erases many social distinctions, for in Alberta of the 1920s the Prince of Wales goes by his first name and socializes with commoners, and the Blood Indian man can speak of himself conversing with royals and with the "young white man" without any sense of social barrier.

It is a new kind of frontier, however. In the article, he offers up models for authentic, as opposed to inauthentic, ways to inhabit this western space. For starters, the remnants of the Old West, as represented by actual working cowboys, are unavailable to the newcomer. It's a closed shop: "All of the genuine cowboys still left on the plains are as pedigreed as a Boston Terrier; that they are known by practically every rancher in the country and that they are the only ones who can get jobs on stock ranches." Dressing like a cowboy won't connote authenticity either, for "the real cowboy dresses less like he is pictured as dressing than those who masquerade as cowboys." Long Lance goes on to describe his encounter with "the world's champion bucking-horse rider" at the Calgary Stampede of 1924. Pete Vandemeer was not among the "one thousand cowboys from Arizona to Alberta riding their mounts in a five-mile pageant through the streets of Calgary" nor at the "head of the Indian contingent," as Long Lance was; rather, he was among the thousands of other cowboys lining the sidewalks along the course of the parade. While most of these cowboys, too, were "gaudily gotten up in what the well-dressed cowhand should wear," Pete "was dressed in a blue serge suit, fresh from the ironing board, white collar and tie, small black hat and carefully shined black shoes."[9] The "real" cowboy, the champion, can only be recognized by those in the know, for he refuses to limit himself to one role, to be told by his clothes. Moreover, clothes can't tell the half of it, for the stampede is full of cowboy poseurs and wannabes.

Long Lance, at the "head of the Indian contingent," presumably is dressed for the role he performs: "real" Indian. We might also presume that Pete Vandemeer wore cowboy attire when he won his title at the Wembly Exposition in London that year. Yet the "authentic" westerner, it seems, need not declare his status sartorially. Even the European royals, who dot Long Lance's article as they do the prairie, have the good sense to dress down. "They are working in the fields in overalls, riding the ranges as ranchers."[10] How then, do we recognize authenticity? What cultural work does it perform? And why does it remain so important in discourses about the West even today? Philip Deloria defines the "authentic" as a

> culturally constructed category created in opposition to a perceived state of inauthenticity. The authentic serves as a way to imagine and idealize the real, the traditional, and the organic in opposition to the less satisfying qualities of everyday life. . . . Because those seeking authenticity have already defined their own state as inauthentic, they easily locate authenticity in the figure of an Other. This Other can be coded in terms of time (nostalgia or archaism), place (the small town), or culture (Indianness). The quest for such an authentic Other is a characteristically modern phenomenon, one that has often been played out in the contradiction surrounding America's long and ambivalent engagement with Indianness.[11]

We recognize authenticity in Long Lance's case by means of the doubled image of iconic Noble Red Man, dressed out in full Plains Indian regalia, along with his image as urban sophisticate, in white tie and tails. Both are necessary for the "authenticity-effect." The first shows Long Lance's link to a Native past, the exotic and adventurous West that tourists, speculators, and ambitious young men seek. The second assures them that their presence hasn't, in fact, killed the first, but that the past, as it were, welcomes modernity and influx with open arms. It is critical then, that Long Lance be the absolute authentic red man in order to make his boosterism seem less exploitive of . . . the red man.

In a period when "friends of the Indian" were reminding white North Americans that pioneer progress had come at the expense of Native peoples, Long Lance was a useful collaborator, inviting white Americans to explore and exploit the last frontier, the Canadian West that had attracted him because of its recent history as a white-free zone. As a "full-blood" Blood Indian, Long Lance could assuage guilt in a way that as a Lumbee, or mixed-blood Native from North Carolina, he never could. Mixed-blood recalled the long story of oppression and the plight of the "vanishing American." North Carolina, with its untold numbers of disenfranchised, de-tribalized, and un-landed Native people, showed all too clearly what happened to "noble" Native culture in the face of continued oppression. As a Blood Indian, Long Lance could invite the new homesteader, including European royalty, as a host invites a houseguest. Long Lance's ideologically tricky maneuvering came at a time when patriotic rhetoric was often anti-Indian, for Indians who reminded whites of a shameful pioneer heritage were akin to traitors. Here, in this convoluted role as both collaborator and defender of Indians, Long Lance's behavior recalls Owens's comments about the mixed-blood's role in frontier discourse, "inhabiting both sides of the frontier plus the middle." [12]

Long Lance was not alone in speaking the enemy's language. Many Native American writers in the nineteenth and twentieth centuries had to play a conventional and iconic role as Indian in order to be heard. In terms of authenticity, such role-playing by "real" Indians reinforces clichéd images as representative of authenticity. Given the inability to demonstrate authenticity outside one's cultural boundaries without such clichéd markers of authenticity, how can we recognize authenticity?

If we return for a moment to Long Lance's encounter with and recognition of the bronc-riding champion, Pete Vandemeer, we might see the trap more clearly. Long Lance, in regalia (or Indian "costume" as it were), finds himself at the Calgary Stampede among the "authentic" cowboys and the inauthentic wannabes. Like Long Lance, most are dressed for this performative occasion, a parade. Their clothing, then, in this context, neither affirms nor denies their authenticity as cowboys. However, the best cowboy, the world champion, refuses the costume of his trade, dressing instead as any urbanite would. But his authenticity is nevertheless validated in spite of his clothing, for his authenticity is so legendary that it announces itself even as he is disguised as an ordinary citizen. Even so, his authenticity also depends upon visual recognition by those in the know—those who know what the world champion bucking-horse rider looks like. In disguise, then, Pete Vandemeer validates both his own authenticity and Long Lance's, for Long Lance recognizes Pete on the street as he passes by in the parade. This second form of authenticity can be recognized only by insiders, who, presumably, don't need the concept of authenticity unless confronted with its opposite—in this case in the form of the outsider or the poseur. Authenticity, then, is a construct primarily for the instruction and social and cultural placement or positioning of outsiders. Long Lance reinforces this use of authenticity, for his *McClure's* article, written to outsiders, is full of tips so that they won't make fools of themselves when they come west. That with these tips they might not give themselves away as tenderfeet suggests that the region where this authenticity ritual takes place already has lost its sense of community and insularity, for if it hadn't, outsiders would be recognized as such regardless of their attire or manner. Authenticity, then, is a marker of the pastness of a cohesive and insular rural, agricultural, or nomadic life. When one can teach or preach authenticity, it is already archaic. Authenticity, from this perspective, although posing as a sign of the antimodern, is always articulated from a position of modernity and serves to devise a better modern social milieu.

In this context, Long Lance's masquerade as a Blood Indian chief is not so much anomalous or exceptional as it is normative or conventional. Yet while such negotiations are common practice for those who want to maintain some position of perceived privilege, its connotations and consequences are different, I think, when initiated by someone outside traditional access to power. Deloria notes that "the fact that native people turned to playing Indian . . . indicates how little cultural capital Indian people possessed at the time." [13]

So, as we return to the "fictional" autobiography, let's consider Long Lance not as a complete imposter but as an Indian man who plays Indian in order to gain cultural capital and to retrain whites in their thinking about Indians. In the process, through his (non)autobiographical writing, Long Lance finds a place to write about his life—his desires, his fears, and his criticisms of a dominant white culture. And this is how he came to publish a fictional or borrowed autobiography.

Originally contracted to write *Long Lance* as a boy's book, his publisher decided to market the book as an autobiography, and Long Lance altered the text accordingly. If Long Lance errs here, or commits a cultural crime as he moves from boy's-book author to autobiographer, it is perhaps because of his own naïveté, which allowed him to believe that he was in fact an artist, an individual, when his value to his publisher was as a cultural exhibit. This erasure has remnants in our own cultural moment, for many contemporary western writers are judged less by their imaginations than by their ability to be lyrically descriptive. We still seem to want our western writers to be native informants rather than creators of fiction.

Long Lance was so successful, I believe, because he both represented the Other and mirrored his white admirers' use of the primitive for modernity's ends. The book's confessional or personal style, then, becomes a necessary component of the comfortable fiction whites have constructed. In other words, the book *must* be presented as first-person narration. Indeed, the few reservations against the book in published reviews indicated that more of the personal should have been included. In his review for the *New York Herald Tribune*, noted anthropologist Paul Radin felt disappointed that Long Lance "consistently refuses to reveal much about his inner self," but that alone authenticates the book, because "no Indian talks much about himself." [14]

Long Lance begins with first-person narration of events ostensibly in Long Lance's childhood, interspersed with ethnographic description of Blood (and other tribes') lifeways. Historical events, often fictionalized or embellished by Long Lance, appear between descriptions of Indian life. Long Lance includes reworked pieces from his journalism career, including interviews and stories gathered in western Canada, often about other tribes. Many of these journalistic stories involve significant departures from the historical record. To these pieces he adds material written by/told by his blood brother from the Blood Reserve, Mike Eagle Speaker. Smith interviewed Eagle Speaker in the 1970s, working through *Long Lance* sometimes page by page. Those interviews are peppered with declarations of "mine" and "I wrote that." According to Eagle Speaker's textual commentary, most of the instances of first-person narration are Eagle Speaker's words or deeds. To Eagle Speaker's recollections of his own childhood, Long Lance sometimes adds bits of lore from other tribes or from other work he had read. Although Mike Eagle Speaker was more than a decade younger than Long Lance (Eagle Speaker was born in 1904), he had been raised traditionally, with elders who had known life in the "old days," before the reserve. While Eagle Speaker had relayed to Long Lance both his *own* experiences and stories he had heard from elders, in *Long Lance* they are interwoven, given either a confusing chronology or a sense of timelessness, depending upon the reader's sensibility. Some aspects of the life depicted by Long Lance were the experiences of a Blackfoot raised in the 1860s, decades before Long Lance's, and Eagle Speaker's birth. Others were within the purview of the younger man. By and large, however, "experts" on Native Americans were untroubled by the mixture of distant and recent past.[15]

Long Lance begins his "autobiography" sounding more like an ethnographer than a Native informant:

> The Indians of whose experience I have written in this book were the last tribes to encounter the white man. The region is the Far Northwest: northern Montana, Alberta, Saskatchewan and British Columbia. Until 1905 Alberta and Saskatchewan were known as the Northwest territories, a wild untamed region of North America, which had seen its first white settlers only twenty years before. The Indians of this vast stretch of high rolling plains still remember the first white man they ever saw. Before that they were a restless, aggressive people who lived as fighting nomads, traveling incessantly from the Missouri River in Montana up eight hundred miles north into the Peace River country; and from the Rocky Mountains east into what is now Manitoba.
>
> The ruling tribe of this wild domain was that of the Blackfeet, known as the "Tigers of the Plains." Upon the signing of the Northwestern Treaty they became permanently divided, and now they live half in the United States and half in western Canada—Montana and Alberta.[16]

Long Lance, ostensibly a Blood (Blackfoot) chief, distances himself from the Indians he writes about, their history, and their place. He refers to "the Indians" and "they," not "my elders" or "we." He mentions first encounters with whites three times in the opening paragraph of his book. Long Lance's "Far Northwest" is remote geographically, but its geographical remoteness functions almost temporally as well. Long Lance's confused chronology works on a mythic rather than historical level. In collapsing the recent with the deeper past, Long Lance revivifies a kind of frontier life that Americans (more than Canadians) were told—by Frederick Jackson Turner and others—had been lost to them. The *Canadian* West here is significant, for the concept of frontier was vital for a much longer period, well into the 1920s.

In Long Lance's estimation, the Blackfeet have many other important distinctions. They were "aggressive," a fighting people, "the ruling tribe" of the region, in fact "Tigers of the Plains." In an era when anyone who was not white could ill afford a temper, or any physical expression of anger, especially in Long Lance's hometown of Winston-Salem, Long Lance's Blackfeet (and indeed the Assiniboines and Crees he writes about) remain fighters long after other peoples of color have been subdued. Long Lance presents this fact as a point of pride here. The Blackfeet are nomadic, refusing boundaries, even national ones, for a very long time. As a child in North Carolina, Long Lance had been trapped by geography, whereas in Blackfeet country Indians cross state, provincial, territorial, and national boundaries routinely. His catalog of the Indians' extensive territory reinforces the idea that freedom of movement is the paramount marker of political freedom, even as he also mentions the division of the Blackfoot Confederacy, for which he gives no date. In fact, the movement across borders was mostly stopped by treaty in 1877, and most Blackfeet were settled on reservations or reserves by the early 1880s. The attraction of nomadic life proves stronger than the need for a reasonably accurate chronology. Sylvester Long was born in December 1890, and Long Lance gave birthdates as late as 1896. Although anyone with a sense of chronology or a timeline at hand would have spotted the temporal discrepancies in Long Lance, apparently the myth proved unassailably attractive. Among the many ethnographers and Indian experts who read the book, none seemed troubled (at least publicly) by the impossibility of Long Lance's story.

The Blackfeet, then, offer Long Lance freedom from whites, borders, and passivity. They are also "the ruling tribe," so at last Long Lance has situated himself in a position of power over not only whites but other Indians as well. While at Carlisle, Long Lance was taunted as inauthentically Indian. Even during his incarnation as an Oklahoma Cherokee, he was distant from a fierce and independent past. As a Blackfoot, Long Lance has a more usable past, and one with a history of domination. He legitimated his own peripatetic behavior as a cultural trait, and he legitimated his own internationalism. Long Lance's self-appointed dual citizenship allows him inaccessibility when needed and the few legal advantages of each nation in a time when Native people's rights received legal sanction slowly and erratically.

Long Lance goes on to explain the allure of his story. He claims that the period of contact between whites and Natives is "the most colorful period in the history of the North American Indian." He can relate stories of these times because they are "the experiences of our old warriors who are still living, but who cannot tell their own stories because they do not speak the white man's tongue." [17] Not unlike the ethnographer, Long Lance positions himself as speaking for the primitive Other. His act, then, is not so much one of appropriation as one of translation. As the transitional Native, Long Lance connects the past (the "old warriors") with the present: Long Lance, the educated Indian, who speaks the "white man's tongue." In fact, Long Lance could understand little of the Blackfoot language, and Mike Eagle Speaker, his principal informant, spoke English fluently.

Like much ethnographic writing, Long Lance's story begins in the first person: "The first thing in my life that I can remember is the exciting aftermath of an Indian fight in northern Montana." The perspective is of the present and of an outsider, for the recollection is of an "exciting aftermath," and the images, such as a small child might have, come after the evaluative language. Already Long Lance is in a time other than his own, for by the 1890s, Canadian Blackfoot Indians did not roam in northern Montana, and intertribal warfare was a thing of the past. The first chapter intersperses personal reflection with tribal practices. In it Long Lance tells of riding at age four, the threat of being made to wear girl's clothing should he fail at being all boy, and the ever-present threat of "a new peril which might spell our doom—the White Man." [18] For Long Lance, the life of a Blackfoot who was his contemporary did not seem authentically Indian, so he sets his story at least twenty to thirty years before his birth in 1890. Again, Long Lance works assiduously to create a pre-contact Indian world. White people may be a rumored threat, but no one has actually encountered one.

In the paragraph that follows the one just quoted, Long Lance again evokes the spectral quality of encounter: "And our fathers themselves were facing a big mystery which they could not fathom: the mystery of the future in relation to the coming of the White Man." Long Lance, born in North Carolina, knows all too well what the "White Man" can do to indigenous culture and the kinds of oppression their contact with people of color engendered. In *Long Lance* he can rewrite the history of contact, wherein he himself becomes emblematic of the survival of the people and their culture. In the process, this assimilated Indian also establishes his own authenticity, much like the process whereby he gained admission to Carlisle. [19] There, as here, he demonstrates an adequately primitive past in order to make himself appropriate for assimilation. This primitive past renders his assimilation more remarkable and more dramatic.

The autobiography, then, by means of the representation of an exotic past, serves to render Long Lance's attributes of the normative white self-made man exotic. Not unlike the mechanism that reveals the "real" cowboy under Pete Vandemeer's urban disguise, the more Long Lance resembles the model of an ambitious white man (a common enough model), the more distinct he becomes. Yet though the model of an assimilationist's dream, Sylvester Long refuses to meld into any one cultural group. In white society he steadfastly remains an Indian, yet he refuses to try to adapt to tribal life in Canada, and he refuses to return to North Carolina.

Working with the borrowed stories from Native informant Mike Eagle Speaker, with his own journalistic pieces, and with a vivid imagination, Long Lance constructs the perfect mythic autobiography, even though it has little chronological value. The autobiography tells a kind of truth, then, more metaphorical—even more allegorical—than factual. Even though the details are not the details of Sylvester Long's life, the autobiography remains an important and telling document. In it Long Lance renders in mythic terms the particularities of his own life, finding in his fabricated stories a mythos that accepts and values the outsider, his transformation, assimilation, and his individual achievement. Long Lance writes his autobiography as a Blood Indian, not a Croatan, a Lumbee, an Eastern Cherokee, an Oklahoma Cherokee, or a Cree, all identities he could claim by birthright or adoption. It is the very westernness of the Blood Indians that appeals to Long Lance. As if a devoted acolyte of Frederick Jackson Turner, Long Lance needs the concepts from Turner's frontier thesis to legitimate his chosen identity. For Long Lance, as for many of his contemporary North Americans (and even those European aristocrats in western Canada), the West provided a space in which to perform authenticity, to garner it, and then to display it for the influx of newcomers in the West, as well as for the folks at home.

Perhaps most surprising here is the way in which Long Lance uses the *Canadian* West, rather than the American West, as the site of the last frontier. Long Lance's story suggests that occasionally we can choose identity as much as it chooses us, and that the West has been an attractive locale for reinvention of one's identity, so much so that the very markers of what is seen to be authentically western are indices of the invention of western identity. Following Long Lance, many of the contemporary West's most authentic writers reenact a form of regional "passing." To be "authentic," then, means to "pass" with an identity that is located.

Notes

My deepest appreciation to Neil Schmitz, Thomas Berninghausen, Julia Watson, Rick Berg, and Donald B. Smith. My own work depends upon theirs.

1. Donald B. Smith, *Long Lance: The True Story of an Imposter* (Toronto: Macmillan of Canada, 1982; Lincoln: University of Nebraska Press, 1983), 147. My terms for Native people of North America will vary throughout the article. During Long Lance's lifetime "Indian" was commonly used. In Canada, usage includes "First Nations," "Native peoples," and "Indians." While many contemporary critics use "Native Americans," several I cite do not. Owens uses both "Native Americans" and "Indians," and Deloria uses "Indians" most frequently. Each term has its politics, a discussion of which is beyond the scope of this article. I use "Blackfoot" when following usage by Long Lance, Donald B. Smith, and other Canadians, and when referring to Canadian tribal groups. I use "Blackfeet" when following usage in Long Lance's text (he was inconsistent), usage in the United States, or when referring to tribal groups in the United States.

2. While Long Lance's birth name is Long, through most of the essay I use his authorial name, Long Lance. Smith's biography offers extensive research on Long Lance's family, and his claims as to their ethnic or racial heritage have been somewhat altered between first and second editions.

3. Louis Owens, *Mixedblood Messages: Literature, Film, Family, Place* (Norman: University of Oklahoma Press, 1998), 12–13.

4. Owens, *Mixedblood Messages*, 25–26.

5. Owens, *Mixedblood Messages*, 39–40.

6. See Philip Deloria's *Playing Indian* and Laura Browder's *Slippery Characters* for two book-length discussions of these processes.

7. The details of Long Lance's life come from Donald B. Smith's carefully researched and updated biography. Smith has added significant new material to the second edition, now titled *Chief Buffalo Child Long Lance: The Glorious Imposter* (Red Deer AB: Red Deer Press, 1999).

8. The article is reproduced in *Redman Echoes*, ed. Roberta Forsberg (Los Angeles: Frank Wiggins Trade School, Department of Printing, 1933), 49.

9. Long Lance, Chief Buffalo Child (Sylvester Long), "Princes Go West, but What of the Young Man without Money?" (1927; reprint, Los Angeles: Frank Wiggins Trade School, Department of Printing, 1933), 50.

10. Long Lance, "Princes Go West," 54.

11. Philip J. Deloria, *Playing Indian* (New Haven: Yale University Press, 1998), 101.

12. Philip Deloria gives a complex reading of the relation between boyhood, outdoor adventure, and the fight over defining patriotism, particularly in the Boy Scouts (see *Playing Indian*, esp. chapter 4); Owens, *Mixedblood Messages*, 40.

13. Deloria, *Playing Indian*, 125.

14. Smith, *Long Lance*, 207.

15. Information on Mike Eagle Speaker is taken from both editions of Smith's biography and from transcriptions of interviews he has deposited at the Glenbow Museum archives.

16. Chief Buffalo Child Long Lance (Sylvester Long), *Long Lance* (1928; reprint, Jackson: University Press of Mississippi, 1995), xxxvii.

17. Long Lance, *Long Lance*, xxxviii. An interesting parallel can be found in the work of James Willard Schultz, a white who first encountered the Blackfeet in 1877, then lived among them off and on for seventy years and was given the name "Apikuni" by the tribe, and went on to make his career as a writer by writing Blackfeet stories. Even as recently as 2002, the University of Oklahoma Press published a new collection of his previously uncollected tales, *Blackfeet Tales from Apikuni's World*.

18. Long Lance, *Long Lance*, 1, 3.

19. Long Lance, *Long Lance*, 3. In order to be admitted to Carlisle, Long Lance needed affidavits supporting his possession of the requisite blood quantum, and he needed to demonstrate proficiency in his "native" language, Cherokee, so that Carlisle could forbid him to speak it at school and teach him English.

8. THE AUTHENTICITY GAME

"Getting Real" in Contemporary American Indian Literature

Susan Bernardin

In 1922 Elsie Clews Parsons, an ethnographer of Hopi, Taos, and other Pueblos, edited a collection of "Indian" tales written by the era's leading anthropologists of American Indians—A. L. Kroeber, Robert Lowie, Franz Boas, Paul Radin, among others—better known for their writing of monographs than of stories.[1] In his introduction to *American Indian Life*, Kroeber explains such a startling departure by heralding fiction's "freedom in depicting or suggesting the thoughts and feelings of the Indian, such as is impossible in a formal, scientific report." In her own preface to the volume, Parsons similarly calls attention to the limitations of available narrative forms about Indians: "Between these forbidding monographs and the legends of [James] Fenimore Cooper, what is there then to read for a girl who is going to spend her life among Indians or, in fact, for anyone who just wants to know more about Indians?"[2] By proposing as possible solution for this "girl's" dilemma a mediating genre between scientific ethnography and elegiac romance, Parsons acknowledged the inseparability of these two seemingly opposed discourses in revealing the "truth" about Indians. In doing so, she both encapsulated and forecast the primacy of authenticity as a cultural value underpinning literature about, and sometimes by, American Indians.

Eighty years later, Parsons's lament hardly seems out of date: a cursory glance at U.S. popular culture registers the ubiquity of the invented Indian. Indeed, mainstream conceptions of American Indians remain in large part unchanged, nourished by a steady diet of such cinematic fare as *Pocahontas* and *Dances with Wolves*, by professional sports team mascots, and by a legion of fraudulent Indian texts shelved in the "Native American section" of bookstores. The ongoing marketability of "Indianness" underscores the tenacity of the nation's attachment to what Gerald Vizenor calls the "bankable simulation" that has "become more important and more significant in America, in the world, than have 'real' people and their experiences."[3] Both everywhere and nowhere in mainstream U.S. society, American Indians are often only visible to non-Natives as commodities and caricatures.

Parsons would also find that once authoritative representations of "the real Indian" produced by her peers have proved to be as fictive as Cooper's

155

romances of the vanishing and vanquished Native. Current articulations of the "New Indian History"—along with those of postmodern ethnography—self-consciously work to dismantle the rhetorical stances of objectivity, distance, and narrative transparency characterizing those formerly "forbidding" monographs. However, with so few Native Americans participating in or being consulted about the making of this "New Indian History" and anthropology, one wonders what might actually be new about these approaches.[4] Meanwhile, academics and activists alike bemoan the public's investment in what Vizenor terms the "absolute fake" at the expense of much-needed attention to ongoing movements of Native political, economic, cultural sovereignty, even as investments in selective notions of "Indianness" have influenced much of the scholarship about Native peoples in the United States.

As Parsons's plea suggests, the vexed relationship between discourses of Native authenticity and narrative representation is an old and overdetermined one, having shaped not only mainstream metanarratives of Native identity but the formation of counter or alternative narratives produced by both foundational and contemporary Native writers. Euro-America's romance with prescriptive notions of the "real Indian" demanded that early Native writers entering dominant print culture negotiate editorial and public demands for moral credibility, narrative veracity, and tribal authenticity with their own literary and political goals. For example, the first known novel written by a Native American, *The Life and Adventures of Joaquín Murieta, the Celebrated California Bandit*, published in California in 1854, was framed by an editorial preface casting its Cherokee author, John Rollin Ridge, as the legendary outlaw's double. Presumably, Ridge's own experiences as witness and participant in post-Removal factional violence among the Cherokee legitimated his western outlaw novel as textually authentic. At the same time, Ridge's own competing interests in social criticism and market appeal converge in a disjunctive text that yokes together formulaic tropes with markers of the historical "real."[5]

Seventy years later, Christine Quintasket, or Mourning Dove, one of the first known Native women novelists and a contemporary of Elsie Clews Parsons, faced similar challenges to her identity as an author during her decade-long effort to publish *Cogewea, the Half-Blood* (1927). Overriding her objections, Quintasket's editor-collaborator, Lucullus McWhorter, vouched for her "native authenticity" by including in his preface a photograph of her in beads and buckskin.[6] In the production of the text itself, McWhorter

continued to cast Mourning Dove as native informant rather than as author, adding ethnographic, editorial, and historical commentaries, even as
he himself resorted to romantic tropes with epigraphs from Longfellow's
"Hiawatha." For her part, Mourning Dove, like Ridge, strategically adapted
the popular genre of western romance in the service of radically defamiliar-
izing readers' expectations of the "romance" of western expansion and the
vanishing Indian. Through the novel's sly reworkings of the genre, in which
cowboys and Indians are one and the same and the open range they "roam"
is allotted reservation land, Mourning Dove debunks the very claims to authenticity advanced by McWhorter in his preface, footnotes, and narrative
impositions.

McWhorter's dual and contradictory reliance on ethnographic and romantic discourse in Mourning Dove's novel is symptomatic of broader cultural confusion surrounding narrative form and Native representation.
From the nation's founding moments, writers consciously turned to Native
American subjects as a means of forging a distinctively American literature.
At the same time, the desire to possess Native Americans *as* narrative subjects fueled the pursuit of Indian autobiographies. Even though many of
these "as-told-to" narratives were solicited, translated, edited, and published by Euro-Americans, they have enjoyed enduring popularity among a
reading public eager to gain access to its notion of "the real thing." Ranging from Black Hawk's narrative to *Black Elk Speaks*, these texts instead register what Renato Rosaldo famously referred to as "imperialist nostalgia"
—a duplicitously elegiac romance of loss and defeat. The popularity of contemporary "as-told-to" autobiographies, such as those by Lame Deer, Mary
Crow Dog, and Leonard Crow Dog, all produced in collaboration with Richard Erdoes, attests to the continued market appeal of Native texts whose
premise is ethnographic and cultural self-disclosure.[7] At the same time,
the "all-American" genre of autobiography has furnished Native writers
both past and present with a powerful form of testimonial and resistance
literature. For example, the genre of the boarding-school memoir, inaugu-
rated by Charles Eastman, Zitkala-Sa, Luther Standing Bear, and others,
sheltered and spread stories of pan-tribal solidarity and survival. Written in
English, these foundational texts were adept in "reinventing the enemy's
language."[8]

However, the struggles faced by early Native writers in English—struggles over control of their stories, over access to dominant print culture, and
over the ever-present dictates of textual and authorial authenticity—con-

tinue to influence the production, marketing, and reception of texts by many contemporary American Indian writers. Despite the recognition and publication of increasingly diverse Native American literary texts, Euro-America's fixation with selective indices of Indian authenticity delimits the kinds of texts circulating in national markets. Those few literary texts published commercially rather than by university or other small presses end up as synecdoches for American Indians, serving as cultural stand-ins for hundreds of distinct nations.

Within a cultural climate whose attraction to alternative or "New Age" spiritual practices has fueled the commodification of American Indian religions, those texts that display signatures of spirituality or of the mythic real have gained particular currency. For example, the recent vogue for "trickster," or what Gerald Vizenor appropriately terms "Coyote kitsch," has threatened to neutralize this complex tribal figure of subversion and creation. Even when texts purposely refuse such reductive readings, their incorporation of trickster figures becomes available for a seemingly digestible experience of ethnic "difference," or what Louis Owens deemed "literary tourism."[9] Ultimately, the publication and national distribution of those texts appearing to reinforce current notions of Native authenticity compound internal debates over authorial and textual authenticity within Native American literary circles.

Such debates have escalated in recent years because, just past the Western millennium, the field of Native American literature inches ever closer to a semblance of institutional legitimacy.[10] The proliferation of college courses, conference panels, listservs, and literary anthologies has intensified the ongoing interpretive and pedagogical double binds faced by scholars of American Indian literatures. As a field undergoing constant formation, Native American literary studies is enmeshed in questions of categorization, value, and representativeness.

Inheriting Parsons's dilemma, many teachers and scholars find themselves caught between the traps of romantic representation still endemic in U.S. culture and the traps of the ethnographic impulse inherited from a now much-maligned anthropological tradition. On the one hand, Joseph Bruchac reminds us that "the Native American view of life as reflected in literature is holistic. Remember that, if you are teaching Native American literature well you are not just teaching literature, you are teaching culture." Kenneth Roemer similarly cautions that "teachers and scholars who ignore the cultural, historical, aesthetic, linguistic and, in the case of oral literatures, the performance contexts of Native texts risk making ludicrous and even sacrilegious mistakes." [11] Without some introduction to Jemez Pueblo and the Diné, for example, the reader of N. Scott Momaday's *House Made of Dawn* will come away with a partial, even impoverished understanding of the novel. Loosened from their cultural matrices, American Indian literary texts become available for (mis)readings that subsume them under universalizing interpretations, thereby subjecting them to yet another form of critical appropriation.

Yet how to attend to such "essential differences," when Andrew Wiget cautions us that the act of reading Native American literature can become a kind of "shadow anthropology," with readers mining texts for nuggets of cultural authenticity? What happens when, as Henry Louis Gates Jr. argues in the broader context of multicultural literature, "literary readings are often guided by the desire to elicit, first and foremost, indices of ethnic particularity, especially those that can be construed as oppositional, transgressive, subversive"? In other words, how to identify and treat the particularities of Native-authored texts without subjecting those texts to anthropological criteria, or resorting to that ultimate badge of authorial authenticity, the book-jacket photograph? [12]

The scholarly and pedagogical challenges of identifying the Native particularities of literary texts often become challenges of identification for students, Native as well as non-Native, who evaluate texts according to their ability to mirror back identifiable images of "Indianness." For my students whose knowledge of contemporary American Indians is often limited to Tomahawk chops and casinos, Native-authored literary texts often function as their first, and perhaps sole, introduction to the universe of treaty rights and other sovereignty concerns, history and politics, and realities of regional and cultural diversity. Not surprisingly, such texts get burdened with the dual role of confronting and dispensing tropes of "Indianness" while also serving as conduits to the real lives and histories of Native peoples. For the Native students from diverse backgrounds and communities who read the same texts in my classes, such texts often need to be real to *their* varied experiences as mixed-bloods or full-bloods living in an array of old and new homelands.

Finally, echoing Jim Northrup's identification of the television as "that window to America / we see you, you don't see us," such texts must respond to the simultaneous visibility and invisibility of Native Americans in the

United States—visible as popular cultural icons and mascots, invisible as members of sovereign nations with distinct histories.[13] Given both the range of readerships and expectations brought to bear on contemporary Native literature, the capacity for any single text to meet them all is simply untenable. All too often, critics, teachers, and students inadvertently end up playing the authenticity game, a circular game in which the identification of a text's "Indian" features gets entangled with assigning that self-same text as culturally informant or race representative.

As a defining problem of Native American literary studies, the concept of authenticity animates enduring and vexing debates over identity (who's Indian), of culture (what's Indian), and of literature (what constitutes American Indian literature). Denoting both the "real thing" and a "claimed or verified origin or authorship," authenticity has long been wielded as a mode of containment. For example, the fiction of blood quantum enacted by the federal government—part of the nineteenth-century discourse of racial purity and the color line—sought to replace indigenous conceptions of tribal membership with racialized and exclusionary ones. By measuring identity through taxonomic indices, the U.S. government set into motion a discourse of purity and impurity in Native identity politics that continues to leave its imprint on the language of membership and belonging in Indian nations. As Chadwick Allen argues in his essay "Blood (and) Memory," "blood quantum enshrines racial purity as the ideal for authentic American Indian identity," adding that "it is not only the federal government or White Americans who pointedly ask, 'How much Indian blood do you have?'" Continuing, Allen cites M. Annette Jaimes: "Indians themselves have increasingly begun to reinforce the race code excluding the genetically marginalized from both identification as Indian citizens and consequent entitlements."[14] An ongoing legacy of colonial thought and its convolutions of legal and political entitlements, authenticity has very real implications for people having to prove their identity for tribal enrollment cards and for Indian nations having to prove their very existence in order to gain federal recognition or title to particular land bases.

In the face of longstanding popular and literary simulations of Indianness, authenticity, to revise a phrase coined by Cornel West, *matters*.[15] In 1991 a researcher discovered that Forrest Carter, author of the highly acclaimed, putatively autobiographical *The Education of Little Tree*, a mixed-blood Cherokee boy's coming-of-age story, was also Asa Carter, a member of white supremacist groups and speech writer for George Wallace. This revelation sparked debate over how this "absolute fake" could have produced such a persuasively "Indian" text. In a provocative *New York Times* magazine essay, " 'Authenticity,' or the Lesson of Little Tree," Henry Louis Gates Jr. argues against using authenticity as an interpretive paradigm for literary texts, claiming that today "its political stakes are relatively trivial." Wary about essentializing ethnic or racial difference, Gates questions the notion of authors standing in for "social constituencies," concluding that "no human culture is inaccessible to someone who makes the effort to understand, to learn, to inhabit another world." Gates's evocation of the "slippery slope" created by unstable and unreliable categories of textual and authorial authenticity is particularly relevant for Native literature, since, in Michael Wilson's words, "perhaps more than any other cultural group in this hemisphere, Native peoples are perceived through the lens of purity and impurity, in the arts, social sciences, and even law." [16]

Yet the political stakes of authenticity, most especially for Native Americans, are far from "trivial." It is precisely because of the dominant culture's pervasive and deeply entrenched pattern of what Philip Deloria calls "playing Indian"—by taking ownership of Native land, history, culture, and now spiritual traditions—that such literary fakes are so insidious. In recent years, writers and editors in Indian Country have "outed" an array of authorial frauds who have generated self-help books, seminars, and novels for eager audiences, their success enabled by reproducing variants of the public's invented Indian. Scholar-writer Craig Womack wonders whether even Native-authored fiction itself—vastly more popular than "non-fiction written by Indians concerning their tribe's land claims or politics"—may play, "in troubling ways, into the vanishing notion by allowing Native people to be fictional but not real?" Perhaps underscoring Womack's concerns, the only recent nonfictional "treatment of land claims or politics" to achieve widespread publicity is Ian Frazier's *On the Rez*, an account of the Pine Ridge reservation by a non-Native writer based in New York. [17]

Given the profitability of "absolute fakes," claims of authenticity have long been available for a variety of moves, spanning from cultural appropriation to tribal self-determination. Yet even when wielded self-consciously, such claims risk the reinscription of the very categorical values they seek to dismantle. Given U.S. culture's longstanding obsession with the discourse of Indian authenticity, David Moore calls its predominance in Native literary studies "at worst a false, or at best, a secondary question," because it "foregrounds colonial relations as the reductive but defining phenomenon of Indian identity, and thus compromises an effort to show more complex dynamics." [18] As such, the authenticity impulse in Native American literary criticism ends up as a strategy of containment, legitimating those texts that appear to reproduce selective definitions of "Indianness," dismissing or demonizing those that challenge them. Parsons's dilemma then, is writ anew in contemporary Native literary studies: interpretive approaches reliant on discourses of authenticity run aground on the shifting grounds of anthropological and romantic language.

While many Native writers have a story about a reviewer who subjects their work to prescriptive criteria of authenticity, some of these very writers have turned similarly critical eyes on the literary productions of their peers. In a well-known example, Leslie Silko's review essay, "Here's an Odd Artifact for the Fairy Tale Shelf," criticizes Louise Erdrich's *The Beet Queen* for its "stylish postmodern prose," which renders insufficient attention to the virulent racism of the communities bordering reservations in North Dakota. Meanwhile, Paula Gunn Allen, in an essay entitled "Special Problems in Teaching Leslie Marmon Silko's *Ceremony*," faults Silko's critically acclaimed novel for being *too* authentic in her inclusion of Laguna ceremonial and sacred materials. [19]

In recent years, debates within the field have reprised longstanding questions within African American literary studies over authorial role and responsibility, narrative form and political content, audience(s), and reception. In different ways, Sherman Alexie, Elizabeth Cook-Lynn, Gloria Bird, Louis Owens, Craig Womack, and others have given shape to the authenticity debate by drawing, redrawing, or dismantling boundary-lines governing the field. In one of the more controversial critical moves in recent years, both Cook-Lynn and Alexie have voiced acerbic criticisms of mixed-blood writers, whom they have claimed are wedded to narratives of invention that reinforce dominant culture's romantic-ethnographic assumptions about American Indians. In 1997 Alexie participated in listserv discussions about Native literature. His frequent posts to the list often pivoted around "what" constitutes authentic Indian literature. One of the more heated exchanges involved determining and policing the relationship between tribal identity and narrative content. For example, Alexie created and then attacked a category of Native writers he labeled "urban, mixed-blood," and academic, whose "tribal knowledge is obtained from the same books, movies, music, and generic cultural touchstones that non-Indians gain their knowledge

from." Separated from the source of authentic Indian identity (the reservation), mixed-blood urban writers, Alexie suggests, attempt to compensate
for this lack by filling "their books with formulaic Indian imagery and non-
Indian critics of Indian lit love it (makes the writing of scholarly papers
much easier)."[20] His critique, then, targeted those writers who, he felt,
were posing as "traditional" and who, in concert with non-Indian scholars,
were guilty of perpetuating romantic tropes of "Indianness."

Alexie's provocative observations of the literary expressions of those he
once termed "less" and "more" Indian on the spectrum of "Indianness" are
akin to those made by Elizabeth Cook-Lynn in her essays "The American Indian Fiction Writer: Cosmopolitanism, Nationalism, the Third World, and
First Nation Sovereignty" and "American Indian Intellectualism and the
New Indian Story." In the latter essay, Cook-Lynn engages in a sustained
polemic against what she calls the "new Indian story" being told by many
contemporary Native writers, excoriating what she terms a "mixed-blood
movement led by those whose tribal past has never been secure." This "literary movement of disengagement" from a communal base of nationalist
concerns, privileges "individual liberation" at the expense of broader efforts of sovereignty and survival.[21] While Alexie has called many of the most
visible Native writers neoprimitivists who churn out the kinds of "Indian
stories" expected by a non-Native readership, Cook-Lynn deplores such
writers for their inability to meet her criteria for politically engaged, nation-
based literature.

Meanwhile, Craig Womack's pathbreaking study of Muscogee (Creek)
literary history enacts Cook-Lynn's call for nation-based literary criticism,
criticism anchored in specific geographical, cultural, tribal histories. At the
same time, Womack argues against the prevalence of the "tainted/untainted
framework" governing Native literary criticism, which, focusing on authors' identities and their texts as hybrid, liminal, and bicultural, marginal-
izes their articulations of "tribal realities."[22] Womack's scholarship, and
that of other Native scholars such as Robert Warrior, marks a crucial shift,
as increasing numbers of Native scholars enter the field and replace earlier
modes of critical, pedagogical, and literary representation. This shift in the
field drives current efforts to decenter critical attention to particular authors
and interpretive approaches that have dominated syllabi, conference panels, and journal submissions. For example, American Indian Quarterly, edited
by Devon Mihesuah, has stated that "until further notice, AIQ is not accepting submissions on Dorris, Erdrich, Harjo, King, Momaday, Owens, Silko,

Welch and identity issues. *AIQ* is seeking submissions on policy, environ-mental protection, treaty rights, forestry, economic development, oral his-tories, AIS programs and activism." A sign of the journal's emphatic refusal of critical projects not aligned with its nation-based mission statement is best shown by the final line: "Submissions dealing with literary criticism must include discussions about Nation-building, empowerment for Na-tives and hope for the future."[23] Such a statement serves as cautionary advice to potential contributors that Native writers canonized by academe are off-limits, as are writers who have been attacked as less "Indian." More broadly, it also reinforces P. Jane Hafen's argument, made in an essay on Sherman Alexie, that critics understand "Native American literature is not simply an exercise in literary theory."[24]

At the heart of these multiple perspectives on the "state" and direction of Native American literature and criticism are ongoing questions that will continue to alternately invigorate and stifle the field: namely, what kinds of relationships should be forged between narrative form, authorial role and responsibility, and the "real"? Such questions necessarily accompany a field so long defined by outsiders. Yet critical debate that pivots around arbitrat-ing a text's "Indianness" can become enmeshed within the very vocabulary of authenticity that it has worked to displace. Moreover, imperatives that in-dividual texts be expected to include both culturally specific and represen-tative experiences of many different kinds of readers promote a monolithic taxonomy of Native reader, writer, and text.

Two contemporary Native writers—Sherman Alexie himself, who has achieved critical acclaim and media fame, and Gerald Vizenor, who has achieved critical acclaim without an accompanying national market—show us how Native writers enter the authenticity game, suggesting how discourses of authenticity might both empower and entrap, subvert and confirm, readers and readings of Native American literature. Their varied approaches to Native authenticity underscore the very real stakes in these debates, as well as their implications for future directions within Native lit-erary studies. Turning, by way of conclusion, to Louis Owens's final novel, *Dark River*, I suggest what might be a paradoxically fruitful relationship be-tween Native and narrative authenticity.

Widely reviewed and marketed, Alexie's prolific literary output—sev-eral volumes of poetry, three short-story collections, and two novels—has garnered him the kind of national press rarely extended to Native writ-ers. Having described himself as "hypocritical and hypercritical," Alexie simultaneously embraces and mocks his public role as "Indian du Jour."[25] His lectures, interviews, essays, and texts repeatedly set up and deflect engrained expectations of representative Native literature. Alexie's short-story collection The Toughest Indian in the World, for example, grapples with questions of sexual orientation and interracial relations in ways that extend and complicate his own previous stands on acceptable content matter for Native-authored texts.

In the book that launched his national literary reputation, The Lone Ranger and Tonto Fistfight in Heaven, Alexie uses a narrative style that neither confronts an outside reader with an emphatically "other" universe of mythic and oral signification nor presents the formidable narrative and epistemological complexity characteristic of texts by Momaday, Silko, Vizenor, and others. Instead, his twenty-two lyrically evocative stories and vignettes offer a deceptively accessible portrait of the Spokane reservation and its inhabitants: one that seemingly hands to readers contemporary stereotypes of Indians only to immediately complicate them. As agent provocateur, Alexie includes characters in The Lone Ranger and Tonto who at first glance fulfill the role of the "drunken Indian," prompting some critics to question his reasons for authenticating a destructive narrative of tragic victimhood. Indeed, Alexie seems to invite such readings by repeatedly using essentialist descriptors for Indians and whites. Moreover, many of Alexie's characters in The Lone Ranger and Tonto themselves fall prey to the tragic role scripted for them by U.S. popular culture. Continually bumping up against both the Crazy Horse model of heroic armed resistance and that of the drunken or stoic "Tonto" Indian, his characters voice the text's overriding, self-reflexive meditation on what it might mean to be a contemporary Indian from a reservation. At the same time, in "The Only Traffic Light," two characters reach for their cooler and edge up against the stereotype of Indian alcoholism, only to remind each other that they are reaching for a Pepsi now, not a beer.

Most strikingly, in contrast to much of contemporary Native literature, The Lone Ranger and Tonto deflects any sustained narrative move toward recovery or reaffirmation of "tradition," community, or culture. Instead, many of Alexie's characters settle for momentary acknowledgments of tribal ties, such as the tenuous bond between Victor and the pariah storyteller Thomas Builds-the-Fire, while calling for imagination as the best survival strategy of all. At once a comic and caustic vision of 1990s Indian life, The Lone Ranger and Tonto refuses the narrative of romantic redemption even as it refuses to fully dismantle the tragic narrative of Indian self-destruction.

In doing so, Alexie has met with criticism for offering what Gloria Bird, a Spokane artist and writer, has called "the exaggeration of despair without context." In her essay "The Exaggeration of Despair in Sherman Alexie's *Reservation Blues*," Bird fears that Alexie's literary and media success encourages readers to treat the Spokane reservation of his fictional terrain as ethnographic or sociological truth, thereby "mistaking it for complete representation." By claiming that in *Reservation Blues* she finds "no evidence of Spokane culture and traditions or anything uniquely Spokane," Bird underscores the danger she sees in the popularity of his fiction and in Alexie himself serving, even if unwillingly so, as a contemporary "race representative." The broader questions she presents in her critique of Alexie's novel, then, are whether Native writers have an authorial responsibility to create a communally accepted discourse of the real in their texts and, if so, whose or which community should be represented and whether certain narrative forms are more effective conduits of "the real." Or, as Bird asks, how to "accurately portray reservation communities without exploiting them?" For Bird, Alexie fails in this task, creating characters who appeal to mainstream audiences because "they are dressed in America's favorite subjects when it comes to Indians: tragedy and despair." [26]

In his essay "Through an Amber Glass: Chief Doom and the Native American Novel Today," Louis Owens poses similar critiques of Alexie's more recent novel, *Indian Killer*, labeling it a member of the "Chief Doom School" of Native American literature, "caricatures inherited from the centuries-old tradition of the doomed, tragic savage." While Owens and Bird view Alexie's fiction as simply dishing up in modern form characters engaging in classic vanishing acts of despair, self-destruction, and tragedy, P. Jane Hafen questions Alexie's positions on identity and belonging. In her essay, "Rock 'n' Roll, Redskins, and the Blues," she writes that "in the world of Indian identity politics, Alexie is uncomfortably essentialist," even as she finds that "he represents real life, and I believe his intended audience consists of real Indians, whoever they may be." [27]

For his part, Alexie has repeatedly called for Native writers to be more accessible and hence more "real" and relevant to the broadest possible audience of American Indians. Part of "getting real" for Alexie involves dispensing with those texts circulating as "the real thing" in classrooms across the country. In a deftly ironic chapter entitled "Introduction to Native American Literature" in *Indian Killer*, Alexie stages much of the current debate over authenticity in Native literary studies. A Spokane character, Marie Polatkin, challenges the authority of her white professor and that of his syllabus, composed of texts whose Native authorship is either absent or deeply compromised: *The Education of Little Tree*, *Black Elk Speaks*, *Lame Deer: Seeker of Visions*, and *Lakota Woman*.[28] As Alexie's chapter makes abundantly clear, at the heart of his writing is an effort to wrest control over the means of Native representation, which for so long has been solely in the hands of non-Natives.

Moreover, Alexie argued in a 1997 interview, in the context of discussing Vizenor's work, that "if Indian literature can't be read by the average twelve-year-old kid living on the reservation, what the hell good is it?"[29] His own interest in eliciting a predominantly Native readership informs his frequent use of what one might call generic signifiers of "Indianness": HUD housing, commodity food, fry bread. In addition, Alexie minimizes attention to tribally specific, geographically anchored locales in favor of these cultural shorthands that both invoke and involve a pan-Indian readership. His related move toward film with *Smoke Signals* (1998), based on a story from *The Lone Ranger and Tonto Fistfight in Heaven*, and, most recently, *The Business of Fancy Dancing* (2002), is part of his concerted effort to reach the broadest possible Native audience, including those "twelve-year-old kids."

Yet those very mechanisms for "getting real" in Alexie's literary lexicon are precisely what Gerald Vizenor writes against, those narratives purporting to be "the real thing." As one of the "urban, mixed-blood, academic" writers under periodic, often severe scrutiny by some Native writers and critics for prose deemed elitist and inaccessible—and hence too attenuated from tribal realities—Vizenor challenges both non-Indians and Indians to break free from the traps of the authenticity impulse. A writer of extraordinary range and energy, Vizenor uses poetry, autobiography, journalism, novels, short stories, and essays to uproot readerly reliance on the truth value of representationality. Profoundly and radically antirealist, Vizenor's prose is *not* going to be readable by many twelve-year-olds, either on or off the reservation. For Vizenor, any efforts to define inevitably entrap; as a result, he reclaims the English language in ways that elude interpretive containment or narrative closure. As such, Vizenor's work is sustained by his contention that "you can't have liberation if you're confined to discourses of the real. Once you're confined to the real, you're trapped; your stories lose their magical power." At the same time, Vizenor confirms that his writing is grounded in realities of colonialism, Anishinaabe history, and philoso-

167

phy: "All the details in my books are as accurately rendered as I can make them."[30]

Arguing that the function of literature "ought to be to continually change and upset, to contradict," Vizenor turns to language itself as a performative and critical site of intervention.[31] Through his shape-shifting wordplay and relentless coinage of new terms ("survivance," "cross-blood," "manifest manners"), Vizenor sets the English language in motion, enacting his efforts to free readers from static poses and precepts. One signature strategy is his citation, incorporation, and juxtaposition of the words of others. While this pastiche format has tended to identify him as a postmodern stylist—in whose work the real is always already constructed—it most notably works to stop the self-perpetuating reliance on notions of authenticity in representations of American Indians.

More specifically, the sheer volume and variety of voices inhabiting his texts—the voices of government and historical documents, anthropology, popular culture, oral stories, non-Native and Native voices from past and present—foil attempts to contain tribal histories, experiences, and stories. For example, in his essay "Postindian Warriors," Vizenor targets what he considers the biggest "occidental invention" in the "word wars": the word *Indian*—a word that never meets up with its intended signifier. As "colonial enactment" and "bankable simulation," the word *Indian*, he argues, has had the power to "reduce the rich complexities of human experience of every tribal group, of every writer coming from a uniquely, distinctly identifiable experience."[32]

As such, the word epitomizes what he has famously referred to as "terminal creeds," those discourses about Native peoples that are static, fixed, and deadening. Beginning with examples of what he calls "manifest manners"—"the notions and misnomers that are read as the authentic and sustained as representations of Native American Indians"—"Postindian Warriors" travels from Lewis and Clark's journals, to New Age novelist Lynne Andrews, to AIM leader/tribal entrepreneur Dennis Banks, and in between cites Jane Tompkins, Larzer Ziff, Wallace Stegner, Scott Momaday, Luther Standing Bear, Jean Baudrillard, and Hannah Arendt.[33] By yoking together such disparate voices, Vizenor offers us a metachorus of contradiction, irony, and conflict rather than a quick narrative fix to problems of narrative representation.

In a related strategic vein, Vizenor's essay tries to break the hold of romantic simulations of "Indianness" through the refrain, "This portrait is not an Indian." Recalling the refrain of his first novel (*Bearheart*)—"What is Indian?"—"Postindian Warriors" first refers to Andy Warhol's silkscreen image of Russell Means, which graces the cover of Vizenor's book *Manifest Manners*, in which this essay appears. The phrase, "This portrait is not an Indian," plays off of the caption of René Magritte's famous and equally playful painting, *Ceci n'est pas une pipe*. Through slight variations of the phrase, such as "This is not an Indian portrait," Vizenor not only teases out his perception of AIM activists "posing" as "real Indians" but teasingly unhitches the word *Indian* from any expected referents. By destabilizing representation itself, Vizenor, in Louis Owens's words, "skewers all of us at one time or another, making us uncomfortably aware of the instability of our own terminal grounds and forcing us to question and re-question all creeds and narratives." [34] Breaking the ground of language itself, Vizenor uproots every culturally ingrained assumption of "Indianness" in an effort to help us all escape the authenticity game.

Alexie's and Vizenor's meditations on authenticity lead us to the endgame of Louis Owens's last novel, *Dark River* (1999). Through its densely woven design of intertextual references to popular culture and tribal politics, to Choctaw and Apache world-renewal stories, the novel itself is a sustained metacommentary on Native and narrative authenticity. Like Vizenor, Owens creates his work out of a patchwork of multiple, conflicting cultural materials. In an indirect response to the "terminal creeds" of Indian authenticity, Owens populates his novel with signs of inclusivity and incorporation: a rooster in an Apache community is named Plymouth Rock; his owner is the formidable Mrs. (John) Edwards.

Most notably, Owens punctures the invented Indian from Puritan times to present-day Hollywood, while claiming the changing sameness of the tribal real. To do so, Owens unravels the entwined discourses of romance and the ethnographic real, embodied within a single character, Avrum Goldberg, a New York anthropologist who has gone more "native" than the Natives, and whose proposal of a grant-funded "traditional" Apache village theme park manifests his misguided efforts to freeze-frame a culture in motion. Another example of Owens's play on the invented Indian is Jesse, an Apache whose scam vision-quest venture backfires when he is shot by militia wannabes while in wolf costume, pretending to fulfill a client's "vision" at the Dark River. In an ironic gesture to another demonized and vanished species, Jesse's masquerade suggests that to play Indian, he must play dead.

The interplay of the novel's twenty-odd major characters is driven by the narrative's own riverine motions, which, like the river of the novel's title, are "ceaselessly changing and moving, but remaining constant."[35] From Sandrine Le Bris, Parisian martial-arts expert and vision quester, to Shorty, the former Hollywood extra whose bursts of Italian make ironic reference to the Italian actors who played Indians in hundreds of westerns, the characters self-consciously view themselves not only *as* characters in intersecting Hollywood and Apache storylines, but even participate in changing the stories they inhabit. Through the latter part of the novel, many of the characters repeatedly invoke cinematic plots, often interrupting their own "lines" to comment on or revise the script they are following. An Apache woman named Allison, for example, complains to the Parisian, "I don't mean to be rude, but this isn't going to be one of those stories . . . where the white person comes in and saves the Indians." Like old Apache stories in the process of renewal in the narrative, the characters remake themselves, deflecting any predictable turn in the metanarrative of Euro-America and Native Americans. As Shorty, the veteran of countless "classic" Indian movies, intones, "you got to avoid cleeshayed plots."[36]

Owens's fluid narrative form, itself an enactment of oral story-making, shapes an ending that defies readers' expectations of closure. In the last few pages, characters debate how to end the novel, trying out different takes and re-takes of the ending. When the villain "hopefully" proposes "killing everybody," "the good guys all dead as hell and the bad guy unpunished," the Parisian dismisses his version of an Indian story as "too postmodern, or too *noir*."[37] Other suggestions for narrative closure are dismissed because they do not accord with Apache stories: in the words of one character, some stories simply can't be "messed with." Through its relentless play on predictable plots, the "end" of *Dark River* is an end in motion, demonstrating the ceaseless impulse to create and renew the world through story. As such, the novel serves as a playfully serious model of how Native writers might work to both exercise and exorcise notions of authenticity.

In "Beads and Buckskins: Reading Authenticity in Native American Literature," Owens contends that "for Native Americans, the term 'Indian' is a deeply contested space, where authenticity must somehow be forged out of resistance to the 'authentic' representation." The paradox of claiming the real thing by refusing discourses of the real also involves creating literary and critical languages that do not reinforce the traps posed by ethnographic and romantic discourse. On this necessity, both Alexie and Vizenor might agree. Alexie claims that "no one has figured out a new way to look at Indian literature," while Vizenor calls for "new critical language to interpret what is a Native American text without depending just upon proof of the author's identity."[38] Whether emanating from dominant culture or from Native literary culture, prescriptive definitions of authenticity feed into ongoing efforts to contain those who dissent from fixed visions of culture and identity. At the same time, they refuse the complexity of literature that by definition participates in multiple narrative and cultural traditions. "Getting real," then, in contemporary Native American literature entails dismantling "terminal creeds" of authenticity while acknowledging the all too real economic, cultural, and political stakes of the authenticity game.

Notes

1. In this essay, I use the terms "Indian," "American Indian," "Native," "indigenous," "Indianness," and "Native American" to signify the shifting political and historical contexts and connotations implied by their respective uses. Each of these terms comes charged with particular debates over identity and resistance to the colonial imposition of names by the dominant culture of the United States. In a recent article entitled "What We Want to Be Called: Indigenous Peoples' Perspectives on Racial and Ethnic Identity Labels," Michael Yellow Bird writes that "no clear consensus exists on which label [Native American or American Indian] is most preferable." While the controversial term "Indian" is more commonly favored by Native peoples than the current academic and media term "Native American," Yellow Bird calls the former into question, particularly when "Indigenous Peoples are reflexively referred to as 'Indians' in the history and social and cultural studies books used in American grade schools, high schools, and universities, as well as in contemporary Hollywood movies, marketing products, and popular fiction and nonfiction books." In Yellow Bird's examples, the old misnomer "Indian" continues to be used by the dominant culture in an unreflexive and objectifying way, even while the colonial associations of the term have been offset by its reappropriation by Indians themselves. Yellow Bird himself argues for the terms "Indigenous Peoples" and "First Nations Peoples" because they signify the "cultural heterogeneity and political sovereignty of these groups." Ultimately, Yellow Bird notes, and many Native peoples would concur, tribally specific names are the most pre-

ferred mode of self and group identification. See Michael Yellow Bird, "What We Want to Be Called," *American Indian Quarterly* 23 (spring 1999): 21–28.

2. A. L. Kroeber, introduction to *American Indian Life*, ed. Elsie Clews Parsons (1922; reprint, Lincoln: University of Nebraska Press, 1991), 13; Parsons, preface to *American Indian Life*, 1.

3. Gerald Vizenor, *Manifest Manners: Postindian Warriors of Survivance* (Hanover NH: University Press of New England, 1994), 11; Hartwig Isernhagen, *Momaday, Vizenor, Armstrong: Conversations on American Indian Writing* (Norman: University of Oklahoma Press, 1999), 102.

4. Until recently, oral histories were viewed by many Euro-American scholars as less objective and hence less reliable than written documents.

5. For an analysis of the dueling agendas within this text, see Louis Owens's *Other Destinies: Understanding the American Indian Novel* (Norman: University of Oklahoma Press, 1990), 32–40.

6. Such appeals recall the history of white patronage of famed fugitive slaves such as Frederick Douglass and Harriet Jacobs, whose texts had to be authenticated by prominent whites.

7. Rosaldo coins this phrase in chapter 3 of *Culture and Truth: The Remaking of Social Analysis* (Boston: Beacon, 1989), 68–87. For a discussion of why the genre of life stories continues to have mainstream market appeal, see Elizabeth Cook-Lynn, "American Indian Intellectualism and the New Indian Story," *American Indian Quarterly* 20 (winter 1996); reprinted in *Natives and Academics: Research and Writing About American Indians*, ed. Devon A. Mihesuah (Lincoln: University of Nebraska Press, 1998), 119–24.

8. More recently, writers such as Scott Momaday, Leslie Silko, Gerald Vizenor, and Ray Young Bear have produced mixed-genre autobiographical narratives that enact the "changing same" of Native orality. The phrase "reinventing the enemy's language" comes from the title of an anthology of Native women's literature edited by Joy Harjo and Gloria Bird. Gerald Vizenor has identified the paradox of affirming tribal survival in the very language of colonial power. In his essay "Shadow Survivance," he claims that "English, that coercive language of federal boarding schools, has carried some of the best stories of endurance" (*Manifest Manners* 106).

9. Isernhagen, *Momaday, Vizenor, Armstrong*, 82; Louis Owens, *Mixedblood Messages: Literature, Film, Family, Place* (Norman: University of Oklahoma Press, 1998), 42.

10. Yet as many Native academics can show, much of this recent institutional acceptance is token, provisional, and contingent. For a related published commentary, see Devon A. Mihesuah's introduction to *Natives and Academics* (1998). In an essay entitled "Calling a Spade a Shovel: Tribal/Ethnic Studies vs. University Policy," Sidner Larson details strategies of containment practiced at the administrative, departmental, and curricular level, strategies aimed at limiting and controlling Native American scholars and studies on college campuses (*Studies in American Indian Literatures* 13 [summer/fall 2001]: 36–48).

11. Quoted in Chris LaLonde, "New Stories and Broken Necks: Incorporating Native American Texts in the American Literature Survey," *Studies in American Indian Literatures* 9 (summer 1996): 11.

12. Henry Louis Gates Jr., "Beyond the Culture Wars: Identities in Dialogue," *Profession* 93 (1993): 8. For critiques of such critical and interpretive turns toward indices of physiognomic authenticity, see Louis Owens, "Beads and Buckskin: Reading Authenticity in Native American Literature" (*Mixedblood Messages* 12–24); and Hartwig Isernhagen's interview with Gerald Vizenor in *Momaday, Vizenor, Armstrong* (77–134).

13. Jim Northrup, *Walking the Rez Road* (Stillwater MN: Voyageur Press, 1993), 104.

14. Chadwick Allen, "Blood (and) Memory," *American Literature* 71 (March 1999): 96, 97; M. Annette Jaimes, "Federal Indian Identification Policy: A Usurpation of Indigenous Sovereignty in North America," in *The State of Native America: Genocide, Colonization, and Resistance*, ed. M. Annette Jaimes (Boston: South End, 1992), 129.

15. I am drawing here on the title of Cornel West's book *Race Matters* (New York: Vintage, 1994).

16. Henry Louis Gates Jr., "'Authenticity,' or the Lesson of Little Tree," *New York Times Book Review*, 24 November 1991, 26; Michael Wilson, "Speaking of Home: The Idea of the Center in Some Contemporary American Indian Writing," *Wicazo Sa Review* 12 (spring 1997): 130.

17. Philip Deloria, *Playing Indian* (New Haven: Yale University Press, 1998); Craig Womack, *Red on Red: Native American Literary Separatism.* (Minneapolis: University of Minnesota Press, 1999), 11. Frazier's *On the Rez* has received considerable critical commentary from such Native writers as

Sherman Alexie, as well as from Native and non-Native scholars. See, for example, the section devoted to reviews of his book in *American Indian Quarterly* 24 (spring 2000): 279–305.

18. David L. Moore, "Cultural Property in American Indian Literatures: Representation and Interpretation," introduction to *American Indian Quarterly* 21 (summer 1997).

19. Leslie Silko, "Here's an Odd Artifact for the Fairy Tale Shelf," *Studies in American Indian Literatures* 10 (1986): 180. Allen felt that *Ceremony* discloses sacred information that should not have been published and hence shared outside the Laguna community. Although many Native and non-Native participants in Native literary studies agree that writers should not disclose religious materials, there is less agreement on which kinds of materials ought to be considered off-limits. See "Special Problems in Teaching Leslie Marmon Silko's *Ceremony*," *American Indian Quarterly* 14 (fall 1990): 379–84.

20. Sherman Alexie, posting to Native Literature listserv, "RE: Message from Sherman Alexie," 12 April 1997 <Nativelit-L@csd.uwm.edu>.

21. Elizabeth Cook-Lynn, "American Indian Intellectualism," 128, 130.

22. Womack, *Red on Red*, 141, 137.

23. See Devon A. Mihesuah, Home page, Northern Arizona University, 7 June 2003 <http://jan.ucc.nau.edu/~mihesuah/>.

24. P. Jane Hafen, "Rock 'n' Roll, Redskins, and Blues in Sherman Alexie's Work," *Studies in American Indian Literatures* 9 (winter 1997): 76–77.

25. In a lecture at the University of Minnesota, Morris, 10 April 2000, Alexie called himself the "Indian du Jour."

26. Gloria Bird, "The Exaggeration of Despair in Sherman Alexie's *Reservation Blues*," *Wicazo Sa Review* 11 (fall 1995): 51, 49.

27. Owens, *Mixedblood Messages*, 82; P. Jane Hafen, "Rock 'n' Roll," 76–77.

28. Patrice Hollrah gives a sustained reading of this chapter, and particularly of the crucial role played by Marie Polatkin, whose character offers up a "political discourse on education, writing, and publication in Native American literature, which demonstrates her resistance to the politics of power." See "Sherman Alexie's Challenge to the Academy's Teaching of Native American Literature, Non-Native Writers, and Critics," *Studies in American Indian Literatures* 13 (summer/fall 2001): 23–35.

29. John Purdy, "Crossroads: A Conversation with Sherman Alexie," *Studies in American Indian Literatures* 9 (winter 1997): 7.

30. Gerald Vizenor, "On Thin Ice, You Might as Well Dance," in *Some Other Frequency: Interviews with Innovative American Authors*, ed. Larry McCaffery (Philadelphia: University of Pennsylvania Press, 1996), 303.

31. Neal Bowers and Charles L. P. Silet, "An Interview with Gerald Vizenor," *MELUS* 8 (1981): 45.

32. Isernhagen, *Momaday, Vizenor, Armstrong*, 84.

33. "Postindian Warriors," *Manifest Manners*, 5–6.

34. Louis Owens, "Introduction: Special Issue on Gerald Vizenor," *Studies in American Indian Literatures* 9 (spring 1997): 1–2.

35. Louis Owens, *Dark River* (Norman: University of Oklahoma Press, 1999), 263.

36. Owens, *Dark River*, 222, 212.

37. Owens, *Dark River*, 282–83.

38. Owens, *Mixedblood Messages*, 13; Purdy, "Crossroads," 7; Isernhagen, *Momaday, Vizenor, Armstrong*, 100.

3. PICTURING HISTORIES

9. EDWARD CURTIS

Pictorialist and Ethnographic Adventurist

Gerald Vizenor

Kevin Gover, the assistant interior secretary, apologized for the many transgressions of the Bureau of Indian Affairs. "This agency set out to destroy all things Indian," he said at a recent anniversary celebration of the agency, according to David Stout of the *New York Times*. "The legacy of these misdeeds haunts us," said Gover. "Our hearts break." [1]

Gover is a member of the Pawnee Tribe. He was born in Lawton, Oklahoma, and graduated from Princeton University and the University of New Mexico Law School. His career and native feats are singular; yet his nominal regrets are ironic after more than a century of federal duplicities, manifest manners, and cultural dominance.

The native story, however, is not only in the text of his apology; the story is in the visual analogies of the large photograph above the news article. Gover is pictured in a decisive pose near a framed portrait of Bear Bull. The Blackfoot was photographed by Edward Curtis, who first visited the tribe at the end of the nineteenth century with George Bird Grinnell.

Gover looks almost to the left in the newspaper photograph. Bear Bull looks to the right of the scene, a pensive, pictorialist profile. Gover bears a studied smile; he is pictured as an approachable native lawyer who wears spectacles, a white shirt, dark necktie, and long hair. Bear Bull is an ancient image, a man of great creases, evident traditions, and coarse braided hair. His lips, slightly parted, are close to a whisper, and his eyes seem to be focused in the distance.

These two natives, a lawyer and a traditionalist, separated by four generations, reservations, and distinctive cultures, are aware of the camera. Credibly, they are both about their survivance poses in the presence of photographers; they are bound by native analogies and the common history of the camera. Gover was photographed by Carol Powers for the news story in the *New York Times*. Bear Bull was captured forever in a picture by Edward Curtis. The analogy of these native images is pictorialist, a double reference to the native past and futurity.

Gover is native, but his apology for the agency was ironic, not cultural; rather, a plaintive, political simulation of the past that should have been made by someone other than a native. Bear Bull stands alone, close to the camera, an aesthetic, pictorial pose, the intended image and idea of the vanished race by Edward Curtis.

Curtis pictures may, in fact, be the choice of more natives than any other photographer. This association, in my view, is aesthetic, not ethnographic; natives, at last, may stand with the visual analogies of artists more than with the language of social scientists.

Curtis, however, presented his photographs, notes, and cultural observations as ethnographic. He argued against those detractors who petitioned the government that he was not a trained ethnographer, and that his work was not decisive. Three generations later the native heirs choose his photographic images for reasons other than the politics of the social sciences. Perhaps natives praise the visual analogy.

Why would natives pose to create a portrait simulation, a pictorial image not their own, for photographic adventurists who later nominate their pictures as the *real*, and the ethnographic documents of a vanishing race?

Perhaps for the money and tricky camera stories.

Why, several generations later, would natives embrace these romantic pictures as real moments of their own cultural memories?

Perhaps the images are a sense of presence, a visual analogy. Or perhaps it is a cult of native remembrance. "In photography, exhibition value begins to displace cult value," wrote Walter Benjamin in *Illuminations*. "But cult value does not give way without resistance. It retires into an ultimate retrenchment: the human countenance. It is no accident that the portrait was the focal point of early photography. The cult of remembrance of loved ones, absent or dead, offers a last refuge for the cult value of the picture." [2]

Richard Kearney argued in *The Wake of Imagination* that the "human ability to 'image' or 'imagine' something has been understood in two main ways throughout the history of Western thought." The first is a "*representational* faculty which reproduces images" of some reality; the second is a "*creative* faculty which produces images" that stand alone. "These basic notions of imagination" refer to "everyday experience" and "artistic practices." [3]

The modernist constructions of culture, with natives outside of rational, cosmopolitan consciousness, are realities by separation, a sense of native absence over presence in history. The absence of natives was represented by images of traditions, simulations of the other in the past; the presence of natives was tragic, the notions of savagism and the emotive images of a vanishing race. The modernist images of native absence and presence, by creative or representational faculties, are the rational binary structures of the other, an aesthetic, ideological disanalogy.

The absence of natives is the simulated presence of the other in the narratives of cultural dominance. The actual presence of natives is ironic in ethnography. "The absence of the Other from our Time has been his mode of presence in our discourse—as an object and victim," observed Johannes Fabian in *Time and the Other*. "That is what needs to be overcome; more ethnography of Time will not change this situation."[4]

The modernist possession of the other, however exotic the fugitive poses, objective reason, and creative images, has no obvious, comparable humanistic worth as an absence, because notions of discovery, theories of evolution and material culture, and other simulations of natives must be new, forever hyperreal even as cultures vanish, otherwise the captured images and museum artifacts would be rated as no more than "courteous kitsch." Ironically, kitschy simulations somehow "authenticate" the bourgeois worth of secular kachinas and doorstop coyotes.[5]

The distinctions and discrepancies of pictorial, ethnographic, and detractive visual images of natives are not easily resolved by cultural evidence, censure, or the politics of identity. Crucial to the resolution of these vagaries of photographic esteem is a visual method of interpretation; a choice of metaphors and visual reason that does not separate natives as the other in an eternal academic disanalogy.

Barbara Maria Stafford argued in *Visual Analogy* for the recuperation of the "ancient and intrinsically visual method of analogy for modern times." Analogy is the "human desire to achieve union" with the other. She pointed out that the "visual arts are singularly suited to provide explanatory power for the nature and function of the analogical procedure."[6]

Edward Curtis created pictorialist images of natives, but most of the interpretations are ethnographic. The creation of visual images, in other words, is represented by linguistic authority. Pointedly, photographic images are bound by the structures of language. Stafford argued that language is a "godlike agency in western culture," and to free "graphic expression from an unnuanced dominant discourse of consumerism, corruption, deception, and ethical failure is a challenge that cuts across the arts, humanities, and sciences."[7]

Semir Zeki likewise observed in *Inner Vision* that "language is a relatively recent evolutionary acquisition, and it has yet to catch up with and match the visual system in its capacity to extract essentials so efficiently."[8]

Analogy is an active, aesthetic, creative connection in the visual arts, and in the sense of natives, analogy is a desire to achieve a human union in visual images rather than a cultural separation in language. Analogy absolves the distance and discrepancies of pictorialist and ethnographic pictures of natives by restoring a sense of visual reason. Bear Bull and Kevin Gover come together by choice and cameras, and by metaphors of similitude in the adventures of native poses.

Analogy "demands that we take seriously the problem of correlation," wrote Stafford. Analogy "is central both to ancient religions and to a modern anthropology of the senses." Analogy is a creative, visual process, but it was "supplanted by the elevation of atomistic difference: the obsession with unbridgeable imparity and the hieratic insistence on insurmountable distance between the material and spiritual realms." Analogy "has the virtue of making distant peoples, other periods, and even diverse contemporary contexts part of our world." Stafford wants to "recuperate the lost link between visual images and concepts, the intuitive ways in which we think simply by visualizing." [9]

Consider the learned theories and studied pictures of natives as the "hieratic insistence" on disanalogy. Ethnology, for instance, became a sacred association in the studies of native cultures. William John McGee, the "ethnologist in charge" at the Bureau of American Ethnology in the late nineteenth century, outlined the goals of his agency in this way: "Ethnologists, like other good citizens, are desirous of raising the Indian to the lofty plane of American citizenship; but they prefer to do this constructively rather than destructively, through knowledge rather than ignorance, through sympathy rather than intolerance." Ethnologists "prefer to pursue in dealing with our immature race the course found successful in dealing with the immature offspring of our own flesh and blood." [10]

Curtis announced similar racialist notions that natives were comparable to children. The notion of natives as immature was a common theory of evolution at the time. Many scientists were involved in a harsh debate over monogenism, a single origin, and polygenism, many origins; these notions of creation were used to explain distinctive native cultures and native resistance to cultural dominance.

Early in the nineteenth century many "critics began to question the monogenetic assumptions, set forth in the Bible, that all mankind shared the same origin," wrote Robert Bieder in *Science Encounters the Indian*. "Increasingly they began to explain Indians' recalcitrant nature in terms of polygenism. To polygenists Indians were separately created and were an inferior species of man." [11]

Natives were first simulated as savages in the common cultural binaries of savagism and civilization. Then, by chicanery, federal treaties, and military means natives were removed to reservations and nominated the vanishing race at the end of the nineteenth century.

American civilization was a cultural manifest, and a religious covenant, over bogus savagism. The "Indian was the remnant of a savage past away from which civilized men had struggled to grow," wrote Roy Harvey Pearce in *Savagism and Civilization*. "To study him was to study the past. To civilize him was to triumph over the past. To kill him was to kill the past. History would thus be the key to the moral worth of cultures." American civilization progressed from "past to present, from east to west, from lower to higher." Pearce pointed out that those "who could not journey to see Indians in person could see them pictured in numerous collections of Indian sketches and portraits." [12]

Edward Curtis was born in Wisconsin in 1868. Naturally, he grew into the literature of natives. He likely read or was aware of dime novels, captivity narratives, and the sensational newspaper stories of the evanescence of the transient savages. As a young man he must have seen sketches of natives and reproductions of portraits by George Catlin and Charles Bird King. Curtis was curious, no doubt, and eager to understand the history and literature of his time.

Curtis opened a photographic studio shortly after he moved with his family, at the end of the nineteenth century, to Puget Sound. Curtis lost his father, and while he assumed the responsibilities of his family, his circumstances improved as a photographer. At the same time, natives lost their land, human rights, a sense of presence, and were pictured as the tragic cultures of a vanishing race. Sitting Bull had been shot by soldiers, and then, two weeks later, hundreds of Ghost Dancers were massacred by Seventh Cavalry soldiers on December 29, 1890, at Wounded Knee. Curtis was a man of nature, a mountaineer and adventurist, but surely he could not have been unaware of newspaper stories about these native miseries. His first pictures must have drawn him into many conversations about natives. Curtis was motivated, after all, to pursue a photographic record of the last natives, and he did so with romantic, pictorial images that ran against the popular notions of the savage.

Many American newspapers created and promoted stories of savagism and the vanishing race. The Civil War, and later the telegraph, changed journalism and the way news was reported. Press associations and "cooperative news gathering" were inspired by the telegraph. War "increased newspaper readership and stimulated new competition between urban newspapers," observed John Coward in *The Newspaper Indian*. Editors "discovered that they could increase their profits when they published stories about major battles," including, of course, conflicts with natives.[13]

Journalists, at the time, were too close to the western adventures of the army, and many thought that native cultures "could be easily known and explained by simple observation," noted Coward. "The 'vanishing Indian' theme was especially popular in the nineteenth century, when native cultures did seem to be fading before the westward rush of white settlement." Clearly, "newspapers played a major role in creating and maintaining popular Indian identities in the nineteenth century." The press, however, was not alone in the promotion of the savage. George Catlin and many other artists, photographers, politicians, and an entire cultural system created the image and historical idea of the tragic savage at the vanishing point.[14]

Sitting Bull, the Lakota healer, for instance, was known largely through simulations and "newspaper representations," especially in the sensational stories on the Battle of the Little Bighorn. The *New York Times* raised a catch question about Sitting Bull: Was he "an extremely savage type, betraying that bloodthirstiness and brutality for which he has so long been notorious?" That savage image of a native humanist was created by strangers. "The Sitting Bull of the papers and the man himself were often worlds apart."[15]

Luther Standing Bear, the author and actor, had graduated from the Carlisle Indian Industrial School and was working at John Wanamaker's department store in Philadelphia when he read in a newspaper that Sitting Bull was scheduled to lecture in the city. "The paper stated that he was the Indian who killed General Custer! The chief and his people had been held prisoners of war, and now here they were to appear" in a theater, Standing Bear wrote in *My People the Sioux*. "A white man came on the stage and introduced Sitting Bull as the man who had killed General Custer," which was not true.

> Sitting Bull arose and addressed the audience in the Sioux tongue,
> as he did not speak nor understand English. He said, "My friends,

white people, we Indians are on our way to Washington to see the Grandfather, or President of the United States. I see so many white people and what they are doing, that it makes me glad to know that some day my children will be educated also. There is no use fighting any longer. The buffalo are all gone, as well as the rest of the game. Now I am going to shake the hand of the Great Father at Washington, and I am going to tell him all these things." Then Sitting Bull sat down. He never even mentioned General Custer's name.

His lecture was translated as the story of the massacre at the Little Big Horn. The white man "told so many lies I had to smile," wrote Standing Bear.[16]

Curtis created his picture The Vanishing Race in 1904. The photogravure, published three years later in the first of his mighty twenty-volume collection, The North American Indian, depicts a column of natives lost in the shadows, a sentimental evanescence. Mick Gidley rightly argues in Edward S. Curtis and the North American Indian, Incorporated that the "ideological thrust of the heritage of photographic pictorialism in Curtis's images worked, almost synergistically, to disguise, even deny, what was, in fact and effect, a seemingly almost endless series of damaging political and economic decisions."[17] These decisions based on agency policies and new federal laws, such as the allotment act that reduced native treaty land by more than half, were carried out in the presence of Edward Curtis.

"The thought that this picture is meant to convey is that the Indians as a race, already shorn of their tribal strength and stripped of their primitive dress, are passing into the darkness of an unknown future," Curtis wrote in the caption to The Vanishing Race. About the same time he wrote in Scribner's Magazine that the "relationship of the Indians and people of this country is that of a child and parent. We will stand convicted for all time as a parent who failed in his duty." He declared that natives were "being ground beneath the wheel of civilization, and though we may be able to justify our claims that advancement and progress demand the extermination of the Indians, we can scarcely justify the method used in this extermination."[18] Curtis, of course, would always be the master of pictures.

Remarkably, this haunting photograph, The Vanishing Race, was created less than a decade after he first aimed a cumbersome view camera at Princess Angeline, the native daughter of Chief Seattle. "I paid the princess a dollar for each picture made," wrote Curtis. "This seemed to please her greatly and with hands and jargon she indicated that she preferred to spend her time having pictures made than in digging clams." [19]

Curtis paid natives to pose; he selected ornaments, vestments, played the natural light, tone, picturesque reflections, and the solitary nature of natives in his pictures. The pictorial images of pensive warriors are simulations of the real, transmuted in visual analogies. The aesthetic poses of natives countered the cruelties of reservations and binaries of savagism and civilization.

"In terms of pictorialist aesthetics, posing contributed positively to the final image," observed Christopher Lyman in *The Vanishing Race and Other Illusions.* "In terms of ethnography, posing did 'injustice to scientific accuracy.'" [20] Curtis paid natives to pose and dance in several simulated ceremonies, but he may not have understood native resistance or the actual tricky scenes he captured. The motion picture of Navajo *Yebechai Prayer,* for instance, was probably transposed by chance, but many natives believe that the dance was reversed as an act of resistance and to protect the sacred. The dancers held rattles in the wrong hand.

Curtis, however, may not have been at the actual ceremonies that he simulated in his pictures. He staged the dances out of season. "Navajo sensibilities" clearly were not his "primary considerations." Curtis used "not only 'phony' costumes, additions, and poses," observed James Faris in *Navajo and Photography,* "but, indeed, in some cases, actual phony Navajo." [21]

Curtis is lauded as a pictorialist but not favorably reviewed as an ethnographic photographer. Yet his pictures are rarely mentioned in historical references to the pictorialists, or Photo-Session, at the turn of the twentieth century in New York City. Curtis was not of the salons or societies that established the aesthetic, pictorial arts of photography; his focus was more ideological, a photographic rescue artist. He posed as an ethnographer out to capture the last images of a vanishing race. To do this, of course, he paid for native poses, staged, altered, and manipulated his pictures to create an ethnographic simulation as a pictorialist. Clearly, he was an outsider, too far removed from the photographic salons to court or count on the ready shows and reviews that had instituted pictorialist photography. Curtis, moreover, had received a five-year endowment from the financier John Pierpont Morgan to produce twenty volumes of *The North American Indian.* The project actually lasted more than twenty years.

Alfred Stieglitz founded the Photo-Session, a group of pictorialist photographers dedicated to expressive, picturesque images and the aesthetic art of creating pictures. "Stieglitz was himself a proponent of what came to be known as 'straight photography,'" noted Christopher Lyman. The "straight" school "asserted that photography had its own pure aesthetics which should not be diluted by extensive manipulation of its process." [22]

Gertrude Käsebier and other pictorialists had once experimented with ethnic and native images, but they soon focused on other subjects. Curtis, on the other hand, was dedicated to natives and the politics of the vanishing race. He visited more than eighty distinct native communities, some more than once, and created more than forty thousand photographs. Most notably, he published twenty volumes of his photogravures, The North American Indian.

Stieglitz and the Photo-Session associated as aesthetic, modernist photographers to advance pictorialist expression, to support the art practice, and to hold exhibitions of pictorial images. Photographic salons were established in several cities, and both "straight" and pictorialist pictures were presented in exhibitions. The New York Times, in a review of an exhibition of photographs at the Montross Galleries in New York in 1912, noted that the "advocates of pure or 'straight' photography feel that by manipulating a print you lose the purity of tone which belongs especially to the photographic medium in trying to get effects that can be more satisfactorily obtained with the painter's brush." [23] Stieglitz was a "straight," photographic impressionist; at the same time he advanced the artistic practices of the pictorialists. These practices countered the common snapshot of popular culture.

John Tagg wrote in The Burden of Representation that photography was rather "common as to be unremarkable" in the late nineteenth century. Pictorialists reacted and sought "to reinstate the 'aura' of the image and distinguish their work aesthetically from that of commercial and amateur photographs." He argued that the revolution was not pictorialist, but a new means of political control. "It was no longer a privilege to be pictured but the burden of a new class of the surveilled," wrote Tagg. [24]

Curtis created simulations of surveillance, the pictorialist pose of ethnographic images. He removed parasols, suspenders, wagons, the actual traces of modernism and material culture in his pictures of natives. Curtis was a pictorialist, but his removal practices were ideological, a disanalogy. He created altered images of the vanishing race at the same time that thousands of native scholars graduated from federal and mission schools. Luther Standing Bear had returned to the reservation as a teacher. Charles Eastman returned as the first native medical doctor on the Pine Ridge Reservation. Curtis may not have noticed native resistance or survivance. Clearly he was an adventurist, sometimes blindsided by his own vanity, debts, and the politics of ethnography. He pursued pictures of an undocumented vanishing race.

"Curtis was concerned about criticism of The North American Indian by professional ethnologists," noted Christopher Lyman. "He explained away their skepticism, however, as a reaction to inflated accounts of his work in the popular press." Curtis "was selling images to a popular audience whose perception of 'Indianness' was based on stereotypes." [25] He was motivated, of course, to remain in the favor of ethnologists.

Curtis created the picture Ogalala War-Party at a time when natives were starving on reservations. Surely he was not insensitive to the adversities of natives, but his pictures reveal only the simulations of the vanishing race. He paid natives to pose as warriors at a time when their rights were denied and their treaties were scorned and evaded by the federal government. Curtis was a dedicated pictorialist, but he assuredly miscarried the ethics of his vested situation on reservations and in native communities. Yes, he was indeed answerable for his time with natives, not by historical revisionism, but because he boldly advanced his career in the presence of native torment and worried hearts.

Lyman noted that Curtis, "like . . . most people of the period, seemed preoccupied with images of Dakota 'hostility.' The caption for Ogalala War-Party explains, 'Here is depicted a group of Sioux warriors as they appeared in the days of intertribal warfare, carefully making their way down a hillside in the vicinity of the enemy's camp.'" Curtis created a simulation of a native absence and an ethnographic presence.

The photogravure In a Piegan Lodge, published in The North American Indian, was retouched by the crude removal of a clock. The original negative pictures the clock in a small box on the ground between two natives. Curtis removed the clock to save a simulation of traditional authority. The picture with the clock has a curious elegance and inspires a visual analogy. The retouched photogravure without the clock is fakery and disanalogy. [26]

Dino Brugioni outlined "four distinct kinds of faked photographs" in Photo Fakery. The first two are the removal and insertion of details; the other two are photomontage and false captions. Curtis was clearly a photographic faker by his removal and insertion of details, and by false captions.

"Photography transcends natural boundaries and verbal language and is probably the most important vehicle for advancing ideas, and ideals, throughout the world," wrote Brugioni. "When a photo is manipulated in any way, truth is compromised; when truth is compromised, distrust begins. Distrust produces a lack of faith in the media," he noted, but photography "has always been manipulated." [27]

Curtis created by strategic manipulations pictures of native disanalogy. Presumably, he was a likable, lonesome adventurist in native communities. He wrote about a sense of natural peace at campsites, but he had been weakened by time, promises, many debts, and the dubious praise of politicians.

Curtis simulated natives as the absolute absence of civilization and modernity. He was a cultural separatist and a racialist of his time. Yet his ethical demerits as a photo faker are not ours. Today, the natives in his pictures, but not the simulated *indians* of his photographic missions, await the recuperation of visual analogy.

Notes

1. David Stout, "No Place for John Wayne at Indian Bureau," *New York Times*, 22 September 2000. Likewise, JoAnn Chase, the executive director of the National Congress of American Indians, was recently photographed in front of an original native portrait by the expressionist painter Fritz Scholder.
2. Walter Benjamin, *Illuminations: Essays and Reflections* (New York: Schocken, 1969), 225, 226. Benjamin pointed out that "as man withdraws from the photographic image, the exhibition value for the first time shows its superiority to the ritual value."
3. Richard Kearney, *The Wake of Imagination* (Minneapolis: University of Minnesota Press, 1988), 15. "The imminent demise of imagination is clearly a postmodern obsession," wrote Kearney. "Postmodernism undermines the modernist belief in the image as an *authentic* expression. The typically postmodern image is one which displays its own artificiality, its own pseudostatus, its own representational depthlessness."
4. Johannes Fabian, *Time and the Other: How Anthropology Makes Its Object* (New York: Columbia University Press, 1983), 107, 154. "Certainly there has been progress in anthropology from mere counting and mapping of

cultural traits toward accounts of culture which are attentive to context, symbols, and semantics," wrote Fabian. "Still, sooner or later one will come upon syntheses of knowledge whose organizing metaphors, models, and schemes are thoroughly visual and spatial."

5. Gerald Vizenor, *Fugitive Poses: Native American Indian Scenes of Absence and Presence* (Lincoln: University of Nebraska Press, 1998), 38. "Modernity, that mirror of science, material culture, and the courier of the other as *indian*, causes the disenchantment of essence, traditional authority, and overruns natural reason. The scrutiny of traditions, however, is never the same in the case of *indians* or natives."

6. Barbara Maria Stafford, *Visual Analogy: Consciousness as the Art of Connecting* (Cambridge: MIT Press, 1999), xv, 2, 3. "I thought it time to develop a sophisticated theory and practice of resemblance rather than continuing endlessly to subdivide distinctions," wrote Stafford. "I also believe the moment ripe to look at the rich and varied imaging or figurative tradition, rather than linguistics, for a connective model of visual rhetoric adequate to our networked, multimedia future."

7. Barbara Maria Stafford, *Good Looking: Essays on the Virtue of Images* (Cambridge: MIT Press, 1996), 5. "In most American university curricula, graphicacy remains subordinate to literacy. Even so-called interdisciplinary 'visual culture' programs are governed by the ruling metaphor of reading," wrote Stafford. "Consequently, iconicity is treated as an inferior part of a more general semantics."

8. Semir Zeki, *Inner Vision: An Exploration of Art and the Brain* (New York: Oxford University Press, 1999), 9, 10, 11. "To equate artists with neurologists, even in the remote sense intended here, may surprise many among them since, naturally enough, most know nothing about the brain and a good many still hold the common but erroneous belief that one sees with the eye rather than with the cerebral cortex," wrote Zeki. "Their language, as well as the language of those who write about art, betrays this view." Donald Hoffman made a similar point in *Visual Intelligence* (New York: Norton, 1998). "Our visual intelligence richly interacts with, and in many cases precedes and drives, our rational and emotional intelligence. To understand visual intelligence is to understand, in large part, who we are," wrote Hoffman. "What you see is, invariably, what your visual intelligence constructs. Just as scientists intelligently construct useful theories based on experimental evidence, so your visual

system intelligently constructs useful visual worlds based on images at the eyes. The main difference is that the constructions of scientists are done consciously, but those of your visual intelligence are done, for the most part, unconsciously" (xi, xii).

9. Stafford, *Visual Analogy*, 51, 61.

10. Hinsley Curtis Jr., *Savages and Scientists: The Smithsonian Institution and the Development of American Anthropology, 1846–1910* (Washington DC: Smithsonian Institution Press, 1981), 236, 281. "But if the Indian were an inferior species of man, what then was his fate? Would the effect of the environment be the same on the Indian as it had been on European man? Were Indians capable of further progress, or had they reached the limits of their potential?"

11. Robert E. Bieder, *Science Encounters the Indian, 1820–1880* (Norman: University of Oklahoma Press, 1986), 11, 12. "But if the Indian were an inferior species of man, what then was his fate? Would the effect of the environment be the same on the Indian as it had been on European man? Were Indians capable of further progress, or had they reached the limits of their potential?"

12. Roy Harvey Pearce, *Savagism and Civilization: A Study of the Indian and the American Mind* (Berkeley: University of California Press, 1988), 49, 110.

13. John M. Coward, *The Newspaper Indian: Native American Identity in the Press, 1820–90* (Urbana: University of Illinois Press, 1999), 16, 17, 20.

14. Coward, *The Newspaper Indian*, 34, 229.

15. *The New York Times*, 10 July 1876. Quoted from *The Newspaper Indian*, by John M. Coward, 159, 190.

16. Luther Standing Bear, *My People the Sioux* (Lincoln: University of Nebraska Press, 1975), 184, 185.

17. Mick Gidley, *Edward S. Curtis and the North American Indian, Incorporated* (New York: Cambridge University Press, 1998), 74, 75. "In essence, the picturesque genre approach to Native American culture, when fused with the ideology of Native Americans as a vanishing race, created images that *naturalized* the predicament faced by indigenous North American peoples at what was, in fact, at the turn of the century, the very nadir of their experience on the Continent," wrote Gidley.

18. Christopher M. Lyman, *The Vanishing Race and Other Illusions: Photographs of Indians by Edward S. Curtis* (New York: Pantheon Books, in association with the Smithsonian Institution Press, 1982), 79. Lyman cited Ed-

ward S. Curtis, "Vanishing Indian Types: The Tribes of the Northwest Plains," *Scribner's Magazine*, June 1906. President Theodore Roosevelt and other government agents expressed similar racialist views about natives. Curtis, it should be remembered, was beholden to Roosevelt for his letter of introduction to John Pierpont Morgan.

19. Gidley, *Edward S. Curtis*, 21. See also Victor Boesen and Florence Curtis Graybill, *Edward S. Curtis: Photographer of the North American Indian* (New York: Dodd, Mead, 1977), 15.
20. Lyman, *The Vanishing Race*, 65.
21. James C. Faris, *Navajo and Photography* (Albuquerque: University of New Mexico Press, 1996), 108, 114, 115, 116. "Curtis tells us he staged the Nightway photographs not because he was there at the wrong time of year but because of the resistance to his photography—a rather minor logistical matter," writes Faris. "The type of resistance is never explained in detail, though we can probably assume it came from assimilationist bureaucrats (Navajo and non-Navajo) who resented Curtis's emphasis and manipulation to achieve some representation of 'aboriginality.'"
22. Lyman, *The Vanishing Race*, 35. "Among the Photo-Sessionists, however, Stieglitz tolerated the often manipulative styles of Edward Steichen and Gertrude Käsebier, and even the visual polemics of Frank Eugene," wrote Lyman. "Although he often spoke to the contrary, Stieglitz's criteria, it appears, had less to do with technique than with the attitudes of the artists and their faithfulness to the elevation of photographic art."
23. Beaumont Newall, *The History of Photography*, 4th ed. (New York: Museum of Modern Art, 1981), 106, 111.
24. John Tagg, *The Burden of Representation* (Amherst: University of Massachusetts Press, 1988), 56, 58, 59. "What Walter Benjamin called the 'cult' value of the picture was effectively abolished when photographs became so common as to be unremarkable; when they were items of passing interest with no residual value, to be consumed and thrown away," wrote Tagg.
25. Lyman, *The Vanishing Race*, 78.
26. Lyman, *The Vanishing Race*, 86, 106.
27. Dino A. Brugioni, *Photo Fakery: The History and Techniques of Photographic Deception and Manipulation* (Dulles VA: Brassey's, 1999), 17, 202. "After the turn of the twentieth century, heavily manipulated photos were produced to create supposed intrinsic and artistic values," wrote Brugioni.

"The photomontage was used as an important propaganda weapon both for and against Nazi Germany. Communists and other nations often rewrote history by removing people and events from photos, despite the fact that copies of the original photos were usually available throughout the world."

10. ANIMAL CALLING/CALLING ANIMAL

Threshold Space in Frederic Remington's *Coming to the Call*

Stephen Tatum

Beauty is nothing but the beginning of terror that we are still just able to bear.

RILKE

Coming to the Call

The end is near, right now and right here: the end of a landform, the end of a day—the end of an animal's life. *Before* this moment, a bull moose browsing the leaves and twigs of willow and poplar and protected by the lengthening shadows of fir and pine trees has heard the hunter's "call," his ventriloquism of the moans and keening whines a moose cow vocalizes during the fall rutting season that, now, is well under way. The layered horizontal lines created by the leveled rifle of the hunter barely visible in the birchbark canoe, by the bull moose's stationary pose on the slightly elevated spit of land, and by the distant horizon's pale lavender or periwinkle band of color—these features incline the visual weight of this 1905 painting by Frederic Remington toward and even beyond the bull moose backlit by the sun, exposed now on the lake's margin. Toward, that is, the slivered wafer of sun dissolving into the distant hills across the lake, its ritual disappearing act both turning this lake's surface into glossy lemon-yellow pools and transforming the rather dense enclosure of trees and brush, nearer to us in the painting's left midground plane, into clustered arcs and serrated towers of deep sienna and ocher shades.[1] While the chromatic register of yellow hues here frames the bull moose's emergent presence before the sun's waning light, it also establishes the painting's swelling autumnal mood—as if, for instance, the deep, glowing, red-orange light lining the horizon of hills forecasts for us the clotted stain of moose blood at this place where land and water meet.

Remington's composition of dark and light passages asks us to imagine a slightly elevated, horizontal line binding together a concealed hunter and his leveled rifle, the silhouetted profile of a bull moose, and a distant range of hills that refract the setting sun's light. In short, our gaze is invited to move from left to right just as we do when reading words printed on a page. To the left, where the sun's light has already retreated and the encroaching darkness seems as certain as the shadows are long, is the immediate past of

194

10.1 Frederic Remington, *Coming to the Call*, 1905.
Oil on canvas, 27¼ × 40¼″ (69.3 × 102.2 cm). Collection William Koch.

the "call" and the hunter's vigil and the moose's day heretofore spent under cover; to the right, where the sun has almost fully dropped below the soft ridgeline, is the immediate future, which is to say "the end"—both of the day and the hunt itself. By following with our eyes the arc of this line from left to right, from an area of darkness to what remains of the day's light, it becomes evident that the painting supplements the moose's static pose with the contours of a fully elaborated narrative sequence, one that moves in time from the hunter's scouting, stalking, and bugled "call," proceeds through his motionless vigil in a canoe on the edge of a lake's cove, and that, finally, will conclude with the kill shot and the labor of butchering. A completed narrative sequence, in fact, that could well include an epilogue displaying either the results of a taxidermist's work with a trophy animal or the photographs attesting to the hunter's prowess for all those clients, associates, and friends who in the future will visit his home, studio, or office back there in the modern urban, industrial world.

Just as still-life paintings function on one level to privilege the difference between possessive humans and the assorted inanimate objects they possess for display and consumption, so too the implied narrative sequence in the traditional hunting painting genre, to which *Coming to the Call* clearly is

10.2 Frederic Remington, *His Second Shot* (*The Last Shot*, altern.), ca. 1902. Halftone illustration, *Collier's Weekly*, 27 September 1902.

affiliated, functions on the most basic level to confirm the difference between inventive, masterful humans and the wild animals who are, finally, mastered both by human calls or lures and by weapons. Even so, *Coming to the Call* seems equally invested in suspending this implied narrative's forward momentum so as, instead, to dwell in the heightened moment of presence that elapses between any before (the "call") and any after (the moose's death). Consider, for starters, how at the painting's center the canoe's prow and its reflection in the water establish a vertical orientation that counters or at least interrupts the horizontal line that arcs from pointed rifle through stationary moose to the setting sun. And, as modeled for us by the idealized holding environment of the birchbark canoe at the painting's center, the painting, tonally speaking, conveys how motion is arrested, stopped amid nature's cathedral of overarching trees and its surround of still water. The bull moose now stands in place, leaning slightly forward, his yearning desire manifested—we can imagine—by his eyes, ears, and nose quietly probing the gathering dusk's dewy air for any sign of the call's maker. A shrouded, solitary hunter sitting silently in his birchbark canoe has just now raised his head and rifle to take aim at this bull moose who has magi-

10.3 Frederic Remington, *Success*, 1889–90. Wood Engraving, *Harper's Monthly*, October 1890. Remington inserts himself into the picture.

cally appeared before his eyes, as if in response to his prayers as well as to his call. So just as the birchbark canoe holds the hunter and just as the distant cusp of hills cradles the sun's descending trajectory, so too are all of us engaged in looking around at things during this moment—not only the hunter and moose but also, by extension, the artist and viewer—held in place, either bathed by an endlessly serene light or concealed by the gathering dark. Neither a standing, newly wounded animal nor a prostrate, dead animal body meets our eyes—unlike the situation, for instance, in *Success*, Remington's picture of the conclusion to a Canadian hunting trip he made with his writer-friend Julian Ralph in December 1889.

Noticing such features while looking at *Coming to the Call* highlights how the painting—amid its dusky yellow surface serenity and its "official" narrative about the human quest for and successful conquest of a wild animal—possesses a haunting *torque* or tensional pressure. There is the overall *torque* resulting from the thematic tension here between the painting's implied bundle of past motion and its explicit, rather coiled present stillness; there is, formally speaking, the *torque* produced by the conflicted energies of its horizontal and vertical lines and vectors. To be sure, we may not register this torque when first beholding this painting, and we may not even understand its source—just as we may not initially see the hunter poised there in the shadows, readying his heart as well as his rifle to take this wild animal's life. But just as the hunter has called out the moose, so too do we essentially call to the painting when beholding it and trying to understand it and the nature of its power. And in the very process of calling to the painting and, at some point registering its thematic and formal torque, we just might find ourselves—like the very moose before our eyes—being "called out" in turn.

So both the painting's varied tensional pull and its dominant trope's inherently ambiguous nature (both calling and being called) foster questions rather than answers and, in the end, trouble or undercut its implied narrative that celebrates human mastery of wild lands and wild animals. Questions such as these: What exactly is the hunter's or the painting's "call"? Just who or what comes to the call—and why? In this drama of the "end," what exactly is the desire that makes one call out or answer the call? *Desire:* as if perhaps the true hunt is that of the mobile eye searching for an *authentic* or genuine "calling" on the contoured margin of a wooded lake as day becomes night? *Desire:* as if the "end" toward which everything in this painting of camouflage and ventriloquism is directed simultaneously constitutes a genesis or advent(ure).

This Sporting Life

A real sportsman of the nature-loving type, must go tramping or paddling or riding about over the waste places of the earth, with his dinner in his pocket. He is alive to the terrible strain of the "carry," and to the quiet pipe when the day is done. The campfire contemplation, the beautiful quiet of the misty morning on the still water, enrapture him, and his eye dilates, his nerves tingle, and he is in a conflagration of ecstasy. When he is going—going—faster—faster—into the boil of the waters, he hears the roar and boom ahead, and the black rocks crop up in thickening masses to dispute his way. He is fighting a game battle with the elements, and they are remorseless. He may break his leg or lose his life in the tip-over which is imminent, but the fool is happy—let him die.

FREDERIC REMINGTON,
"Black Water and Shallows" (1893)

Let man's better nature revel in the beauties of existence; they inflate his soul. The colors play upon the senses—the reddish-yellow of the birch-barks, the blue of the water, and the silver sheen as it parts at the bows of the canoes; the dark evergreens, the steely rocks with their lichens, the white trunks of the birches, their fluffy tops so greeny green, and over all the gold of a sunny

day. It is my religion, this thing, and I do not know how to tell all I feel con-
cerning it.

FREDERIC REMINGTON,
from *Crooked Trails* (1898)

Coming to the Call first appeared as a two-page color halftone spread in the 19 August 1905 issue of *Collier's Weekly*, a little over four years before Remington's untimely death from peritonitis caused by a burst appendix. He probably painted *Coming to the Call* during the early summer of 1905 at Ingleneuk, the island retreat in Chippewa Bay on the St. Lawrence River that he had purchased five years earlier. There, in his studio outbuilding nestled in the birch trees on the Canadian side of the island, Remington devoted the summer to completing the bulk of his paintings and sculptures for that year's gallery shows or commissioned work. And there, in the evening after supper, he would usually paddle out on the river or into the nearby bays in his Rushton canoe and float in the evening twilight, sketching and taking color notes to aid his ongoing studio work with what had become his late-career passion: nocturnes.

In 1905 alone, Remington produced eight pictures of men in canoes on bodies of water, five of them set with the muted light of sunset and the moon and stars, or the veiled light of a rainstorm, or the gray floating mist of a winter day. Moreover, as the quotations above indicate, Remington not only rendered his love of paddling, whether in whitewater streams or on still lakes, in his visual artwork. He also published written accounts of his canoeing adventures with rod and gun, these for the most influential national magazines and journals. Just as *Coming to the Call* indirectly comments on Remington's other art and his writings having to do with the subject of canoes, hunters, and wild animals, so too does his prose discourse about such subjects help us better understand what appears within this particular painting's frame. This is because his writing's linear narrative sequences and explicit authorial commentary unpack the key thematic issues that Remington, due to the demands of the painting medium, condensed or layered onto the canvas surface in the more spatial form of visual metaphors.

Living as we do now in the strong wake of the romantic sublime, Remington's verbal rendering of the aesthetics of risk, this sporting "thing" he calls "my religion," may easily seem commonplace, even banal. Yet amid his awkward syntax ("going—going—faster—faster") and clunky diction ("greeny green"), it is curious that Remington declines, say, to specify the

10.4 Frederic Remington, Untitled compositional sketch, n.d.
Ink on paper, $3\frac{1}{4} \times 4\frac{1}{2}$".
Courtesy Frederic Remington Art Museum, Ogdensburg NY.

contents of his "real" sportsman's "dinner in the pocket." Nor does this painter, nominally so invested with what he calls "the play of colors," write very specifically about tones and shades of color during his canoe trips. And I find it curious, or at least noteworthy, how the notoriously overweight Remington in his prose discourse typically reduces his persona's corporeal presence to that of a disembodied, roving eye. As we can see in these representative passages, his gaze moves in graduated increments around the natural scene, responding to the succession of basic colors it registers from nearby (the canoe), then on to the middle distance over the water and to the shapes seen on the shoreline, and then upward to take in the overarching "gold of a sunny day." Remington's concentration on the natural world's power to stimulate his nerves and soul thus dilutes or denies the visceral response his body presumably would register to what he calls "the strain of the carry." As a result, a certain *connoisseurship of feeling* comes to predominate in his prose discourse. The point here is that it is precisely this desire for and this capacity to experience a heightened connoisseurship of feeling that, in the end, identifies the *real* or authentic sportsman—not so much his skill with paddle, rod and reel, or with shotgun and rifle.

What, if anything, should we make of this aestheticizing of the canoeing adventure?

For one thing, this projection of the overall processual flow of sensory experience as a matter of the eye and of consciousness—as if corporeality were not only a given but an obstacle to the desired inflation of one's "better nature"—reveals that any luxuriating in "the beauties of existence" depends on the sportsman's retreat from material luxuries and civilized contrivances, which is to say those things that insulate one's central nervous system and potentially enlightened soul from nature's stimulus.[2] Couched in the language of "rapture" and "ecstasy," Remington's prose suggests that any return to the simple, primitive life in order to achieve a desired sensory and spiritual tumescence ("dilation" of the eye, "inflation" of the soul) will depend upon the "real" sportsman's circulation and movement. The mobility of Remington's gaze provides an analogy for or epitomizes his social and geographic mobility to travel, which is to say his freedom from the necessity of work so as to "tramp" the "waste places of the earth" with his available leisure time. Both the religion of nature and the hoary ideal of the simple life articulated and forwarded by Remington's writings about sporting adventures—and, by extension, by his paintings and illustrations of hunting and fishing episodes—thus assume a sense of class privilege or entitlement.

During Remington's infancy an increasingly romanticized religion of nature—evident in the establishment of Yosemite National Park and in a vogue of landscape painting and local-color descriptive writing—functioned in part to offer a healing antidote for a nation recovering from the agony of the Civil War. During Remington's maturity, however, such an ardently expressed desire to return to a more authentic sensory and spiritual life in the woods, lakes, and rivers of nature's nation largely functioned to allay the anxieties of dominant professional-managerial class males who, like Remington, were anxious about the massive social and cultural transformations accompanying the rise of urban industrial modernity. As T. J. Jackson Lears has shown in his social history No Place of Grace, for instance, prominent antimodernist men (and a few women as well) distrusted the increasing luxury, banality, and domestication of American culture at the turn of the twentieth century. They sought "to endow weightless modern experience with gravity and purpose" by fervently promoting the martial ideal, adventurous travel, competitive sports (such as the collegiate football Remington played at Yale), and of course the hunting exploits we see frequently

depicted in Remington's art and writing. Stories about warrior types became extremely popular subjects for the reading public at the end of the
nineteenth century, with the result that the signatures of such intrepid
writer-adventurers as Rudyard Kipling, Robert Louis Stevenson, Theodore
Roosevelt, Owen Wister, Jack London, and—of course—Frederic Remington were famous in the popular culture of industrial America.[3]

With this context in mind, then, both Remington's prose discourse on
the thrills of paddling in remote waters and the visual metaphors for the
hunting moment depicted in *Coming to the Call* might be said to forward explicitly and implicitly the virtues of a retreat from urban luxury and orna-
mentation in order to refashion, as Theodore Roosevelt would with his
"strenuous life" ethos, the era's masculine ideology. And with regard to
hunting and other sporting adventures, such refashioning linked gender
with class anxieties. As cultural and environmental historians have also recently noted, the dominant professional-managerial class of Anglo-Saxon
America effectively wielded an ideology of the honorable, sporting hunt
with seasonal and bag limits against the putatively more brutal and crass
primitive accumulation hunting practices of the lower classes, indigenous
tribal peoples, and newer immigrants from eastern and southern Europe.
Along with the progressivist idea of the honorable hunt governed by an
ethic of "fair play" and the "clean" kill, then, what Remington calls the *real*
sportsman's feeling response to the "beauties of existence" discloses,
among other things, his particular class fraction's promotion of the sporting hunt's aesthetic and spiritual—not its commercial—value as part of its
struggle to maintain hegemony.[4]

However Remington's verbal and visual discourse might be saturated
with markers of class difference, perhaps the oddest feature of Remington's
aestheticized ethos of adventure is its implicit assumption that the authentic life desired by the "real" sportsman is not just something one simply
does—or, if one has been dealt a bad hand since birth, simply endures—
until it mercifully comes to an end. *Real* life, that is, turns out not to be
something one just lives in, through, or around, like the air humans breathe
or the water through which fish swim. Rather, an authentic "real" life turns
out to be something that can be—and in fact has to be—improved upon,
capitalized on as if it were an investment tendered for maximum dividends
on the stock exchange of being. So what one is born into isn't "real" life, so
to speak—it's just the everyday same old, same old. As we now say, to be a
truly alive, authentic person, much less a "real sportsman," one must needs

go out and "get a life"—through acts that, ironically, turn out to be different only by degree, not kind, from the very ethos of consumption predominant in the metropolis from which one has fled in search of experiential intensification. So in the end achieving an authentic existence does not only constitute a sort of desirable "future" investment on the stock exchange of being. The desired intensification of life—in Remington's rhetoric, that moment of transformation from the calm to the tingle, from the closed off to the dilated, and from the inert to the inflated—always remains somewhere else from where one is, is always located, both temporally and spatially, at a distance.[5] So you must go get it, seek it out—hunt for it. Acquire it—just as Remington acquired all those artifacts of American Indian life during his various travels in search of the right exotic subjects to compensate for an otherwise drab everyday existence.

But here's the curious thing: all this questing for an authentic life that will inflate one's soul, tingle one's nerves, and dilate one's eye—all this patently acquisitive desire is, finally, paradoxically bound up with passivity and submission as well as with aggressivity and dominance. Look again at the passages leading off this section of the essay. Remington's narrative persona scans the natural scene and marks with his eye the panoply of hues and the variegated shapes of natural objects, particularly the rocks and trees that signify his courting of danger as well as of beauty. Yet just as clearly this roving eye registers how it is captured by the dancing "play of colors," just like a canoe is described both as carving a wake with its gliding passage and, simultaneously, being caught by a silver sheen of the water at its bow. The point is that as the distracting clutter of the social world falls away during his heightened recall of sensory and, in the end, soulful exhilaration, all the fetching colors, textures, and motions of the natural world won't stand still to be simply ravished by Remington's vampiric eye. Rather, they are described as also penetrating and possessing—preying upon—this willing communicant. For Remington, then, the "real" sportsman's visual feasting on the world evolves into the pleasure of being consumed by its reciprocating presence. As a result, an authentically real life thus appears to be both a mode of stalking or seeking and a mode of being stalked or enraptured. Paradoxically, as if describing the throes of sexual passion, the rapturous coming "alive" signaled by the eye and soul's tingling, inflation, dilation, in collusion with the canoe's rhythms and speed, eventually climaxes with the egotistical flameout Remington terms the "conflagration of ecstasy."[6]

Animal Calling/Calling Animal

Men have only had an unconscious since they lost a territory. . . . The uncon-
scious is the individual structure of mourning in which this loss is incessantly,
hopelessly replayed—animals are the nostalgia for it.

JEAN BAUDRILLARD

In Remington's 1901 treatment of the moose-hunting theme, a native guide using birch bark rolled up in the shape of a cone is portrayed calling to a moose on behalf of a hunter who has hired the guide and now sits forward in the canoe, cradling his rifle in anticipation of a moose's appearance. Why does or how can the "call" itself signify something at all, for the hunter as well as for the moose? How is it possible that the hunter's call prompts an answer from the wild animal represented in the painting's scene?

One obvious answer is that in order for there to be a "call" at all, the moose's signifying system, how it understands and specifically communicates with the world, must be invoked: hence the hunter's or the guide's practice of putting certain sounds and breath patterns together in certain rhythmic sequences so as to create the call. In the act of calling to the wild animal, though, the hunter's call of course can never duplicate the animal's call in the manner of an *exact* likeness (as if that were possible, since by definition decoys, lures, and calls are cultural constructions masquerading as natural signs). Rather, the successful call seems to work as the caller assembles a sequence of sounds that eventually operate, in W.J.T. Mitchell's words, "as an artificial sign that is not a sign, an icon that is an 'equivalent' rather than a 'likeness.'"[7] If considered as an "equivalent to" rather than a precise "likeness of" something, then, the "call" works because the prey animal apparently does not have the cognitive ability to see or hear something simultaneously as both "there" and "not there." Humans, by contrast, with a certain cognitive maturity, are able to see both the colored surface and the figurative form of, say, an artwork (the "there") and understand them as together constituting an image or representation of, say, a moose (the "not there"). This represented animal is literally "there" in the artform, exists on its painted surface—but at the same time, of course, this image is neither equivalent to the color and the lines deployed by the artist nor even to the animal out there beyond the frame in the world. For humans, the cognitive (and cultural) ability to make this distinction between image and thing realizes a certain degree of freedom; but because in "coming to the

10.5 Frederic Remington, *Calling the Moose* (*The Call to Death*, altern.), 1901. Oil on canvas, 26½ × 39½″ (67.3 × 100.3 cm). Courtesy R. W. Norton Art Gallery, Shreveport LA.

call" a bull moose thinks it sees or hears the things themselves and cannot, to its peril, distinguish them from the images of things, this animal being occupies a position of "lack" in relation to the human's mode of knowing and having a world.

Thus in this anthropocentric scenario, which one could trace in the Western intellectual tradition from Aristotle through Heidegger, human freedom depends in some significant way upon the ability of our species to create images and representations in words, pigment, stone, and bronze— and taxidermy. These potentially offer any given individual an advent into what Heidegger calls "the Being of being as such," for like the successful "call" itself such images and representations—while never offering exact replicas of the originals out there in the natural world—potentially compensate for the tyranny of time's passing and for our special human knowledge of death's certain advent.[8] And, if considered as a type of image or representation, the hunter's imitative "call" not only discloses the *performative* nature of human identity. Since the purpose of the "call" is to *regulate* the prey animal's body movements, it also discloses the working out of an

205

elemental human desire for power and mastery. As if in confirmation of Heidegger's thesis about the animal's "lack" of being in this regard, the suspended hunting moment rendered in *Coming to the Call* conceivably fantasizes the event of the hunter's advent into "the Being of being as such," thanks to his artifice with and mastery over the things of the natural world.

Yet surely a problem exists with regard to this formulation of the "call" and this definition of the animal being as always existing in a position of "lack." Is it truly the case that power and mastery only flow in one direction, in this case from the human hunter kneeling in the shadows to the prey animal suddenly exposed in a clearing at land's end? Consider, for starters, the painting's overall grammar of looking: the painter has looked at a canvas, with the result that a moose is represented as looking; the artist's counterpart on the canvas surface, the represented hunter, has been and is looking—and right now is sighting in his rifle; and beyond the picture frame, a viewer looks, too—and perhaps looks away and looks back again as if compelled by a magnetic field's attraction and repulsion. To say that such acts of looking might produce pleasure doesn't seem so far-fetched if we first recall that both literally and metaphorically the "call" itself connotes an invitation for the bull moose to mate during rutting season (and there is the obvious phallic nature of the rifle's shape and action, its flash and discharge of heated energy seeking to penetrate another's body). From this perspective, the overall drama of desire in *Coming to the Call* entwines the act of calling an animal out for visual inspection with the pleasure devolving from the libido's gaining of access to the world through the organ of the eye, the human's performative call and gaze regulating one of what Remington calls "the beauties of existence."

Still, as James Elkins reminds us, inherent in any surveillance operation is this dynamic: "Like a bullet, the gaze shoots out toward the object; but the act of killing changes the killer, and like a bullet, light travels back from the object to the observer. When it comes to seeing, objects and observers alter one another, and meaning goes in both directions."[9] Like the light traveling back from the object to the observer, altering both in the process, calling out the animal via a simulated shape or sound conceivably entails one's simultaneously being called out by the animal and its environs. To call out the animal is thus not only to cast over it a spell that merges Eros with death. It is also potentially to have such a spell cast over oneself, which is to say both one's body and one's psyche—as if one's own "primitive" interior wilderness as well as one's body were being summoned out for inspection in answering the "call." As we saw to be the case with regard to the paradox of the "real" sportsman being both a consumer of and being consumed by the natural world's danger and beauty, calling forth and gazing at the wild animal simultaneously depends upon one's very immersion in and submission to the sensuous natural world—a speaking *to*, not *about*, this beguiling external world to the degree that one can become aligned with its material rhythms, textures, and tones.

So *Coming to the Call* renders a drama of desire for power. Yet through the trope of the "call" and its predominant motif of surveillance, one that implicates viewer and artist as well as the hunter and moose in the scene, this drama of desire conceivably is not simply about human command and control. If it can be said to be "about" anything at all, perhaps it is as much about the nature and the limits of exchange and even kinship. And it is this latter prospect that identifies for us how this wild animal and its environs conceivably ought to be seen as embodying a realm of plenitude, not lack— at least in comparison to the human mode of knowing and being in the world. Through its metaphor of the "call" the painting, rightly seen, registers *both* the regulation of the animal body's movements by a masterful human *and* a perennial human longing for an unmediated relationship with an authentic "something" or some "things" believed to be already lost or in danger of becoming lost; or with a perceived more authentic "something" or some "things" that have yet to be controlled and owned, like other wild animals and "the waste places of the earth," both of these ardently pursued because of their reputed ability to complete the human self's being in the world, to redeem *its* feeling of "lack." So even as *Coming to the Call* dramatizes formally and thematically a human mastery of nature through the appropriative acts of hunting and the creation of artistic images (the painting, the photograph, the mounted trophy head), the painting's dominant trope of the call also suggests Remington's (and his culture's) deep-seated anxiety about losing contact with the *thereness of things as things*, of losing touch with the "there" of real life due to the seduction of the "not there" realized by the assorted simulacra mediating our everyday lives. Better to be, at least in the imagination if not in reality, one of Remington's "men with the bark on," primitivist types whose uncurried hides and physical lives full of danger seemingly inoculated them against the modern dominant-class males' debilitating mental introspection. Better to have one's nerves tingle out there in the presence of the wild than to be, well, nervous.

This is why, in 1905, concerned about his standing in the art world and wondering if what he termed his "capital"—that is, the subject matter of the U.S. westward experience—had any currency in a swarming modern era epitomized for him by "the derby hat, the smoking chimneys, the cordbinder, and the thirty-day note" and "the conventionalities—the cooks and the dudes and the women"—this is why an obese, alcoholic Frederic Remington fantasizes in a letter to his friend Jack Summerhayes that "birchbarks and injuns are for me." [10] Ironically, of course, any arduous and repetitive seeking after the authentic life by means of actual adventures and projective identification with "wild" animals and "wild" men is bound up with the destruction of the very thing or things thought necessary to alleviate one's alienation. Hence the haunting paradox of Remington producing images and representations that were, like the call, supposed to disguise and conceal their nature as artificial signs so as to provide the "equivalent" of what was believed to be authentic experiences in the midst of a weightless modern world. Hence Remington's obsessive return to the hunt as a primal scene of union between warrior males and the redemptive natural world. Indeed, through its cuts and seams and points of incision by various edged forms (tree limbs, canoe prow, palmate antlers, serrated edge of land), Coming to the Call conjures up a deceptively serene topography of contact and sacrificial exchange involving a specifically male-male encounter.

The adventurer desires to escape from the cooks and the dudes and the women back home in order to recover an authentic real life through an encounter with the natural world's representative animal patriarch. Perhaps this deadly calling and hiding and seeking will lead to the advent of the "real" sportsman. And yet, as emblematized here by the bull moose and the flood of yellow light and water, it may be that the natural world's profligate creativity and potency will also bring into the light—as does the mythological story of Saturn slaying his father Cronos with a scythe—the hunter's underlying anxiety about his belatedness or secondariness. [11] So as much as it purports to be a painting about conquest and control, then, about a hunter's genesis—his being called out as well as the moose's body—on this threshold between night and day, life and death, Coming to the Call also testifies to the haunting presence of experiential loss: the loss of a wild territory, both in the external and internal worlds; the loss of an intimate contact with real life—even the loss of secure paternity, symbolized by the animal patriarch and the sun disappearing behind the horizon of hills.

The Hunter-Artist and the King of the Woods

We go to the Island just as soon as the ice goes out and I'm going on a six weeks canoe trip this Fall in Canada that will beat anything since Noah's cruise. I'm d——— tired of paint & clay and want to see the big river and the moonlight and hear Pete Smith (my man) tell how he got through the winter.

FREDERIC REMINGTON
to Jennings S. Coxe Jr., 14 April 1905

A hunter with a rifle and a prey animal in the forest; the figurative device of the "call"; a leitmotif of incision and being incised, this manifested by the suture of pitch on the canoe's side, by the gazes of hunter and moose, and by the smooth skin of yellow pigment that highlights, through contrast, the darker topography of points and edges, seams and sutures. And whose yellow, pooled stillness in the foreground promotes reverie, establishing a medium for the unconscious, whose *shadow figure* has emerged in the middle distance as a dark, defamiliarized animal form conjuring up our evolutionary animal heritage. If we can say that we *see* these things for sure, then I think we can also begin to understand how Remington successfully transformed (what could have been) a conventional hunting painting into a rather stylized visual rendering of the solitary male hunter's initiation into the kingship of the woods, a ritual process that Richard Slotkin has termed the myth of "regeneration through violence."[12]

In keeping with the pagan sense of the forest as a primal birthplace of nations as well as of individuals, the processual mythic narrative describing the hunter's retreat to and eventual return from the primitive natural environs of moose, wolf, and bear symbolically represents a desire for *origins* or foundations: there is the hunter-aspirant's genealogical quest to recover the authentic ground of his identity, or to establish a purer ethics grounded in "natural" law, or to redeem a vision of the larger national mission. From this perspective, *Coming to the Call* not only embeds the class conflicts and cultural anxieties of Remington's progressive era; its brooding yellows and overall dusky atmosphere also offer, by means of their displacement into the ritual hunt and its attendant myth of regeneration through violence, visual correlates of the artist's (and perhaps a viewer's) psychic ambivalence.

As Brian Jay Wolf suggests in his study of Thomas Cole's paintings, an artist's figurative reliance on sunset and twilight atmospheres often signals the presence of "the *memory of a primal trauma* too deep to be recognized and too painful to be ignored." In such instances, Wolf remarks, "sunset becomes the governing metaphor for these transactions by providing a threshold region sufficiently dark to prevent either detection or naming of the original forces, and yet light enough to allow their engagement and re-working." [13] If regarded as obliquely registering through its haunting absences and twilight-cast shadows the artist's deep-seated anxiety about losing contact with an authentic "real" life, then *Coming to the Call* could be said, following Wolf's lead, to illustrate Remington's general engagement with and working through—in his present moment—of that "primal trauma" broadly known as separation anxiety. Refracted through the imagery and mythic narrative pattern of the ritual hunt's quest to assimilate the natural world's potency and fertility, Remington's painterly engagement with and reworking of the memory of a "primal trauma" comes to center on the camouflaged figure kneeling in the canoe. This hunter whose "calling" to and looking at the moose and its environs recapitulates or mimics the activity of the artist. This shrouded hunter figure, in short, exists as the artist's (and the viewer's) surrogate.

Thinking about the hunter as a surrogate figure for the artist leads me to say that the official fantasy the painting promotes is this: that through either a firearm or artist's brush—both linear, wooden, relatively small (in comparison to the world they front) instruments or tools of the hand—the (re)sources of the natural world from which they have been made will be incorporated and transformed (an animal into "meat," oil and pigment into a painting). Thought about as dramatizing an initiation into and an assimilation of the big wood's creative or reproductive powers and energies—at least as these get embodied by the animal patriarch who has come to the call—the ritual hunt assayed in *Coming to the Call* presents the hunter as the surrogate artist's engagement with and working through an elemental anxiety of influence. As keyed for us by the painting's title and trope of the "call," this elemental anxiety of influence centers on the drama of finding one's true "calling," which is to say with one's realizing both an autonomous and an authoritative personal and vocational identity. Here we might well recall how in the absence of warfare, the blood sport of hunting—and its cultural representations—has always provided both a process and a stage for a culture to determine status, honor, rank, or privilege.

All the evidence scholars and biographers have gathered indicate that Remington experienced episodic crises with regard to his artistic status and his work's value in the critical as well as the commercial marketplace. On one level, this news is hardly surprising, for in the absence of wealthy individual patrons Remington depended entirely for his living on contracts with magazines for illustrations and on gallery sales of his paintings and sculpture. In the last decade of his life Remington befriended the painter Childe Hassam and other American impressionists living in the northeastern United States. The rather ambitious paintings of his last few years reveal his internalization and revision of some of their techniques and aesthetic philosophies in his bid to be recognized as an *artist*, not merely as a successful commercial illustrator of outdoor adventures in the West or the "North Country"—subjects that in the last couple years of his life were increasingly regarded by his *Collier's Weekly* editors as irrelevant to the magazine's new look and the country's new age. Such a view, much less the irritation Remington felt about his being denied membership in the National Academy, basically only confirmed his long-held belief that the "serious" art-critical establishment was overly reluctant to accord *western* American subject matter attention as serious art.

Moreover, in the midst of his most creative outpouring of painting and sculpture, during what turned out to be the last four years of his life, from 1905 to 1909, Remington on at least four separate occasions burned up numerous paintings and studies on board that did not, he believed, begin to fulfill his emerging artistic direction. Whose existence, he thought, would plague his bid for artistic recognition and acceptance. At one point he called his existing early work "enemies come to haunt me," and further admitted that he felt helpless when such works were offered for sale to the public: "I would buy them all if I were able and burn them up." This volatile nexus of artistic production and gender and vocational identity appears in shorthand form in the December 1904 letter Remington wrote to the art critic Royal Cortissoz, who had praised the artist's recent exhibition of work at the Noë Gallery in New York. Remington valued Cortissoz's favorable response, remarking in this letter that the creative process is not only an extraordinarily difficult one. Its very existence, it seems, depends upon supportive audiences who can appreciate the artist's risk-taking: "At times we [artists] are inclined to set back in the breeching if someone don't say something nice. A good word at times is a lot of comfort." On one level, the key phrase to be "set back in the breeching" epitomizes how Remington's overall conception of creativity was a phallic one centering on the issue of potency or powerlessness (i.e., "the breeching" describes a loaded weapon that may not fire its load without the spark of a good critical word). Metaphorically, though, the phrase also discloses his awareness of and anxiety both about secondariness (to be relegated to a position in the rear behind the firearm's barrel or bore) and about the fragile nature of the creative process ("setting back" as a delay in or failure to load the breech with ammunition).[14]

Whatever pleasures, terrors, anxieties, nervousness, and powerless feelings that circulated through Remington's being in his drive for autonomous recognition from past and present paternal influences and authorities are seemingly engaged with, negotiated, and worked through in the complex pastoral moment dramatized in Coming to the Call, in which the artist's surrogate hunter figure returns to nature so as to appropriate the rival animal king symbolically representing the primitive, patriarchal origin or source of potency and fertility. In this painterly elaboration of the ritual hunt pattern, in short, the desired power over and assimilation of the animal patriarch's fertility and potency amounts to what in psychoanalytic discourse would be termed a refusal of secondariness or belatedness. From this perspective, the hunter as a surrogate artist figure—by means of his camouflage and his call's mimicry—yearns to consume powerful, external male imagoes (the bull moose, the sun) so they are not simply the endpoint of his libidinous identification but rather internalized sources testifying to his authority and power, his authenticity. (Re)sources, that is, that will enable, underwrite, and sustain his creative endeavors. (Re)sources that will be both genuine and generative. "Genuine" in the sense that by wearing the hide or displaying the trophy head or even by painting the animal, the hunter-artist will make visible a direct, unbroken line of descent or patrimony—as in the old folk custom that spawned the word "genuine" (with its connotations of "pure" and "true"), where a father places his infant on his knee to acknowledge publicly his paternity. "Generative" in the sense that any new creativity— say, the writing or the painting about adventure—will testify to the hunter-artist's successful internalization and displacement of the primal creative authority embodied by the natural world and its potent animal king.

Projecting through its camouflage of shadows and brilliant yellows an underlying anxiety over secondariness and belatedness as well a desire for mastery and control, it is as if, in Coming to the Call, Remington, through his surrogate hunter figure, strategically confirms his initiation into an authorized, authentic vocational identity, (re)enacts the advent of finding his true "calling," in the process strategically resolving in fantasy both his internal and the external world's doubts or uncertainties as to his stature as a real artist and a real man. The atmosphere of the ritual hunt that saturates the ar-

10.6 Photograph from Remington's collection.
Courtesy Frederic Remington Art Museum, Ogdensburg NY.

rested drama of surveillance in *Coming to the Call* would thus seem to have at least two valences: on the one hand, there is the male hunter-artist's ritual enchantment by and encounter with a rival patriarchal figure, the animal king of the woods, the aggressive assimilation of whose potency will both testify to the hunter-artist's status and sustain his creative powers; on the other hand, there is the hunter-artist's identification with (as we have seen in the discussion of the call's dual nature) and immersion in the maternal body's life-giving powers, the more-than-human, telluric holding environment of water and trees that sustains the animal patriarch.

With regard to this second valence, the hunter-artist's withdrawal into the darkness at this threshold moment reveals his strong desire to immerse himself in and appropriate this symbolic maternal realm's generative powers so as to inaugurate an *alternative* masculinist scenario of creative (re)production. Exactly foreshadowing this substitution of the hunter-artist's creative work for nature's "beauties of existence" is the drama of reflection in the lower foreground of *Coming to the Call*. In cutting down and out and striving to simplify things in his quest for "Big art," Remington arranges the scene as a theater of clean, reflective surfaces. In this theater of reflection such things as the canoe's reflected prow, the *copy* itself, appear to be as substantially real and compelling of our attention as the original or supposedly precedent form, just as the artist's overall disposition of light and color will come to substitute for the sunlight fading in the western sky.

So as the hunter-artist buries the world's matter—the prey animal buried by the hunter, the primed canvas buried by the artist's paint—the action of the rifle and of flat or round brush at the same time brings into the light (to use the literal meaning of the word "illustration") a new substitute or replacement sun. So here the visual furrow in the air "breeched"—to use Remington's verb in his letter to Royal Cortissoz quoted earlier—by the hunter's gaze, by the horizontal line of his rifle and the future trajectory of its bullet, and by the vertical shape and stark edge of the canoe's prow— this pathway projects both an identification with and incorporation of the sources of creative power embodied both by the earth's motherbody and by the logos of the sun that, just now, just now, begins to disappear behind the hills.

The Story of Where the Sun Goes

Or is beauty itself an intricately fashioned lure, the cruelest hoax of all?
ANNIE DILLARD

Like hunting, looking is a form of directed desire. And like the call, looking is a dynamic activity saturated with ambiguity: just looking at something may lead to our being looked at in return, a being hunted by, a being preyed or played upon by the external world's gaze. In the very act of looking at still water or at the hypnotic flames of a campfire or at a scarf of cloud formations moving off in the distance, we just might find ourselves—like the cowboys, soldiers, hunters, and Indians in several of Remington's late paintings—enthralled by that which both meets and unfolds before our eyes and also returns our gaze. And if considered as an analogue for hunting, our directed looking for "something"—regardless of whether that "something" be a painted bull moose or a cartoon Bullwinkle—may well lead, as it does in the stylized ritual hunt invoked by *Coming to the Call*, to a trying out and even reciprocal exchange of identities between observer and observed. So its luminous yellow hues rendering the sun's light and simultaneously harboring the shadow of death not only convey the seductive pleasure value of darkness. They also display how the entwined acts of looking as hunting and hunting as looking knead together the pleasures associated with both aggressive desire and passive reverie.[15]

Of course, looking is not only connected with "pleasure-value," whether that be defined, as it is here, as the play of light and color at day's end or as an escape from the world's prying eyes into that secret refuge provided by the gathering dark and canopy of trees. Both for the observer as well as for the observed, looking can in fact be painful: some sights surely cause us to avert our eyes; some acts of looking in fact desire to control—if not also to inflict pain on—the objects being scrutinized. Indeed, recognizing how "just looking" might well constitute a painful as well as a pleasurable act, I must now recognize that in answering the painting's call, in lingering before its beautiful lure of yellow, I have to a large degree averted my eyes from the agonizing end its title, form, and content anticipate. So for better or worse, and with some surprise—for I am not a hunter—I have found myself trying to account for how this painting's visual rhetoric calls its beholders to dwell—like the hunter and artist who also have looked or are caught out looking at this bull moose on this lake's edge—in a threshold space of *ambivalence*. Thus, to speak of affective response, both identification and estrangement, both attraction and repulsion, get sutured together as surely as do light and shadow in the painting's arrested moment.

As a result of this dynamic of looking, does not the painting itself—and the act of looking at the painting—establish a *dual* pathway for desire and longing, a pathway that just might, when all is said and done, constitute the painting's *true* subject? On the one hand, *Coming to the Call* might be said to promote a rather narcissistic drive for self-preservation, this simple impulse satisfaction manifesting itself through the hunter-artist's imitation and then appropriation of the natural world and its animal king's power. And yet, on the other hand, the painting discloses a rather powerful drive for intimacy, this fantasized striving for relations or kinship materialized whenever one is called out and caressed by this external world's exceeding wonder and mystery, its panoply of colors and forms flooding one's being. If the former pathway for desire leads one toward the pleasure of mastery and control, the latter pathway for desire engages one with the rather tender mercies that follow on relinquishing control, on acknowledging one's ultimate dependency on this very world that, time and time again, calls us out to marvel at its exceeding beauties and attend to its varied terrors. As a result, both in the painting itself and in the sustained act of looking at the painting, time is not the only thing momentarily arrested. Mastery and control, possession and conquest—although these strong desires are surely courted as our gazes travel the pathways carved out by Remington's brushwork, they are also endlessly deferred. So the pathology of control and power characteristic of Remington's work is everywhere on this particular canvas surface leavened by underlying anxieties about relations and relating—and about remaining in contact with some purportedly authentic natural ground that will confirm the artist's masculine authority and sustain his artistic creativity.

Having said all this, however, I find there is at least one further point to make about this painting in which hunting is one form of looking and looking is one form of hunting. When all is said and done, the hunter's fate—like that, finally, of the artist and the viewer who also behold this moose—is never truly to see the moose. That is, even though the moose answers the call and enters the clearing, it can never really occupy the precise location the hunter wants it to occupy in order to gratify the specific needs and desire that have brought him—this hunter in this canoe at this twilight moment near this year's end—to this place. As we see here, in fact, the moose always looks elsewhere, does not figuratively and cannot literally return the hunter's possessive gaze. So the hunter's action of calling and gazing and shooting can never truly overcome the primal separation evident in the bull moose's inevitable failure to show himself, to be truly there for the hunter. And there is more: as signaled by his camouflaged presence, the hunter-artist for his part can never really fully and truly be "there" for the moose either. Precisely because his being is (indeed, how can it not be?) essentially overdetermined by his overweening desires and by his culture's way of making sense of the world, he cannot and does not now truly show himself—which is to say, let his full being stand exposed, in the fullest sense of that word, to or before this enchanted avatar of nature's potent power.[16]

This misfire of gaze and being, so to speak, constitutes the underlying mystery and the challenge and—I must now recognize—the haunting defeat Coming to the Call registers even as its arrested moment officially forecasts regenerative success for the hunter in making meat and an artist in making a painting—and perhaps even a viewer in making sense of that painting. Remington's and my own coming to the "call" and being called out in turn on one level constitute an obsessive, renewed longing to recover that powerful authentic "something" out there glittering on the horizon, say that totem animal or fetishistic object, the possession of which promises to complete and legitimate our identities and claims to competency, much less power, in an increasingly alien, disenchanted world. Remington is seemingly caught out in the open here grasping with his imagination, gaze, and brush after the visual image or verbal representation that will attest to his climatic dwelling with or in "authentic" reality, his having been and continuing to be a *real* sportsman and artist, just as I am right now caught out in the open, grasping with my words and accumulating sentences to describe Remington's own yearning to commune with authentic existence. Of course, what any of us possesses in the end, if not actually also from the beginning of this hunt, is—like the "call"—a "likeness," not an equivalent. Despite anyone's best (or worst) efforts, this hunt for authenticity never truly ends: the adventurous escape from the world of simulacra is and can never be truly realized, no matter how strong the desire and no matter how capable the eyes and hands and imagination.

As a result, I have come to regard Remington's official vision of a capable male in control of and somewhat liberated from the world's determining influences as serving to *alibi* for a masculine subjectivity never truly in full control and never apparently sufficient and complete unto itself. The illusion Remington conjures up before our eyes is one of mastery, power, and control; the reality puncturing that illusion at the point of the painting's various sutures and edges and joins is that of fragility and turmoil, a subtle dread or foreboding—*as if what one is called to do here, in the final analysis, is to witness the moment of one's own death as well as the advent of one's being through an animal's sacrifice.* So to my mind the painting's features, metaphors, and forces, even as they loom up before our eyes in this visual fable of strong desire, necessarily falter on the very threshold space they compose and in which they can be said to dwell. Such features, metaphors, and forces necessarily falter on this threshold space and moment because of their inherent ambiguities and connotations of ambivalence. And because, finally, no antidote exists for this hardest fact of our shared temporal existence, the very fact emblematized here by the end of land, by the end of day, and by the coming end of the animal's life. This is the fact that that time—under whose sway the hunter, artist, and viewer mutually pursue their looking as hunting—is nothing if not a careful and relentless thief of life.

To strive to compete with or double the sun's light, as the painter's cadmium yellow pigment does; to strive to compete with or double nature's creative powers, as the painting's image does—in short, to strive to assimilate and to double for the sun not only connotes a desire to imitate its power. It also means, at some unknown future moment, to emulate the sun's fated daily disappearance from the scene.[17] Thus, the drama of the desire for the authentic life in *Coming to the Call* can offer at best only an illusory advent of mastery and possession. Can at best only provide triage for a fatal wound, temporary balm for the envious eye lured into forgetting that the end of all looking is foreshadowed for us by this very sun's daily decline in the sky. If anything, then, both the line of sight that links hunter and moose and the painterly composition that foregrounds a containerlike canoe and an enveloping yellow fluid combine with Remington's leitmotif of concealment and exposure, of hiding and seeking, so as to offer nothing, finally, nothing in the end but loss and absence. And so here, amidst the stark clarity of its edges — say, the outline either of a canoe's prow reflected in the water or of a bull moose's palmate antlers grasping the evening air — this painting uncannily comes to define the beautiful yet terribly brittle *pathos* that saturates all of Remington's major paintings.

Notes

1. Originally purchased at Remington's 1905 exhibition of new work at the Noë Art Galleries in New York City, *Coming to the Call* was brought to auction at Sotheby's on 10 December 1970. Part of the estate of Matilda R. Wilson, of Meadow Brook Hall in Rochester, Michigan, it then sold for $150,000. Fourteen years later, on 30 May 1984, it was again brought to auction at Sotheby's, this time selling for $550,000. See *Art at Auction: The Year at Sotheby's and Parke-Bernet, 1970–71* (New York: Viking, 1971), and *Important American Paintings, Drawings, and Sculpture* (New York: Sotheby's Parke-Bernet, 1984), 12–13. The catalog text for the 1984 auction characterizes the painting as depicting the sky of "early morning." Technically speaking, real hunters out there hunting real moose in the real world find that both sunrise and sunset are the best times for hunting. Because of the lemon-yellow hues and the particular cast shadows in this painting, and because of Remington's habit at Ingleneuk to paddle out on Chippewa Bay in his canoe after dinner and take color notes or draw sketches at sunset and under the moonlight, I am rather inclined to regard this painting as depicting a moment near or at sunset.

2. Remington theorized that the secret to creating what he called "Big art" lies in "the process of elimination. Cut down and out—do your hardest work outside the picture, and let your audience take away something to think about—to imagine" (qtd. in Peggy and Harold Samuels, *Frederic Remington: A Biography* [Austin: University of Texas Press, 1985], 347–48).

3. For a helpful discussion of the iconography of the landscape school with regard to the construction of national identity, see Simon Schama, *Landscape and Memory* (New York: Knopf, 1995), 197–200; and David Miller, "The Iconology of Wrecked or Stranded Boats in Nineteenth-Century American Culture," in *American Iconology*, ed. David C. Miller (New Haven: Yale University Press, 1993), 186–208. For a thorough discussion of what he terms the "antimodernist" critique of the developing features of urban industrial society, see T. J. Jackson Lears's *No Place of Grace* (New York: Pantheon, 1981).

4. In addition to Remington's class and political affiliations (and personal acquaintance of course with Roosevelt), these are the moral and environmental themes present in such productions as his essay "Policing the Yellowstone" (*Harper's Weekly*, 12 January 1895) and his 1906 series of paintings for *Collier's* entitled "The Tragedy of the Trees"; see Mike Davis, *Ecology of Fear: Los Angeles and the Imagination of Disaster* (New York: Henry Holt, 1998), 221–26.

5. My thoughts on Remington's rendering of this ethos of acquiring and maximizing "real" life so as to live truly (and well) have been helped along by Richard Brodhead's analysis of Henry James's work (Lecture, University of Utah, 27 April 2000).

6. As part of his discussion of Carl Rungius's wild-game and hunting art, Alexander Nemerov reminds us how turn-of-the-century discourse about hunting frequently displayed sexual connotations in rendering the ecstasy about the moment of "release" or the kill. See his "Haunted Supermasculinity: Strength and Death in Carl Rungius's *Wary Game*," *American Art* 13, no. 3 (fall 1999): 2–31. My argument extends Nemerov's point to suggest that the motif of the hunt in *Coming to the Call* relays a deep-seated anxiety about (and desire for) autonomous male reproduction and fertile creativity that would rival maternal reproductivity.

7. W.J.T. Mitchell, *Iconology: Image, Text, Ideology* (Chicago: University of Chicago Press, l986), 91.

8. Qtd. in Jacques Derrida, "On Eating Well," in *Who Comes After the Subject?* ed. Eduardo Cadava, Peter Connor, and Jean-Luc Nancy (New York: Routledge, 1991), 111–12. Derrida focuses on Heidegger's claim that the animal possesses its world in the mode of a "not having." Heidegger means by this phrase "not-having" that the animal's openness to the world—which is why they appear to us to be smart or nervous or sad— is nevertheless a "not-having" in the crucial sense that the animal re-

mains "deprived on account of having access neither to the world of man that he nonetheless senses, nor to truth, speech, death, or the Being of being as such."

For Remington, whose letters reveal his obsessive concern with his art's marketplace value and his standing among his artistic peers, the aesthetic residue sedimented in his "big art" efforts would hopefully testify to and guarantee an enduring recognition of his enduring genius, even as his body decomposed in its grave and his oil pigments faded and cracked in museums and private collections. This, at any rate, is the utopian desire underwriting his creativity, whether in the end that be defined as his bronzes or his paintings. See his letters to Owen Wister as reproduced in Vorpahl, *My Dear Wister: The Frederic Remington–Owen Wister Letters* (Palo Alto: American West, 1972); and also in Allen P. Splete and Marilyn D. Splete, *Frederic Remington—Selected Letters* (New York: Abbeville Press, 1988).

9. James Elkins, *The Object Stares Back* (New York: Harcourt Brace, 1996), 43.

10. As Remington writes his friend Jack Summerhayes in 1904, "I go on a big canoe trip in September. Nippissing or Winnepeg Lake—don't know which—birch bark & injuns for me" (qtd. in Splete and Splete, *Frederic Remington*, 348.

11. See Elkins, *What Painting Is* (New York: Routledge, 1998), pages 64 and 76, for a discussion and an image of the vaulting, prowlike symbol for Saturn's scythe in the alchemical tradition, which abstractly looks like Remington's signature's cursive t and n.

12. See Bettelheim, *The Uses of Enchantment: The Meaning and Importance of Fairy Tales* (New York: Vintage, 1977), 75–76, on the potential symbolic meanings of wild or primitive animal figures; see Richard Slotkin, *Regeneration Through Violence: The Mythology of the American Frontier* (Middletown CT: Wesleyan University Press, 1973), 146–79.

13. Bryan Jay Wolf, *Romantic Re-Vision: Culture and Consciousness in Nineteenth-Century American Painting and Literature* (Chicago: University of Chicago Press, l982), 218; emphasis added.

14. Splete and Splete, *Frederic Remington*, 358. In his *The Eastern Establishment and the Western Experience* (New Haven: Yale University Press, 1968), G. Edward White valuably introduces the idea of identity crisis and oedipal conflict in the lives of Remington, Roosevelt, and Wister by following, largely, the theories of identity formation developed by Erik Erikson in the wake of Freud. With regard to Remington, White's argument centers

mostly on the crises in vocational identity that Remington went through during his late-adolescent years and its resolution in his decision to become an artist, a decision that was resisted by his own father, his mother, and his future father-in-law.

15. *The Story of Where the Sun Goes* is the title of a 1907 Remington oil on canvas, also printed as a color halftone reproduction in the 23 November 1907 *Collier's Weekly*. My thoughts on this topic are generally indebted to James Elkins's discussion of the nature of seeing in his *The Object Stares Back*. Of particular relevance in this context is his chapter 3, "Looking Away, and Seeing Too Much," 86–124.

16. For more on the notion of the "envious eye" and on the dynamic of gazing and misrecognition, see Jacques Lacan, *The Four Fundamental Concepts of Psycho-Analysis*, ed. J. A. Miller, trans. A. Sheridan (Harmondsworth: Penguin, 1979), 113–16.

17. A painting entitled *The Story of the Sun Sleep*, referenced in the artist's ledger book, was apparently exhibited at the Noë Art Galleries in 1904, the year prior to the completion of *Coming to the Call*. No image of this 1904 painting is known to exist, as Peter H. Hassrick and Melissa J. Webster point out in *Frederic Remington: A Catalogue Raisonné of Paintings, Watercolors and Drawings* (Cody WY: Buffalo Bill Historical Center in association with University of Washington Press, 1996), 2:772. More specifically, this series of comments about the consequence of striving to double the sun is generally influenced by J. Hillis Miller's discussion of J.M.W. Turner's art in *Illustration* (Cambridge: Harvard University Press, 1992), 132–33.

11. "CAMERAS AND PHOTOGRAPHS WERE NOT PERMITTED IN THE CAMPS"

Photographic Documentation and Distortion
in Japanese American Internment Narratives

Melody Graulich

Variations of my title quotation recur again and again in the literature written by Nikkei—people of Japanese descent living in the United States or Canada—about their imprisonment during World War II. The narrator of Joy Kogawa's *Obasan*, for instance, comments that "our cameras—even Stephen's toy one that he brought out to show them when they came—are all confiscated." "We are the despised rendered voiceless," she adds, "stripped of car, radio, camera and every means of communication." Yet the remark of absence—cameras taken away, forbidden—usually leads to an assertion of a right to presence, to voice, to self-representation. In Miné Okubo's *Citizen 13660*, the line "cameras and photographs were not permitted in the camps" is immediately followed by "so I recorded everything in sketches, drawings, and paintings." In *The Invisible Thread*, Yoshiko Uchida includes one of her paintings, captioned: "Since we were not allowed to have cameras, I painted this scene of a dust storm in Topaz." [1]

Texts about camp life present cameras and photography in an ironic tension. On the one hand, as Susan Sontag says, "Photographs furnish evidence. Something we heard about, but doubt, seems proven when we're shown a photograph of it." Nikkei writers use family album photographs to document their "Americanness" and documentary photographs of internment camps, taken by outsiders, to show what "really" happened. Yet Sontag also points out that "photography implies that we know about the world if we accept it as the camera records it. But this is the opposite of understanding, which starts from not accepting the world as it looks." [2] This line is particularly poignant and ironic for Nisei who were not "accepted" as citizens because of the way they "looked."

Their experiences led Nikkei writers and visual artists to anticipate Sontag's insight, to challenge the photographic record, exploring the erasure of Japanese Americans in various ways and the distortion of their experiences. They provide, in effect, new captions and frames for old photographs, raising questions about the historical uses to which photographs have been put and about what photographs can help us to understand. While work on

11.1 Miné Okubo, Untitled drawing from *Citizen 13660* (page 12).
Reproduced courtesy of Seiko Buckingham.

photography by Sontag, John Tagg, Laura Wexler, and others can offer illu-
minating contexts for understanding ambivalent representations of photographs, the Nikkei themselves provide theoretical approaches and insights
into contemporary issues of representation, the gaze, and documentary
"evidence." Okubo presents one undeniable example in figure 1. Her understanding of the role of the objectifying gaze is clear without the caption:
"The people looked at all of us, both citizens and aliens, with suspicion and
mistrust." [3]

If a contemporary American has any idea what the camps built to "as-
semble" and "intern" Japanese Americans during World War II looked like
or has an image of the internees themselves, the viewpoint was probably
defined by the lens of one of the government photographers who documented the process of internment: Dorothea Lange, Clem Albers, Russell Lee, and others. Because of the wide circulation of similar photographs, images by Lange (fig. 2), Albers (fig. 3), and an unknown War Relocation Agency photographer (fig. 4) will look familiar even if you've never
seen them. [4]

Of course, there are hundreds of these War Relocation Agency photographs, and I have selected these images, unfairly, with a point in mind.

11.2 Dorothea Lange, Grandfather and grandchildren awaiting evacuation bus, Hayward CA, 8 May 1942.
Records of the War Relocation Authority, National Archives no. RG 210.

They suggest that while these liberal veterans of the Work Projects Administration era were certainly sympathetic to the Nikkei, their finest work—or perhaps the work most often reproduced and circulated—sometimes seems to use Japanese Americans and their experiences as props to support an ironic political statement about American hypocrisy. As Anthony W. Lee argues in Picturing Chinatown, photographs of Asian Americans and the spaces they inhabit "speak most directly to the needs, desires, and assumptions of their makers." These call forth the word "plight." The images reflect persistent representations of Asian Americans. As Gary Okihiro has argued, "Asians have [frequently] been depicted as victims, most promi-

11.3 Clem Albers, Child awaiting evacuation.
Records of the War Relocation Authority, National Archives.

nently as objects of exclusion in the nineteenth-century Anti-Chinese movement and as 'Americans betrayed' in the twentieth-century concentration
camps. The pervasiveness of that portrayal has prompted Roger Daniels to
write: 'Asians have been more celebrated for what has happened to them
than for what they have accomplished.'"⁵

Some WRA images seem to be more about "America" (perhaps with a k)
than about the experience of the internees. I don't question the sincerity of
Lange and Albers and others; unlike most North Americans, they recognized that the Nikkei were indeed victims of racism and of a government
eager to consolidate support for a war effort, and they used their cameras
to attempt to intervene by providing images with overt political content. As
Sontag says, however, understanding can only come from "not accepting
the world as it looks," a point Nikkei writers insist upon. In these images
the individual is subsumed to the political statement. In *The Burden of Representation*, John Tagg comments on what he calls "the gaze of the state."
"Documentary photography," he says, "inscribed relations of power in representation which were structured like those of earlier practices of photo-

11.4 Photographer unknown, Japanese American girl in front of flag. Records of the War Relocation Authority, National Archives.

documentation: both speaking to those with relative power about those positioned as lacking, as the 'feminised' Other, as passive but pathetic objects capable only of offering themselves up to a benevolent, transcendent gaze, the gaze of the camera, and the gaze of the paternal state."⁶

In Lange's famous photograph *Dust Storm, Manzanar* (fig. 5), the "transcendent gaze" is apparent, revealed through aesthetics and framing and through editorial content. Note the perfectly balanced composition, probably cropped, the heavy irony of the flag directly in the middle foreground, proudly waving against the majestic mountains above the desert plain, reaching up into the spacious skies. My own heavy-handed irony suggests how readily this image conjures slogans of United States nationhood, identifies the Nikkei as a "people betrayed," and casts them in the role of victim. The flag dominates; the few miniscule people are hardly noticeable. The lack of people is certainly "realistic"—they'd have taken cover—but nevertheless the Nikkei are erased, dwarfed by this mythic American land-

11.5 Dorothea Lange, *Dust Storm, Manzanar*.
Records of the War Relocation Authority, National Archives.

scape with its patriotic refrains, almost invisible, powerlessly buffeted by the storms of history.

Perhaps this ironic reading is the product of today's political consciousness, however, for in *On Photography*, Sontag uses WRA images in particular as her example of how the "meaning" of photographs is not stable but contextual. She suggests that the politics of the 1960s allowed "many Americans, . . . looking at the photographs Dorothea Lange took of Nisei on the West Coast being transported to internment camps in 1942, to recognize their subject for what it was—a crime committed by the government against a large group of American citizens. Few people who saw those photographs in the 1940s could have had so unequivocal a reaction; the grounds for such a judgment were covered over by the pro-war consensus. Photographs cannot create a moral position, but they can reinforce one—and can help build a nascent one." In fact, whatever the photographer's intentions, the photograph's meanings are contingent and contextual. As Martha Sandweiss points out, "the original artist often could not control the associations that adhered to his picture by the time it reached a public audience." The moral and historical influence of a photograph—whether of a young woman kneeling by a body at Kent State, of an (allegedly staged) group of soldiers raising a flag at Iwo Jima, or of a row of blindfolded Taliban prisoners at Guantánamo Bay—is the result of its circulation: it has been chosen for reproduction—by magazine editors, newspeople, television producers, government officials, academics—either because it tells the story they wish to tell or because it seems to embody a self-contained story. As Sandweiss says, photography has seemed "uniquely suited to capturing those fleeting moments that emblematized or distilled complex activities," but the tendency to focus on "the individual image" as representing a "significant decisive moment" creates a historical record heavily dependent upon symbolism.[7]

There *are* images in which, to quote Lucy Lippard from another context, the "photograph becomes the people photographed," in which the internees have been "freed from the 'ethnographic present'—that patronizing frame that freezes personal and social specifics into generalization. . . . They are 'present' in part because of their undeniable personal presence." Many appear in Ansel Adams's *Born Free and Equal*. In this book, published in 1944 in the midst of the war, Adams had a clear political generalization to make: he was determined to represent internees as "loyal Americans." The man in figure 6 takes up a full page, but his name is not revealed. Consistent with one of Adams's major themes—the Nikkei's varied occupations and work ethic—the caption is "A Woodworker." Yet Bert K. Namura —as he was later identified—projects an "undeniable personal presence" and individuality.[8] Although Adams certainly seeks to make a statement, his subjects gaze back and take control of the photograph. Perhaps demonstrating the truth of Sontag's observation, *Born Free and Equal* is difficult to find because copies were publicly burned in protest.[9]

Yet comparing Adams to another Manzanar photographer reveals the differences between an insider's and outsider's view. Most of my earlier images are of the assembly process rather than life in internment camps. Photographers were restricted in what they were allowed to photograph in the camps, "forbidden to photograph the guard towers, the guards, or the barbed wire." In an ingenious reading, Armor and Wright suggest Adams responded to the restrictions by implication. Figure 7, *City in the Desert*, they argue, "implies the existence of the guard towers, because it was taken from one."[10]

11.6 Ansel Adams, *A Woodworker* (Bert K. Namura).
Library of Congress no. A35 tol M445B 303235.

Yet a photograph exists of one of the Manzanar towers, taken by the camp's resident photographer, internee Toyo Miyatake. At a time when Japanese Americans were forbidden even to own cameras, let alone bring them into the camps, Miyatake, who had worked for years as a professional photographer in Los Angeles, sneaked a lens into Manzanar and built his own wooden camera, initially taking shots secretly. In figure 8, the focus is on the interior life, on the subjective private response to public events; when the gaze is turned outward, the viewer looks through the eyes of experience and sees the world from within, as we can see in Miyatake's shot of the symbol of power that dominated his daily view in Manzanar.[11]

Miyatake's title, *Watchtower*, focuses our attention on the idea of surveillance—and, following Foucault, the concept of discipline—not surprisingly a dominant theme in internment art. The technological circle at the top of the tower, echoing the moon in the background, is a spotlight,

11.7 Ansel Adams, *City in the Desert.*
Library of Congress no. A351 Tol 3M 04 BX 303235.

suggesting exposure. Yet the watchtowers—and there are many more in paintings, such as George Matsusaboro Hibi's *Watch Tower* and Kenjiro Nomura's *Guard Tower*—manage to reverse Foucault's concept of surveillance. The internees do not internalize the position of authority. They look up, out, expressing a subjectivity resistant to, indeed reversing, governmental scrutiny. The dominating phallic images of surveillance against an empty landscape lead inevitably to the question, Who (or what) is being guarded from whom? They remind viewers of images where two photographers take aim at each other; but they also recall W. E. B. DuBois's perceptive description of how the minority American lives in a world "which yields him no true self-consciousness, but only lets him see himself through the revelation of the other world. It is a peculiar sensation, this double-consciousness, this sense of always looking at one's self through the eyes of others, of measuring one's soul by the tape of a world that looks on in amused contempt and pity." [12]

The watchtower images spotlight the doubled viewpoint that runs throughout internment art. Many themes come together in the story of Kango Takamura, who drew figure 9, *Our Guard in the Watchtower Became a Spring Baseball Fan*, while "detained" in a prison camp at Santa Fe. Trained as

11.8 Toyo Miyatake, *Watchtower*. Reproduced in *Our World*, ed. Diane Honda.
Reproduced courtesy of the Miyatake Family.

a photographer, Takamura worked as a photo retoucher in RKO Studios in Hollywood. He was sent to the prison camp because before Pearl Harbor he had agreed to sell a Japanese friend a surplus movie camera from the studio. Under surveillance by the FBI, he was accused of selling the camera to the Japanese Army and arrested. In an interview after the war, the man who "touched up" film described the complex negotiations he made as he attempted to capture his point of view: "As you know, we cannot use any camera. So I thought sketching's all right. But I was afraid not supposed to sketch. Maybe government doesn't like that I sketch. . . . So I work in a very

11.9 Kango Takamura, *Our Guard in the Watchtower Became a Spring Baseball Fan.*
JARP collection, Department of Special Collections,
Charles E. Young Research Library, UCLA.

funny way purposely, made these funny pictures. . . Little by little, I sketch
more like a photograph." [13]

Along with the guard towers, the WRA also erased the barbed-wire fences
from the public record, refusing to allow photographs of them, but internees found a way to comment, sometimes satirically, on their containment. In *Farewell to Manzanar*, for instance, Jeanne Wakatsuki Houston describes her brother Woody's "American Swing Band," who sing—

> Oh, give me land, lots of land
> Under starry skies above,
> Don't fence me in.
> Let me ride through the wide
> Open country that I love
> Don't fence me in. [14]

With her typical wit, Okubo comments, "When the evacuation came, I
said, 'God has answered my prayers.' All my friends asked why don't I go
East instead of going to Camp. I said, 'No, I'm going camping.'" Okubo,
who saw black comic ironies everywhere, has taught me to see them too.

11.10 Chiura Obata, *Regulations*.
Reproduced courtesy of the Obata Family.

One of the most interesting ironies is that those largely unpopulated, "desolate," hard-to-reach areas favored by the War Relocation Agency for internment camps are now favored locations for backcountry camping trips, memorialized in snapshots. Like Okubo, other internees commented ironically on those old western standbys turned into nationalistic symbols, spacious skies and mountain majesties, through the way they framed them. In figure 10, Chiura Obata's *Regulations*, the fence denies the woman and her children access to the space of the national imaginary, squeezing them into a constricted corner, the strong diagonal emphasizing divisions within the nation, yet they assert their presence by dominating the foreground.[15]

11.11 Estelle Ishigo, *Boys with Kite*.
Reproduced courtesy of JARP collection, Department of Special Collections,
Charles E. Young Research Library, UCLA.

If mountains characteristically symbolize freedom in American mythology, here we see sharp, barbed boundaries bifurcating the space, emblems of division, reminding me of the history of barbed wire in the West, of the border fence that extends into the ocean at Tijuana, of Matthew Shepherd's crucifixion on a fence in "The Equality State." Yet some challenge the fence and what it symbolizes, as do the young boys in figure 11, Estelle Ishigo's *Boys with Kite*. In an address at Topaz Art School in 1943, George Matsusaboro Hibi claimed a symbolic role for the mountains: "Training in art maintains high ideals among our people, for its object is to prevent their minds from remaining on the plains, to encourage the human spirit to dwell high above the mountains." [16] The fence blocks the boys' aspirations, but like most immigrants, they are ready to climb over the obstacles constructed by racism and nationalism.

Like the guard towers and fences, the camera becomes an instrument of surveillance and control throughout internment literature. Yoshiko Uchida's father had clearly been under surveillance by the FBI before Pearl Harbor, since he was one of the Issei arrested on December 8, 1941, and taken immediately to a prison camp in Montana. As he and others were interviewed about their "loyalties," Uchida tells us, "some were photographed full-face only, while others were photographed in profile as well, and it was immediately rumored that those photographed twice would be detained as hostages." With no accurate information and no control over their own movements, Uchida's family appropriately saw the government as all powerful and attempted to interpret its inexplicable actions: they took as a hopeful sign that he was "one of those who had been photographed only once." [17] Indeed, Dwight Uchida was eventually allowed to join his family at Topaz—but no one knew why he was transferred when others were not.

We can infer Dwight Uchida's experience from figure 12. Because he answered "no, no" to questions 19 and 20 on the "loyalty questionnaire," Kosaka Takaji was sent from Topaz to Tule Lake, by 1943 transformed from an "internment camp" to a prison for those the WRA planned to "repatriate" to Japan. As did Franz Boas in his photographs of American Indian prisoners and Louis Agassiz in photographs of African Americans, WRA officials apparently sought to define identity through measurement. In fact, fear of passing had been a recurrent theme throughout the war. As early as December 22, 1941, Life magazine devoted an article to "How to Tell Japs from the Chinese." [18] Their advice was apparently deemed ineffective since one of the most repeated justifications for internment was that white Americans could not "distinguish between loyal and disloyal Japanese"—remarks that read, in context, like polite versions of "they all look alike." Three distinguished lawyers asked by Attorney General Biddle to express their opinions on the constitutionality of evacuation argued in a memorandum in 1942 that "since the Occidental eye cannot readily distinguish one Japanese resident from another, effective surveillance of the movements of particular Japanese residents suspected of disloyalty is extremely difficult if not practically impossible." Yet Germans and Italians did not have to be interned because "the normal Caucasian countenances of such persons enable the average American to recognize particular individuals by distinguishing minor facial characteristics." (The lawyer responsible for this argument, Benjamin V. Cohen, "with tears in his eyes," later showed a colleague "a newspaper picture of a little Japanese American boy leaning out of the evacuation train window and waving an American flag.") [19] In 1943 the WRA was still having difficulty telling Nikkei apart and so took photographs like figure 12 in an effort to obstruct "troublemakers" from "passing" as "loyal Japanese" and to keep track of those repatriated in case they ever attempted to return from Japan.

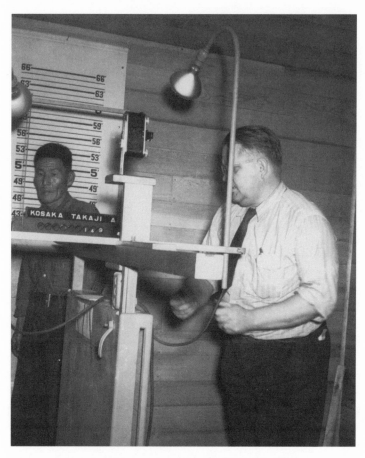

11.12 Photographer unknown, *Kosaka Takaji.*
War Relocation Authority, National Archives no. 210-G-16G-20.

Once again, Okubo recognized the implications of such photographic
practices and satirized them in her illustrations, anticipating current theoretical writers like Tagg. Figure 13 comes from near the end of her book, as
she is photographed before she is allowed to leave the camp. Here Okubo
shows the use to which the U.S. government puts photography: as a means
of keeping track of those whose place in the body politic is somehow suspect. She draws herself as the object of a mug shot. The framing device resembles an instrument of torture—or perhaps a box into which every face
must be disciplined to fit. Of what is she accused? Her narrative caption

11.13 Miné Okubo, Untitled drawing from *Citizen 13660* (page 207).
Reproduced courtesy of Seiko Buckingham.

reads: "After plowing through the red tape, through the madness of packing again, I attended forums on 'How to Make Friends' and 'How to Behave in the Outside World.' I was photographed."[20] Just in case she didn't know how to behave in the outside world . . .

Like Miyatake, however, Okubo also turns the gaze around. In figure 14, we watch her watching the spies: "Day and night Caucasian camp police walked their beats within the center. ("Caucasian" was the camp term for non-evacuee workers.) They were on the lookout for contraband and for suspicious actions."[21] Here, prisoners behave suspiciously by playing a popular card game, "Go," which was outlawed by camp officials who considered it gambling. Throughout *Citizen 13660* Uchida challenges the way others saw and represented her: she includes herself in each of her drawings, thus claiming her right to self-representation and providing herself with a sympathetic gaze—and in the worst conditions she never presents herself or others as pitiful. In her drawings she effectively resists "double consciousness," always looking at herself through her own eyes.

11.14 Miné Okubo, Untitled drawing from Citizen 13660 (page 60).
Reproduced courtesy of Seiko Buckingham.

As Okubo and Uchida demonstrate, the critique of photographic representations of internment I have developed was anticipated by internees themselves. For instance, early in *Desert Exile*, Uchida comments on the Issei's "great propensity for taking formal photographs to commemorate occasions ranging from birthdays and organizational get-togethers to weddings and even funerals. I suppose this was the only way they could share the event with their families and friends in Japan, but it also resulted in many bulging albums in our households." Images like figure 15 and passages like this one "normalize" the Issei, containing their "difference"— they are still connected to Japan—within the frame of their middle-class American ordinariness. Photos of Uchida in a kimono and playing with her dog, "Laddie," presented together on the same page, reinforce the same duality (fig. 16). These images operate in several ways in *Desert Exile*. As Marianne Hirsch suggests in *Family Frames*, family albums explore the "space of contradiction between the myth of the ideal family and the lived reality of family life," showing us more readily "what we wish our family to be" than "what it is not." In Uchida's family album, the pre-war photographs offer a prelapsarian vision of the Uchida family, underscored by the

11.15 Unknown photographer, *Uchida Family Portrait.*
Reproduced courtesy of Bancroft Library, University of California, Berkeley.

11.16 Unknown photographer.
Yoshiko Uchida in Kimono and *Yoshiko Uchida with Her Dog, Laddie.*
Reproduced courtesy of Bancroft Library, University of California, Berkeley.

text, a recurrent motif in internment art. In the early 1940s, for instance, Henry Sugimoto painted several versions of an image he called "My Papa." Using national imagery as ironically and effectively as did Lange, Sugimoto paints in the background a lushly productive truck farm in central California; in the foreground, a man clad in overalls is led away from his crying family by two suited men. Into the prelapsarian pastoral enter the agents of the omnipotent government—and the Nikkei are exiled from Eden. Uchida highlights the contradiction between the myth of the ideal family and the lived reality of family life, but like Sugimoto, she demonstrates that the contradiction is the result of historical, not psychological, forces.[22]

As she lost control of her freedom of movement, so did Uchida lose control over her visual self-representation after her family's internment at Tanforan and Topaz. The "reality" of family life is suggested by an unattributed Lange image of an unidentified young woman in a doorway to a stable at Tanforan. As we turn the pages of *Desert Exile*, moving from conventional private photographs to another FSA photograph of a newsstand, the headlines screaming "OUSTER OF ALL JAPS IN CALIFORNIA NEAR," we learn that the family album could not contain the Issei's and Nisei's "difference," and we trace the disjunction between the private story and the public text—in this case a newspaper headline—and recognize how entangled they are, what they reveal. As Jo Spence and Patricia Holland point out, "Family photography can operate at [the] junction between personal memory and social history."[23]

Negotiating between the private and the public, writers like Uchida nevertheless use official public documents—photographs, letters, internment orders, proclamations, laws—to authenticate what happened, to provide "proof." My own photographic story demonstrates that Sontag is right when she suggests that photographs can "furnish evidence," particularly of suppressed histories. I was born in 1951 in Salinas, California, in a coastal valley about ninety miles south of San Francisco. If you haven't heard of Salinas, next time you buy head lettuce or cauliflower, look at its wrapper; check out the source of your basket of strawberries. The Salinas Valley produces a substantial portion of the United States' winter vegetables. Salinas is best known for having—some claim—the world's largest rodeo and the world's longest underground river.

In 1941 Salinas had a population of about 15,000; some 2,000 Nikkei lived in the Salinas Valley, the largest ethnic population, many of them successful farmers. Salinas was the home base of the influential Growers and Shippers Vegetable Association, which had long actively fueled anti-Japanese sentiments and actions. In 1941 they recognized an opportunity to get rid of their competition and sent representatives to Washington to lobby for internment: "We're charged with wanting to get rid of the Japs for selfish reasons," said Austin Anson. "We might as well be honest. We do. It's a question of whether the white man lives on the Pacific Coast or the brown men. They came into this valley to work, and they stayed to take over." The association president, E. M. Seifert Jr., argued that "for the protection of future generations of Californians and Americans, no Japanese, even though he be born in America, should be permitted to own land."[24] In 1943 the Salinas Chamber of Commerce conducted a questionnaire of approximately 775 residents. Asked "how many persons [their] vote definitely represents," they claimed to speak for over ten times that number. The central question was, "Do you believe it desirable that Japanese who are considered loyal to the United States be permitted to return to the Pacific Coast states during the war?" The survey includes only one "yes" answer, from attorney George D. Pollack. Not surprisingly, as historian Sandy Lydon says, by "all accounts, for the returning Japanese community, the Salinas Valley was the worst." By 1950 only 162 Nikkei had returned to Salinas.[25]

Despite winning the "Daughters of the American Revolution" American history award in junior high school in 1965, I was well into my twenties before I found out about the internment of Japanese Americans.

Many years later, in 1997, I was doing primary research on internment in the National Archives. Reading the Poston, Arizona, yearbook, I noticed that most of the seniors would have graduated from my own high school, Salinas High, had they not been interned. Looking at their faces, I realized suddenly that they were my father's classmates. He would have graduated with them in 1945, had he not run off to join the Merchant Marines and been sent to Japan as part of the occupation force.

The next day I went to the Library of Congress to look at Farm Security Administration and War Relocation Administration photographs. One folder of Russell Lee's photos was labeled "Salinas." As I looked at the photos, I saw that there had been an assembly camp in Salinas, at the famous rodeo grounds. Lee took numerous photos of the Salinas Armory, where the Nikkei were assembled—and where my 1969 graduation dance was held. Figure 17, one of Lee's shots from May 1942, shows Salinas Valley Nikkei waiting to be bused to the rodeo grounds.

11.17 Russell Lee, Salinas CA, May 1942.
Japanese Americans waiting for transportation to reception center for evacuees
from certain West Coast areas under United States Army war emergency order
[inside Salinas Armory Building]. Farm Securities Administration Collection,
Library of Congress negative no. 72498-D.

That night I called home and asked some questions I had never thought
to ask. Yes, my father had had a number of friends who were interned; one
had taught him to play bridge. Yes, my mother knew about the rodeo
grounds. My much-beloved grandfather had helped to build the barracks
there.

As I mentioned, the Salinas Valley is defined by its best-known geographical feature, the world's longest underground river, which provided
the title for the only history of Salinas I'd read until I encountered the yearbook and Lee's photographs. Only through the intervention of photographs
did I finally read of Salinas's long underground history. As Laura Wexler
points out, photographs can "expose alternative histories." [26]

Yet FSA and WRA photographs, including several by Lee, in the photographic archive in the Library of Congress and National Archives, can "furnish evidence" for various stories and storytellers. On that same research
trip, I came upon figures 18, 19, 20. As John Berger puts it, photographs are

11.18 Russell Lee, Los Angeles CA, April 1942.
The evacuation of Japanese Americans from West Coast areas under U.S. Army
war emergency order. Waving good-bye to friends and relatives who are leaving
for Owens Valley. Farm Securities Administration Collection,
Library of Congress negative no. 13291-M4.

11.19 Photographer unknown, Arcadia CA, April 1942.
All baggage is inspected before newcomers enter the
Santa Anita Park assembly center for evacuees of Japanese ancestry.
Official OWI photograph, National Archives, D-5067.

11.20 Photographer unknown, Lone Pine CA, May 1942.
Three Japanese American girls with suitcases who have just arrived by train
from Elk Grove and who will be transported by bus from Lone Pine to Manzanar,
a War Relocation Authority center where they will remain for the duration of the
war. Records of the War Relocation Authority, National Archives no. D-531.

"irrefutable as evidence, but weak in meaning." What do these images "mean"? As Berger and others point out, titles or captions are often applied to photographs to stabilize meaning. The captions provided by most government-sponsored photographers were neutral, letting the images speak for themselves. For figure 18, for instance, Lee provided these words: "The evacuation of Japanese-Americans from West Coast areas under the U.S. Army war emergency order. Waving good-bye to friends and relatives who are leaving for Owens valley." [27] While even this understated caption points to the contradictions the photograph tacitly records between smiling faces in the foreground, in line with the disinterested symbol of power, and the somber faces in the background, apparently less cheerful about "waving good-bye to friends and relatives," Uchida and other internee writers offer much more explicit captions to dispute interpretations of the photographic record.

Internee writers use photographs to confront their readers with "reality," but at the same time they undermine the authority of such public representations. In *Nisei Daughter*, Monica Sone exposes the "truth" captured by photographs: "Newspaper photographers with flash-bulb cameras pushed busily through the crowd. One of them rushed up to our bus, and asked a young couple and their little boy to step out and stand by the door for a shot. They were reluctant, but the photographers were persistent and at length they got out of the bus and posed, grinning widely to cover their embarrassment. We saw the picture in the newspaper shortly after and the caption underneath it read, 'Japs good-natured about evacuation.'" The photographer is manipulative, but the author of the caption, ignorant of cultural differences, supremely confident of his ability to imagine the emotions of others, and certainly aware of what would sell papers, provides an interpretation so patently absurd that Sone lets it speak for itself. While an onlooker herself, she feels no need to describe the reality of the young couple's feelings. Yet implicitly she suggests how photographs often cannot record the discrepancies between the public face and private self. In another version of the same scene, this time from the inside, Mitsuye Yamada makes that point more explicit in a poem called "Evacuation": "As we boarded the bus / bags on both sides . . . / the *Seattle Times* / photographer said / Smile! / so obediently I smiled / and the caption the next day / read: / Note smiling faces / a lesson to Tokyo." [28]

Internment texts are filled with passages and imagery calling our attention to differences between representations from without and from within—whether in images or words—to the erasure of private subjectivity in public exposures. In *Desert Exile*, Uchida describes "a friend" who told her "that the Army had come to take films of her mess hall, removing the Japanese cooks and replacing them with white cooks for the occasion. She was so infuriated by this deception that she refused to go to her mess hall to eat while the films were being made." This scene recalls an earlier anecdote that records her self-consciousness about her erasure from groups associated with nationalistic identity. She is the only Japanese American girl in a "Girl Reserve" unit at her junior high school when a photographer comes to take a picture for the local newspaper: "The photographer casually tried to ease me out of the picture, but one of my white friends just as stubbornly insisted on keeping me in. I think I was finally included, but the realization of what the photographer was trying to do hurt me more than I ever admitted to anyone." Her use of photographs in her text and her editorial comments on them illustrate how, in Alan Trachtenberg's words, photographs "shift and slide in meaning": "They may seem to offer solid evidence that objects and people exist, but do they guarantee what such things *mean*? The lesson of the photograph, as early photographers came quickly to learn, was that meanings are not fixed, that values cannot be taken for granted, that what an image shows depends on how and where and when, and by whom, it is seen." [29] Exposing the ways the public record misrepresented and erased their bodies and their feelings, Sone, Yamada, Uchida, and Okubo let us know that seeing should not be believing and does not necessarily lead to understanding.

In many ways, they seek to show us what the images mean to them. With their sensitivity to doubled points of view, from outside and inside, internment writers also recognize the power of photographs as repositories of memory. Anthony Lee suggests that "we should see the needs and desires of the less represented as structuring absences [that] appear in the fissures, emphases, [and] ellipses" of the photograph. As in my story about Salinas's unspoken history, photographs sometimes seem to speak through silence. In *Obasan*, the narrator has "no words" from her mother, who vanished in a trip to Japan just before the war began, only "old photographs" from which she pieces together her past. Wakako Yamauchi, who worked as a photo processor to support her writing after she left the camps, sees in "old photographs of the mass evacuation . . . the mirror of our tragedy." To avoid what DuBois describes as "always looking at one's self through the eyes of others, . . . measuring one's soul by the tape of a world that looks on in amused contempt and pity," many "remain silent about our camp experience," she suggests, to "ask that you not indulge us with pity, neither then nor now. The fact of our survival is proof of our valor. And that is enough." [30]

Internees often left their history underground. Years after living at Manzanar, Jeanne Wakatsuki Houston associated even a photographer with "evidence" of what had happened to her. "In 1966," she writes, "I met a Caucasian woman who had worked for one year as a photographer at Manzanar. I could scarcely speak to her. I desperately wanted to, but all my questions stuck in my throat. This time it was not the pain of memory. It was simply her validation that all those things had taken place." Like Yamauchi, Houston remained silent about her camp experience for many years. Only when she turned to an "old 1944 yearbook put together at Manzanar High School" could she face the past and begin to tell her story. "It documented the entire camp scene," she says, "the graduating seniors, the guard towers, the Judo pavilion, the creeks I used to wade in, my family's barracks. As the photos brought that world back, I began to dredge up feelings that had lain submerged since the forties. I began to make connections I had previously been afraid to see." [31]

Through its "documentation" of the "entire camp scene," the yearbook calls forth memories, feelings, connections, subjective responses that flow beneath the surface of the photographs. Houston richly suggests these subjective responses, and the understanding she comes to, through *descriptions* of the photographs that led her to see the connections she "had previously been afraid to see." She mentions several images from the yearbooks, but three seem especially suggestive. The first is overtly political and activist: just as the camps closed, "the high school produced a second yearbook, *Valediction 1945*, summing up its years in camp. The introduction shows a page-wide photo of a forearm and hand squeezing pliers around a length of taut barbed wire strung beneath one of the towers" (fig. 21). Houston lets the political message speak for itself, but her descriptions of the images on the final pages of the 1943–44 yearbook, both taken by Toyo Miyatake, elliptically convey the subjective connections and ambiguities she finds in her past. "Finally," she says, there are "two large blowups, the first of a high tower with a searchlight against a Sierra backdrop." This is figure 8, Miyatake's "Watchtower," which I've already discussed as an image of oppressive surveillance by the all-powerful government; along with the fences, the watchtower served as a major symbol of the Nikkei's imprisonment. Yet the image Houston describes in most detail presents an "alternative history" of camp life. It was a two-page endsheet, showing a wide path that curves among rows of elm trees. White stones border the path. Two dogs are following an old woman in gardening clothes as she strolls along. She is in the middle distance, small beneath the trees, beneath the snowy peaks. It is winter. All the elms are bare. The scene is both stark and comforting. This path leads toward one edge of camp, but the wire is out of sight, or out of focus. The tiny woman seems very much at ease. She and her tiny dogs seem almost swallowed by the landscape, or floating in it (fig. 22). [32]

In Houston's reading of this final image, "both stark and comforting," Toyo Miyatake focuses not on the "wire" but on a woman in a private moment of reflection, "very much at ease." He does not expose her, violate her privacy, but he does reveal to Houston—and she to me—her powerful self-possession. Speaking through silence to Miyatake and then to Houston,

11.21 Toyo Miyatake, Pliers cutting wire at Manzanar.
Reproduced in *Our World*, ed. Diane Honda.
Reproduced courtesy of the Miyatake Family.

who makes me see with her eyes, the "tiny woman" makes a big claim for the right to self-definition.

For Houston, photographs do indeed furnish evidence, but they prompt emotional responses and personal understanding rather than provide historical documentation. Through readings of these three photographs, she claims multiple positions of power, connecting the political and the personal: the power to turn the searchlight around, back on a reprehensible and illegal governmental act; the power to cut through the literal and symbolic barriers of racism; and the power to reject being represented as a

11.22 Toyo Miyatake, Woman walking dogs.
Reproduced in *Our World*, ed. Diane Honda.
Reproduced courtesy of the Miyatake Family.

stereotypical object of pity or a victim. Their meaning, she seems to suggest, is hers to claim.

Aware that the meaning of photographs is created collaboratively, in a particular and ever-changing historical moment, Nikkei writers and artists develop photographic absences and offer alternative archives; describe photographs as duplicitous documents, revealing and concealing; gaze at them and critique them; reproduce them and resist them; re-frame and re-caption them in their own interpretations and words. They know that photographs can tell a story, many stories; they question whose stories they tell—and insist upon telling their own. Adding their captions and images to the national album produces a more capacious historical archive where no single photograph carries the weight of too much symbolic meaning, where Lange's vision of Manzanar is complicated and enhanced by Miyatake's.

Notes

1. Joy Kogawa, *Obasan* (New York: Doubleday, 1983), 85, 111; Miné Okubo, *Citizen 13660* (1946; reprint, Seattle: University of Washington Press, 1983), ix; Yoshiko Uchida, *The Invisible Thread* (Englewood Cliffs NJ: Julian Messner, 1991). The painting appears in a group of illustrations between pages 52 and 53.

2. I have struggled with terminology to describe the "camps." I consider them concentration camps, where innocent people were illegally imprisoned, without due process, but because that term is so thoroughly associated with the Holocaust, it is sometimes misleading, as it would be had I used it in my title. I have most often used the term "internment camps" or "camps" because that is the term used by the writers I discuss, but I have attempted to use strong verbs—"imprisoned" rather than "detained," for instance—to make clear what was really happening there. Susan Sontag, *On Photography* (New York: Delta, 1977), 5, 23.

3. Okubo, *Citizen 13660*, 12.

4. These three images are courtesy of the Library of Congress, as are figure 5 by Lange and figure 17 by Lee.

5. Anthony W. Lee, *Picturing Chinatown: Art and Orientalism in San Francisco* (Berkeley: University of California Press, 2001), 8; Gary Okihiro, *Margins and Mainstreams: Asians in American History and Culture* (Seattle: University of Washington Press, 1994), 151.

6. John Tagg, *The Burden of Representation: Essays on Photographies and Histories* (Minneapolis: University of Minnesota Press, 1993), 12.

7. Sontag, *On Photography*, 17; Martha A. Sandweiss, "Views and Reviews: Western Art and Western History," in *Under an Open Sky: Rethinking America's Western Past*, ed. William Cronon, George Miles, and Jay Gitlin (New York: Norton, 1992), 195; and Martha A. Sandweiss, "Undecisive Moments: The Narrative Tradition in Western Photography," in *Photography in Nineteenth-Century America*, ed. Martha A. Sandweiss (New York: Harry N. Abrams, 1991), 98.

8. Lucy Lippard, introduction to *Partial Recall*, ed. Lucy Lippard (New York: New Press, 1992), 35; Ansel Adams, *Born Free and Equal: The Story of Loyal Japanese-Americans* (New York: U.S. Camera, 1944), 43. Namura is identified by John Armor and Peter Wright in *Manzanar*, a history of the camp, accompanied by a collection of Adams's photographs, and with commentary by John Hersey (New York: Times Books, 1988), 37. Adams did not renew his copyright on *Born Free and Equal* and gave his images to the Library of Congress. The number for this image is A35 Tol 4M45B 303235.

9. Armor and Wright, "The Photographers of Manzanar," *Manzanar*, xviii.

10. Armor and Wright, "The Photographers of Manzanar," xx. *City in the Desert* appears on xix. In *Born Free and Equal*, it appears on 26–27 (Library of Congress number A351 Tol 3M04BX 303235).

11. Miyatake's *Watchtower* originally appeared in the 1944–45 Manzanar High School yearbook, *Valediction 1945*. It also appears near the end of the unpaginated reprint of the 1943–1944 *Manzanar, Our World*, along with other images from the 1944–45 yearbook and informational updates. The reprint was edited by Diane Yotsuya Honda, a high-school yearbook teacher. Copies are available directly from her at 8765 North Sierra Vista, Fresno CA 93720. I thank the family of Toyo Miyatake for permission to reproduce his photographs.

12. W. E. B. DuBois, *The Souls of Black Folk* (1903), in *The Oxford W. E. B. DuBois Reader*, ed. Eric J. Sundquist (New York: Oxford University Press, 1966), 102.

13. *Our Guard in the Watchtower* reproduced courtesy of UCLA Special Collections; Deborah Gesensway and Mindy Roseman, *Beyond Words: Images from America's Concentration Camps* (Ithaca: Cornell University Press, 1987), 119–20. Even today most Americans do not realize that the WRA created separate "prison camps" for men suspected of espionage; one was located at Santa Fe. Takamura was eventually transferred to Manzanar. After the war, he returned to his job at RKO studios, publicly welcomed back by the president, and worked there another twenty-five years.

14. Jeanne Wakatsuki Houston and James D. Houston, *Farewell to Manzanar* (Boston: Houghton Mifflin, 1973), 74. Because *Farewell* is a memoir about Jeanne's experience, I refer to her as the author for economy's sake.

15. Quoted in Gesensway and Roseman, *Beyond Words*, 66; I reproduce Obata's *Regulations* courtesy of the Obata family. For more Obata images, see *Topaz Moon: Chiura Obata's Art of the Internment*, ed. Kimi Kodani Hill (Berkeley: Heyday Books, 2000).

16. *Boys with Kite* reproduced courtesy of UCLA Special Collections. Ishigo was a Caucasian married to a Nikkei; she petitioned the government to be interned with him at Heart Mountain; the privately published *Lone Heart Mountain* contains her writings and sketches about life there. Quoted in Hill, *Topaz Moon*, 70.

17. Yoshiko Uchida, *Desert Exile: The Uprooting of a Japanese-American Family* (Seattle: University of Washington Press, 1982), 50–51.

18. Courtesy National Archives, photo no. 210-G-16G-20 (WRA Collection); the fullest exploration of the horrific events at Tule Lake is in Michi Nishiru Weglyn, *Years of Infamy: The Untold Story of America's Concentration Camps* (Seattle: University of Washington Press, 1976). Audrie Girdner and Anne Loftis, *The Great Betrayal: The Evacuation of the Japanese-Americans During World War II* (London: Collier-Macmillan, 1969), 11. Girdner and Loftis continue, "The faces portrayed were those of a benevolent Chinese public servant, Ong Wen-hao, and a Japanese warrior, General Hideki Tojo. After discussing physiological differences, the article concluded, 'An often sounder clue is facial expression, shaped by cultural, not anthropological, factors. Chinese wear rational calm of tolerant realists. Japs, like General Tojo, show humorless intensity of ruthless mystics.' Little wonder that some Japanese were reported to be wearing 'I am Chinese' buttons" (11).

19. Although this point was repeatedly made, this particular quote comes from Los Angeles county manager Wayne R. Allen, justifying "the dismissal of all county workers of Japanese descent," quoted in Peter Irons, *Justice at War: The Story of the Japanese Internment Cases* (Berkeley: University of California Press, 1983), 40–41, 54, 55.

20. Okubo, *Citizen 13660*, 207.

21. Okubo, *Citizen 13660*, 60.

22. Uchida, *Desert Exile*, 19, 36 (family photo), 37 (Kimono and Laddie); Uchida images reproduced courtesy of the Bancroft Library, University of California at Berkeley. Marianne Hirsch, *Family Frames: Photography, Narrative, and Postmemory* (Cambridge: Harvard University Press, 1997), 8. Sugimoto did many versions of this painting. One appears in Gesensway and Roseman, *Beyond Words*, 31.

23. Uchida, *Desert Exile*, 54; quoted in Hirsch, *Family Frames*, 13.

24. Quoted in Morton Grodzins, *Americans Betrayed: Politics and the Japanese Evacuation* (Chicago: University of Chicago Press, 1949), 27; quoted in Girdner and Loftis, *The Great Betrayal*, 104.

25. Document labeled "Salinas. Chamber of Commerce. Survey of Attitudes of Salinas Citizens toward Japanese-Americans During World War II" (R.979.476, Special Collections, John Steinbeck Library, Salinas, California); Sandy Lydon, *The Japanese in the Monterey Bay Region: A Brief History* (Capitola CA: Capitola Books, 1997), 27.

26. Laura Wexler, *Tender Violence: Domestic Visions in an Age of U.S. Imperialism* (Chapel Hill: University of North Carolina Press, 2000), 5.

27. John Berger, *Another Way of Telling* (New York: Pantheon, 1982), 92. The caption is attached to the photograph in the Library of Congress. According to James Curtis, Roy Striker, head of FSA photographic division, "had his photographers follow contemporary social science techniques in captioning their images. Subjects photographed, like citizens interviewed, remained anonymous" (*Mind's Eye, Mind's Truth:* FSA Photography Reconsidered [Philadelphia: Temple University Press, 1989], 49).

28. Monica Sone, *Nisei Daughter* (Seattle: University of Washington Press, 1953), 170–71; Mitsuye Yamada, *Camp Notes and Other Poems*, 2nd ed. (Latham NY: Kitchen Table/Women of Color Press, 1992), 13.

29. Uchida, *Desert Exile*, 92, 41; Alan Trachtenberg, *Reading American Photographs* (New York: Hill and Wang, 1989), 19–20.

30. Lee, *Picturing Chinatown*, 287; Kogawa, *Obasan*, 218; Wakako Yamauchi, preface to a poetry reading, quoted in Dorothy Ritsuko McDonald and Katherine Newman, "Relocation and Dislocation: The Writings of Hisaye Yamamoto and Wakako Yamauchi," in *Seventeen Syllables*, ed. King-Kok Cheung (New Brunswick NJ: Rutgers University Press, 1994), 130.

31. Houston, *Farewell to Manzanar*, 134, ix.

32. Houston, *Farewell to Manzanar*, 97, 74–75.

4. REIMAGINING PLACE

12. AUTHENTICITY, OCCUPANCY, AND CREDIBILITY

Rick Bass and the Rhetoric of Protecting Place

Scott Slovic

Thirteen or fourteen years ago, the state of Nevada switched to a new license plate on motor vehicles: it's white with blue lettering and faint local images of bighorn sheep, craggy mountains, and Joshua Trees. The funny thing is how residents of the state who own the previous simple blue license plate with white letters have, almost universally, kept those old plates, switching them from car to car as they update their personal transportation. There's something intriguing about this desire to demonstrate longevity, to state proudly through one's license plate, "I'm a long-timer, not a Johnny-come-lately." It's strange to think that people who've lived in that place less than a decade can presume to be longtime residents.

I notice a similar tendency whenever I'm with a group of strangers, such as a new group of students at the beginning of the semester, and self-introductions are made; invariably, a few people will announce, "I'm Tom so-and-so or I'm Linda such-and-such, and I'm a native Nevadan." It's as if nativeness—or long residency, the next best thing—is a special badge of honor in a state that had almost no stable Euro-American population a century ago (Las Vegas had a population of 40 in 1900) and where you're more likely to pass ghost towns, depopulated remnants of various mining booms and busts, than bustling, living communities when you drive the six hundred miles or so from the northern to the southern end of the state. So you'll have to forgive me for being so interested in this issue of occupancy and authenticity, this question of belonging. I've lived in Reno for nine years now. A newcomer in Nevada is in good company, but we know we're outsiders. This is an interesting dimension, in certain ways, of western environmental writing, too. And in this essay I'll try to begin probing this literary and cultural issue, first in a general way and then by examining the work of Rick Bass, one of the major contemporary environmental writers of the American West.

Many contemporary American environmental writers have come recently to think of themselves not merely as "nature writers" (with "nature" coding for "non-human") but rather as "community writers," artists who regard their work as an act of exploring and reforming *relationships* in the broadest sense of that word, encompassing both the human and the non-human. For writers in the American West, however, *community* is a vexed and complicated concept.

Unlike authors such as Robert Finch on Cape Cod or Scott Russell Sanders who lives in Bloomington, Indiana, western writers find themselves particularly compelled to come to terms with mobility and transience and new-residency in order to explain their roles as people speaking for and about such communities as the Yaak Valley in Montana and Finn Rock, Oregon. Charles Wilkinson, in *The Eagle Bird: Mapping a New West* (1992), points out that "communities in the West have less cohesiveness than any region in the country. Our towns lack the stability and sense of community found, for example, in villages in New England and the Midwest. To quote Patricia Nelson Limerick, . . . 'Indians, Hispanics, Asians, blacks, Anglos, business people, workers, politicians, bureaucrats, natives, and newcomers, we share the same region and its history, but we wait to be introduced.'"[1] Yet Wilkinson, after several pages of documenting the tendency toward community fragmentation and violent social conflict in the West, shifts into a more optimistic assertion as his chapter, called "Toward an Ethic of Place," continues:

> Still, we can ameliorate these problems. We deserve and can achieve more stable, tight-knit communities, communities bound together by the common love of this miraculous land, of this region the likes of which exists nowhere else on earth. We can do much better.
>
> We need to develop an ethic of place. It is premised on a sense of place, the recognition that our species thrives on the subtle, intangible, but soul-deep mix of landscape, smells, sounds, history, neighbors, and friends that constitute a place, a homeland. An ethic of place respects equally the people of a region and the land, animals, vegetation, water, and air. It recognizes that westerners revere their physical surroundings and that they need and deserve a stable, productive economy that is accessible to those with modest incomes. An ethic of place ought to be a shared community value and ought to manifest itself in a dogged determination to treat the environment and its people as equals, to recognize both as sacred, and to insure that all members of the community not just search for but insist upon solutions to fulfill that ethic.[2]

I quote at length because I find it intriguing that a law professor, in a book devoted to regional environmental law and policy, should argue so forcefully, so eloquently, for precisely the "ethic of place" that so many literary artists in the West are also seeking to articulate and advocate. Most readers of this book could, I'm sure, name a number of favorite western writers who routinely—and in some cases *incessantly*—devote themselves to evoking the "soul-deep mix of landscape, smells, sounds, history, neighbors, and friends" that Wilkinson mentions as the defining features of "place." Perhaps the reason western writers have been so stalwart in recent decades as supporters of the process of rethinking our relationship to the land is that many of these writers are themselves, in relative terms, newcomers to the places they write about—and the recentness of their arrival contributes both to the vigor of their engagement with fresh landscapes and, sometimes, to the palpable sense of insecurity they express when they find themselves speaking in defense of these new homelands. In spite of this newcomer's innocence and uneasiness, however, there is a striking attitude of responsibility and commitment—the zealous devotion of converts—in the way dozens of western environmental writers depict and explore and fight for the places they inhabit and visit.

This zeal—this intensity—has inspired many of these writers to seek new, surprising audiences for their work. Indeed, the earlier domains of literary expression have been exploded in recent years as various writers— Terry Tempest Williams, Robert Michael Pyle, David Quammen, Gary Nabhan, Rick Bass, Barry Lopez, and Gary Snyder, for example—have pushed their preoccupations with natural history and environmental conservation, sometimes aggressively apropos and sometimes arcane, into such unlikely forums as the pages of *House Beautiful* and the halls of Congress. The goal of this work is nothing short of revolution—a revolution in how Americans consider what it means to inhabit the planet, to occupy this globe in an authentic, meaningful, ethical way; and a revolution in what we regard as the proper place of literary language. Somehow, the naïve idealism and passionate excitement of the newcomer—an idealism and excitement that emerge even among western writers, like Terry Tempest Williams, who come from old western families—have inspired these authors to target the most impenetrable minds and pages and buildings for their words and ideas. A few years ago, I received from Terry a package of journal articles and a note that read, "Here is an example of how our work is infiltrating law reviews and legal briefs regarding public policy." To me, this implies a new

259

form of "literary occupancy"—a nascent inhabitation of legal discourse by the literary arts. More on this later. A few weeks after Terry's packet arrived, David Quammen, the Bozeman, Montana, science journalist, included the following statement to me in a long e-mail message: "Among the firmest of my professional convictions is that a writer who wants to influence how humans interact with landscape and nature should strive to reach as large an audience as possible and NOT preach to the converted. That means, for me, flavoring my work with entertainment-value, wrapping my convictions subversively within packages that might amuse and engage a large unconverted audience, and placing my work whenever possible in publications that reach the great unwashed."[3]

What I'd like to begin developing in this essay is an idea about the pervasive uncertainty in western environmental writing regarding sense of place and attachment to place and what I see as a parallel uncertainty about the "place" of literature in our culture, about the potential social ramifications of environmental literature. What is "authentic" literature? Where does literary expression properly belong and where does our society need story and image to defy conventions of discourse? I will conclude with an extended examination of the regional conflations and uncertainties that emerge in the stories and essays of one of the West's most prolific contemporary writers, Rick Bass, exploring how issues of occupancy and authenticity pertain to his efforts to protect wild places.

Readers may sense in western literature a certain defensiveness or an eager disclaiming of indigenousness. Bass, for instance, begins his first Yaak Valley book, *Winter: Notes from Montana* (1991), by scrambling to authenticate his prior contact with a Yaak-like place: "I'd been in the mountains before," reads the opening line of this book about his first winter in northwestern Montana. Barry Lopez, for his part, opens a 1995 essay entitled "Occupancy" by stating, "Sandra and I arrived in the spring of 1970," both confessing that he is not native to the McKenzie River Valley in Oregon where he resides and suggesting that, by western standards, he and his wife have been around awhile. Alison Deming, in her 1995 essay collection *Temporary Homelands*, explicitly avoids any claims to long-term residency, instead making a virtue of transience; "I wanted to write an honest book about my relationship with nature," she states, "not to offer theories or prescriptions for what that relationship ought to be. . . . I wanted to understand the places, events, and ideas in my own experience that seem most significant in shaping that relationship, and to explore the quality of reflection that certain loved places seem to induce. This book, finally, is about one thing—re-constructing an intimacy with nature. We live in a time of radical loss—loss of space, places, tribes, and species. Loss of a sense of belonging in and to a place. Loss of continuity and coherence." At the outset of his recent book *About This Life*, Lopez urges a young writer "to learn another language, to live with people other than her own, to separate herself from the familiar. Then, when she returns, she will be better able to understand why she loves the familiar, and will give us a fresh sense of how fortunate we are to share these things."[4] In a sense, Lopez is offering the advice that he would give to a younger version of himself, a blueprint for someone aspiring to become "a writer who travels." This transient sensibility not only reinforces one's attachment to the familiar, as he states, but constantly breaks the crusts of social conformity, the ruts of complacency, against which environmental writers, particularly in the West, are prone to militate. Travel itself is a way not only to gain new adventures and collect experience but to ritualize loss and disorientation, to force one's mind to create new maps of meaning. The mind thus destabilized and invigorated tends to see through established structures and patterns, even upon returning home.

Let me backtrack a bit and talk about the words *occupancy* and *authenticity*. *Occupancy* suggests the old dictionary in my office, implies not just physical presence in a particular place or building but *ownership*—even legal possession—of an object or a dwelling. *Authenticity*, on the other hand, implies reliability, genuineness, and validity. Much contemporary environmental writing in the West aims, in part, to validate the author as spokesperson for a particular place or community, often straining to overcome the historical fact of the author's newness and relative lack of legal or economic commitment to the place or community. Even more interesting, though, is the moral paradox that many of these writers encounter when they seek to assert their engagement with particular places while—more or less—avoiding the ethical faux pas, from the stereotypical "green" perspective, of land ownership and resource extraction. Despite the fact that many western writers, sooner or later, come to purchase plots of land and build houses—as Bass and his family have done in the Yaak, as Lopez has done alongside Oregon's McKenzie River, and as Gary Snyder has done on the western slope of the Sierra Nevadas—this is often done in the spirit of creating "temporary homelands," to borrow Alison Deming's locution. These writers don't view themselves as possessors and controllers of the places where they live but rather as co-inhabitants just passing through. Either that, or as

Snyder put it in a 1996 Jim Lehrer *News Hour* interview, the goal of such "occupancy" is to live an ecologically responsible life, a life devoted to the preservation of land and community, maintained as if one expected to be present for the next ten thousand years.

One of the great, brief articulations in recent western environmental writing of the moral dubiousness of "ownership" and occupancy in this region appears in the title essay of William Kittredge's 1987 collection, *Owning It All*: "The teaching mythology we grew up with in the American West is a pastoral story of agricultural ownership. The story begins with a vast innocent continent, natural and almost magically alive, capable of inspiring us to reverence and awe, and yet savage, a wilderness. A good rural people come from the East, and they take the land from its native inhabitants, and tame it for agricultural purposes, bringing civilization: a notion of how to live embodied in law. The story is as old as invading armies, and at heart it is a racist, sexist, imperialist mythology of conquest; a rationale for violence—against other people and against nature." [5] So what's the point of criticizing this mythology of agricultural ownership or any of the other western mythologies that have guided not only Kittredge's generation that came of age in the 1930s and 1940s but younger generations of westerners as well? What is the goal of a book like *Owning It All*?

Kittredge extends his criticism of the prevailing, traditional land ethic in the West as follows, indicating the practical goals of literature (his own writing and that of other contemporary authors): "In the American West we are struggling to revise our dominant mythology, and to find a new story to inhabit. Laws control our lives, and they are designed to preserve a model of society based on values learned from mythology. Only after re-imagining our myths can we coherently remodel our laws, and hope to keep our society in a realistic relationship to what is actual." We've got a chicken-and-egg scenario here. What takes priority, law or story, government or art and imagination? Kittredge, not surprisingly, argues that the imagination forges the cultural values that, in turn, lead to law and public policy. I believe the point of his critique of the dominant mythology of ownership and exploitation in the West, a critique that could surely be applied to any other region of the country, is to exhort himself and his fellow writers to understand the responsibility they bear in evoking their lives, their places, their visions of social reform. Authenticity, in this context, means taking responsibility. In his essay "Language, Law, and the Eagle Bird," also part of the 1992 book called *The Eagle Bird*, Charles Wilkinson, too, argues that a language revolution is one of the keys to achieving a revolution in environmental policy. "If the language among the people changes," he writes, "the language in the law books will change. One task is to add new kinds of words to balance out a vocabulary now dominated by board feet and cost-benefit analyses. The other task is to enrich existing words. When we hear a forester comment that timber harvesting will 'sustain the productivity of the land,' we should ask, 'Productivity for voles?' When enough westerners understand that concept, law and policy will fall into line."[6] How shall westerners in general, Americans more generally still, as well as people throughout the world begin to consider concepts and words such as "productivity" and "value" from the perspective of voles? We can begin to see an answer to this by reading Terry Tempest Williams's "A Man of Questions: A Tribute to Wallace Stegner," published in a 1997 issue of the University of Utah's *Journal of Land, Resources, and Environmental Law*; by examining how David Hoch and Will Carrington Heath begin their 1997 article "Tracking the ADC: Ranchers' Boon, Taxpayers' Burden, Wildlife's Bane" in the journal *Animal Law* by quoting the entirety of Williams's short essay "Redemption"; and by Williams's decision to print her cryptic, mythicized narrative "Bloodlines" in the small anthology, *Testimony*, that she and Stephen Trimble distributed to all members of the U.S. House and Senate in 1995. These writings by Williams are, on the whole, oblique and exploratory, full of questions rather than answers, poetry rather than measurements, uncertainty rather than certainty. When anthropologist Terre Satterfield and I conducted an interview in April 1998 with the ethnobotanist and nature writer Gary Nabhan, he told us he regards story as "a zone of tension," a form of language that facilitates understanding because it obstructs easy, linear thinking.

Authentic occupancy in the American West requires accepting our geography and our language as zones of tension. More and more western writers, including the various people I've mentioned here, are realizing that it is their responsibility—and by extension the responsibility of critics and teachers—to find ways of getting their language not only to occupy the minds of academics in classrooms and conference hotels but also to live in law journals and courtrooms and corporate boardrooms—and this is what's happening today.

As we speak, one of the major authors of the West continues to lift his voice in an effort to protect wild places and wild species in this region, but he does so from a stance of contingency and uncertainty, from a personal viewpoint that constantly raises questions of belonging and occupancy. Although Rick Bass has now lived in the Yaak Valley in the far northwestern corner of Montana for the past seventeen of his forty-six years, although people are far more likely to refer to him as a "Montana writer" than as a "southern writer," and although his books are not placed in the "Mississippi authors" section at Square Books in Oxford, Mississippi, Bass remains an artist for whom the southern experience and, more specifically, southern landscapes, are deeply generative. His environmental activism became a notable part of his life only after the move to Montana, and yet his southern origins remain unmistakable in his work. Doubts about Bass's "regional affiliation," so to speak, appear also in the recent scholarly literature, with Michael Kowalewski claiming him as a western author in *Reading the West: New Essays on the Literature of the American West* and Robert H. Brinkmeyer Jr. reclaiming him as a southern author in *Remapping Southern Literature: Contemporary Southern Writers and the West*. Brinkmeyer explains at length how Bass's view of western wilderness is, in a sense, part of the author's continuing process of releasing himself from and reconciling himself to his southern past. Regarding *Winter*, the critic states: "In a hopeful and ironic dismissal of the past, rare in Southern writing, Bass . . . wholeheartedly embraces the American dream of leaving history behind, of fleeing west into a new world of possibility and potentiality." What interests me, however, is the fact that Bass's westward migration is not merely a flight "into a new world of possibility and potentiality" but rather a process of gaining better, fiercer moral purchase on the interaction between American society and the natural world. By gaining a fresh, firm grip on his own relationship to the physical world, the author aspires to create for himself an authentic, believable voice. By moving geographically to the outer edge of American culture—not only from south to west but from city to remote mountains—Bass assumes the potent rhetorical role that George P. Landow, in *Elegant Jeremiahs*, attributes to the "sage." As Landow puts it, "The style, tone, and general presentation of the wisdom speaker derive from the fact that his often anonymous voice resides at a societal and cultural center; it purports to be the voice of society speaking its essential beliefs and assumptions. In contrast, the style, tone, and general presentation of the sage derive from the fact that his voice resides at the periphery; it is . . . an eccentric voice, one off center." [7]

In a strange and interesting way, Rick Bass's work combines the familiarity and acceptability of the "wisdom speaker" with the radical aggressiveness of the sage. He writes from the standpoint of a husband and a father and someone who loves his family and his home, but he also writes as someone who loves animals and wild, uncomfortable, and even (sometimes) ugly places. One of the central themes of Bass's work, both his fiction and his nonfiction, beginning with the 1985 work *The Deer Pasture* and continuing to the present, is the desire to find, to experience, to appreciate a "wild home." This is, of course, an oxymoron—it's a tension, an incompatibility, one of several that Bass lives with every day. Look through his work, and you'll see again and again various characters—or the author's various personae—both relishing wild, manic feats of energetic joy and hunkering down in quest of a safe haven to call "home." Where might it be possible to find a "wild home"? How might it be possible? These are what I take to be the questions at the core of this writer's work.

When I interviewed Bass in 1993 for the journal *Weber Studies*—an interview reprinted in Alan Weltzien's book *The Literary Art and Activism of Rick Bass*—there was one particular section of that conversation that's always stuck out in my mind because of the weirdness of what Bass said and because I had to wonder if it were actually true—even possible. We were discussing his writing about the Yaak (remember he'd lived there only six years or so at the time, and his books about the Yaak, starting with *Winter* in 1991, had been out for no more than two years), and I asked if he was concerned that by publicizing the Yaak he might lure hordes of Winnebagoes into his remote, rugged part of the world—or worse yet, if his writing might inspire the hordes to clamor for new roads into the Kootenai region of northwest Montana and southeast British Columbia. So I asked if all of this celebratory writing about the Yaak uses this particular area as a "kind of place, not as a homing beacon." [8]

He responded, "Oh goodness, yeah. It's ugly. I mean, it's a homing beacon for me because it's home, but it's ugly, it's not a place people want to go visit. It's got clearcuts and it rains a lot and you can't see anything, there are no vistas. It's an ugly place to visit—it's an okay place to live. It's a perfect place for me to live because it's just what fits my warped mind, the twisted contours of brain—what are those things called?—the loops and coils. . . . Anyways, it fits, it's a good fit for me, but it probably wouldn't be for anyone else in the world." [9] I've never forgotten the idea, expressed here, that there might be a single, perfect place for a particular individual—the right place for the right mind. I try to imagine, perhaps over-literally, how the clearcuts and rain and the lack of vistas somehow "fit" the "loops and coils" of this one man's brain. It occurs to me that this is a statement from someone trying very hard to justify and explain, for himself as much as for anyone else, why he came to choose, with the whole world a possibility, this particular place to make his home. He's articulating a sort of myth of the perfect home. To me, though, even his brief, derogatory description of the Yaak in the above statement sounds a lot like a description of where he'd just come from, the interlaced pastures and dense woods of Mississippi.

Now I want to throw out a phrase, "geographical isomorphism," that I used quite a bit when I was studying the distinguished German explorer Alexander von Humboldt. Humboldt traversed the globe in the late 1700s and through the first several decades of the nineteenth century, from the Orinoco Basin in South America to the steppes of Siberia, and one of his main interests was the extraordinary similarities among certain kinds of places in vastly different parts of the world—the llanos of South America, the Great Plains of North America, the steppes of Russia, and the grasslands of South Africa, for instance. I think it's plausible to argue that, for Rick Bass, the Yaak Valley of northwest Montana is a wild (and more mountainous) replica of the overly populated and domesticated landscape of Mississippi, and Mississippi represented a less urban, somewhat hillier version of the woods and bayous he grew up with in Houston. Far from being a "Montana author," truly wedded to the distinctiveness of the intermountain West, Bass is a southern writer, someone whose taste for place was formed in Houston, the Texas Hill Country two hundred miles west of Houston, and the mixed pine and hardwood forests of Mississippi and Alabama, who eventually lighted out for a wilder version of his southern home.

To offer just a brief recap for those of you not familiar with Bass's geographical movements, he lived primarily in Houston, Texas, while growing up, with regular November hunting trips to Gillespie County, where he developed much of his affinity for both the natural world and storytelling. In the mid-1970s, as a high-school senior, Bass visited Logan, Utah, in order to take a scholarship test at Utah State—something about Logan and Logan Canyon captivated him, and he decided to attend college at Utah State. He graduated with a degree in petroleum geology in 1980 and took a job in Jackson, Mississippi. The job in petroleum prospecting involved a lot of desk work but also some tramping around in the backwoods of east-central Mississippi and northern Alabama. Bass, who'd studied nature writing and literary nonfiction with Thomas J. Lyon at Utah State, began writing in a serious way while he was living in the Jackson area in the early 1980s—so he was immersed in the Mississippi landscape as he worked to re-imagine himself as an artist. He relates this process in his 1999 book, *Brown Dog of the Yaak*. In the summer of 1987 Bass and his then-girlfriend, Elizabeth Hughes, a Mississippian, got in his old truck, together with their two hound dogs, and drove west and north until they found a place that felt right—they stopped just short of the Canadian border. (This is all described in the book *Winter*.) For four years they lived as caretakers at the Fix Ranch in the Yaak Valley, before buying land in 1991 and building their house on it. More recently, using money brought in by selling his personal papers to the natural-history special collection at Texas Tech University (where his papers now join those of Barry Lopez, William Kittredge, David Quammen, Pattiann Rogers, and other major environmental writers), Bass has bought additional land surrounding the lot purchased in 1991, further insolating himself and his family from expected land development in the area.

Bass's early books—*The Deer Pasture, Wild to the Heart, Oil Notes*, and *The Watch*—are mostly about his family's Hill Country hunting lease ("the deer pasture"), Houston, and fictional and actual adventures in Mississippi, Alabama, and North Carolina. Repeatedly, in the nonfiction, we see Bass physically located in one place while dreaming of another. Often this takes the form of nostalgic self-realization, as if his true self will emerge in how much he misses what he's left behind—people, landscapes, wild experiences. His first book, *The Deer Pasture* (1985), begins in precisely this vein, as he recounts his move from Logan, Utah, to Jackson, Mississippi, with friends and family placing bets on how long it would take him to quit his job and move back to the mountains. "When I left school for Jackson," he writes,

> I was able to stuff everything I owned in the back of my little Rabbit. It was a sad feeling, very frightening, actually, leaving the security of the mountains, traveling downhill like that, out of the crispness of the high country and into the hot torpor of the flatlands, but it was also a good feeling, being able to contain myself and all my possessions in one small orange car that would go forty-two miles on a gallon of gas. I believe I even hummed a little as I drove.
>
> Whistling in the dark.
>
> When I got to Jackson, I was glad I had brought the little cedar tree [from the Texas Hill Country]. It was a pretty one, and until I found a tiny one-room cell of an efficiency apartment to stay in, it so completely filled my hotel room with the sappy, sprightly clean

smell of the deer pasture that upon awakening in the morning, for the first few seconds I would forget where I was. Or rather, where I wasn't.[10]

Much of Bass's writing, both the early southern-focused books and the more recent volumes centered in Montana, exhibits the particular form of place-writing that Lawrence Buell has called "the aesthetics of the not-there." In other words, Bass has an intriguing tendency to describe one place in terms of, or in relation to, another. Buell argues that Henry David Thoreau does much the same thing in *Walden*, using elements from exotic European landscapes and other parts of the world to characterize the local features of Concord. In Bass's case, though, I would say the purpose of such landscape juxtapositions, couplings, and transpositions is to evoke a sense of yearning, a restless urge to find his true place in the world, and possibly his truest self. So, upon arriving in Mississippi, he savored the smells of his potted Hill Country cedar. Eventually, he planted his tree "in the center of the City Hall flower garden, right beneath the statue of Andrew Jackson."[11] As he recounts in the preface to *The Deer Pasture*, he'd spend lunch and coffee breaks in Mississippi visiting the cedar tree—"I . . . close my eyes and take deep, satisfied breaths; it smells so good," he writes.[12] Quite a powerful display of the aesthetics—the identity-forming process—of the "not-there."

For me, some of the most memorable early pieces of Bass's writing also exhibit this powerful yearning to be somewhere else. These are the essays called "The Shortest Route to the Mountains" and "On Camp Robbers, Rock Swifts, and Other Things Wild to the Heart," from the 1987 book *Wild to the Heart*.

"The Shortest Route to the Mountains" is about how you can experience mountain wildness without actually getting to true western mountains. In this essay, Bass, then still working in Jackson, tells the story of an August escape from the steamy city. Since he doesn't have enough time to go all the way to the mountain West, he heads north, to Hot Springs, Arkansas, taking the "shortest route to the mountains." As gradually becomes clear in this collection, though, the author is not seeking just a specific place in the world, a specific geography, but a certain quality of experience that he calls "wild." Synonyms for "wild" would be intensity, passion, richness, energy, freedom, and sensation. The irony of "Shortest Route to the Mountains" is that Bass begins to experience "wild" things before he's gone far from Jackson and before he's left ordinary, fast-food civilization. The essay opens with a rapturous description of a strawberry milkshake: "The trouble with buying a strawberry milkshake from the Lake Providence, Louisiana, Sonic Drive-In on the left side of Highway 65 going north through the Delta, north to Hot Springs, Arkansas, is that you have got to tag the bottom with your straw and then come up a good inch or so if you want to get anything, the reason being that the Lake Providence Sonic uses real strawberries and lots of them in their shakes." [13] The first three paragraphs rhapsodize about such a milkshake, the joy of this experience accented by the withering heat and humidity of the Mississippi Delta in August. The next several pages of this brief essay offer vivid details of the northward drive, as the narrator stays in his car, sinfully pleased to have the windows rolled up and the air conditioner on. The piece ends with the speaker anticipating his arrival at Hot Springs the following day, but the shortest route to the mountains and what they entail has already been enjoyed through the sensations of the trip itself—the milkshake and the other sensations of the drive. This is sheer Thoreauvian "home-cosmography," relishing the local as if it were the longed-for exotic.

Sometimes, though, it's not enough to stay nearby—the actual, authentic mountains are required. This is the point of "On Camp Robbers, Rock Swifts, and Other Things Wild to the Heart," which recounts the story of Bass's thirty-six-hour, round-trip drive from Jackson, Mississippi, to the Pecos Wilderness Area just west of Las Vegas, New Mexico, in 1981. Unlike "Shortest Route," which focuses on the richness of the drive itself, "On Camp Robbers" elides the drive and opens with the narrator already in the mountains. "I've been waiting a long time for this," he tells us. "Jackson, Mississippi, is the best place for me to make a living, but there's this one small problem. There are no mountains. There aren't even any aspen. . . . That's why I'm here—to drink in the mountains and the aspen for a brief Fourth of July vacation." One is struck by the calmness, the non-franticness of the prose, which belies the frenzied journey from Mississippi to New Mexico and back again. Predictably, the New Mexico mountains are placed in relief against the landscape he's just left: "After I woke I shouldered my pack, yawned, consulted my topo map, scarcely believing my luck—just yesterday I was in hot humid flat Mississippi!—and headed up a ridge toward where I hoped the trailhead to Hermit's Peak would be." He continues to write about the mountains, even these mountains he's never seen before, as if he's come home to a long-lost favorite place: "On my way through the aspen I snack on the last of the sausage and biscuits (sweet madeleine!) and suddenly, all is well. Job pressures are gone, as are worries that I might never see aspen or feel the rough wild texture of the mountains on the palms of my hands again. I am back home again, for a couple of days anyway. The sausage and biscuit is always the real beginning of the best part of the trip; I always save one for this purpose. Everything before that last Grand-mother's homemade biscuit is Getting There; everything afterward is There Itself." [14]

The Proustian reference—sweet madeleine—reinforces the power of nostalgia for Bass's imagination. What has been lost or left behind, and then regained, at least momentarily, at least by way of a surrogate or a sym-bol, takes on a richness of meaning not possessed by objects, places, or re-lationships newly acquired. The Deer Pasture thus assumes a mythic elu-siveness for Bass, as a place loved magically for a brief period of time each autumn, in the company of his family, in pursuit of natural experiences (not just through hunting) and the primal bonds of story, and then this place is left behind when the family returns to Houston. The mountain West, first experienced in Logan, Utah, is lost to the author when, giving in to young-adult responsibility, he takes his first job in Mississippi and drives "down-hill" to the office in the city in the humid flatlands.

But nostalgia can work in opposite directions. When I refer to ideas such as "geographical isomorphisms" or "the aesthetics of the not-there," I'm not just thinking of how Bass, in his southern writings, looks for traces of mountain wildness in the South or describes certain aspects of the South with language he associates with the non-South or even uses the South as a foil against which to celebrate the yearned-for mountain West. What's also fascinating about Bass's life and work is how he and Elizabeth have chosen to live in a part of the mountain West that resembles certain aspects of their southern experience—clear-cut, rainy, and relatively vista-less—and, further, how Bass's descriptions of the Yaak could, with minor tweak-ing, sound like descriptions of southern landscapes. One of Bass's most evocative and eloquent essays since the move to Montana in 1987 is the piece he wrote in 1993 for the Nature Conservancy's anthology of writings on favorite, endangered places, *Heart of the Land*, which appeared in 1995; the essay, called "On Willow Creek," waxes nostalgically about the Texas Hill Country and mourns, both explicitly and metonymically, the death of Bass's mother, which occurred shortly before he traveled down to Texas to work on the essay. Three years after he wrote "On Willow Creek," Bass's collection of essays, *The Book of Yaak*, came out. One could make a thorough study of southern-esque descriptions of Montana landscapes in this volume, but when I picked up the essay recently it took only few minutes to find a passage in the essay called "The Value of a Place," near the beginning of the book, where the Yaak is celebrated in terms that could just as easily be applied to Mississippi, or Houston, if not to the Hill Country:

> The cycle of dying trees giving birth to living ones—we're all familiar with this, familiar with the necessity of rot, and diversity, in an ecosystem: the way that the richness, or tithing, of rot, and the flexibility, the suppleness, of diversity, guarantees that an ecosystem, or any other kind of system, will have a future. I like to walk—and sometimes crawl—through the jungle up here, examining the world on my hands and knees—watching the pistonlike rise and fall of individual trees—noticing the ways they block light from some places and funnel or focus light into other places—watching the way, when the weaker trees fall, that they sometimes help prop up and brace those around them. Other times the fallen trees crash all the way to the ground to become fern-beds, soil-mulch, lichen pads. It's not a thing we can measure yet, but I like to imagine that each different tree, after it has fallen, gives off a different quality of rot—a diversity even in the manner in which nutrients are released to the soil. The slow rot of a giant larch having a taste to the soil, perhaps, of bread; the faster disintegration of ice-snapped saplings tasting like sugar, or honey. The forest *feasting* on its own diversity, with grace and mystery lying thick everywhere.[15]

When I read this passage about the Yaak, I find myself thinking of the character Buzbee in the title story of Bass's 1989 collection, *The Watch*, a seventy-seven-year-old man who's disappeared into the piney woods and swampy bottomlands of central Mississippi. Although there are few sustained natural descriptions like the one I've given from *The Book of Yaak*, there are many references in the story "The Watch" to fecundity and rot, in both the land and the human imagination. I can tell these two texts, one located in the mountains of Montana and the other set in the woods and bayous of Mississippi, come from the same pen. I suppose this is why, whenever I refer to "the Montana writer Rick Bass," I find myself hesitating slightly, knowing that wherever Bass might be living, whatever landscape he's writing about, he's also still "a southern author."

So, one might ask, how does Bass seek to gain moral and political credibility as a defender of wilderness in the mountain West when he continues to write in a "southern voice," from a "southern sensibility," intuitively relying upon the "aesthetics of the not-there"? I began this essay by emphasizing the extraordinary and sometimes comical value placed on long-term occupancy in western states such as Nevada. Implicit in any discussion is the idea that a native or longtime resident possesses more authority, more credibility, than the newcomer in any issue of public debate. However, the reality is that most residents of the western mountain states are relative newcomers, straining to be at home, to develop a sense of attachment and caring in places where we might have dwelled, physically, for only a period of months and seldom for more than a decade. For the first decade or so of his life in Montana, Bass's literary representation of the West was particularly notable for its reliance upon the "aesthetics of the not-there," a trope that can be understood as an effort to make the strange familiar, the not-home home. In other words, this is a technique for boot-strapping oneself into a condition of belonging.

More recently, some surprising new rhetorical shifts have occurred in Bass's work, and I would like to conclude by briefly discussing how these shifts have contributed to the author's authentic, pleasing voice and vision and, at the same time, have made his conservation efforts even more credible and convincing than before. Bass's two presentations at the Orion Society's June 1999 millennial extravaganza, Fire & Grit, mark the emergence of a newly detached and philosophical Rick Bass and the return of the charmingly antic storyteller whose comedic sensibility, evident early on in The Watch, had become increasingly submerged in activist angst and frustration by the mid-1990s. The essay "The Community of Glaciers" recounts Bass's efforts on behalf of a small "pro-roadless group" in the Yaak, which resulted in the author's shocking dismissal from the volunteer steering committee by a vote of thirty-nine to three. "Wearier, if not smarter," he writes, "I have retreated to the far perimeters of the community, for now. The place where everyone wants me, the place where perhaps even the landscape wants me, and hell, perhaps even the place where, when all is said and done, I myself want to be—though it does not feel that way to me." The essay proceeds to contemplate the processes by which social change and glacial erosion occur, especially the concept of glacial slowness and imperceptibility. "I do not mean to dismiss our little fires, nor our fiery hearts," he concludes: "I mean only to remind us all that our lives, our values, are a constant struggle that will never end, and in which there can never be a clear 'victory,' only daily challenge." [16] This sounds like the world-weary statement of a wilderness warrior now retired from the battlefield rather than the desperately fierce whoops of *The Book of Yaak* and *Fiber*. And yet, taken in context, "The Community of Glaciers" can be seen as an effort to retrench and gain perspective, a gathering up of wisdom and resolve for the next phase of the artist-activist's life.

The day before he presented "The Community of Glaciers" at Fire & Grit, Bass read a hilarious, self-mocking essay called "Bear Spray Stories," subtly setting up his audience for the more sober critique of activist hubris. "Every time I get sprayed, I have to laugh. It's like, how dumb can I get? But each time it happens, I tell myself it won't happen again: that there's no way I'll make that mistake twice," he writes. Beneath the guise of a series of slapstick stories, Bass seems to be stating a powerful message for artists and activists and everyone else: life is funny, painful, uncontrollable, and sometimes all too predictable. Things don't always work out as we want or expect, but it's important to keep striving, loving, and believing.

These two recent essays illustrate a surprising discovery that Bass seems to have made in his quest for an authentic, credible literary voice, a voice that might gain him leverage in the landscape debates of the American West. He has discovered that beyond and beneath a more specific regional authenticity are certain familiar and perhaps universal human passions and concerns. "The Community of Glaciers" and "Bear Spray Stories" seem to acknowledge and accept the author's lingering and perhaps insurmountable outsiderness—and in doing so they tap into the sense of unbelonging that many of Bass's readers are likely to feel. Although Bass certainly would not have wished to be voted out of the Yaak Valley Forest Council any more than he would intentionally squirt himself with pepper spray, these experiences of alienation and ineptitude have, in the hands of a brilliant storyteller, become the inadvertent means of achieving a kind of authentic humanity that will inspire future readers and listeners to take up the cry, "Don't hack the Yaak," "Nevada is not a wasteland," and various other slogans and phrases that indicate a growing ethic of responsible occupancy in the American West.

Notes

1. Charles Wilkinson, *The Eagle Bird: Mapping a New West* (New York: Pantheon, 1992), 135–36.

2. Wilkinson, *The Eagle Bird*, 138–39.

3. Terry Tempest Williams, note to author, 19 May 1988; David Quammen, e-mail to author, 28 May 1988.

4. Rick Bass, *Winter: Notes from Montana* (Boston: Houghton Mifflin, 1991), 1; Alison Deming, *Temporary Homelands: Essays on Nature, Spirit and Place* (New York: Picador, 1996), xiii–xiv; Barry Lopez, *About This Life: Journeys on the Threshold of Memory* (New York: Knopf, 1998), 14.

5. William Kittredge, *Owning It All* (Saint Paul MN: Graywolf, 1987), 62–63.

6. Kittredge, *Owning It All*, 64; Wilkinson, *The Eagle Bird*, 15–16.

7. Robert H. Brinkmeyer Jr., *Remapping Southern Literature: Contemporary Southern Writers and the West* (Athens: University of Georgia Press, 2000), 81; George P. Landow, *Elegant Jeremiahs: The Sage from Carlyle to Mailer* (Ithaca: Cornell University Press, 1986), 23.

8. Scott Slovic, "A Paint Brush in One Hand and a Bucket of Water in the Other: Nature Writing and the Politics of Wilderness. An Interview with Rick Bass," *Weber Studies* 11, no. 3 (fall 1994): 21.

9. Slovic, "A Paint Brush," 21.

10. Rick Bass, *The Deer Pasture* (New York: Norton, 1985), x.

11. Lawrence Buell, *The Environmental Imagination: Thoreau, Nature Writing, and the Formation of American Culture* (Cambridge: Harvard University Press, 1995), 68; Bass, *The Deer Pasture*, xi.

12. Bass, *The Deer Pasture*, xi.

13. Rick Bass, *Wild to the Heart* (New York: Norton, 1987), 15.

14. Bass, *Wild to the Heart*, 38, 40, 40–41.

15. Rick Bass, *The Book of Yaak* (Boston: Houghton Mifflin, 1996), 11.

16. Rick Bass, "The Community of Glaciers" (essay presented at Fire & Grit, Shepherdstown, West Virginia, June 1999).

13. AUTHORING AN AUTHENTIC PLACE

Environmental and Literary Stewardship in Stegner and Kittredge

Bonney MacDonald

This essay attempts to come to terms with lines from Wallace Stegner that have puzzled me for some time. In *This Is Dinosaur*, he wrote that a "place is nothing in itself. . . . It has no meaning . . . except in terms of human perception, use and response." In *Where the Bluebird Sings to the Lemonade Springs*, he also remarked that "no place, not even a wild place is a place until it has had that human attention that at its highest reach we call poetry." Wild places needing our *use* or our *poetry*? How could Stegner, author of "The Wilderness Letter" and so many works advocating land conservation in the West, say such things? Isn't the wilderness in the arid and fragile West, especially after all it has suffered from humans' extractive practices, better off without us?[1]

The answer, from what Stegner suggests, is not so simple. Along with William Kittredge, Stegner mourns the irreversible damage done to western lands; and yet, with Wendell Berry, he insists on certain human responsibilities. For Stegner, as for Berry, places are intimately connected to humans' labor and language. In fact, Stegner's environmental ethic, stemming from his self-defined anthropocentrism, advocates responsible preservation and stewardship.[2]

Further, Stegner's stewardship ethic parallels his—as well as Kittredge's—attempts to preserve the West's regional literature and sense of place. Just as western land was often destroyed by the carelessness born of an Old West myth of limitless resources and extractive practices, so too has western literature and the West's sense of place suffered from that frontier myth. Westerners, both authors tell us, cling to an outmoded myth because they lack an identity in the present. We not only await restored western ecosystems, we also await, as Kittredge puts it, a new regional literature to "inhabit."[3] I want to suggest that the responsibility to enact careful land use, based in Stegner's model for stewardship and careful use, is linked to the responsibility of authorship and naming that Stegner and Kittredge advocate for western literature and place. If an older, frontier-based West is gone, both authors nonetheless find hope: authentic western places can emerge when we work the land responsibly with our hands as well as our words.

Western Lands

Both Stegner and Kittredge grew up before the consequences of settlement were obvious. In Kittredge's boyhood West, "possibility [was still] the oldest American story. . . . Promises of paradise for the taking." Growing up in Oregon's Warner Valley, before it "all went wrong," Kittredge loved his ranch, finding a "coherency I loved, [and] a place which was mine" (OA 68, 11). The region's beauty came as much from the land itself as from the satisfaction gained from working it; he relished the "luminous, . . . glowing, radiant and permeable mornings," as the family rebuilt "dams across swales in the hay meadows." In building that "perfect agricultural place," the Kittredge family was carrying on an old myth: "The story begins with a vast continent, . . . capable of inspiring us to reverence and awe. . . . A good rural people come from the East . . . and tame it for agricultural purposes, bringing civilization" (OA 7, 11, 57, 63).

The West, seemingly poised to be "hope's native home, the youngest and freshest of America's regions, [seemed] magnificently endowed with the chance to become something unprecedented and unmatched in the world." Unfortunately, however, in the urge to plant and settle, we followed "arrogant pipedreams," acting upon the landscape with the "force of a geological agent" (WBS xv, xvii, 47). As Kittredge recalls of his family's ranch, "it all went dead, over the years. . . . We had reinvented our valley according to the most persuasive ideal given us by our culture, and we ended with . . . a dreamland gone wrong" (OA 61).

In the last throes of this delusion, those who believed the story held on tight—to ownership and to profit. Kittredge describes how his grandfather set large cage-traps for migrating magpies each summer. His grandfather would fetch his 12-gauge and drive down to the traps in his "ancient gray Cadillac." The "ritual was slow and dignified, and . . . as inevitable as one shoe after another." The old man would stare at the birds and then step out of the sedan, "the pockets of his gray gabardine suit-coat . . . bulging with shells." Through the cage's chicken-wire, "he would kill them one by one, taking his time." When asked to explain this methodical slaughter, he simply replied, "Because they're mine" (OA 65–67). Clinging less to dreams of ownership than to dreams of plenty and profit, Stegner's father continually gambled on the next bonanza. After running a Reno gambling joint, "when he was close to down and out, . . . he did one last desperate and damaging thing." With land in California, he hired "a crew to cut down all [the land's] two-hundred-year-old oaks and sell them off as firewood" (WBS xxi).

Both Kittredge and Stegner lament the damage done in the "conquest of acreage," and they both offer visions of preserving and renewing the western lands they love. Kittredge, as Scott Slovic has noted, offers "confessions of destruction," and his goal is "nothing short of revitalizing and revivifying the physical world" (TC 82, 86). Stegner, of course, also articulates a land ethic and pleads for compassion and preservation. His commitment to the land, as T. H. Watkins writes, was strong, "a visceral thing." From his work at the Interior Department with Stewart Udall, to his involvement in the Sierra Club and the Wilderness Society, Stegner exhibited an unfailing concern for western places. He voiced, as Ann Ronald puts it, an "emotional attachment to the land" and a "consistent . . . ecological awareness."[4]

However, in the midst of Stegner's conservationist works, Ronald notes inconsistencies: "One would expect any good conservationist," she writes, "to embrace adaptation while disdaining engineering" and the manipulation of land. In *One Way to Spell Man*, however, Ronald finds puzzling remarks: we need, Stegner writes, a "land ethic that unites science, religion and human feeling." It sounds, as Ronald rightly comments, "strangely out of place — naming something akin to technology, something many conservationists would blame rather than embrace." Certainly, any conservationist would share this surprise. Stegner is connecting a land ethic with three distinctly *human* concerns — science, religion, and human feeling. Continuing this focus on humans' actions and views, he writes that "natural beauty is nothing until it comes to the eye of the beholder. . . . We cannot even describe a place except in terms of its human uses."[5]

What Stegner intends in these jarring statements equating land's value with human use and perception is *not* that wilderness itself is not sacred but that we have only our human perceptions and needs through which to see it: "Incorrigibly anthropocentric as we are, we can only respond humanly." This humanism leads directly to Stegner's view of how to proceed with wild places and damaged lands: stewardship. The term does not endorse domination and taking whatever we want. Instead, it prescribes caring for the land around us, especially in the wake of previous damage: "Land is a heritage as well as a resource, and ownership suggests stewardship, not exploitation."[6]

Stegner advocates continued, human involvement in nature for two reasons. First, we must responsibly clean up the lands that we have damaged. We have misused our powers and have put profit and greed above common sense and good local practice. Despite this misuse, however, as

Ronald writes, Stegner still "assumes an ongoing need for man's participation in things environmental because, as he well knows, whole ecological systems no longer remain intact. For what the anthropocentric has already manipulated, the anthropocentric must accept responsibility for." As Stegner insists, we must "apply to ourselves and our habitat the intelligence that has endangered both. That means drastically and voluntarily . . . husbanding, building and nourishing, instead of squandering and poisoning."[7]

A second reason for Stegner's "rational view of stewardship" comes from his agreement with Wendell Berry over the inevitability of our anthropocentric outlook. Nature, Berry proposes in "Preserving Wildness," is "*somewhat* hospitable to us, but it is also absolutely dangerous" (HE 138). It comes down to matters of responsible use and the human starting point: "To use or not to use nature is not a choice available to us; we can only live at the expense of other lives. Our choice has rather to do with how and how much to use" (139). Berry even goes so far as to allow self-interest into the equation: "Certainly self-interest has much wickedness to answer for, and we are living in just fear of it; nevertheless, we must take care not to condemn it absolutely" (147). We must, of course, share the planet with "each other and other creatures," but to survive, we must also "use it somewhat at the expense of other creatures. We must acknowledge both the centrality and the limits of our self-interest" (148). We must be able to distinguish, as William Cronon puts it, between "*abuse and use.*"[8]

Berry, in fact, calls for a balance between the civilized and the wild, which, odd as it sounds, depends on a responsible anthropocentrism. The "greatest danger," he thus explains, "lies in our dislike of ourselves as a species": "This is an understandable dislike—we are justly afraid of ourselves—but [we must still] act out of a proper self-interest and genuine self-respect as human beings. . . . We must [recognize] . . . that it is not natural to be disloyal to one's own kind" (HE 149).

Here, the echoes of Stegner are clear: our human perspective and our responses to our places are *what we begin with.* We cannot, Berry concludes, exit ourselves: "A common complaint . . . is that humans think the world is 'anthropocentric,' or human-centered. I understand the complaint; the assumptions of so-called anthropocentrism often result in gross and dangerous insubordination. And yet I don't know how the human species can avoid some version of self-centeredness; I don't know how any species can. An earthworm, I think, is living in an earthworm-centered world" (HE 148).

Berry's definition of place comes from a corresponding agricultural and domestic perspective. For him, wilderness is vital and must be cared for; in the final analysis, however, it is not our *daily* home. Our places of belonging are tended, tilled, and often built. Wild places are not our homes, and there is even a "bad reason" to go to them. "We must not," Berry warns, go to the wild "to escape the ugliness and dangers of the present human economy, . . . and we must not go there to escape ourselves" (HE 18).

To idealize the wild, as Cronon has argued, can compromise the environment "that for better or worse we call home." Too, since many of our environmental problems begin in our settled places, "we need an environmental ethic that will tell us as much about *using* nature as about *not* using it." [9] For Cronon, as for Berry, the made, the cultured, and the tilled are our home places.

Related to this emphasis on the domestic, Stegner recalls Berry's claim that if "you don't know where you are, you don't know *who* you are" (WBS 199). I would add that, for Stegner and Berry, the converse also holds true: if you don't know *who* you are, you cannot know *where* you are. That is, if you cannot acknowledge your own human needs and position, you cannot know how to regulate your living and your (responsible) use of your surroundings. If we are to act responsibly and compassionately toward our environments, we need to know them as places; and to know them as places, Stegner argues, is to begin, at least, with our human perspective: "Deep ecologists warn us not to be anthropocentric, but I know no way to look at the world, settled or wild, except through my own eyes. I know that it wasn't created especially for my use, and I share the guilt for what members of my species . . . have done to it. But I am the only instrument that I have access to by which I can enjoy the world and try to understand it. So I must believe that, *at least to human perception*, a place is not a place until people have been born in it, grown up in it, lived in it, . . . experienced and shaped it" (201).

Stegner's stewardship, and his abiding love for western lands, comes out of this human-centered vision. Anthropocentrism, for all its excesses, and stewardship, for all its misuse, remain the foundation of Stegner's and Berry's land ethic. For them, imaginative responses to and manual labor on the land constitute our authentic relations with place.

Western Stories

If dependence on the "enfranchising myth" of pastoral, agrarian ownership destroyed western lands, it also damaged the West's literature, communities, and sense of place (OA 157). As Stegner tells us, overuse of land created mobility and a resulting lack of community: "Deeply lived-in places are the exceptions rather than the rule in the West. For one thing, all western places are new; for another, many of the people who established them came to pillage . . . rather than to settle for life. When the pillaging was done, . . . they moved on." The Turnerian model of continual movement and progress collapsed into its inevitable consequences: rootlessness and transience. In the continually shifting settlement patterns, still reenacted today, American individualism has not been corrected by "belonging" (WBS xvi–xvii, 72).

If Stegner explains the evolution of wind-blown, transient towns, Kittredge tells us about the lives within them, and the picture is not pretty. Victims of (and participants in) a "mythology of ownership" live lives of uncharted, unstoried desperation. Part critic and part sympathizer, Kittredge urges us not to judge too quickly: "So many people in the American West are hurt, and hurting. . . . Rednecks originate out of hurt and a sense of having been discarded and ignored by the Great World. . . . They lose faith and ride away into foolishness, striking back. . . . [They feel] used and cheated and disenfranchised. . . . Any one of them might yearn for a nurse, a double-wide, a blue roan Appaloosa, and a sense of place in a country that left [them] behind" (OA 81–83).

In Kittredge's portraits of fallen lives in fallen towns, locals live in the West's "amputated present" (WBS 193). Among the disenfranchised, witness Davis Patten, who on February mornings trudges through three feet of snow and works his feed-sled, pulled by Belgian geldings. After a hard day in insulated coveralls, dreaming about an unattainable Caterpillar D-6, he sits with his wife, Loretta, drinking bourbon-laced coffee. From their Barca-Loungers, they watch "people laughing and joking in bright Sony color. . . . [Soon he will drift off and then] wake to the white noise from a gray screen. It is important to have a sense of this. There are many lives, this is just one, but none are the lives we imagine when we think of running away to the territory" (OA 87).

If Davis Patten works hard on his farm, other casualties of a fallen myth work and live hard on the oil rigs, drift off to sleep in bars, and move on to the next job. Part-time settlers and full-time drifters, these roughnecks create bizarre homesteads in the outlying Ragtown before picking up and moving on. Kittredge recalls one worker who lived in his truck, which he heated with a Coleman stove, and another who lived outside of his truck: "one of the boomers . . . hauled back about three thousand dollars worth of motel furniture from a wholesale outlet, everything but a TV, and set up housekeeping in the sagebrush around a fire ring. He lived there like a crowned king of the imagination until October. . . . He left the stuff sitting, and headed back to winter in Texas[,] . . . everything on rubber, and open roads" (OA III–12).

These western towns remind us that the old myth hasn't been successful for a very long time. The dream about taming wilderness has collapsed, and "simple individuals can find nothing to defend, nothing to reap but the isolation implicit in their stance, nothing to gain for their strength but loneliness." Community and belonging has been left behind and these westerners, once again, "yearn for . . . a sense of place in a country that left [them] behind" (OA 89, 83).

What they have, of course, is a frontier myth that they haven't been able to renounce. And for some time, Kittredge tells us, western writers were not much better off, producing western novels and tales that were "petrified" and irrelevant. In film and fiction, nostalgia kept western writing stunted for too long, offering a "western past [that was] mythicized almost out of recognizability" (SMW 199). Western writers, as Elliot West points out, had "no story to help them understand . . . things around them . . . [and] no way to know who in the world they were." [10] The "old mythology [didn't] work anymore" so that, as Kittredge puts it, we live in a "transitional time," "struggling to revise our dominant mythology and find a new story to inhabit" (OA 68, 64).

Seeking just such a story for himself, Kittredge finds inspiration on his family's land. At the mouth of an abandoned cave, Kittredge looks for "signs" that will help forge a "story of who I would be." He begins digging with a shovel and turns up a fragment of woven rush matting from long-ago Indians. On a nearby lava outcropping, he notes more signs of Native labor—a number of twelve-inch holes ground into the rock: "The holes are like bowls, and once *worked* into the outcropping they could not be destroyed. . . . For me, like the crumbling woven mat, that stone worn to the shape of the *work* came to exist as a metaphor. . . . I think of it as a quite classical recognition in which I began to sense the legitimacy of an urge to tell *stories*" (OA 78–79, emphasis added). Linking manual labor and stories, the telling of tales—repeatedly and with new turns—works the lives and land we live on just as Native labor reshaped the stone. "I have learned," Kittredge explains, "to understand *writing as useful* precisely as that broken bit of woven mat and those bowls worn in the fundamental stone were useful to me" (OA 79, emphasis added).

Kittredge implies that writing, like his shovel, is a practical, daily tool. Stones and stories—both serve as tools for digging out and creating a sense of place. Digging, or what Thoreau would pun as mining a claim, creates a form of emotional ownership, a needed departure from the claims and owning strategies of Kittredge's grandfather and the Old West. When Thoreau, playing off of mine and claim, announces in *Walden* that "here I will begin to mine," he equates his own experiment in writing with the physical work of digging: "The intellect is a cleaver; it discerns and rifts its way into the secret of things. . . . My head is hands and feet . . . [and] my instinct tells me that my head is an organ for burrowing, as some creatures use their snout and fore-paws, and with it I would mine and burrow my way through these hills. I think that the richest vein is somewhere hereabouts." [11]

Like Thoreau, Kittredge intuits that the richest region is right under his feet. Further, his attempts at redefining myths about claim and ownership remind us that newly perceived or newly storied places establish a claim just as much as, if not more than, any legal deed. Playing with claim and ownership, once again, Thoreau reports that because he has seen neighboring farms he has as good as "bought [them] all." "In imagination [he] bought all the farms in succession" and talked with the farmers about their lands. He "took everything but a deed . . . took [their] word[s] for their deed[s]" and was better off for it. Words and tools, storytelling and building a home place, come together in Kittredge's understanding of writing and "storytelling as the *art of constructing* road maps, ways home to that ultimate shelter" (OA 103, emphasis added). For Kittredge, words are tools with which to build places and construct dwellings. For this reason, Kittredge, writing on Stegner, asserts that "there is no such thing as a landscape, there are only the processes of nature, and those of location, which in humans derive so largely from . . . storytelling." [12] For Stegner and Kittredge, there is no such thing as a place until it has been lived in and died in, and until tales about those lives and deaths have accrued.

With this ability of the writer to create a sense of place, we come close to a kind of literary stewardship. As the true steward tends the land for long-term health and sustainability, so too must the regional writer tend and cultivate the land with words. Reaching back to Wendell Berry, Stegner equates poetic cultivation of place with the "knowledge of place that comes from working it in all weathers, making a living from it, suffering from its catastrophes, . . . valuing it for the profound investment of labor and feeling that

you . . . put into it. [Berry] is talking about the knowing that poets special-
ize in" (WBS 205). For Stegner, Berry's physical work on the farm and a
poet's working of words about the land are both forms of cultivation that
create place. Thus, as Stegner claims in a line worth repeating: "No place . . .
is a place until it has had that human attention that at its highest reach we
call poetry. . . . No place is a place until things that have happened in it are
remembered in history, ballads, yarns, legends or monuments. Fictions
serve as well as facts" (WBS 205, 202).

Names

Someone said my real name to me
Last night. Someone whispered
To me, before I know, the name he knew
Me to become last night . . .
And I rose easily to my name
As if over the rim of the earth at dawn,
Exhumed and spacious, shining
In his arms . . .

PATTIAN ROGERS, "The Power of Sun"

In Stegner's human- and writer-oriented model, new stories emerge when
they are told and retold; new myths emerge as we describe, name, and
build. That Daniel Boone "killed a bear at a certain spot in Kentucky did not
make it a place. It began to be one, though, when he remembered the spot
as Bear Run, and other people picked up the name and called their settlement after it . . . and when children had worn paths through its woods to a
schoolhouse or swimming hole" (WBS 202).

Provided that they are not merely arbitrary geographical markers but
connected to events and particulars of a place, names on landscapes help
construct the kind of places that Stegner envisions. Explaining this in his
Wisdom Sits in Places, Keith Basso asks how named places function among
the Western Apache. Basso finds that place-names perform cultural and
ethical work because they carry instructional tales that stay with the name.
Such tales, delivered in shorthand by "speaking with place-names," help
"people live right." [13]

For example, Basso tells of a young Apache ranch hand, Talbert Paxton,
who normally led an upright life. After a failed love affair, however, he went
on a binge of carousing, chasing women, and drunkenness. When Paxton

returns to the field, sober and ready to work, Basso overhears what he initially thinks are "total non-sequiturs": "So! You've returned from Trail-Goes-Down-Between-Two-Hills!" And from another: "So! You got tired of walking back and forth!" (wsp 112–13). As Basso learns, at this location long ago, a "bad-living" man who drank and chased women once learned a lesson. Two beautiful Apache girls stationed themselves on two hills and shouted out sexual invitations. The man, desperate for one and then the other, exhausted himself by running back and forth between the hills. The place-name, when spoken to Paxton, did the "interactional work" (wsp 75). As Scott Momaday puts it, speakers of place-names "*appropriate* their landscapes, to think and act 'with' them." [14] Such an utterance "is a way of *appropriating* portions of the earth" (wsp 143).

Using names on the land, of course, does not always find such positive press. Naming—and the projecting, thereby, of human perception onto nature—has also been construed as an unjustified act of power over nature. The Adamic naming of the land, according to Lynn White Jr., constitutes a destructive act of human-centered power. In "The Historical Roots of Our Ecologic Crisis," White claims that humans' exploitative attitudes and practices began with the "victory of Christianity over paganism," and specifically with the human-centered vision licensed by the creation story. Linking Adamic naming with power, he writes, "Man *named* all the animals, thus establishing his *dominance* over them. God planned all of this explicitly for man's benefit: . . . no item in the physical creation had any purpose save to serve man's purposes. . . . Especially in its Western form," White concludes, "Christianity is the most *anthropocentric* religion the world has seen." [15]

My purpose in citing White, here, is not to assess his theology but to address the links he identifies between naming, anthropocentrism, and domination. For White, naming nature constitutes a selfish appropriation exclusively for human benefit. Keeping in mind Basso's work on naming, and recalling Stegner's and Berry's remarks on our inevitable human-centered outlook, I turn to the unlikely subject of animal training to ask whether naming and abusive power or domination are necessarily linked.

In her *Adam's Task: Calling Animals by Name*, Vicki Hearne, poet and philosopher, discusses the intricacies of dog- and horse-training. [16] In this philosophical and practical discussion of the language of training and command, Hearne asks what gives us the right to command another being. She reasons that, in uttering commands, we must also be willing to obey; she insists that we must mean what we say; and she concludes that, if a command is truly suited to an animal, that animal will respond by bringing its best self forward. For Hearne, provided the name matches the creature, names call animals into being. And in a counter to White's equating of naming and domination, Hearne offers her version of the creation story: "In the beginning, God gave 'dominion over the fish of the sea, and over the foul of the air, and over every living thing that moveth on the earth.' Adam gave names to the creatures, and they all responded to their names without objection, since in this dominion to command and to recognize were one action. There was no gap between the ability to command [or name] and the full acknowledgement of . . . the being so commanded. . . . Then Adam and Eve failed in obedience, and in this story to fail in obedience is to fail in authority" (AT 47).

Our situation today, with respect to the land, is analogous. As Berry and Stegner remind us, we have good reason to fear our power and to shun all excesses of anthropocentrism. We have, indeed, abused the earth, and our commands and names on the land have violated those landscapes. As Stegner, Kittredge, and Berry would all agree, we need a renewed sense of place. And places, as Basso reminds us, are human constructions and appropriations. We must be sure that the authority by which we name and build those places is truly a commitment to the nature of the land. We must "bear the consequences of our speech," as Hearne says—bear the commitment, that is, implicit in all working or naming of nature.

In fact, we may not have another option. For to pretend that we do not have authority or do not engage in naming or commanding is an act of denial: "We are in charge already, like it or not . . . [and we] assume authority over each other constantly, or at least we better do so if only to be able to say 'Duck!' at the right moment. . . . A refusal to give commands or to notice that commands are begin given is often a refusal to acknowledge a relationship, just as is a refusal to obey." To train a dog well, a trainer—to borrow from Heidegger—must listen to the dog's being, must be capable of "beholding [the] dog" (AT 49). And to name the land and create place, humans must be similarly committed to the particulars of the landscape. To do so is to obey the limits of one's dominion and to recognize the essence of the land.

Adam's Task argues that responsible authority is central to "our relationships, logically essential to speaking, and that talking depends on the possibility of command." This account of training and naming is useful, as well, as a model for speaking place-names. To work the land with our hands or to name it with our words, we must be cautious as well as willing to acknowledge our already-present authority. How else, Hearne asks, can we say "'Turn in your papers on Tuesday' or 'take one pill after each meal' . . . or 'Marry me!' What gives us the right to say 'Fetch!'? Something very like reverence, humility and obedience" (AT 76).

The caution and reverence, then, as well as the courage and commitment it takes to call another by name is tremendous. It is this kind of responsible working of words and land that, Stegner argues, remains necessary for creating place. Stegner's fascination with what Basso would call "speaking place names" emerges in his comments on George Stewart's *Names on the Land*, a book that focuses on "how names are given." "Nobody," Stegner writes, "ever wrote such a book . . . before; nobody has written one since" (WBS 167, 158).

Long before Indians and Europeans, Stewart begins, "the land stretched away without names." [17] With the arrival of humans, tribes gave names to the land and "laid their bones by the hills and streams they had named." Most of these were "little names, known only to those who lived nearby, of ponds and swamps and creeks and hills." These names—emerging out of "time and place, blood and language"—grew out of the place itself and the lives of the people. Names, that is, not only retold and preserved human events, they also reflected the land itself. These place-names "prefigured something of what was to be . . . and the thing and the name were one" (NL 3, 4–5).

Stegner praises *Names on the Land* for describing how, in naming, "we went about putting our marks on the continent, and . . . added ourselves to the continent and the continent to ourselves." Stewart understood, Stegner concludes, in an echo of Basso, "that nothing is comprehended . . . until it has been given a name." When we live in a named place, provided that we do so responsibly, we know where we belong. And when we know *where* we are—as Stegner paraphrases Berry—we can know *who* we are (WBS 157, 168, 199).

Authentically Authored Places
The word *author* comes out of an adaptation of the Latin *auctor*, formed from *augere*, which means to make grow. According to the OED, an author is a person who "originates or gives existence" to something; one "who gives rise to or causes an action . . . or condition of things"; and "one who has authority over others." Relatedly, the word authority, with ties to the French

autorité but also taken from the Latin *auctor*, connotes the "power to influence action, opinion, belief"; the "right to command"; and the "power to inspire belief." The term authentic, coming from the Greek, does not originate with either of these terms. However, in fifteenth-century usage, it was linked with the Latin *auctor*. The OED further notes that the "development of [its] meaning is [rather] involved, and influenced by medieval Latin and French." The word authentic, the OED concludes, seems to "combine the ideas of 'authoritative' and 'original.'" Authenticity itself, then, seems to be part made and part given.

My claim, here, etymologically hinging on the fifteenth-century combining of author and authentic, and thematically related to this combined meaning of made and given, suggests that the authentic can, in part, be created or authored. A regional writer giving a name or a story to a land calls the given particulars of that place into being and authors a story or a place in which to dwell. Like Heidegger's authentic Being, whose "authenticity is 'hidden' but nonetheless given 'beforehand,'" a place becomes a place to dwell through language and attention. If a place-name truly fits the land and the people, the name, as with authentic *Dasein*, "genuinely exemplifies its being."[18]

And so, the labor of authoring opens up a dwelling place and helps us move into belonging. After all, perception of a given place, Stegner writes, is a "human creation," and words on the land can help make a "civilization to match the scenery." If "no place is a place . . . until it has had that human attention that at its highest reach we call poetry," and if we need that sense of place, then writers—Whitman-like—are poised to give voice and language to their lands (wbs xv, 205). Like environmental stewards tending the land, writers can work and steward the land with words and names, creating new stories to inhabit. When western writers give words to landscapes and author newly perceived dwelling places, the region can change from space to place. It is through such labors of language on the land that "the West [can] realize itself" and, rising to its name, become the "geography of hope" so resonantly called forth by Stegner's own naming (wbs 116, xv).

Notes

1. Wallace Stegner, ed., *This Is Dinosaur: Echo Park and Its Magic Rivers* (New York: Knopf, 1955); Stegner, *Where the Bluebird Sings to the Lemonade Springs: Living and Writing in the West* (New York: Penguin, 1992) (henceforth wbs); Stegner, "The Wilderness Letter," in *The Sound of Mountain*

Water (Lincoln: University of Nebraska Press, 1985), 145–53 (henceforth SMW).

2. Ann Ronald, "Stegner and Stewardship," in *Wallace Stegner: Man and Writer*, ed. Charles E. Rankin (Albuquerque: University of New Mexico Press, 1986), 87–103.

3. William Kittredge, *Owning It All* (St. Paul: Graywolf Press, 1987), 64 (henceforth OA).

4. William Kittredge, *Taking Care: Thoughts on Storytelling and Belief*, ed. Scott Slovic (Minneapolis: Credo, 1999), 23 (henceforth TC); T. H. Watkins, "Reluctant Tiger: Wallace Stegner Takes Up the Conservation Mantle," in *Wallace Stegner and the Continental Vision*, ed. Curt Meine (Washington DC: Island Press, 1997), 141–61; Ronald, "Stegner and Stewardship," 88, 89.

5. Ronald, "Stegner and Stewardship," 91; Stegner, *One Way to Spell Man* (Garden City: Doubleday, 1982), 177 [also quoted in Ronald, "Stegner and Stewardship," 91]; Ronald, "Stegner and Stewardship," 91; Stegner, *This Is Dinosaur*, 15 [also quoted in Ronald, "Stegner and Stewardship," 94–95].

6. Stegner, foreword to *The Grand Colorado*, by T. H. Watkins et al. (Palo Alto CA: American West, 1969), 10 [also quoted in Ronald, "Stegner and Stewardship," 95]; Wallace Stegner and Page Stegner, *American Places* (Moscow ID: University of Idaho Press, 1983), 143 [also quoted in Ronald, "Stegner and Stewardship," 96].

7. Ronald, "Stegner and Stewardship," 101; Stegner, "Conservation Equals Survival," in *Crossroads*, ed. Tom E. Kakonis and James C. Wilcox (Lexington MA: D. C. Heath, 1972), 128 [also quoted in Ronald, "Stegner and Stewardship," 101].

8. Ronald, "Stegner and Stewardship," 100; Wendell Berry, *Home Economics* (New York: Farrar, Straus & Giroux, 1987), 137 (henceforth HE); William Cronon, "The Trouble with Wilderness; or, Getting Back to the Wrong Nature," in *Uncommon Ground: Rethinking the Human Place in Nature*, ed. William Cronon (New York: Norton, 1996), 85.

9. Cronon, "The Trouble with Wilderness," 85.

10. Wallace Stegner, *The Sound of Mountain Water*, 192; Elliot West, "Stegner, Storytelling and Western Identity," in *Wallace Stegner*, ed. Rankin, 62.

11. Henry David Thoreau, *Walden* (New York: Time Inc. Book Division, 1962), 96.

12. Thoreau, *Walden*, 79; Kittredge, "The Good Rain: Stegner and the Wild," in *Wallace Stegner*, ed. Rankin, 39.

13. Pattiann Rogers, *Firekeeper* (Minneapolis: Milkweed, 1994), 231–33; Keith Basso, *Wisdom Sits in Places: Landscape and Language Among the Western Apache* (Albuquerque: University of New Mexico Press, 1996), 47 (henceforth WSP).

14. Quoted in Basso, *Wisdom Sits in Places*, 75.

15. Lynn White Jr., "The Historical Roots of Our Ecologic Crisis," Address to the American Association for the Advancement of Science, December 26, 1966.

16. Vicki Hearne, *Adam's Task: Calling Animals by Name* (New York: Knopf, 1987) (henceforth AT).

17. George R. Stewart, *Names on the Land: A Historical Account of Place-Naming in the United States* (New York: Random House, 1945), 3 (henceforth NL).

18. Jacob Golumb, *In Search of Authenticity: From Kierkegaard to Camus* (New York: Routledge, 1995), 89.

14. "GENEALOGY IS IN OUR BLOOD"

Terry Tempest Williams and the Redemption of "Native" Mormonism

Joanna Brooks

Most of my ancestors came west early, and it seems to me that they did so to scatter themselves. This holds true for the Okies of my father's side and for the Basque *californios* of my mother's, but it was not so for the Dorton line, my maternal grandmother's family. Early English converts to the Mormon Church, they came from Manchester in the 1850s and 1860s, across ocean and plains, to Utah and southern Idaho, as participants in a broader Mormon gathering to Zion. Today, this gathering continues as my mother, an expert genealogist, collects the names of earlier Dortons as well as the names of other ancestors who never set foot in Utah. These names are grouped in families, bound together in "Books of Remembrance," and sent for safekeeping to a church-owned vault in a granite hillside east of Salt Lake City. A Mormon "Book of Remembrance" does not serve the authenticating purpose other pedigrees might. One cannot claim membership in the church upon the "discovery" of a Mormon great-grandmother. Our genealogies find, with each generation back, fewer and fewer Mormon ancestors and none before the founding of the Church of Jesus Christ of Latter-day Saints in 1830.

This essay examines the relationship between identity, genealogy, and authenticity as negotiated by white Mormons in the contemporary American West. Classic sociological studies of Mormonism such as Thomas O'Dea's *The Mormons* (1957) and Jan Shipps's *Mormonism: The Story of a New Religious Tradition* (1985) have addressed issues of Mormon identity by characterizing Mormons as a distinctive subculture or ethnic group. For example, Shipps argues that "by virtue of a common paradigmatic experience as well as [geographical] isolation," Mormons "have acquired an ethnic identity so distinct that it sets the Saints apart in much the same fashion that ethnic identity sets Jews apart." Similarly, the *Harvard Encyclopedia of Ethnic Groups* (1980) catalogs Mormons as a distinct ethnicity with a characteristic "ethnic consciousness." More recently, Patricia Nelson Limerick has proposed Mormon ethnic identity as a valuable alternative model for understanding ethnicity in the West and America at large. She finds in Mormonism a structural parallel between the "search for religious belief" and the "search for ethnicity," a parallel that emphasizes faith rather than phenotype or genotype as a basis for identification.[1] According to Limerick, the Mormon model of identity suggests that all American ethnicities are the products of common beliefs and desires. However, if a distinctive Mormon ethnicity did emerge in the American West during the late nineteenth and early twentieth centuries, that identity faces new pressures in the contemporary era. Dramatic church growth in Central America, South America, and Asia means that white English-speaking American westerners now constitute a minority of Mormon church membership. Meanwhile, Armaund Mauss observes that the ethnic features of Mormon identity have faded in the twentieth century due to assimilation or "an obvious convergence between Mormons and their host societies in North America." Finally, renewed emphases on orthodoxy within the institutional church have narrowed the definition of authentic Mormonism and endangered the notion of an inalienable ethnic Mormonism.[2]

This essay is thus premised on my sense that Mormon history and Mormon theology have fostered distinctive processes of identification and authentication among white Mormons in the American West. If Patricia Limerick finds Mormon models of identity to be instructively alternative, I would like to point out that they are also deeply contested and mediated by the politics of the institutional church. Given the rise of Mormon neo-orthodoxy and the growth of the worldwide church, ethnic rather than institutional Mormon identities have become a refuge for those who find themselves outside the narrowing bounds of orthodox Mormonism—especially liberals, intellectuals, feminists, and gays and lesbians. For these marginalized Mormons, identity is not necessarily maintained through the cultural practices associated with the programs of the institutional church. Rather, what provides many marginal Mormons in the contemporary American West with a continuing sense of identity is our deep, intractable, and distinctively Mormon family histories. Our genealogies root us in Mormonism, however uncertain our relationships to the present and future institutional church may be.

Contemporary Mormon culture assigns to genealogy a range of values, theological and cultural, orthodox and renegade. Its narrowest definition pertains to Mormon temple worship: genealogical research permits church members to identify ancestors for baptism, marriage, and other proxy ordinances that take place in Mormon temples worldwide. By a more elegant theological account, genealogy and temple ordinances "seal" families together across generations and across time. Many Mormons experience a tremendous sense of connection to their ancestors as they do genealogical and temple work on their behalf. Indeed, Mormon tradition is rich with stories of visitations by ancestors who express gratitude for genealogical work done and offer comfort or protection to their descendants. For some contemporary Mormons in the American West, genealogy can also be a source of cultural prestige or distinction, especially when one can boast of several lines of Mormon pioneers or seven generations of church membership. In Utah, Idaho, Arizona, and California, local chapters of the "Daughters of the Utah Pioneers" promote this legacy; similarly, the state of Utah celebrates "Pioneer Day" every July 24. Other Mormons read their genealogies against the grain, discovering beyond sacralized birthdates and granite gravemarkers evidences of a stubbornly unrepentant human past. Mikal Gilmore, brother of convicted multiple murderer Gary Gilmore, reads his Mormon family history as "legends memorializing pioneer ancestors who probably, behind all the inflated and pious myths, were really hard-asses and sons-of-bitches."[3] Considered in all its unorthodox and orthodox permutations, then, Mormon genealogy can be viewed as the effort to establish and maintain a discursive relationship with the past. It is therefore a potent resource for those who would attempt to establish and maintain a relationship to Mormon identity, even as the orthodox configurations of that identity constrict.

An outstanding literary example of this genealogical application is *Refuge: An Unnatural History of Family and Place* (1991), by Terry Tempest Williams. Williams is a natural historian, an environmental activist, and a Utah Mormon with deep pioneer roots. As a personal-ecological treatise in the tradition of Edward Abbey's *Desert Solitaire* (1968), *Refuge* has won broad environmentalist and eco-feminist audiences, but it is also a work with specifically Mormon significance as a genealogical "Book of Remembrance." As its subtitle announces, *Refuge* documents the interplay of natural and unnatural forces in shaping identity, family, landscape, and individual survival. It chronicles the spring of 1983, when massive flooding of the Great Salt Lake turned city streets into navigable rivers and, in a loss felt more sensibly by Williams, overtook the Bear River Bird Refuge, displacing hosts of endangered birds. That same spring, Williams's mother—a "downwinder" resident of southern Utah exposed to fallout from aboveground nuclear testing in Nevada—succumbed to breast cancer. Against a backdrop of loss and desolation, against the malevolent forces she holds responsible for her mother's death, Williams negotiates in *Refuge* a new relationship, a new covenant with her land, her people, and her family. "As a Mormon woman of the fifth generation of Latter-day Saints," she writes, "I must question everything, even if it means losing my faith, even if it means becoming a member of a border tribe among my own people."[4] She weighs her genealogy against her allegiance to the institutional church and establishes for herself a space on the margins of orthodox Mormonism but still firmly within the provenance of her cultural history.

With this bold declaration, Williams joined a growing "border tribe" of Mormons displaced by a rising tide of institutional antifeminism and neoorthodox retrenchment in the early 1990s. The flood point came in the years immediately following the publication of *Refuge* in 1991. Brigham Young University fired Professor Cecilia Konchar Farr in 1993 after Farr spoke on a pro-choice platform *as a Mormon woman* at a NOW-sponsored rally in Salt Lake City. Later that year, seven other scholars and feminists were disfellowshipped or excommunicated from the Mormon Church; several more feminist faculty members—including Professor Gail Houston—were fired or voluntarily resigned from Brigham Young University.[5] Their stories expose the "unnatural" quality of Mormon identity: even if you're "born in the covenant" to Mormon parents, raised within the culture, and baptized at eight years of age, you can still be made an exile.

Mormon "identity" is a historically contingent, highly contested, and perpetually tenuous construct. This tension derives primarily from the complex relationship between membership in the Mormon Church and affiliation with Mormon culture. Church membership is ecclesiastically regulated, institutionally maintained, and revocable; Mormonism is sustained otherwise—in memory, desire, faith, discourse, performance, and community. Mormonism originated as a voluntary religious association, and it continues in the dynamic relationship between institutional and individual histories. The history of the Mormon Church—from its organization in upstate New York in 1830—is a story of conscientiously developed and carefully mediated cultural differentiation. In the 1840s church practices such as economic communitarianism and plural marriage materialized the differences between Mormons and their neighbors. Widespread suspicion toward esoteric and Masonic-related elements of Mormon belief further deepened the cultural divide. Soon Mormons established their own settlements, first in Ohio and then in Illinois and Missouri as local violence and political hostility spurred removal and relocation. With their westward exodus to Utah in 1846–1847, beyond the established boundaries of the United

States, Mormons established a firm religious, cultural, and geographical distance between themselves and their national origins. The state of "Deseret" soon had its own currency, its own alphabet, and its own system of government. Reports of Brigham Young's "desert empire" drew suspicion from U.S. president James Buchanan, who ordered federal armies to march on Utah in 1857. The "Utah War" never escalated to armed conflict, but perceptions of Mormons as a distinct protonational entity and sometimes as a distinct race persisted through the early twentieth century.

Mormons have maintained their cultural difference even though geographic and demographic bounds of the community have been radically reshaped by a crosscurrent of forces. The church's official abolition of polygamy in 1890 and Utah's subsequent admission to statehood brought Mormons back into American political commerce; since then, the church's vigorous missionary program and rapid expansion in Central and South America have made national boundaries increasingly irrelevant to the Mormon concept of "Zion." And if nineteenth-century travel writers once characterized the Mormon race by its English converts' pale faces and narrow features, this phenotype no longer applies except to a minority of church members still residing in the geographical Utah-Idaho-Arizona corridor. Still, Salt Lake City remains the headquarters of the Mormon Church and the geographical center of Mormon life. Diasporic patterns of Mormon settlement and the tremendous growth of the international church have strengthened the power of church policies to determine who is considered a "member" and who is not. Abstinence from coffee, tea, tobacco, and alcohol are now significant markers of Mormon identity, although our grandparents might remember that more than a few souls in their small Utah towns kept a coffee pot on the stove and "Jack Mormons"—smokers and drinkers—were considered Mormons still. Increasingly, conservative politics have come to index orthodoxy. In the early and mid-twentieth century, Utah Mormons emphasized their Americanness with a patriotism that inclined to John Birch Society politics. More recently, the church has committed its membership and resources to political campaigns against the Equal Rights Amendment and gay marriage. The radical history of Deseret and a strong but little-known legacy of Mormon feminism notwithstanding, many contemporary American Mormons now articulate their difference from "worldly standards" in language that seems allied with that of the religious right.[6]

The stakes of Mormon identity politics are high for those who write and publish: public Mormonisms that do not accord with the culture's most conservative self-concepts are seen sometimes as a threat to the church itself. In his defense of gay Mormon poet Timothy Liu, Bryan Waterman observes: "The near-ethnic flavor of nineteenth-century Mormonism is giving way to a constructed identity aligned closely with (voluntary) activity in the institutional church."[7] Liu's choice to include in his poetry both elements of gay experience and references to Mormon culture situate him as a prodigal son of Mormonism. Mormon feminist writers like Terry Tempest Williams need not confess departure from a Mormon lifestyle to be considered unorthodox or even heretical. The very act of speaking out independently and publicly *as a Mormon woman* can be seen as inappropriate to patriarchal society. This antagonism has been intensified by institutional retrenchment and neo-orthodoxy, which emphasizes absolute and unquestioning obedience to church officials. Thus, as an independent, broadly public, woman-authored text about Mormon experience and belief, *Refuge* by its very existence challenges institutionally based and orthodox concepts of Mormon identity.

The substance of Williams's testimony in *Refuge* complements its form and redoubles the anti-neo-orthodox challenge. In the book's oft-reprinted epilogue, "The Clan of One-Breasted Women," Williams testifies that unquestioning obedience to a sovereign institutional power is dangerous if not lethal. She reviews the history of above-ground nuclear testing in Nevada and Southern Utah and the outcomes of cases filed against the United States by "downwinder" cancer victims. These suits were ultimately rejected under the doctrine of "sovereign immunity," interpreted by the court to absolve the government of responsibility for the public-health impact of its nuclear testing program. Williams connects the doctrine of sovereign immunity, Mormon orthodoxy, and downwinder mortality:

> In Mormon culture, authority is respected, obedience is revered, and independent thinking is not. . . . For many years, I have done just that—listened, observed, and quietly formed my own opinions, in a culture that rarely asks questions because it has all the answers. But one by one, I have watched the women in my family die common, heroic deaths. . . . Fear and inability to question authority that ultimately killed rural communities in Utah during atmospheric testing of atomic weapons is the same fear I saw in my

> mother's body. Sheep. Dead sheep. The evidence is buried. I cannot
> prove that my mother, Diane Dixon Tempest, or my grandmothers,
> Lettie Romney Dixon and Kathryn Blackett Tempest, along with my
> aunts developed cancer from nuclear fallout in Utah. But I can't
> prove they didn't.[8]

Williams acknowledges that it is impossible to establish definitively, under the doctrine of sovereign immunity and in accordance with legal and scientific standards, the truthfulness of her experience and of the experience of her foremothers. Hers is a family history that the government dare not authenticate, a radicalizing story that defies official sanction.

Her legacy and testimony *as a Mormon woman* pose similarly fundamental challenges to institutional neo-orthodoxy. Sonia Johnson, a Mormon feminist and ardent Equal Rights Amendment activist, who was excommunicated in 1979, put it this way: "In a patriarchy, to preach equality is to preach treason. To preach such a doctrine in a patriarchy is to preach the most powerful of all heresies. Feminists are heretics, then, and traitors."[9] If so, then according to a strictly institutional (or neo-orthodox) ideology of Mormon identity, Mormon feminism itself is impossible. (Both our sympathizers and our critics, from conservative Mormons to non-Mormon feminists, have said as much.) Yet we who call ourselves Mormon feminists persist against this reductive identity politics. It may be impossible for the institutional church to abide our testimonies or legitimate our Mormonisms; still, we continue to claim the authority of our experience. Retrenchment and neo-orthodoxy have put Mormon feminism under terrific strain. Some of us choose to continue quietly in full activity in the institutional church; some of us negotiate our church activity on a provisional, day-to-day basis; some of us maintain our affiliation to Mormonism exclusively through non-official associations. Those who write and publish do so mindful of repercussions through church discipline or excommunication. The challenge, then, is to find a way of establishing authority and securing identity *as a Mormon woman*, independently of institutional sanction.

Williams alternates between implicit and explicit discourses to communicate her engagement with Mormonism. What she cannot say with ecclesiastical authority, she attempts to say with professional authority as a natural historian. The multistranded plot allows her a similar poetic flexibility. It parallels the flooding of the Great Salt Lake, the displacement of endangered birds from the Bear River Refuge, Diane Dixon Tempest's intensifying struggle with cancer, and the author's deepening anguish; each chapter opens with an indexical reading of the Great Salt Lake's rising water level. Williams also applies the discourse of natural history to claim for herself an inalienable Mormonism rooted in family and place. After all, no matter how unorthodox her ideas, no one can deny the author's Mormon pioneer ancestors nor her family's long residence in Utah. "Genealogy is in our blood," she writes. "As a people and as a family, we have a sense of history. And our history is tied to land."[10] It is a curious conceit—this "genealogy in the blood"—one which borrows from biological race theory and the discourse of blood quantum. In Williams's case, the blood does not communicate Mormon genes but rather Mormon "genealogy," or a discursively constructed historical consciousness. By inscribing her Mormonism as "genealogy in the blood," Williams naturalizes her identity, absorbing religious belief and cultural affiliation into the marrow of the body. This *native* Mormonism establishes a basis for sovereignty of conscience.

The idea of native Mormonism is compelling for the "border tribe." It preserves Mormonism's ethnic sensibility, and it supplants the power of the institutional church to determine Mormon identity. But the language of Mormon nativism, sovereignty, and tribalism has its liabilities as well, especially as it uncritically mimics American Indian political discourses. "As a people and as a family, we have a sense of history," Williams writes, "and our history is tied to land." While it is true that Mormon history predates American history in Utah—Mormon pioneers arrived in 1847, and Utah passed from Mexican to American colonial control under the Treaty of Guadalupe Hidalgo in 1848—Utah was Indian before it was Mexican, Mormon, or American. Mormons tend to remember ourselves as an oppressed people driven into the desert rather than as settler-colonists and oppressors in our own right, and this exceptionalist concept of Mormon-Indian relations structures our historical memory. Mormon-Indian exceptionalism derives in part from theology: the Book of Mormon identifies the indigenous peoples of America as descended from the tribes of Israel, and some Mormons (both white and Native) maintain that American Indians are descended from Book of Mormon peoples. Our exceptionalism also derives from historical experience, as Mormon settlers interacted closely with Utah tribes. Brigham Young's stated Indian policy was explicitly (though not exclusively) ameliorationist: as he explained in December 1854, "It was manifestly more economical and less expensive, to feed and clothe, than to fight them."[11] Still, whether by feeding, fighting, or proselytizing, colonization by Mormons has done violence to indigenous communities in Utah, Idaho, Arizona, and elsewhere.

Refuge fails to remember this violence in its history of Mormon settlement. It records the arrival of handcart pioneer companies with no mention of Indian-white interaction; its account of Brigham Young's "colonial economics" in Brigham City, Utah, says nothing of "feeding" or "fighting." However, Indians—more dead than living—and Indianness do figure significantly in the text as the objects of ethnography and natural history. Williams participates in a long tradition of fantastic anthropology and primitivistic modernism by displacing questions of identity, authenticity, culture, custom, and survival onto indigenous peoples. Her purposes are self-protective: this strategy allows Williams to evade a direct interrogation of Mormonism. It permits her to escape the double-bind of being both curator and *object*, avoiding disclosures that could expose her to ecclesiastical repercussions.

Refuge was not the first book in which Williams turned to "Indian country" for instruction. In *Pieces of White Shell: A Journey to Navajoland* (1984), Williams points out that both Navajos and Mormons are migrants, "relative newcomers" to the "Four Corners" region; both are "caught between modernization and tradition"; both are "spiritual," emphasizing the sacredness of place and family. Despite these similarities, she recognizes the wrongs of simply appropriating Indian culture: "I am not suggesting we emulate Native Peoples—in this case, the Navajo. We can't. We are not Navajo. Besides, their traditional stories don't work for us. It's like drinking another man's medicine. Their stories hold meaning for us only as examples. They can teach us what is possible." She asks "Navajo holy-man" Herb Blatchford if it is "inappropriate for a non-Indian to use Indian stories to illustrate a land ethic." "No, it does not offend me," he replies. "But it may some." These conscientious considerations about "Indian stories" do not prevent a romantic reliance on Indian sites and artifacts in *Refuge*. Over the course of the narrative, Williams makes several trips to archaeological dig sites. Each artifact she unearths or encounters—petroglyphs in Anasazi State Park, the "disintegrating" skulls of Kwakiutl Indians on a "remote island" off the coast of Vancouver, a ceremonial birdfoot necklace belonging to the now "extinct" Frémont—seems to teach her about the enduring power of culture or the essential spirit of place. At a Frémont dig in the flatlands west of Salt Lake City, Williams imagines the artifacts in the hands of their original owners. "Can't you see them dancing around the fire dressed in feathers with the shrill cry of bone whistles in the air?" she asks a companion on the dig. He replies, "And where are these feathered robes and bone whistles now?" The party of archaeologists refashions the past on the last night of their expedition; they craft fake birdfoot necklaces from plastic forks and "dance wildly like tribesmen around the fire," "singing songs . . . never heard before." [12] Fantastic anthropology assures her—if temporarily— that dry bones do in fact live.

Representations of Indianness undergo a meaningful shift when death calls Williams home from the dig site. (Williams's mother passed away in January 1987, and her grandmothers in November 1988 and June 1989.) Relics lose their power to fascinate, and she becomes more self-conscious about her curatorial habits. Back in Salt Lake City, after her mother's death, she spots at a "trading post" a pair of deerskin moccasins, "ankle-high and fully beaded, including the soles, which were an intricate design of snakes." An unnamed bystander, who identifies herself as Cherokee, observes that they are "burial moccasins." Indeed, the storekeeper explains, a Shoshone woman brought them in to sell, having made two pairs for her grand-mother's funeral. Williams does not buy the moccasins. Instead, she de-scribes the way Mormons dress their dead—ceremonial white dress, slip-pers, apron, and veil. A few days later, she views a display of hollow eggshells at the Utah Museum of Natural History with a critical eye: "This collection is a sacrilege, the exposed medicine bundles of a tribe." [13] Here, *Refuge's* long catalog of artifacts—petroglyphs from disappeared tribes, trading-post moccasins, amputated bird limbs, empty eggshells, magic dust, ashes—ends. Williams relinquishes Indian grave goods and assumes the burden of her own culture.

The tremendous loss of three foremothers devolves upon her complete responsibility for her ancestry and their legacy. She declares herself "a woman rewriting my genealogy" and redirects her engagement with Mor-monism. It is advice of the author's grandmother and "spiritual mentor" Mimi that prompts this confrontational turn. Before death, Mimi interprets for Williams her experience of passing a large, cancerous uterine tumor: "When I looked into the water closet and saw what my body had expelled, the first thought that came into my mind was 'Finally, I am rid of the ortho-doxy.' My advice to you, dear, is do it consciously." Williams reflects upon her grandmother's uneven resistance to Mormon orthodoxy: Mimi had "read herself out of Mormonism" into Jungian psychology and "Eastern re-ligious thought," but she "voted for Ronald Reagan twice." The clandestine and arcane provided no protection against nuclear fallout, nor against the politics that produced it. Williams concludes, "If I am to survive, I must let my secrets out." [14]

This moment comes in *Refuge*'s epilogue, "The Clan of One-Breasted Women." Williams witnesses that she quietly nursed her mother, her aunts, and her grandmothers through their cancers and to their graves. She concludes that silence is fatal and commits herself to "question everything," "even if it means becoming a member of a border tribe among my own people." This epilogue is an act of testimony, a traditionally Mormon discursive mode. Our churches reserve the first Sunday service of the month for the congregational "bearing of testimony"; as in a Quaker silent meeting, individuals deliver impromptu testimonials of faith. By an unspoken understanding, only orthodox voices are heard in testimony meetings. To bear an unorthodox or an anti-orthodox testimony in an institutional context characterized by retrenchment is to negate one's authority and to endanger one's place within the congregation, even the church. Exposure, like complicity, can be harmful to the Mormon "border tribe." Consequently, in the latter half of the epilogue, Williams takes cover in the veiled language of dreamscape. "One night," she writes, "I dreamed women from all over the world circled a blazing fire in the desert," to dance, drum, and sing a song "given to them by Shoshone grandmothers." Soon, the women sense "tremors" from nuclear testing. "Stretch marks" appear on the land. Bombs become "stillborns." Wearing "Mylar" and "clear masks," the women walk through the desert toward town to protest, to testify that "to deny one's genealogy with the earth was to commit treason against one's soul." When "soldiers" arrest them and lead them away, "blindfolded and handcuffed," they sing up "reinforcements" with the Shoshone song. [15] This is a surrealist rendition of the Nevada Desert Experiment, an annual interfaith civil-disobedience campaign in which protesters "cross the line" onto "government-owned" testing grounds in southeastern Nevada. The testing grounds are located within Shoshone tribal land and "trespassers" carry with them "permits" granted by tribal authorities. Williams's account of the protest amplifies both its authentically tribal and its performative "Indian" aspects.

The act of playing Indian has a significant but checkered cultural history. As Philip J. Deloria perceptively observes, white Americans have performed Indianness to inaugurate, indigenize, and revitalize national identities. Some have attempted to remedy their spiritual ills by mimicking Indian religious practices; these "whiteshaman" poets and Men's Movement "warriors" have drawn well-deserved criticism. George Lipsitz identifies another species of this phenomenon in his study of New Orleans Mardi Gras Indians. He argues that this adoption of Indianness as a disguise, though it may seem simply an "escapist . . . appropriation, colonization, or eroticization of difference," can "provide protective cover for explorations of individual and collective identity. Especially when carried on by members of aggrieved communities—sexually or racially marginalized "minorities"—these detours may enable individuals to solve indirectly problems that they could not address directly." [16] I would cautiously apply this understanding to *Refuge*'s surrealist closing scene: Williams locates in an "Indian"-tinged "native" Mormonism a refuge from the impossibilities of orthodoxy.

There is a specifically Mormon cultural history of "playing Indian" that inflects this "border tribe" performance, as refugees throughout Mormon history have "played Indian" in the face of crisis. The "Danites," a vigilante group formed in response to anti-Mormon mob violence—violence that crested with Missouri governor Lillburn Bogg's 1838 "Extermination Order"—reportedly disguised themselves as Indians. Though the original band dissolved when the Mormons left Missouri, "Danites" persisted as a figure both in Mormon culture and the national imagination. In literature about Mormon Utah, including novels by Arthur Conan Doyle, Zane Grey, and Robert Louis Stevenson, as well as Richard Burton's 1862 Utah travelogue, *City of the Saints*, they come to represent an element of Mormonism inassimilable to nationalist norms. Danite vigilantes were not the only Mormons to play Indian. Frontier writer John Young Nelson reported finding a "tremendously tall," "painted" white man among a band of Utes in 1859: "[He] asked me in broken English where I was going, and if I was a Mormon. . . . [I] guessed he was one of the fanatical renegade-destroying angels, whose mission was to kill every white man not belonging to the sect, and particularly those who were apostates." After passing the evening with the group, Nelson revised his opinion: this man was not a Danite but "had been driven out of the Mormon community for some crime, and had found refuge with these Utes." Other marginal Mormons sought end-times refuge among the Paiutes of northern Nevada during the Ghost Dances of 1890. These "millennialists" believed that the year 1890 and the revitalization of American Indians signaled the return of Christ. Reports that "the whites and the Indians danced together" led some government officials to accuse the Mormons of inciting the "craze." [17]

The history of this Mormon cultural type reveals two seemingly contradictory facets to its character: one renegade, one defender of the faith. This is the contradiction of the "border tribe" as well. Williams finds herself outside her "own people" not necessarily because of unbelief but because of the particular and historically contingent politics of the cultural center are inhospitable or even hostile to her "native" Mormonism. She flees into the wilderness not to forget, but to remember. As a Book of Remembrance, *Refuge* claims genealogy for the Mormon margins. It posits a non-institutional, "native" Mormonism: an identity both inherited and constructed, natural and unnatural, which persists in the act of remembering.

Notes

1. Thomas S. O'Dea, *The Mormons* (Chicago: University of Chicago Press, 1957); Jan Shipps, *Mormonism: The Story of a New Religious Tradition* (Urbana: University of Illinois Press, 1985), 187 n.23; "Mormons," in *The Harvard Encyclopedia of Ethnic Groups*, ed. Stephan Thernstrom (Cambridge: Harvard University Press, 1980), 720–31; Patricia Nelson Limerick, *Something in the Soil: Legacies and Reckonings in the New West* (New York: W. W. Norton, 2000), 254.

2. Armaund Mauss, "Identity and Boundary Maintenance: International Prospects for Mormonism at the Dawn of the Twenty-First Century," in *Mormon Identities in Transition*, ed. Douglas Davies (London: Cassell, 1996), 9–19; Armaund Mauss, "Mormons as Ethnics: Variable Historical and International Implications of an Appealing Concept," in *The Mormon Presence in Canada*, ed. Brigham Card et al. (Edmonton: University of Alberta Press, 1990), 348; Kendall White, *Mormon Neo-Orthodoxy: A Crisis Theology* (Salt Lake City: Signature Books, 1987).

3. Mikal Gilmore, *Shot in the Heart* (New York: Doubleday, 1994), 59.

4. Terry Tempest Williams, *Refuge: An Unnatural History of Family and Place* (New York: Vintage, 1991), 286.

5. "BYU Fires Two Controversial Faculty Members," *Sunstone* 16, no. 5 (July 1993): 74–77; Martha Nussbaum, *Cultivating Humanity: A Classical Defense of Reform in Liberal Education* (Cambridge: Harvard University Press, 1997); and Bryan Waterman and Brian Kagel, *The Lord's University: Academic Freedom and Religious Orthodoxy* (Salt Lake City: Signature Books, 1998).

6. On historical and contemporary Mormon feminism, see the landmark essay collection *Women and Authority: Re-emerging Mormon Feminism*, ed.

Maxine Hanks (Salt Lake City: Signature Books, 1992). The "re-emergence" of contemporary Mormon feminism was spurred in part by the Mormon Church's organized opposition to the Equal Rights Amendment. Sonia Johnson's autobiographical *From Housewife to Heretic* (Garden City: Doubleday, 1981) chronicles Mormon feminism in the 1970s.

7. Bryan Waterman, "'Awaiting Translation': Timothy Liu, Identity Politics, and the Question of Religious Authenticity," *Dialogue: A Journal of Mormon Thought* 30, no. 1 (spring 1997): 168.

8. Williams, *Refuge*, 285–86.

9. Johnson, *Housewife*, 162–63.

10. Williams, *Refuge*, 14.

11. B. H. Roberts, *A Comprehensive History of the Church* (Salt Lake City: Deseret News Press, 1930), 4:50.

12. Terry Tempest Williams, *Pieces of White Shell: A Journey to Navajoland* (New York: Scribner's Sons, 1984), 2–3; Williams, *Pieces of White Shell*, 5, 135–36, 187–89.

13. Williams, *Refuge*, 234, 262.

14. Williams, *Refuge*, 241, 246, 273.

15. Williams, *Refuge*, 286, 287–89.

16. Philip Deloria, *Playing Indian* (New Haven: Yale University Press, 1998); Wendy Rose, "What's All This Fuss About Whiteshamanism Anyway?" in *Coyote Was Here: Essays on Contemporary Native American Literary and Political Mobilization*, ed. Bo Scholer (Aarhus, Denmark: SEKLOS, 1984); Ward Churchill, *Fantasies of the Master Race* (Maine: Common Courage Press, 1992); and Ward Churchill, *Indians R Us?* (Maine: Common Courage Press, 1994); George Lipsitz, *Dangerous Crossroads: Popular Music, Postmodernism, and the Poetics of Place* (London: Verso, 1994), 62.

17. Rebecca Foster Cornwall and Leonard J. Arrington, "Perpetuation of a Myth: Mormon Danites in Five Western Novels, 1840–90," BYU Studies 23 (spring 1983): 147–65; John Young Nelson, Fifty Years on the Trail: A True Story of Western Life (1889; reprint, Norman: University of Oklahoma Press, 1963), 140–41, 141; Lawrence G. Coates, "The Mormons and the Ghost Dance," Dialogue 18, no. 4 (winter 1985): 89–111); Garold Barney, Mormons, Indians and the Ghost Dance Religion of 1890 (Lanham MD: University Press of America, 1986); and James Mooney, The Ghost Dance Religion and the Sioux Outbreak of 1890 (Lincoln: University of Nebraska Press, 1991).

15. AUTHENTIC RE-CREATIONS

Ideology, Practice, and Regional History
along Buena Park's Entertainment Corridor

Hsuan L. Hsu

It is the event that is primary, not the things or even our directed thoughts about them. And it is in the place/time of the event that the audience takes part, becoming co-creators of social meaning. Authenticity is located in the event.

SPENCER R. CREW and JAMES E. SIMS,
"Locating Authenticity: Fragments of a Dialogue," 1991

A billboard off of the 101 Freeway in Los Angeles advertises Knott's Berry Farm as "The Theme Park Californians Call Home," implicitly contrasting its regional emphasis and local appeal with nearby Disneyland's more cosmopolitan attractions. At the same time, promotional literature boasting that "The Difference Is Real" at Knott's claims that, unlike Disneyland's fantasy-spaces (often based on animated films), Knott's Berry Farm—along with the other attractions on Buena Park's "Entertainment Corridor" —offers visitors "authentic" historical and ethnographic facts.[1] Indeed, the phrase even suggests that Knott's presents authentic representations not only of historical phenomena but of "difference" itself. A survey of the corridor's offerings—dancing Indians, jousting knights, waxen statues of movie stars, anthropological "oddities," and a berry farm turned Ghost Town—reveals that this claim to authenticity is closely tied to two apparently unrelated themes: on the one hand, Knott's Berry Farm, Wild Bill's Western Diner Extravaganza, the Covered Wagon Motel, and Po'Folks Restaurant represent the history of the American West—the very terrain on which these attractions are located; on the other hand, Medieval Times Dinner and Tournament and the Ripley's Believe It or Not! Museum offer ethnographic exhibitions of African, Asian, and Spanish cultures—cultures that seem entirely foreign to the West. This paper explores the ways in which these juxtaposed representations of America's internal and foreign frontiers relate to an ideology that uses supposedly authentic representations to gloss over cultural differences and historical complexities.

Insofar as the Entertainment Corridor describes its buildings, artifacts, and performances somewhat oxymoronically as "exact replicas" and "au-

15.1 Map of Knott's Berry Farm.
Reproduced by permission of the Buena Park Convention
and Visitors Office.

thentic representations," the notion of authenticity serves the ideological
function of enabling fixed representations to pass for actual experiences of
"otherness." At the same time, a narrative of historical justification effaces
every trace of the violence and inequality that characterize America's past
(and present) encounters with other cultures. Knott's Berry Farm's themed
areas illustrate the ways in which the park's "realism" depend upon a re-
duction of history to stereotyped images: Ghost Town represents a frontier
mining town; Fiesta Village "salutes" "California's Hispanic heritage"; Indian Trails denotes "the park area saluting and preserving the art and heri-

tage of Native Americans"; the Boardwalk recreates a California beach re-
sort of the 1920s; Camp Snoopy's miniature mountains and trees "evoke the
grandeur of Yosemite"; and Wild Water Wilderness "recaptures the magnificent beauty of a California wild river park of the early 1800s."[2] The law-
less boom town, California's beaches, bloody battles with Mexicans and Indians, and the threatening grandeur of the wilderness are reduced to an
outdoor shopping mall (Ghost Town) and an effort to recapture something
that never even existed ("a wild river park of the early 1800s")—as though
the wilderness were already a tamed and cultivated "park" when American
settlers first encountered it.

In fact, the American frontier was characterized by crime, corruption,
and often racially motivated violence. W. Eugene Hollon reports that "the
history of every Western state is replete with lawlessness," and describes
a diverse assortment of criminals, including "claim jumpers, miners, cowboys, cattle rustlers, Indian haters, Border ruffians, Mexican banditti, mule
skinners, railroad workers, highwaymen, racial bigots of various colors,
professional outlaws, homicidal maniacs, and hired gunslingers. Each
group had more than a speaking acquaintance with violence, for the rough
life on the frontier prior to 1900 produced scant recognition of the law as
law."[3] Little trace of these "individual types" remains in Ghost Town and
the recreated nineteenth-century saloon at Wild Bill's: at best the outlaws,
miners, and prostitutes represented here have only a "speaking acquaintance" with violence—they are either hired performers or inanimate statues. The corridor's Native Americans and Hispanics appear primarily as
English-speaking tribal dancers and mariachis, although their cultures
have been largely displaced by American expansion. (Of course, the park's
operations depend upon a largely Hispanic—and not always Anglophone
—maintenance staff, part of whose business it is to remain as inconspicu-
ous as possible.) Moreover, both Knott's and Wild Bill's disregard differences *among* Native Americans: Wild Bill's features a Hopi Ring Dance
performed to an Apache hymn sung by a member of the Cheyenne tribe,
while Indian Trails at Knott's juxtaposes three dancers from different tribes
with "authentic" tepees and a totem pole. By advertising Indian Trails as
Knott's Berry Farm's Native American "Interpretive Center," the park foregrounds entertainment value as the primary meaning or "interpretation" of
Native American cultures. A Mayan temple contains the entrance to the
roller coaster Jaguar!, while Montezooma's Revenge—a roller coaster that
"zooms" forward and backward through a full loop in less than a minute—

playfully alludes to Spain's brutal conquest of Montezuma's Aztec civilization. Wild Bill's presents another such pun in its publicity slogan, blatantly announcing its project of effacing frontier violence: instead of showing how the West was won, the attraction invites tourists to "come discover how the West was FUN!"

Such attempts to recover the "heritage" of Hispanic and Native American cultures for the purpose of entertainment merely re-cover or conceal both present-day and historical tensions: Walter Knott's own grandparents, for example, engaged in several battles with "hostile Indians" during their journey from Texas to California following the Civil War.[4] The military and imperialist connotations of Knott's Berry Farm's "salutes" and "tributes" to Mexicans and Indians ironically register the very history of violence they are attempting to disavow. "Saluting and preserving the art and heritage of Native Americans," after all, indulges in what Renato Rosaldo calls "imperialist nostalgia"—a hypocritical reaction in which "people mourn the passing of what they themselves have transformed." The very name of Knott's Berry Farm exemplifies this logic of nostalgia: when he marketed fruits that his own family had cultivated, Walter Knott referred to his growing business as "Knott's Berry Place": it was not until 1947—well after the founding of the Chicken Dinner Restaurant (1937), which served thousands of dinners a night, and the cyclorama entitled "The Covered Wagon Show" at Ghost Town (1940)—that the park was renamed "Knott's Berry Farm."[5] In other words, the Knotts renamed it a "Farm" precisely during the period when the reputation and income of the restaurant and theme park were beginning to eclipse those of the farm itself. Misrepresentations of benevolent—or at least harmless—Native Americans similarly "preserve" and "salute" cultures that the United States expropriated or exterminated. Ripley's Believe It or Not! Museum and Medieval Times Dinner and Tournament offer analogous misrepresentations of foreign cultures: the museum's "authentic replicas" of African fetishes, Siamese twins, and Spanish Inquisitors' torture devices exaggerate the "unbelievable" strangeness of "primitive" peoples; Medieval Times reenacts a medieval Spanish joust that likewise primitivizes California's former colonizers.

However, the corridor's primary object of consumption remains the American frontier, the peripheral national space that resonates with all these representations of cultural "otherness." Though geographically contiguous with southern California, the historical frontier described in Frederick Jackson Turner's landmark study was radically different from Buena

Park's ordered and controlled suburbia: "The frontier is productive of individualism. . . . The tendency is anti-social. It produces antipathy to control, and particularly to any direct control." For Turner, the frontier involves not a preservation but a rejection of the past, a departure from society into unexplored regions, a willingness to engage in physical labor and possibly violent conflicts with Native Americans and outlaws. His essay concludes that "movement had been [the frontier's] dominant fact"—that the unrestricted mobility offered by the West produced the "dominant individualism" he claims to be characteristic of American democracy.[6] Knott's and Wild Bill's reflect a very different version of the frontier, one located not beyond but in the midst of the metropolis. Here, the frontier is purged of crime, risk, and mobility: signs demarcating restricted areas, security guards, surveillance cameras, and conspicuous placards reserving "the right to refuse service to anyone" impose more control in spaces of tourism than in the city proper.[7] In another departure from historical facts, Ghost Town refrains from serving alcohol even in its "authentic" saloons: "Walter wanted the Berry Farm always to be a place of good fellowship for entire families . . . a park in which children would never have to see either drinking or drunkenness." Surrounded by employees at work—or at least "performing" the roles of laborers—visitors do nothing but watch: the Calico Mine Ride offers a tour of an artificial silver mine in which electronically animated "miners" appear to be hard at work. One press release boasts that "all across Knott's Ghost Town, there's a lot to learn from . . . talented craftspeople at work—an artisan at her wheel, spinning yarn; a blacksmith laboring at his forge. All are eager to talk about their crafts and their lives."[8]

Although it still functions as a sort of escape from social constraints, Knott's seems to be diametrically opposed to the revisionary attitude toward the past described by Turner. Instead, Walter Knott appealed to the frontier as a tradition that ought to be recovered and preserved: he built Ghost Town—the first of the park's themed areas—because he "thought people [during the Great Depression] needed to be reminded of the pioneering spirit. He could build something on the berry farm to be both a monument to the early-pioneers—including his parents—and an educational diversion." Ironically, however, this appeal to the frontier Ghost Town involves the most radical of historical revisions: for actual "ghost towns" are defined by their lack of inhabitants, economy, and wealth. Insofar as the ghost town embodies the stagnant and abandoned residue of the "pioneer spirit," Knott's appropriates the frontier in the form of its corpse, transforming it from a unstable, marginal region of uncontainable mobility into a frozen, "preserved" tradition.[9] It simultaneously resurrects and dehistoricizes the ghost town with an infusion of "history" repackaged as amusement: the promotional literature oxymoronically claims that "Ghost Town brims with vital, living history." Walter Knott's re-presentation of frontier life confirms Turner's announcement of the closing of the frontier by simultaneously "saluting" it and banishing its most essential feature.[10]

Despite all these ideological deviations from historical complexities, however, Knott's persuasively asserts its authenticity by collapsing distinctions between fact and fiction. A reconstructed nineteenth-century Kansas schoolhouse, where Umberto Eco overheard "one tourist ask his wife if the children were real or 'fake,'" provides an eloquent example of the theme park's principle of authenticity. A placard on its wall reads: "Mr. Knott bought the school, outhouse, and playground at an auction, had them dismantled, and and [sic] trucked here in 1952. To facilitate reconstruction, numerous drawings and photographs were made of the school, both interior and exterior[,] enabling the plasterer to duplicate exactly the cracked and worn walls. The original building has been changed from white to red, and a bell tower added." This sign registers no disjunction between the detailed drawings and photographs used "to duplicate exactly the cracked and worn walls" and the gratuitous change in color and addition of a bell tower. Flaws and improvements alike serve to certify the schoolhouse's "authenticity."

Other attractions along the corridor deploy different rhetorics of authenticity. The Movieland Wax Museum's description of a replicated scene from *Gone with the Wind*, for example, reads: "Authenticity is the key word here. Even though it is never seen, Hattie is wearing a long red petticoat, a gift from Rhett. The gazebo was actually on a Georgia plantation and moved and reassembled at Movieland." Despite the caption's assurance, the statue itself reveals no trace of the fetishized red petticoat: one cannot resist repeating Rhett's act of undressing Scarlett with his eyes ("He looks as if . . . as if he knows what I look like without my shimmy!") By arousing the viewer's desire (both erotic desire and the desire for authenticity), the petticoat's invisibility paradoxically enhances its effectiveness: in effect, the scenario promises to be more authentic than it appears. Captions boasting that "Greta Garbo's magnificent gown is an exact duplicate of the original which cost $35,000 and took 125 hours to sequin by hand" and that the reproduction of Barbra Streisand's gown cost $4,000 cite extravagant cost and labor as further guarantors of authenticity. Conversely, Eco claims that the Ripley's Believe It or Not! Museum employs a purely visual rhetoric of authenticity: "The authenticity the Ripley's Museums advertise is not historical, but visual. Everything looks real, and therefore it is real; in any case the fact that it seems real is real, and the thing is real even if, like Alice in Wonderland, it never existed." [11] Whereas Knott's and Movieland depend upon captions to establish their historical and corporeal authenticity, tourists at Ripley's fetishize the (often duplicated or reconstructed) oddities they see rather than "real" historical specimens.

Whether guaranteed by cost, detail, or sensationalism, authenticity along the Entertainment Corridor is largely a rhetorical effect. Whatever their specific messages, the very abundance of both textual captions and visual supplements (backgrounds, informational pamphlets, dioramas, etc.) reinforces each object's authenticity-effect. Ghost Town presents the most obvious example of simulacral overkill: the Old Trails Hotel from Prescott, Arizona, "an authentic saloon," the Denver and Rio Grande Railroad, a replica of the Bird Cage Theater in Tombstone, Arizona, and the schoolhouse from Beloit, Kansas, were all transplanted to Knott's Berry Farm in order to provide "an authentic setting" for a "cyclorama" depicting a wagon train painted by the Austrian artist Paul von Klieben. This eclectic aggregate of original buildings, replicas of original buildings, and fictional embellishments seems all the more persuasive for being composed of so many heterogeneous elements. Yet, at the same time that the overabundance of reproductions and commentaries produces an authenticity-effect, their heterogeneity and the superficiality of their content actively undermine the direct, unmediated presence expected of an authentic artifact. Georges van den Abbeele explains that "the marker, while constitutive of the sight in its supposedly unmediated authenticity, is what, through the diacritical act of its marking, perpetually removes or defers the sight from any undifferentiated immediacy." Since most of the Entertainment Corridor's sights are replicas or simulations, markers of authenticity play a crucial role in establishing a discursive "aura" even as their overabundance removes any possibility—or expectation—of "undifferentiated immediacy."

This deferral of the unmediated "original" destabilizes authenticity as much as it asserts it. After all, do tourists really believe in the corridor's often blatantly stereotypical representations? Do they leave Knott's persuaded that the frontier was a safe, predictable "park," the Native Americans eager exhibitors of their uprooted culture? Or can visitors experience the corridor's ideological representations skeptically? To simply dismiss the corridor as an ideological space would be to repeat its conservative move, effacing the potential forms of mobility and destabilization that are in fact inseparable from experiences of that space. For even the corridor's ideologically determined attractions are subject to different interpretive traversals; tourist attractions are not static representations but open-ended spaces that both accommodate and respond to the experiences of individual visitors. Individual spaces embody a different principle of authenticity—one that is just as significant as the authenticity-effects produced by the corridor's reductive images, yet falls outside their reach.

If the corridor's attractions are fantasy spaces that trivialize and efface conflicts and differences, no one dwells in the fantasy for long. According to Walter Benjamin, even the nineteenth-century Parisian *flâneur* was never entirely deceived by the city's fascinating displays: "The deepest fascination of this spectacle lay in the fact that as it intoxicated him it did not blind him to the horrible social reality." At Knott's and the Movieland and Ripley's museums, tourists are continually on the move from one attraction to the next, seldom resting for more than a few minutes at a time. Without these continual active movements on the part of their visitors, the attractions couldn't influence anybody; yet these very movements involve a subversive mobility that individualizes the corridor's spaces. Because every particular experience produces a different "interpretation" of the corridor, its ideological representations do not imprison visitors so much as they provide a field for the enactment of their individual traversals.[12]

Thus, tourists can carry on a continual negotiation with its ideological architecture on the most practical of levels—simply by avoiding and frequenting different parts of the corridor. In the last few decades, this interaction between the corridor and its visitors has produced several architectural revisions: the alligator farm established across the street from Knott's moved to Florida in 1982; the Palace of Living Arts, whose waxen statues representing the subjects of famous paintings both fascinated and baffled Eco, closed in 1982; and the Adultland xxx movie theater was replaced by the more "respectable" Studio Theater in 1997. Knott's and Movieland are also in a state of continual transition, adding new attractions on an annual basis in response to popular demand. As Alan Bryman puts it in his comments on the Disney theme parks, "The parks are not inert texts. Walt always said that the parks would never be finished. . . . Not only have new attractions been continually added (while others have been dropped), but also many have been changed and redesigned."[13] In Buena Park as well as at Disneyland, the relative popularity of respective attractions, reflected in attendance statistics, exerts a considerable influence on this continual process of revision. Van den Abbeele explains that, advertisements and institutional signs aside, "[the tourist's] activity is also a marking" of a given sight: "both 'society' and the individual tourist are implicated in the marking process [and] neither is fully in control of it." Tourists continually re-mark attractions simply by visiting them in the course of specific itineraries, purchasing or not purchasing souvenirs and interpreting pre-existing markers in various ways. A journey that included Knott's and Wild Bill's and another that moved from Wild Bill's to Adultland, for example, would produce two very different "readings" or realizations of the corridor's offerings: the former would emphasize the theme of the American West, while the latter might view the scantily clad saloon dancers at Wild Bill's as a prelude to Adultland's pornographic films.[14]

In a sense, then, every tourist reenacts the individualistic, revisionary drives of the American frontier in the very process of traversing the corridor. Although it often represents the frontier—as well as foreign cultures—through static themes and icons, particular experiences of the corridor reintroduce the continual change and radical mobility that Turner ascribes to the frontier. To criticize the corridor only on the level of its reductive representations would be to concede that the frontier can only be represented as a static object rather than put into practice as an individualized and potentially transformative performance.

In fact, there is more to the corridor than its two-dimensional representations of historical and cultural specificities. For even a theme park ultimately depends upon the people who traverse it, and the ways in which they do so: "The interior space of the [theme] park is not designed to be contemplated from a privileged point of view, but to be traversed. The park necessitates mobility." Michel de Certeau argues that even so quotidian an activity as walking constitutes an active "process of *appropriation* of the topographical system . . . a spatial acting-out of the place." Whether driving down the corridor or walking amongst its attractions, tourists in motion exert an unsettling effect on urban space: "[Walking] develops its effects, proliferates, floods private and public spaces, undoes their readable surfaces, and creates within the planned city a 'metaphorical' or mobile city, like the one Kandinsky dreamed of: 'a great city built according to all the rules of architecture and then suddenly shaken by a force that defies all calculation.'"

The notion of a "metaphorical" city refers to a space experienced from a moving vehicle (*metaphorein* is "to carry across") rather than from an abstract and disembodied point of view. A negativity that "undoes . . . readable surfaces" reintroduces the mobility of Turner's frontier into the city. Indeed, both Jane Holtz Kay and William Fulton have identified automobiles and suburban expansion as modern versions of Turner's frontier.[15] Tourists traversing landscapes designed in the service of ideology—from Walter Knott's authentic architectural replicas to Movieland's recreated film stills—re-introduce mobility by their very act of passing through.

On the surface, Knott's Berry Farm's roller coasters seem to provide only a superficial caricature of de Certeau's spatial practices. For with all their velocity, loops, and sudden swerves, high-speed rides remain mere performances of danger and transgression. A host of warnings, height restrictions, seat restraints, and even the rails themselves constantly remind visitors that there is no safer or more constrained form of movement. Proper behavior on these rides is strictly enforced: speakers announce rules in several languages, and transgressions are punished by forced removal from the park. Ironically, since roller coaster casualties are statistically far rarer than automobile casualties, getting to and from the theatricalized "danger" of amusement parks is really much more dangerous than the rides themselves. Unlike walking and driving, roller coasters do not involve any "real" motion: the rides end up where they begin. Nevertheless, roller coaster riders deliberately pursue the feeling of vertigo: they lose all sense of direction and perspective, both during the ride and for a period of time thereafter. In a chapter entitled "Vertigo," Kathleen Kirby writes that "we go into the funhouse willingly to experience a state of confusion [and] with the intention of deranging our usual ways of knowing."[16] In other words, the theme park creates a sense of vertigo that, by deranging the (ideological) foundations of knowledge, enables visitors to revise their understanding of its representations. Roller coasters at Knott's—including the Corkscrew (featuring the world's first 360-degree loop), Montezooma's Revenge (whose very name refers to both "zooming" speed and a vernacular phrase for something akin to nausea), and Boomerang (which turns riders upside down six times in less than a minute)—produce a sort of social vertigo that sets the park's ideologically determined representations in motion in such a way that knowledge itself becomes shifting and indeterminate.

By means of the revisionary or "re-creational" activities of walking, driving, and roller coaster riding, tourists perform individual and "authentic" traversals of the corridor. Indeed, even the "sedentary" attractions—Wild Bill's, Medieval Times, and the recently removed Adultland theater—offer a sort of vicarious mobility. Medieval Times offers disorientation in the form of fast horses, archaic language, and an insistence that guests eat with their bare hands; Adultland's pornographic films represent what may be the most transgressive of genres—one that has extravisual designs on viewers' bodies. And the very designation of Wild Bill's as an "Extravaganza" suggests that mere spectatorship can constitute a sense of transgressive mobility or "extra-vagrancy." Indeed, one of Turner's most vivid descriptions of the frontier involves a form of quasi-cinematic spectatorship grounded in travel: "Each [type of settler] passed in successive waves across the continent. Stand at the Cumberland Gap and watch the procession of civilization, marching single-file—the buffalo following the trail to the salt springs, the Indian, the fur-trader and hunter, the cattle-raiser, the pioneer farmer—and the frontier had passed by. Stand at the South Pass in the Rockies a century later and see the same procession with wider intervals between." The process of witnessing this "procession" of civilization rhetorically transports the viewer to famous western landmarks, so that the very act of watching the frontier "pass by" vicariously reenacts the frontier's westward movement—from the Cumberland Gap to the South Pass and beyond. A similar process of extra-vagant spectatorship may be at work in the corridor's ethnographic spaces "representing" Spain, China, Africa, and Central America as well as the American West. More than a two-dimensional amalgamation of unrelated "foreign" spaces, the corridor may also embody a utopian space as defined by Louis Marin: "Utopia as process is the figure of all kinds of frontiers, displacing, by the practice of its travels, all representation." [17]

Still, can the distinction between ideology and subversion simply be mapped onto an opposition between representation and individual practice? Do individual itineraries have any greater claim to "authenticity" than the nostalgic representations that disavow past and present inequalities? Isn't a distanced or cynical experience of the corridor, which ironically emphasizes the arbitrary nature of its ethnic stereotypes, merely a repetition of that disavowal on another level—a disavowal of representations that disavow violence? According to Van den Abbeele, such a disavowal involves not a subversion but rather a common topos of the rhetoric of tourism: "The tourist's desire for authenticity is an individualistic one in which he seeks to appropriate that authenticity for himself as opposed to the other tourists (simply 'the tourists,' since the tourist rarely considers himself to be one) who can render the sight inauthentic by their mere presence." In response to an ideology that fetishizes frozen icons of the frontier, does a theory that overvalues spatial practices merely fetishize a different type of authenticity ascribed to movement itself? Spatial practices may allow for the inscription of ironic detachment, individual preferences, and disoriented experiences of space, but to what extent can they disorient the corridor's spaces themselves?[18]

After all, as M. Christine Boyer points out, fetishizing automobiles did not prevent the futurists from buying into fascist ideology, and, by the 1960s, "The freedom of mobility and the exhilaration of speed that the automobile once promised the Futurists had turned into an illusion. Instead, the open road led to the scrap heap, junkyard, used-car lot, parking lot, drive-in bank, shopping center, or gas station." Despite the freedom of movement they seem to offer, automobiles are always also tools of ideology, vehicles of drive-in consumerism. They also serve to cut people off from the ugly effects of urban stratification: "The view from a car's windows is our prime experience of urban space at a time when few dare to walk the city's mean streets or explore its unmapped terrains."[19] If the corridor is most easily visited by car, then the majority of its visitors are "cut off" from the realities of its street life (approaching Knott's from any street other than Beach Boulevard, one sees only the impenetrable wall that isolates the park from pedestrian contact with the city around it).

Nor do the displacement, fragmentation, and condensation of space associated with automobiles necessarily subvert urban modes of control. In fact, Boyer suggests that such disorienting effects merely reproduce the corridor's removal of experience from its historical or mnemic context: "Discussions about topographical amnesia, about unpredictable collisions, ruptures, elisions, or deformations of visual material, enable us to understand why Dean MacCannell argues that the emblematic icon for postmodernity should be the automobile, not architecture, as has been commonly assumed. It is the automobile that not only contributes to the fragmentary nature of contemporary experience, but also expedites a failure of memory and hastens the eclipse of time by speed."[20]

Such an erasure of collective memory and time does not subvert but actually supports the corridor's project of erasing historical conflicts: the very destabilization of historical space results in an increased desire for a stable and totalizing representation of regional "history" and identity.

"Since memory is actually a very important factor in struggle," Foucault warns, "if one controls people's memory, one controls their dynamism. And one also controls their experience, their knowledge of previous struggles."[21] This suggests that, by fragmenting our spatial experiences, mobility actually contributes to the administration of urban space. If ideology cannot "control" people's memory, it can at least cajole them into voluntarily displacing, fragmenting, and disfiguring memory beyond recognition.

Slavoj Žižek points out a similar ambivalence when he argues that postmodern irony, with all its displacements and fragmentations, remains complicit in capitalist ideology: "In contemporary societies, democratic or totalitarian . . . cynical distance, laughter, irony . . . are, so to speak, part of the game." According to Žižek, irony remains ineffectual insofar as, whether or not one knows better (i.e., that tourism is tied to imperialist ideology or that driving contributes to the dissolution of collective memory), one participates in the ideological "game" all the same. Knott's Berry Farm's own history supplies an exemplary illustration of cynical participation in the ideology and economy of capitalism. According to Nygaard, Walter's wife, Cordelia, refused to open a restaurant at Knott's from the very beginning: "'No. I'll not go into the restaurant business,' she assured [Walter]. But quite possibly it was at that moment that another idea was born, for today the restaurants at Knott's Berry Farm are among the most popular eating places in all of Southern California." Nygaard's smug account implies that Cordelia began planning a restaurant precisely "at that moment"—at the very moment of denial. Later, Nygaard reports the following exchange:

> "But I do have an idea. . . . It won't be to run a restaurant, but I think we might try serving chicken dinners. There would just be the usual potatoes and vegetables, of course, but no selections. Just chicken dinners."
>
> "But you said no restaurant!" Walter was completely nonplussed, little realizing that when a good wife said, "No," she often meant, "Yes," or possibly just "Perhaps." At any rate, without intending to engage in it, the Knotts were in the restaurant business in 1934.[22]

Despite Cordelia's vehement disavowal of having anything to do with the restaurant business, the Knotts were in fact running a restaurant by 1934. Cordelia's cynical distance—her emphatic disavowal of capitalist enterprise—does not dislocate ideology: as Nygaard observes, a discursive "no" does often mean a "yes" for all practical purposes, or at least "perhaps." In the end, authenticity or "resemblance" boils down to economics: "On Thanksgiving, 1937, they served 1,774 dinners. Even Cordelia had to admit to herself that even if they would not have a restaurant, they did have a mighty close resemblance to one. . . . Mighty close indeed." [23]

This "mighty close resemblance"—the principle of the functioning simulacrum—accounts for another level of individual practice along the Entertainment Corridor. Terry Van Gorder, the president and CEO of Knott's, explains that "Our guests interact with operating antiques; they participate in real ways." It is not just a matter of false consciousness—believing that a smiling Cherokee employee performing a Hopi ring dance means that all American Indian tribes are not only intact, but thriving; instead, Van Gorder points to the fact that the reconstructed saloons, shops, and restaurants at Ghost Town are so realistic that they actually transact business with visitors. These attractions not only represent the frontier as a fantasy space— they also incorporate visitors into that fantasy. Hence, Eco observes that the tourist at Knott's "finds himself participating in the fantasy because of his own authenticity as a consumer; in other words, he is in the role of the cowboy or the gold-prospector who comes into town to be fleeced of all he has accumulated while out in the wilds." Whereas Eco concludes that "the hallucination operates in making the visitors take part in the scene and thus become participants in that commercial fair that is apparently an element of the fiction but in fact represents that substantial aim of the whole imitative machine," Van Gorder's remark and Cordelia Knott's repeated denials make it clear that there is no *hallucination* operating here at all. [24] Visitors are no less aware that the corridor is out for profit than Cordelia was conscious that she in fact ran one of southern California's most successful restaurants.

By means of audience participation, the corridor incorporates tourists into its representational field: at Medieval Times, the champion chooses his "Queen of Love and Beauty" from the audience; performers at Wild Bill's descend from the stage to sing and flirt with audience members, and then choose partners to square dance with on stage; and at the heart of Movieland's labyrinth of reproduced cinematic scenes, visitors confront a waxen representation of a tourist wearing a sweatshirt and hat with the Movieland logo whose camera flashes periodically. Each of the attractions offers souvenir photographs of visitors sitting with a wax statue of George Burns, meeting a medieval count and countess, [25] or screaming as they fall fifty feet in a log boat; often, these photographs are taken at points of entry and exit as a sort of ritual of initiation and departure that incorporates the tourist's body into the realm of mechanical reproduction, so that whether one actually purchases them or not is almost beside the point. The practice of exhibiting and selling photographs of visitors taken by automatic cameras at the climactic moments of roller coasters exemplifies one of the most poignant forms of audience incorporation. These photographs usually present grotesque images of visitors simultaneously smiling and screaming, desperately grasping safety handles or waving their hands in the air while being constrained by bulky mechanized bars—they are frozen portraits of people denied movement, frightened, blurred by speed, but enjoying themselves in spite of everything.

In none of these instances do tourists need to "believe" the corridor's representations: they are already addressed, framed—literally *photographed* as participants. Criticizing Louis Althusser's notion that "ideology consists in the very fact that the people 'do not know what they are really doing,' that they have a false representation of the social reality to which they belong," Slavoj Žižek claims that, on the contrary, people are often perfectly aware of the social conditions that their actions serve to perpetuate: "On an everyday level, the individuals know very well that there are relations between people behind the relations between things. The problem is that in their social activity itself, in what they are *doing*, they are *acting* as if money, in its material reality, is the immediate embodiment of wealth as such. They are fetishists in practice, not in theory." Belief is not the issue at Ripley's; simply by paying for admission, visitors are already complicit—on the level of practice— in fetishizing each of the oddities exhibited, whether they "Believe It or Not." This distinction between theoretical and practical belief is reflected by vernacular terms for belief that involve economic notions of "buying," "being invested in," or "putting stock in" an argument or idea. The motto of the Ripley's Museum can thus be completed as follows: "Believe it or not, you've already bought it!" Similarly, the dinner theaters induce arbitrary divisions of the audience to compete with one another in screaming, applauding, and otherwise exhibiting their enjoyment as loudly and convincingly as possible.[26] Whether one really enjoys oneself or not is beside the point: rather, what matters is how happy one can *act*. It doesn't matter that the jousts are choreographed, Native Americans didn't really dance in neon costumes, or the artifacts at Ripley's are reproductions, for all these attractions impose the injunction, "Whether you believe it or not, enjoy yourself!"

(This recalls Jacques Lacan's point that the superego—the agency that internalizes the law—insists above all on enjoyment: "The briefest way to render the superego paradox is the injunction 'Like it or not, enjoy yourself!'" Medieval Times's commemorative program issues this very command: "His Grace [the Count of Perelada] decrees that you have fun.")[27] Whether cynically, naïvely, or enthusiastically, every visitor at the Entertainment Corridor's attractions engages in some form of compulsory "pleasurable" consumption.[28] Theoretical distance makes no practical difference: tourism, like capitalism, incorporates its denial and assimilates its Other.

Turner's association of the frontier with notions of self-determination and unconstrained mobility doesn't adequately acknowledge capitalism's strategy of incorporating its frontier. In fact, William Cronon's criticism of Turner in *Nature's Metropolis* suggests that the foremost theorist of the frontier actually has several ideas in common with Walter Knott, a politically reactionary appropriator and simulator of the frontier. Like Knott, who built his amusement park to remind people of the "pioneering spirit," "Turner, the historian, looked backward with some nostalgia from an urban-industrial world he feared was losing touch with its rural democratic roots." According to Cronon, Turner also misrepresents the frontier, for western cities actually "grew in tandem with the countryside and played crucial roles in encouraging settlement from a very early time. City and country formed a single commercial system, a single process of rural settlement and metropolitan economic growth. To speak of one without the other made little sense." Cronon cites the perspective of Chicago's urban "boosters" as a more accurate alternative to Turner's frontier thesis: "Turner's Chicago rose to power only as the frontier drew to a close, whereas the boosters' Chicago had been an intimate part of the frontier almost from the beginning. . . . Urban-rural commerce was the motor of frontier change." Cronon also cites a thought experiment by nineteenth-century farmer Johann Heinrich von Thünen, in which successive frontiers develop as "concentric agricultural zones" forming around an abstract, ideal city that sits "in the midst of an endless and uniformly fertile plain." Inverting Turner's quasi-cinematic montage of westward waves as seen from the Cumberland Gap and South Pass, Cronon explains that "one has only to imagine [von Thünen's] central city in a nineteenth-century American setting . . . and then travel outward through the surrounding rural countryside, to experience an odd sense of déjà vu. Leaving the city and its factories behind, one first passes through a zone containing densely populated farm settlements practicing intensive forms of agriculture. . . . As one travels farther west, these intensive farms gradually give way to newer and more sparsely settled communities. . . . Farther west still, these give way to the open range, where ranchers and cowboys raise animals rather than crops. . . . Seen from the midst of the city . . . frontier and metropolis turn out to be two sides of the same coin." [29]

Paradoxically, it is not Cronon's urban perspective but rather Turner's nostalgic transcendental eye planted in the Cumberland gap that refuses to travel. Although Turner valorizes the continual mobility of the frontier, he ultimately observes the passage of civilization from fixed, panoramic points: "*Stand* at Cumberland Gap. . . . *Stand* at South Pass." On the other hand, von Thünen, who imagines a fixed city set in a uniform plain, uses the metaphor of a traveling eye. The writers' rhetorical modes of vision clash with the principles they endorse, problematizing any simple opposition between an abstract, stationary city and a disorienting, transitory frontier. The corridor not only represents the frontier as "Seen from the midst of the city": it also represents it in the midst of the city of Buena Park. Cronon's revision of Turner's thesis suggests that there is no definitive boundary (or "frontier") between the city and its frontier: the agricultural production of the frontier and the commercial exchange of the metropolis are mutually constitutive.

For Marin, the frontier does not embody mobility or transition at all, but the antithetical characteristic of stability. Juxtaposing two early definitions of the word "frontier," which denoted a defensive "front" opposed to a state's threatening enemies as well as the expanding limits of an aggressive kingdom, Marin argues that "the frontier defines a state of equilibrium and balance between the opposing forces of expansion and resistance." Marin's frontier, unlike those of Frederick Jackson Turner and Walter Knott, comprises a relatively stable "state" (political as well as physical) of equilibrium. He describes both the frontier and the utopia as an absolutely neutral space ("the 'other' of any place"), rather than something either radically subversive or nostalgically reactionary: "*Outopia* is a paradoxical, even giddy toponym since as a term it negates with its name the very place it is naming. . . . Utopia at the dawn of our modernity could be the name of the horizon that, as we have seen, makes the invisible come within the finite, all this by a strange nominal *figure* of the frontier (horizon, limit), that is to say, a name that would constitute a distance, a gap neither before nor after affirmation [and negation], but 'in between' them; a distance or a gap that does not allow any affirmation or negation to be asserted as a truth or a falsehood. Ne-uter, this is the radical of the frontier (limit, horizon) as well as that of Utopia." [30]

The corridor's utopian attractions present an ideology that cannot be simply affirmed or negated: all negations participate in the ambivalence of Cordelia Knott's denial ("I am not in the restaurant business"), which turns out to be homophonous with the affirmation, "I am Knott . . . in the restaurant business." Spatial practices may indeed disorient and negate the spaces of ideology, but they simultaneously reinforce them by giving rise to new visible historical boundaries and markers. The moment a possible trajectory is chosen and put into practice, that trajectory can be observed and mapped. Furthermore, the most common individual practice in the corridor remains the economic transaction, the contractual agreement that to some extent ratifies or "buys" its ideological caricatures. Even the greatest excesses of disorienting leisure take the form of an economic exchange, so that every frontier at some level belongs to a network of commercial transactions rooted in the city. Cronon's metaphor—that city and frontier are "two sides of the same coin"—aptly depicts the two types of space as always already circumscribed by money. Both reductive representations and individual practices are subsumed under what may be the corridor's most authentic—because unavoidable—practice: paying to have fun.

The city's incorporation of its frontier—whether it be the frontier of foreign cultures, pornographic films, the American West, or vertiginous roller coasters—ultimately renders the two opposed elements indistinguishable. The city blends with its surroundings to such an extent that, as an advertisement published by the California Office of Tourism boasts, "even the land and the ocean themselves look new" in Orange County:

> It's a theme park—a seven-hundred-and-eighty-six-square-mile theme park—and the theme is "you can have anything you want."
>
> It's the most California-looking of all the Californias: the most like the movies, the most like the stories, the most like the dream.
>
> Orange County is Tomorrowland and Frontierland, merged and inseparable. 18th-century mission. 1930s art colony. 1980s corporate headquarters.
>
> There's history everywhere: navigators, conquistadors, padres, rancheros, prospectors, wildcatters. But there's so much Now, the Then is hard to find. The houses are new. The cars are new. The

stores, the streets, the schools, the city halls—even the land and the ocean themselves look new. . . .

Come to Orange County. It's no place like home.[31]

"No place like home" points to both the absolute neutrality of Marin's *Ou-topia* ("no place") and the *unheimlich* ("not home-like") quality of a Ghost Town whose ruined buildings have been artificially restored to life.[32] Orange County is both "not" like home and all the more homelike precisely on account of its strangeness. This blurring of frontiers between the uncanny, utopian theme park and the conventional comforts of home may help account for the enigmatic roadside billboard that advertises Knott's Berry Farm as "the theme park Californians call home." These advertisements for Orange County and Knott's encourage people not only to experience displacement (both physical displacement and historical displacement from the violent expropriations that made suburbia possible) but to actively seek out and purchase the experience of homelessness.

Notes

I'm grateful to William Handley for his advice in this and other undertakings, and to the Buena Park Library and public relations representatives at Medieval Times, Wild Bill's, and Knott's.

My epigraph by Spencer R. Crew and James E. Sims is from *Exhibiting Cultures: The Poetics and Politics of Museum Display*, ed. Ivan Karp and Steven Lavine (Washington DC: Smithsonian Institution Press, 1991), 174.

1. Dana Hammontree, "Knott's Berry Farm 1997: The Difference Is Real" (Buena Park CA: Knott's Public Relations Department, Jan. 1997), 1.

2. Dana Hammontree, "Knott's Berry Farm 1997: The Difference Is Atmosphere" (Buena Park: Knott's Public Relations Department, Jan. 1997), 2–3. The series of press releases claiming that, at Knott's, "The Difference Is . . ." atmosphere, food, shopping, learning, and simply "Real," replaces historical "differences" with arbitrary factors focusing on the two primary themes of authenticity and consumption. These two factors come together in the visitor's mass consumption of "authentic" narratives of historical justification.

3. W. Eugene Hollon, *Frontier Violence: Another Look* (New York: Oxford University Press, 1974), vii.

4. Norman Nygaard, *Walter Knott: Twentieth-Century Pioneer* (Grand Rapids MI: Zondervan Publishing House, 1965), 17.

5. Renato Rosaldo, *Culture and Truth: The Remaking of Social Analysis* (Boston: Beacon Press, 1989), 69; Rosaldo glosses this term as follows: "A person kills somebody, and then mourns the victim. In more attenuated form, someone deliberately alters a form of life, and then regrets that things have not remained as they were. . . . At one more remove, people destroy their environment, and then they worship nature" (69–70). "Knott's Berry Farm: 1920–1997 Timeline" (Buena Park CA: Knott's Public Relations Department, 1997), 1.

6. Rosaldo, *Culture and Truth*, 71–72; Frederick Turner, "The Significance of the Frontier in American History," in *The Frontier in American History* (Tucson: University of Arizona Press, 1986), 30, 37.

7. Compare Michael Sorkin, "See You in Disneyland," in *Variations on a Theme Park*, ed. Michael Sorkin (New York: Farrar, Straus & Giroux, 1992), 210: "The abiding theme of every park is nature's transformation from civilization's antithesis to its playground."

8. Nygaard, *Walter Knott*, 89; Dana Hammontree, "Knott's Berry Farm 1997: The Difference is Learning" (Buena Park CA: Knott's Public Relations Department, Jan. 1997), 2; Marjorie Scott, "History: Knott's Berry Farm" (Buena Park CA: Knott's Public Relations Department, n.d.), 3.

9. Such an act of dehistoricization or de-temporalization is even more evident at Movieland, where each motion picture is metonymically reduced to a static, "representative" shot replicated in lifeless wax; Georges Van den Abbeele, "Sightseers: The Tourist as Theorist," *diacritics* 10, no. 4 (winter 1980), 7; Don DeLillo's description of the most photographed barn in America provides an elegant fictional account of touristic markers: "Once you've seen the signs about the barn, it becomes impossible to see the barn. . . . We're not here to capture an image, we're here to maintain one. Every photograph reinforces the aura. . . . We've agreed to be part of a collective perception" (Don DeLillo, *White Noise* [New York: Penguin, 1985], 12–13).

10. Hammontree, "Real," 1; compare M. Christine Boyer's commentary on Maurice Halbwach's distinction between history and collective memory: "History fixes the past in a uniform manner; drawing upon its difference from the present, it then reorganizes and resuscitates collective memories and popular imagery, freezing them in stereotypical forms" (M. Christine Boyer, *The City of Collective Memory* [Cambridge MA: MIT Press, 1996], 66–67).

11. See Victor Fleming et al., *Gone with the Wind*, Selznick International Pictures, 1939; Umberto Eco, *Travels in Hyperreality*, trans. William Weaver (Orlando: Harcourt Brace, 1986), 16. Since von Klieben's work is not conspicuous outside of Knott's, his artistic authority seems to derive from his designation as "Austrian." Otherwise, a *foreign* artist of little or no repute would hardly seem qualified to illustrate "authentic" scenes from the *American* frontier.

12. Walter Benjamin, "The Paris of the Second Empire in Baudelaire," in *Charles Baudelaire*, trans. Harry Zohn (London: Verso, 1997), 59. The metaphor of an Entertainment "Corridor" registers this combination of containment and "otherness": a corridor is both an enclosed hallway and a transitional space—"A strip of territory of a state running through another [foreign] territory" (*A Supplement to the Oxford English Dictionary*, ed. R. W. Burchfield [Oxford: Clarendon Press, 1972], 1:645). The word's etymology (from *correre*, "to run") also involves a paradoxical transformation of speed into a static space.

13. Alan Bryman, *Disney and His Worlds* (London: Routledge, 1995), 83. As a child, I used to spin the turnstiles repeatedly, watching the counters that record the popularity of each attraction register my passage a number of times.

    Eco describes the Palace of Living Arts with characteristic sarcasm: "The Palace reproduces in wax, in three dimensions, life-size and, obviously, in full color, the great masterpieces of painting of all time. Over there you see Leonardo, painting the portrait of a lady seated facing him: She is Mona Lisa, complete with chair, feet, and back. Leonardo has an easel beside him, and on the easel there is a two-dimensional copy of *La Gioconda*: What else did you expect?" (Eco, *Travels in Hyperreality*, 18).

14. Van den Abbeele, "Sightseers," 10. At the same time, however, the corridor imposes restraints and incentives to influence people's itineraries. It is impossible, for example, to see the shows at both Wild Bill's and Medieval Times in one night, since the performance times overlap. On the other hand, Ripley's and Movieland offer discounted joint tickets to encourage people to visit both attractions on the same day.

15. Anne-Marie Eyssartel and Bernard Rochette, *Des mondes inventées: Les parcs à thème* (Paris: Éditions de la Villette, 1992), 77, my translation; Michel de Certeau, *The Practice of Everyday Life*, trans. Steven Rendall (Berkeley: University of California Press, 1988), 97–98, 110; Jane Holtz Kay, *Asphalt Nation* (New York: Crown, 1997), 144; and William Fulton, *The Reluctant*

Metropolis: The Politics of Urban Growth in Los Angeles (Point Area CA: Solano Books, 1997), 344. Automobiles significantly outnumber pedestrians and buses along Beach Boulevard, and Knott's initial berry stand began as a roadside attraction: "A roadside stand was built on Grand Avenue, an extension of the center street of Buena Park, down which came motorists from more northerly areas heading to and from the beaches" (H. A. Chamberlain, "From Coyotes to Commerce: Beginning of the Berry Farm," in *Buena Park News Independent* [August 27, 1972], A-2).

16. Kathleen Kirby, *Indifferent Boundaries: Spatial Concepts of Human Subjectivity* (New York: Guilford Press, 1996), 107.

17. Turner, "The Significance of the Frontier," 12; Louis Marin, "Frontiers of Utopia: Past and Present," *Critical Inquiry* (spring 1993), 417.

18. Van den Abbeele, "Sightseers," 7. He explains that "current visitors to Paris may find it fashionable, for example, to ignore famous sights such as the Eiffel Tower or the Louvre in order to find the 'real' French life in little-known parts of the city." Recent theorists of nomadism have a problematic tendency to set up nomadic movement—that is, movement without reference to a destination or endpoint—as a utopian endpoint for their arguments. Rosi Braidotti's claim that "rethinking the bodily roots of subjectivity is the *starting point* for the epistemological project of nomadism," for example, projects a linear and somewhat predictable itinerary from this starting point to the destination of nomadism conceived as an oppositional project (*Nomadic Subjects, Embodiment and Sexual Difference in Contemporary Feminist Theory* [New York: Columbia University Press, 1994], 3, emphasis added). Van den Abbeele follows a similar path when he moves from Dean MacCannell's semiotics of tourism to the convenient conclusion that "the nomad can no more be said to be moving than not moving since there is no longer any fixed point of reference in regards to which movement can be either perceived or measured" (14).

19. M. Christine Boyer, *Cybercities: Visual Perception in the Age of Electronic Communication* (New York: Princeton Architectural Press, 1996), 219. MacCannell also observes that, however subversive and empowering driving promises to be, in the end "we have stayed within the lines, while controlling a device we know is capable of violating boundaries, racing down sidewalks, crashing through the glass front of any office, shop, or restaurant"; Dean MacCannell, *Empty Meeting Grounds: the Tourist Papers* (London: Routledge, 1992), 189; Boyer, *Cybercities*, 219–20.

20. Boyer, *Cybercities*, 218.

21. Michel Foucault, "Film and Popular Memory," in *Foucault Live (Interviews 1966–84)*, trans. John Johnston, ed. Sylvere Lopringer (New York: Semiotext[e], 1989), 92.

22. Slavoj Žižek, *The Sublime Object of Ideology* (London: Verso, 1989), 28; Nygaard, *Walter Knott*, 71 (all dialogue from Nygaard's book is of dubious origin, since the author's only citation for them is a vague reference to interviews conducted with Walter Knott in 1965); Nygaard, *Walter Knott*, 76.

23. Chamberlain, *Buena Park News Independent*, 4 October 1972, A-2.

24. Hammontree, "Real," 1; Eco, *Travels in Hyperreality*, 42, 43.

25. The program maintains that "Don Raimundo and his wife, Dona Maria, are not fictional characters. They are, in fact, the real ancestors of the owners of the Medieval Times Dinner & Tournament." To further justify the "reality" of its owners, Medieval Times points out that it has even adopted or "inherited" the medieval system of inheritance. Each ritual photograph taken with these characters acknowledges their aura in practice, if not in theory. "Commemorative Program" (Buena Park CA: Medieval Times Dinner & Tournament, Dec. 1995), 6.

26. Žižek, *Sublime Object of Ideology*, 31. At Medieval Times, each audience section cheers for a particular knight. An advertising supplement describes a similar procedure at Wild Bill's: "Separated into four groups— the sheepherders, townsfolk, ranchers and desperados—the crowd takes part in whooping competition and joins in for singing in the round." Julie Price, "Updated Re-Print of Advertising Supplement H," press release, in *Discover Orange County: Daily News* (Orange County CA: Nov. 29, year unspecified).

27. "Some of the curiosities in the Ripley's Museums are unique; others, displayed in several museums at once, are said to be authentic duplicates. Still others are copies. The Iron Maiden of Nuremberg, for example, can be found in six or eight different locations, even though there is only one original" (Eco, *Travels in Hyperreality*, 15); Slavoj Žižek, *The Plague of Fantasies* (London: Verso, 1997), 173; "Commemorative Program," Dec. 1995, 1. The corridor often combines its spectacles with both literal and metaphorical (economic) consumption: Medieval Times and Wild Bill's both combine dinner with theater, and one informational pamphlet, citing Cordelia Knott's Chicken Dinner Restaurant and the popularity of Knott's Berry Farm's pies and preserves, boasts

that, at Knott's, "The Difference Is Food" (Dana Hammontree, "Knott's Berry Farm 1997: The Difference Is Food" [Buena Park CA: Knott's Public Relations Department, Jan. 1997]).

Ripley's exhibits a photograph of "Three Ball Charlie"—a man who could whistle while holding three tennis balls in his mouth—as well as an impressive reproduction of Leonardo da Vinci's *Last Supper* composed entirely of browned toast. Every site includes at least one gift shop, and another pamphlet—this one entitled "The Difference Is Shopping"—insists that, far from being mere "afterthoughts" or "sidelights," Knott's Berry Farm's shops are "all creatively planned to add distinctive flavor to the Knott's Experience" (Dana Hammontree, "Knott's Berry Farm 1997: The Difference Is Shopping" [Buena Park CA: Knott's Public Relations Department, Jan. 1997], 1).

28. Scott, "History: Knott's Berry Farm," 3.
29. William Cronon, *Nature's Metropolis: Chicago and the Great West* (New York: W. W. Norton, 1991), 47–48, 50–51.
30. Marin, "Frontiers of Utopia," 408, 411.
31. Quoted in Edward W. Soja, *Thirdspace: Journeys to Los Angeles and Other Real-and-Imagined Places* (Cambridge MA: Blackwell, 1996), 237.
32. On the uncanny, see Sigmund Freud, "The Uncanny," in *The Standard Edition of the Complete Psychological Works of Sigmund Freud*, ed. and trans. James Strachey (London: Hogarth Press, 1953–74) 17:218–56.

Adams, Ansel. *Born Free and Equal: The Story of Loyal Japanese-Americans.* New York: U.S. Camera, 1944.

Adams, Henry. *Selections: Democracy, Esther, Mont Saint Michel and Chartres, The Education of Henry Adams.* Ed. Ernest Samuels and Jayne N. Samuels. Library of America ed. New York: Literary Classics of the United States, 1983.

Adorno, Theodor. *The Jargon of Authenticity.* Trans. Knut Tarnowski and Frederic Will. Evanston: Northwestern University Press, 1973.

Alexander, Ruth Ann. "Elaine Goodale Eastman and the Failure of the Feminist Protestant Ethic." *Great Plains Quarterly* 8 (1988): 89–101.

Alexie, Sherman. Posting to Native Literature listserv. "RE: Message from Sherman Alexie." 12 April 1997 <Nativelit-L@csd.uwm.edu>.

Allen, Chadwick. "Blood (and) Memory." *American Literature* 71, no. 1 (March 1999): 93–116.

Allen, Paula Gunn. "Special Problems in Teaching Leslie Marmon Silko's *Ceremony.*" *American Indian Quarterly* 14, no. 4 (fall 1990): 379–86.

"American Section: The Heye Collection." *University of Pennsylvania: The Museum Journal* (June 1910): 11–12.

Anderson, Benedict. *Imagined Communities: Reflections on the Origin and Spread of Nationalism.* London: Verso, 1983.

Anderson, Nancy K. "'Curious Historical Artistic Data': Art History and Western American Art." In *Discovered Lands, Invented Pasts: Transforming Visions of the American West.* Ed. Jules D. Prown et al. New Haven: Yale University Press, 1992. 1–35.

Antelyes, Peter. *Tales of Adventurous Enterprise: Washington Irving and the Poetics of Western Expansion.* New York: Columbia University Press, 1990.

Armor, John, and Peter Wright. *Manzanar.* New York: Times Books, 1988.

Art at Auction: The Year at Sotheby's and Parke-Bernet, 1970–71. New York: Viking, 1971.

Atwater, Caleb. *Remarks Made on a Tour to Prairie du Chien; thence to Washington City, in 1829.* 1831. Reprint, New York: Arno Press, 1975.

Atwood, Margaret. *Survival: A Thematic Guide to Canadian Literature.* Toronto: Anansi, 1972.

Bartram, William. *Travels Through North and South Carolina, Georgia, East and West Florida.* Facsimile of the 1792 London edition. Intro. Gordon DeWolf. Charlottesville: University Press of Virginia, 1980.

Bass, Rick. "Bear Spray Stories." Paper presented at Fire & Grit, Shepherds-town WV, June 1999.

———. *The Book of Yaak*. Boston: Houghton Mifflin, 1996.

———. *Brown Dog of the Yaak*. Minneapolis MN: Milkweed Editions, 1999.

———. "The Community of Glaciers." Paper presented at Fire & Grit, Shepherdstown WV, June 1999.

———. *The Deer Pasture*. New York: Norton, 1985.

———. "On Willow Creek." In *Heart of the Land*. Ed. Joseph Barbato and Lisa Weinerman. New York: Pantheon, 1995.

———. *The Watch: Stories*. New York: Norton, 1989.

———. *Wild to the Heart*. New York: Norton, 1987.

———. *Winter: Notes from Montana*. Boston: Houghton Mifflin, 1991.

Basso, Keith. *Wisdom Sits in Places: Landscape and Language Among the Western Apache*. Albuquerque: University of New Mexico Press, 1996.

Bederman, Gail. *Manliness and Civilization: A Cultural History of Gender and Race in the United States, 1880–1917*. Chicago: University of Chicago Press, 1995.

Benjamin, Walter. *Illuminations: Essays and Reflections*. New York: Schocken Books, 1969.

———. *The Paris of the Second Empire in Baudelaire*. In *Charles Baudelaire*. Trans. Harry Zohn. London: Verso, 1997.

Bennett, Mildred R. *The World of Willa Cather*. 1953. Reprint, Lincoln: University of Nebraska Press, 1961.

Bentley, D. M. R. *The Gay]Grey Moose: Essays on the Ecologies and Mythologies of Canadian Poetry, 1690–1990*. Ottawa: University of Ottawa Press, 1992.

Berger, John. *Another Way of Telling*. New York: Pantheon, 1982.

Berlant, Lauren Gail. *The Anatomy of National Fantasy: Hawthorne, Utopia, and Everyday Life*. Chicago: University of Chicago Press, 1991.

Berry, Wendell. *Home Economics*. New York: Farrar, Straus & Giroux, 1987.

Bettelheim, Bruno. *The Uses of Enchantment: The Meaning and Importance of Fairy Tales*. New York: Vintage, 1977.

Bieder, Robert E. *Science Encounters the Indian, 1820–1880*. Norman: University of Oklahoma Press, 1986.

Bird, Gloria. "The Exaggeration of Despair in Sherman Alexie's *Reservation Blues*." *Wicazo Sa Review* 11, no. 2 (fall 1995): 47–52.

Black, Max. *Models and Metaphors: Studies in Language and Philosophy*. Ithaca: Cornell University Press, 1962.

Boas, Franz. "The Aims of Ethnology." In *A Franz Boas Reader: The Shaping of American Anthropology, 1883–1911.* Ed. George Stocking. Chicago: University of Chicago Press, 1982.

———. *The Mind of Primitive Man.* New York: Macmillan, 1911.

———. "Recent Anthropology II." *Science,* 15 October 1943, 334–37.

Boesen, Victor, and Florence Curtis Graybill. *Edward S. Curtis: Photographer of the North American Indian.* New York: Dodd, Mead, 1977.

Bohlke, L. Brent, ed. *Willa Cather in Person: Interviews, Speeches, and Letters.* Lincoln: University of Nebraska Press, 1986.

Bold, Christine. *Selling the Wild West: Popular Western Fiction, 1860 to 1960.* Bloomington: Indiana University Press, 1987.

Booth, Annie L., and Harvey M. Jacobs, eds. *Environmental Consciousness— Native American Worldviews and Sustainable Natural Resource Management: An Annotated Bibliography.* Chicago: Council of Planning Librarians, 1988.

Boyer, M. Christine. *The City of Collective Memory: Its Historical Images and Architectural Entertainments.* Cambridge: MIT Press, 1996.

———. *Cybercities: Visual Perception in the Age of Electronic Communication.* New York: Princeton Architectural Press, 1996.

Braidotti, Rosi. *Nomadic Subjects: Embodiment and Sexual Difference in Contemporary Feminist Theory.* New York: Columbia University Press, 1994.

Brinkmeyer, Robert H., Jr. *Remapping Southern Literature: Contemporary Southern Writers and the West.* Athens: University of Georgia Press, 2000.

Browder, Laura. *Slippery Characters: Ethnic Impersonators and American Identities.* Chapel Hill: University of North Carolina Press, 2000.

Brown, E. K. *On Canadian Poetry.* Toronto: Ryerson Press, 1943.

———. *Willa Cather: A Critical Biography.* New York: Alfred A. Knopf, 1953.

Brown, Michael F. *The Channeling Zone: American Spirituality in an Anxious Age.* Cambridge: Harvard University Press, 1997.

Brugioni, Dino A. *Photo Fakery: The History and Techniques of Photographic Deception and Manipulation.* Dulles VA: Brassey's, 1999.

Brumble, H. David. *American Indian Autobiography.* Berkeley: University of California Press, 1988.

Bryman, Alan. *Disney and His Worlds.* London: Routledge, 1995.

Buell, Lawrence. *The Environmental Imagination: Thoreau, Nature Writing, and the Formation of American Culture.* Cambridge: Harvard University Press, 1995.

Butala, Sharon. "The Reality of the Flesh." In *Writing Saskatchewan: Twenty Critical Essays*. Ed. Kenneth G. Probert. Regina: Canadian Plains Research Centre/University of Regina, 1989. 96–99.

Calder, Alison. "'The Nearest Approach to a Desert': Implications of Environmental Determinism in the Criticism of Canadian Prairie Writing." *Prairie Forum* 23 (1998): 171–82.

Carr, Helen. *Inventing the American Primitive: Politics, Gender and the Representation of Native American Literary Traditions, 1789–1936*. New York: New York University Press, 1996.

Cather, Willa. *My Ántonia*. Ed. Charles Mignon. Willa Cather Scholarly Edition. Lincoln: University of Nebraska Press, 1994.

———. *O Pioneers!* Ed. Susan Rosowski and Charles Mignon. Willa Cather Scholarly Edition. Lincoln: University of Nebraska Press, 1992.

———. *Stories, Poems, and Other Writings*. New York: Library of America, Viking Press, 1992.

Cawelti, John G. *The Six-Gun Mystique*. Bowling Green: Bowling Green University Press, 1971.

Chalfant, Edward. *Better in Darkness: A Biography of Henry Adams, His Second Life, 1862–1891*. Hamden CT: Archon Books, 1994.

———. *Both Sides of the Ocean: A Biography of Henry Adams, His First Life, 1838–1862*. Hamden CT: Archon Books, 1982.

———. *Improvement of the World: A Biography of Henry Adams, His Last Life, 1891–1918*. North Haven CT: Archon Books, 2001.

Chalykoff, Lisa. "Overcoming the Two Solitudes of Canadian Literary Regionalism." *Studies in Canadian Literature* 23, no. 1 (1998): 160–77.

Chamberlain, H. A. "From Coyotes to Commerce." Articles serialized in *Buena Park News Independent* (Aug. 23, 1972, to Apr. 18, 1973): A-2.

Churchill, Ward. "A Little Matter of Genocide: Native American Spirituality and New Age Hucksterism." *Bloomsbury Review* 8, no. 5 (Sept./Oct. 1988).

Clifford, James. *The Predicament of Culture: Twentieth-Century Ethnography, Literature, and Art*. Cambridge: Harvard University Press, 1988.

Clifford, James, and George E. Marcus, eds. *Writing Culture: The Poetics and Politics of Ethnography*. Berkeley: University of California Press, 1986.

Cohen, Ted. "Metaphor and the Cultivation of Intimacy." In *On Metaphor*. Ed. Sheldon Sacks. Chicago: University of Chicago Press, 1978. 1–10.

Colacurcio, Michael. "The Dynamo and the Angelic Doctor: The Bias of Henry Adams' Medievalism." *American Quarterly* 17 (1965): 696–712.

―――. "Idealism and Independence." In *Columbia Literary History of the United States*. Ed. Emory Elliott. New York: Columbia University Press, 1988. 207–26.

Colton, Calvin. *Tour of the American Lakes, and among the Indians of the North-West Territory*. London: Frederick Westley and A. H. Davis, 1833.

Comer, Krista. *Landscapes of the New West: Gender and Geography in Contemporary Women's Writing*. Chapel Hill: University of North Carolina Press, 1999.

"Commemorative Program." Buena Park CA: Medieval Times Dinner and Tournament, Dec. 1995.

Conder, John J. *A Formula of His Own: Henry Adams' Literary Experiment*. Chicago: University of Chicago Press, 1970.

Cook, Nancy. "The Scandal of Race: Authenticity, *The Silent Enemy*, and the Problem of Long Lance." In *Headline Hollywood: Scandal and Cinema*. Ed. David Cook and Adrienne MacLean. New Brunswick NJ: Rutgers University Press, 2001.

Cook-Lynn, Elizabeth. "The American Indian Fiction Writer: Cosmopolitanism, Nationalism, the Third World, and First Nation Sovereignty." *Wicazo Sa Review* 9, no. 2 (fall 1993): 26–36.

―――. "American Indian Intellectualism and the New Indian Story." *American Indian Quarterly* 20, no. 1 (winter 1996): 57–76; reprinted in *Natives and Academics: Researching and Writing about American Indians*. Ed. Devon A. Mihesuah. Lincoln: University of Nebraska Press, 1998. 111–38.

Cooley, Dennis. Introduction to *Inscriptions: A Prairie Poetry Anthology*. Ed. Cooley. Winnipeg: Turnstone, 1992. xv–xvii.

―――. *The Vernacular Muse*. Winnipeg: Turnstone, 1987.

Coward, John M. *The Newspaper Indian: Native American Identity in the Press, 1820–90*. Urbana: University of Illinois Press, 1999.

Crane, Hart. *The Bridge: A Poem*. New York: Liveright, 1970.

Crew, Spencer R., and James E. Sims. "Locating Authenticity: Fragments of a Dialogue." In *Exhibiting Cultures: The Poetics and Politics of Museum Display*. Ed. Ivan Karp and Steven Lavine. Washington DC: Smithsonian Institute Press, 1991.

Cronon, William. *Nature's Metropolis: Chicago and the Great West*. New York: Norton, 1991.

―――. "The Trouble with Wilderness: Or Getting Back to the Wrong Nature." In *Uncommon Ground: Rethinking the Human Place in Nature*. Ed. William Cronon. New York: Norton, 1996.

Cronon, William, George Miles, and Jay Gitlin, eds. *Under an Open Sky: Re-thinking America's Western Past*. New York: Norton, 1992.

Cuming, Fortescue. *Sketches of a Tour to the Western Country, through the States of Ohio and Kentucky; a Voyage down the Ohio and Mississippi Rivers, and a Trip through the Mississippi Territory, and Part of West Florida*. 1810. Reprint, Cleveland: Arthur H. Clark, 1904.

Curtis, Edward S. "Vanishing Indian Types: The Tribes of the Northwest Plains." *Scribner's Magazine*, June 1906.

Curtis, James. *Mind's Eye, Mind's Truth:* FSA *Photography Reconsidered*. Philadelphia: Temple University Press, 1989.

Davey, Frank. "A Young Boy's Eden: Notes on Recent Canadian 'Prairie' Poetry." *Reading Canadian Reading*. Winnipeg: Turnstone, 1988.

Davis, Mike. *Ecology of Fear: Los Angeles and the Imagination of Disaster*. New York: Henry Holt, 1998.

Daymond, Douglas, and Leslie Monkman, eds. *Towards a Canadian Literature: Essays, Editorials, and Manifestos*. 2 vols. Ottawa: Tecumseh, 1985.

De Certeau, Michel. *The Practice of Everyday Life*. Trans. Steven Rendall. Berkeley: University of California Press, 1984.

Decker, William Merrill. *The Literary Vocation of Henry Adams*. Chapel Hill: University of North Carolina Press, 1990.

DeLillo, Don. *White Noise*. New York: Viking Penguin, 1985.

Deloria, Phillip. *Playing Indian*. New Haven: Yale University Press, 1998.

Deming, Alison Hawthorne. *Temporary Homelands: Essays on Nature, Spirit and Place*. 1994. Reprint, New York: Picador U.S.A., 1996.

Derrida, Jacques. "On Eating Well." In *Who Comes After the Subject?* Ed. Eduardo Cadava, Peter Connor, and Jean-Luc Nancy. New York: Routledge, 1991.

Dewart, Edward Hartley. "Introductory Essay to *Selections from Canadian Poets*." 1864. Reprinted in *Towards a Canadian Literature: Essays, Editorials, and Manifestos*. Ed. Douglas Daymond and Leslie Monkman. Ottawa: Tecumseh, 1985. 1:50–59.

Diggins, John. "'Who Bore the Failure of Light': Henry Adams and the Crisis of Authority." *New England Quarterly* 58 (1985): 165–92.

Dillard, Annie. *Pilgrim at Tinker Creek*. New York: Harper & Row, 1974.

DuBois, W.E.B. *The Souls of Black Folks*. 1903. *The Oxford W.E.B. DuBois Reader*. Ed. Eric J. Sundquist. New York: Oxford University Press, 1966.

Dusinberre, William. *Henry Adams: The Myth of Failure*. Charlottesville: University Press of Virginia, 1980.

Eastman, Charles. *From the Deep Woods to Civilization: Chapters in the Autobiography of an Indian*. 1916. Reprint, Lincoln: University of Nebraska Press, 1977.

———. *Indian Boyhood*. 1902. Reprint, Lincoln: University of Nebraska Press, 1991.

———. *Indian Heroes and Great Chieftains*. 1918. Reprint, Lincoln: University of Nebraska Press, 1991.

———. "Language of Footprints." *St. Nicholas*, January 1917, 267–69.

———. "'My People': The Indians' Contribution to the Art of America." *The Red Man*, December 1914, 133–40.

———. "Recollections of the Wild Life." *St Nicholas*, December 1893, 129–31; January 1894, 226–28; February 1894, 306–8; March 1894, 437–40; April 1894, 513–15; May 1894, 607–11.

———. *The Soul of the Indian: An Interpretation*. 1911. Reprint, Lincoln: University of Nebraska Press, 1980.

Eastman, Elaine Goodale. *Sister to the Sioux*. Ed. Kay Graber. Lincoln: University of Nebraska Press, 1978.

———. *The Voice at Eve*. Chicago: Bookfellows, 1930.

———. *Yellow Star: A Story of East and West*. Boston: Little, Brown, 1911.

Eco, Umberto. *Travels in Hyperreality*. Trans. William Weaver. Orlando fl: Harcourt Brace Jovanovich, 1986.

Edwards, Elizabeth. *Anthropology and Photography, 1860–1920*. Hew Haven: Yale University Press, 1992.

Edwin, James. *Account of an Expedition from Pittsburgh to the Rocky Mountains, Performed in the Years 1819 and '20*. Philadelphia: H. C. Carey and I. Shea, 1822–23.

Egan, Timothy. "Indian Reservations Bank on Authenticity to Draw Tourists." *New York Times*, 21 Sept. 1998.

Elkins, James. *The Object Stares Back*. New York: Harcourt Brace, 1996.

———. *What Painting Is*. New York: Routledge, 1998.

Evans, Estwick. *A Pedestrious Tour, of Four Thousand Miles, through the Western States and Territories, during the Winter and Spring of 1818*. Cleveland: Arthur H. Clark, 1904.

Eyssartel, Anne-Marie, and Bernard Rochette. *Des mondes inventés: Les parcs à thème*. Paris: Éditions de la Villette, 1992.

Fabian, Johannes. *Time and the Other: How Anthropology Makes Its Object*. Columbia University Press, 1983.

Fairbanks, Carol. *Prairie Women: Images in American and Canadian Fiction.* New Haven: Yale University Press, 1986.

Faris, James C. *Navajo and Photography.* Albuquerque: University of New Mexico Press, 1996.

Flint, Timothy. *Recollections of the Last Ten Years.* 1826. Reprint, New York: Alfred A. Knopf, 1932.

———, ed. *Western Monthly Review.* Cincinnati, 1827–30.

Flood, Renee Sansom. *Lost Bird of Wounded Knee: Spirit of the Lakota.* New York: Scribner, 1995.

Foucault, Michel. "Film and Popular Memory." In *Foucault Live (Interviews 1966–84).* Ed. Sylvere Lopringer. Trans. John Johnston. New York: Semiotext(e), 1989. 92.

Freud, Sigmund. "The Uncanny." In *The Standard Edition of the Complete Psychological Works of Sigmund Freud.* Ed. and trans. James Strachey. London: Hogarth Press, 1953–74. 17:218–56.

Frye, Northrop. *The Bush Garden.* Toronto: Anansi, 1971.

———. Conclusion to *Literary History of Canada.* Ed. Carl F. Klinck et al. Toronto: University of Toronto Press, 1965. 821–49.

———. Criticism and Environment." In *The Eternal Act of Creation: Essays 1979–1990.* Ed. Robert D. Denham. Bloomington: Indiana University Press, 1993. 139–53.

Fuller, William Henry. *H.M.S. Parliament or The Lady Who Loved a Government Clerk.* In *Canada's Lost Plays.* Ed. Anton Wagner and Richard Plant. 1880. Reprint, Toronto: CTR Publications, 1978. 1:158–93.

Fulton, William. *The Reluctant Metropolis: The Politics of Urban Growth in Los Angeles.* Point Area CA: Solano Books Press, 1997.

Gass, Patrick. *A Journal of the Voyages and Travels of a Corps of Discovery, under the Command of Capt. Lewis and Capt. Clarke.* 1807. Reprint, Dayton: Ells, Claflin, 1847.

Gates, Henry Louis, Jr. " 'Authenticity,' or the Lesson of Little Tree." *New York Times,* 24 Nov. 1991, 26–30.

———. "Beyond the Culture Wars: Identities in Dialogue." *Profession 93* (1993): 6–11.

Gesensway, Deborah, and Mindy Roseman. *Beyond Words: Images from American's Concentration Camps.* Ithaca: Cornell University Press, 1987.

Gidley, Mick. *Edward S. Curtis and the North American Indian, Incorporated.* New York: Cambridge University Press, 1998.

Gilmore, Mikal. *Shot in the Heart.* New York: Doubleday, 1994.

Girdner, Audre, and Anne Loftis. *The Great Betrayal: The Evacuation of the Japanese-Americans During World War II.* London: Collier-Macmillan, 1969.

Golumb, Jacob. *In Search of Authenticity: From Kierkegaard to Camus.* New York: Routledge, 1995.

Gone with the Wind. Dir. Victor Fleming et al. Selznick International Pictures, 1939.

Goodale, Dora, and Elaine Goodale. "Poems by Two Little American Girls." *St. Nicholas,* December 1877, 109–10.

Granatstein, J. L. *Yankee Go Home? Canadians and Anti-Americanism.* Toronto: HarperCollins, 1996.

Grodzins, Morton. *Americans Betrayed: Politics and the Japanese.* Chicago: University of Chicago Press, 1949.

Hafen, P. Jane. "Rock and Roll, Redskins, and Blues in Sherman Alexie's Work." *Studies in American Indian Literatures* 9, no. 4 (winter 1997): 71–78.

Hall, James. *Legends of the West.* 1832. Reprint, Cincinnati: Applegate and Company, 1857.

———. *Letters from the West; Containing Sketches of Scenery, Manners, and Customs; and Anecdotes Connected with the First Settlement of the Western Sections of the Unites States.* 1828. Reprint, Gainesville fl: Scholars' Facsimiles and Reprints, 1967.

———. *Sketches of History, Life, and Manners in the West; Containing Accurate Descriptions of the Country and Modes of Life, in the Western States and Territories of North American.* Cincinnati: Hubbard and Edmands, 1834.

———, ed. *Western Monthly Magazine.* Cincinnati, 1833–36.

———, ed. *The Western Souvenir, a Christmas and New Year's Gift for 1829.* Cincinnati: N. and G. Guilford, 1829.

Hammontree, Dana. "Knott's Berry Farm 1997: The Difference Is Atmosphere." Press release. Buena Park ca: Knott's Public Relations Department, Jan. 1997.

———. "Knott's Berry Farm 1997: The Difference Is Food." Press release. Buena Park ca: Knott's Public Relations Department, Jan. 1997.

———. "Knott's Berry Farm 1997: The Difference Is Learning." Press release. Buena Park ca: Knott's Public Relations Department, Jan. 1997.

———. "Knott's Berry Farm 1997: The Difference Is Real." Press release. Buena Park ca: Knott's Public Relations Department, Jan. 1997.

———. "Knott's Berry Farm 1997: The Difference Is Shopping." Press release. Buena Park ca: Knott's Public Relations Department, Jan. 1997.

Handley, William R. *Marriage, Violence, and the Nation in the American Literary West*. Cambridge: Cambridge University Press, 2002.

Harbert, Earl N., ed. *Critical Essays on Henry Adams*. Boston: G. K. Hall, 1981.

———. *The Force So Much Closer to Home: Henry Adams and the Adams Family*. New York: New York University Press, 1977.

Harrison, Dick. *Unnamed Country: The Struggle for a Canadian Prairie Fiction*. Edmonton: University of Alberta Press, 1977.

Haslam, Gerald. "Introduction: Western Writers and the National Fantasy." In *Western Writing*. Ed. Haslam. Albuquerque: University of New Mexico Press, 1974. 1–15.

Hassrick, Peter H., and Melissa J. Webster. *Frederic Remington: A Catalogue Raisonné of Paintings, Watercolors and Drawings*. 2 vols. Cody WY: Buffalo Bill Historical Center in association with the University of Washington Press, 1996.

Hearne, Vicki. *Adam's Task: Calling Animals by Name*. New York: Knopf, 1987.

Hertzberg, Hazel W. *The Search for an American Indian Identity: Modern Pan-Indian Movements*. Syracuse: Syracuse University Press, 1971.

Hildreth, James. *Dragoon Campaigns to the Rocky Mountains. By a Dragoon*. 1836. Reprint, New York: Arno Press, 1973.

Hill, Kimi Kodani, ed. *Topaz Moon: Chiura Obata's Art of the Internment*. Berkeley: Heyday Books, 2000.

Hirsch, Marianne. *Family Frames: Photography, Narrative, and Postmemory*. Cambridge: Harvard University Press, 1997.

Hoch, David, and Will Carrington Heath. "Tracking the ADC: Ranchers' Boon, Taxpayers' Burden, Wildlife's Bane." *Animal Law* 3 (1997): 163–87.

Hoffman, Charles Fenno. *A Winter in the West*. New York: Harper and Brothers, 1835.

Hoffman, Donald. *Visual Intelligence*. New York: W. W. Norton, 1998.

Hoffmann, Karen A. "Identity Crossings and the Autobiographical Act in Willa Cather's *My Ántonia*." *Arizona Quarterly* 58, no. 4 (winter 2002): 25–50.

Hollon, W. Eugene. *Frontier Violence: Another Look*. New York: Oxford University Press, 1974.

Honda, Diane Yotsuya, ed. *Our World*. Reprint of the 1944–45 Manzanar High School Yearbook. Privately printed.

Houston, Jeanne Wakatsuki, and James D. Houston. *Farewell to Manzanar*. Boston: Houghton Mifflin, 1973.

Hutcheon, Linda. *The Canadian Postmodern: A Study of Contemporary English-Canadian Fiction.* Toronto: Oxford University Press, 1988.

Important American Paintings, Drawings, and Sculptures. New York: Sotheby's & Parke-Bernet, 1984.

Irons, Peter. *Justice at War: The Story of the Japanese Internment Cases.* Berkeley: University of California Press, 1983.

Irving, Washington. *A Tour on the Prairies.* 1834. Reprint, New York: Pantheon, 1967.

Isernhagen, Hartwig. *Momaday, Vizenor, Armstrong: Conversations on American Indian Writing.* Norman: University of Oklahoma Press, 1999.

Jacknis, Ira. "The Ethnographic Object and the Object of Ethnology in the Early Career of Franz Boas." In *Volkgeist as Method and Ethic: Essays on Boasian Ethnography and the German Anthropological Tradition.* Ed. George W. Stocking Jr. Madison: University of Wisconsin Press, 1996.

Jacobson, Joanne. *Authority and Alliance in the Letters of Henry Adams.* Madison: University of Wisconsin Press, 1992.

Jaimes, M. Annette, ed. *The State of Native America.* Boston: South End, 1992.

Jordan, David. *New World Regionalism: Literature in the Americas.* Toronto: University of Toronto Press, 1994

──────, ed. *Regionalism Reconsidered: New Approaches to the Field.* New York: Garland, 1994.

Jordy, William H. *Henry Adams: Scientific Historian.* New Haven: Yale University Press, 1952.

Kaledin, Eugenia. *The Education of Mrs. Henry Adams.* Philadelphia: Temple University Press, 1981.

Kaplan, Amy, and Donald E. Pease, eds. *Cultures of U.S. Imperialisms.* Durham: Duke University Press, 1993.

Kaplan, Harold. *Power and Order: Henry Adams and the Naturalist Tradition in American Fiction.* Chicago: University of Chicago Press, 1981.

Karttunen, Frances. *Between Worlds: Interpreters, Guides, and Survivors.* New Brunswick: Rutgers University Press, 1994.

Kay, Jane Holtz. *Asphalt Nation.* New York: Crown Publishers, 1997.

Keahey, Deborah. *Making It Home: Place in Canadian Prairie Literature.* Winnipeg: University of Manitoba Press, 1998.

Kearney, Richard. *The Wake of Imagination.* Minneapolis: University of Minnesota Press, 1988.

Kelly, Ursula. *Marketing Place: Cultural Politics, Regionalism, and Reading.* Halifax, Nova Scotia: Fernwood, 1993.

339

Kern, Stephen. *The Culture of Time and Space, 1880–1918.* London: Weidenfeld & Nicolson, 1983.

Kirby, Kathleen M. *Indifferent Boundaries: Spatial Concepts of Human Subjectivity.* New York: Guilford, 1996.

Kittredge, William. "The Good Rain: Stegner and the Wild." In *Wallace Stegner: Man and Writer.* Ed. Charles E. Rankin. Albuquerque: University of New Mexico Press, 1986. 87–103.

———. *Owning It All.* Saint Paul MN: Graywolf, 1987.

———. *Taking Care: Thoughts on Storytelling and Belief.* Ed. Scott Slovic. Minneapolis: Milkweed, 1999.

Kluckhohn, Clyde. "The Personal Document in Anthropological Science." In *The Use of Personal Documents in History, Anthropology, and Sociology.* Ed. Louis Gottschalk, Clyde Kluckhohn, and Robert Angell. New York: Social Science Research Council, 1945.

Knopp, Lisa. *Field of Vision.* Iowa City: University of Iowa Press, 1996.

"Knott's Berry Farm: 1920–1997 Timeline." Press release. Buena Park CA: Knott's Public Relations Department, 1997.

Kogawa, Joy. *Obasan.* New York: Doubleday, 1983.

Kolodny, Annette. *The Land Before Her: Fantasy and Experience of the American Frontiers, 1630–1860.* Chapel Hill: University of North Carolina Press, 1984.

———. "Unearthing Herstory: An Introduction." In *The Ecocriticism Reader.* Ed. Cheryll Glotfelty and Harold Fromm. Athens: University of Georgia Press, 1996.

Kreisel, Henry. "The Prairie: A State of Mind." In *Essays on Saskatchewan Writing.* Ed. E. F. Dyck. Regina: Saskatchewan Writers Guild, 1986. 41–58.

Kroetsch, Robert. *The Lovely Treachery of Words: Essays Selected and New.* Toronto: Oxford University Press, 1989.

Krupat, Arnold. *Ethnocriticism: Ethnography, History, Literature.* Berkeley: University of California Press, 1991.

———. *For Those Who Come After: A Study of Native American Autobiography.* Berkeley: University of California Press, 1985.

Lacan, Jacques. *The Four Fundamental Concepts of Psycho-Analysis.* Ed. J. A. Miller. Trans. A. Sheridan. Harmondsworth: Penguin, 1979.

LaLonde, Chris. "New Stories and Broken Necks: Incorporating Native American Texts in the American Literature Survey." *Studies in American Indian Literatures* 8, no. 2 (summer 1996): 7–20.

Landow, George P. *Elegant Jeremiahs: The Sage from Carlyle to Mailer.* Ithaca: Cornell University Press, 1986.

Lane-Fox Pitt-Rivers, A. *The Evolution of Culture and Other Essays.* Oxford: Clarendon Press, 1906.

Langness, L. L. *The Life History in Anthropological Science.* New York: Holt, Rinehart and Winston, 1965.

Lears, T. J. Jackson. *No Place of Grace: Antimodernism and the Transformation of American Culture, 1880–1920.* New York: Pantheon, 1981.

Lee, Anthony W. *Picturing Chinatown: Art and Orientalism in San Francisco.* Berkeley: University of California Press, 2001.

Lee, Dennis. "Cadence, Country, Silence: Writing in Colonial Space." In *Towards a Canadian Literature: Essays, Editorials, and Manifestos.* Ed. Douglas Daymond and Leslie Monkman. Ottawa: Tecumseh, 1985. 2:497–520.

Lee, Hermione. *Willa Cather: Double Lives.* New York: Vintage, 1991.

Leonard, Zenas. *Narrative of the Adventures of Zenas Leonard, a Native of Clearfield County,* PA, *Who Spent Five Years Trapping for Furs, Trading with the Indians, &c., &c., of the Rocky Mountains: Written by Himself. Clearfield* PA: D. W. Moore, 1839.

Levenson, J. C., et al., eds. *The Letters of Henry Adams.* 6 vols. Cambridge: Harvard University Press, 1982–88.

Leverenz, David. *Manhood and the American Renaissance.* Ithaca: Cornell University Press, 1989.

Levin, David. *History as Romantic Art: Bancroft, Prescott, Motley, and Parkman.* Stanford: Stanford University Press, 1959.

Lewis, Nathaniel. *Unsettling the Literary West: Authenticity, Authorship, and Western American Literature.* Lincoln: University of Nebraska Press, 2003.

Limerick, Patricia Nelson. *Legacy of Conquest: The Unbroken Past of the American West.* New York: Norton, 1987.

———. "The Real West." In *The Real West.* Commentary by Patricia Nelson Limerick. Intro. Andrew E. Masich. Denver: Civic Center Cultural Complex, 1996. 13–22.

———. *Something in the Soil: Legacies and Reckonings in the New West.* New York: W. W. Norton, 2000.

Lippard, Lucy. Introduction to *Partial Recall.* Ed. Lucy Lippard. New York: New Press, 1992.

Lipsitz, George. *Dangerous Crossroads: Popular Music, Postmodernism, and the Poetics of Place.* London: Verso, 1994.

Littlefield, Daniel F., Jr., and Lonnie E. Underhill. "Renaming the American Indian: 1890–1913." *American Studies* 12 (1971): 33–45.

Longacre, Joseph B., and James Herring, eds. *The National Portrait Gallery of Distinguished Americans.* 4 vols. Philadelphia: H. Perkins, 1834–39.

Long Lance, Chief Buffalo Child (Sylvester Long). *Long Lance.* 1928. Reprint, Jackson: University Press of Mississippi, 1995.

Lopez, Barry. *About This Life: Journeys on the Threshold of Memory.* New York: Knopf, 1998.

———. "Occupancy." *Orion* (spring 1995): n.p.

Lydon, Sandy. *The Japanese in the Monterey Bay Region: A Brief History.* Capitola CA: Capitola Books, 1997.

Lyman, Christopher M. *The Vanishing Race and Other Illusions: Photographs of Indians by Edward S. Curtis.* New York: Pantheon Books, in association with the Smithsonian Institution Press, 1982.

MacCannell, Dean. *Empty Meeting Grounds: The Tourist Papers.* London: Routledge, 1992.

Mandel, Eli. "Writing West: On the Road to Wood Mountain." In *Trace: Prairie Writers on Writing.* Ed. Birk Sproxton. Winnipeg: Turnstone, 1986. 39–53.

Marcus, George E., and Michael M. J. Fischer, eds. *Anthropology as Cultural Critique: An Experimental Moment in the Human Sciences.* Chicago: University of Chicago Press, 1986.

Marin, Louis. "Frontiers of Utopia: Past & Present." *Critical Inquiry* 19, no. 3 (spring 1993): 397–420.

McCourt, Edward. *The Canadian West in Fiction.* Rev. ed. Toronto: Ryerson Press, 1970.

McDermott, John Francis. *Seth Eastman: Pictorial Historian of the Indian.* Norman: University of Oklahoma Press, 1961.

McDonald, Dorothy Ritsuko, and Katherine Newman. "Relocation and Dislocation: The Writings of Hisaye Yamamoto and Wakako Yamauchi." In *Seventeen Syllables.* Ed. King-Kok Cheung. New Brunswick NJ: Rutgers University Press, 1994. 129–41.

McGee, Thomas D'Arcy. "Protection for Canadian Literature." In *Towards a Canadian Literature: Essays, Editorials, and Manifestos.* Ed. Douglas Daymond and Leslie Monkman. Ottawa: Tecumseh, 1985. 1:43–45.

M'Clung, John A. *Sketches of Western Adventure: Containing an Account of the Most Interesting Incidents Connected with the Settlement of the West, from 1755–1794.* 1832. Reprint, Dayton OH: L. F. Claflin, 1850.

McNaught, Kenneth. *The Penguin History of Canada*. Rev. ed. London: Penguin, 1988.

Meine, Curt, ed. *Wallace Stegner and the Continental Vision*. Washington: Island Press, 1997.

Mihesuah, Devon A. "Voices, Interpretations, and the 'New Indian History': Comment on the *American Indian Quarterly*'s Special Issue on Writing about American Indians." *American Indian Quarterly* 20, no. 1 (winter 1996): 91–108.

Miller, David C. "The Iconology of Wrecked or Stranded Boats in Nineteenth-Century American Culture." In *American Iconology*. Ed. David C. Miller. New Haven: Yale University Press, 1993. 186–208.

Miller, J. Hillis. *Illustration*. Cambridge: Harvard University Press, 1992.

Milner, Clyde, ed. *A New Significance: Re-Envisioning the History Of the American West*. New York: Oxford University Press, 1996.

Mitchell, Lee Clark. *Westerns: Making the Man in Fiction and Film*. Chicago: University of Chicago Press, 1996.

Mitchell, W.J.T. *Iconology: Image, Text, Ideology*. Chicago: University of Chicago Press, 1986.

Moffitt, John F., and Santiago Sebastian. *O Brave New People: The European Invention of the American Indian*. Albuquerque: University of New Mexico Press, 1996.

Momaday, N. Scott. *The Man Made of Words: Essays, Stories, Passages*. New York: St. Martin's, 1997.

Moore, David. "Introduction: Special Issue on Cultural Property." *American Indian Quarterly* 2, no. 4 (fall 1997): 545–54.

Moreland, Kim. *The Medievalist Impulse in American Literature: Twain, Adams, Fitzgerald and Hemingway*. Charlottesville: University Press of Virginia, 1996.

Morgan, Lewis Henry. *Ancient Society*. 1877. Reprint, Cambridge: Harvard University Press, 1964.

Murphy, John J. *My Ántonia: The Road Home*. Boston: G. K. Hall, 1989.

———, ed. *Critical Essays on Willa Cather*. Boston: G. K. Hall, 1984. Murray, Charles Augustus. *Travels in North America during the Years 1834, 1835, & 1836. Including a Summer Residence with the Pawnee Tribe of Indians, in the Remote Prairies of the Missouri, and a Visit to Cuba and the Azore Islands*. 2 vols. London: Richard Bentley, 1839.

Nelson, John Young. *Fifty Years on the Trail: A True Story of Western Life*. 1889. Reprint, Norman: University of Oklahoma Press, 1963.

Nemerov, Alexander. "Haunted Supermasculinity: Strength and Death in Carl Rungius's *Wary Game*." *American Art* 13 (fall 1999): 2–31.

Newall, Beaumont. *The History of Photography*. 4th ed. New York: Museum of Modern Art, 1981.

Newfield, Christopher. "The Politics of Male Suffering: Masochism and Hegemony in the American Renaissance." *Differences* 1, no. 3 (1989): 55–87.

Northrup, Jim. *Walking the Rez Road*. Stillwater MN: Voyageur Press, 1993.

Nygaard, Norman E. *Walter Knott: Twentieth Century Pioneer*. Grand Rapids MI: Zondervan Publishing House, 1965.

O'Brien, Sharon. *Willa Cather: The Emerging Voice*. New York: Oxford University Press, 1987.

Office of Indian Affairs. *Annual Report of the Commissioner of Indian Affairs*. Washington DC: GPO, 1905.

Okihiro, Gary. *Margins and Mainstreams: Asians in American History and Culture*. Seattle: University of Washington Press, 1994.

Okubo, Miné. *Citizen 13660*. 1946. Reprint, Seattle: University of Washington Press, 1983.

Owens, Louis. *Dark River*. Norman: University of Oklahoma Press, 1999.

———. "Introduction: Special Issue on Gerald Vizenor." *Studies in American Indian Literatures* 9, no. 1 (spring 1997): 1–2.

———. *Mixedblood Messages: Literature, Film, Family, Place*. Norman: University of Oklahoma Press, 1998.

———. *Other Destinies: Understanding the American Indian Novel*. Norman: University of Oklahoma Press, 1992.

Parker, Amos A. *Trip to the West and Texas, Comprising a Journey of Eight Thousand Miles, through New-York, Michigan, Illinois, Missouri, Louisiana and Texas, in the Autumn and Winter of 1834–5: Intersperced with Anecdotes, Incidents, and Observations*. Concord NH: White and Fisher, 1835.

Parker, Samuel. *Journal of an Exploring Tour Beyond the Rocky Mountains*. 1838. Reprint, Moscow ID: University of Idaho Press, 1990.

Parsons, Elsie Clews, ed. *American Indian Life*. 1922. Reprint, Lincoln: University of Nebraska Press, 1991.

Pattie, James O. *The Personal Narrative of James O. Pattie of Kentucky During an expedition from St. Louis, through the Vast Regions between That Place and the Pacific Ocean, and Thence Back through the City of Mexico to Vera Cruz, During Journeying of Six Years, etc.* Ed. Timothy Flint. 1833. Reprint, Cleveland: Arthur H. Clark, 1905.

344

Pearce, Roy Harvey. *Savagism and Civilization: A Study of the Indian and the American Mind*. Berkeley: University of California Press, 1988.

Peterson, Erik. "An Indian, An American: Ethnicity, Assimilation and Balance in Charles Eastman's *From the Deep Woods to Civilization*." *Studies in American Literatures* 4 (1992): 145–60.

Pollock, Sharon. *Walsh*. In *Modern Canadian Plays*. Ed. Jerry Wasserman. Vancouver: Talonbooks, 1993. 1:233–71.

Porter, Carolyn. *Seeing and Being: The Plight of the Participant Observer in Emerson, James, Adams, and Faulkner*. Middletown CT: Wesleyan University Press, 1981.

Porter, Frank W., III. *Strategies for Survival: American Indians in the Eastern United States*. New York: Greenwood, 1986.

Potyondi, Barry. *In Palliser's Triangle: Living in the Grasslands, 1850–1930*. Saskatoon: Purich, 1995.

Pratt, E. J. "Towards the Last Spike." In *Poets Between the Wars*. Ed. Milton Wilson. Toronto: McClelland and Stewart, 1966.

Pratt, Mary Louise. "Fieldwork in Common Places." In *Writing Culture*. Ed. James Clifford and George E. Marcus. Berkeley: University of California Press, 1986. 27–50.

————. *Imperial Eyes: Travel Writing and Transculturation*. New York: Routledge, 1992.

Pratt, Richard Henry. "The Advantages of Mingling Indians with Whites." In *Americanizing the American Indians*. Ed. Francis Prucha. Cambridge: Harvard University Press, 1973.

Price, Julie. "Undated Re-Print of Advertising Supplement H." Press release. *Discover Orange County (California): Daily News*, Nov. 29, year unspecified. Single page.

Purdy, John. "Crossroads: A Conversation with Sherman Alexie." *Studies in American Indian Literatures* 9, no. 4 (winter 1997): 1–18.

Quantic, Diane Dufva. "The Unifying Thread: Connecting Place and Language in Great Plains Literature." *American Studies* 32, no. 1 (1991): 67–83.

Radin, Paul. "Personal Reminiscences of a Winnebago Indian." *Journal of American Folklore* 26 (1913): 293–318.

Rankin, Charles E., ed. *Wallace Stegner: Man and Writer*. Albuquerque: University of New Mexico Press, 1986.

Remington, Frederic. "Policing the Yellowstone." In *The Collected Writings of Frederic Remington*. Ed. Peggy and Harold Samuels, Garden City NY: Doubleday, 1979. 169–75.

Reynolds, Guy. *Willa Cather in Context: Progress, Race, and Empire*. New York: St. Martin's, 1996.

Richards, I. A. *The Philosophy of Rhetoric*. New York: Oxford University Press, 1936.

Ricou, Laurie. *Vertical Man/Horizontal World: Man and Landscape in Canadian Prairie Fiction*. Vancouver: University of British Columbia Press, 1973.

Riley, Glenda. *Women and Nature: Saving the "Wild" West*. Lincoln: University of Nebraska Press, 1999.

Roberts, B. H. *A Comprehensive History of the Church*. 4 vols. Salt Lake City: Deseret News Press, 1930.

Robinson, Forrest G., ed. *The New Western History: The Territory Ahead*. Tucson: University of Arizona Press, 1997.

Rogers, Pattiann. *Firekeeper*. Minneapolis: Milkweed Editions, 1994.

Ronald, Ann. "Stegner and Stewardship." In *Wallace Stegner: Man and Writer*. Ed. Charles E. Rankin. Albuquerque: University of New Mexico Press, 1986. 87–103.

Rosaldo, Renato. *Culture and Truth: The Remaking of Social Analysis*. Boston: Beacon Press, 1989.

Rosowski, Susan J. *Birthing a Nation: Gender, Creativity, and the West in American Literature*. Lincoln: University of Nebraska Press, 1999.

Rowe, John Carlos. *Henry Adams and Henry James: The Emergence of a Modern Consciousness*. Ithaca: Cornell University Press, 1976.

———, ed. *New Essays on "The Education of Henry Adams."* New York: Cambridge University Press, 1996.

Runte, Alfred. *National Parks: The American Experience*. Lincoln: University of Nebraska Press, 1997.

Ruoff, A. LaVonne Brown. "American Indian Literature." In *A Literary History of the American West*. Fort Worth: Texas Christian University Press, 1987.

———. *American Indian Literatures*. New York: Modern Language Association, 1990.

Rusk, Ralph Leslie. *The Literature of the Middle Western Frontier*. 2 vols. New York: Columbia University Press, 1925.

Salinas Chamber of Commerce. "Survey of Attitudes of Salinas Citizens toward Japanese-Americans During World War II." R.979.476. Special Collections, John Steinbeck Library, Salinas, California.

Samuels, Ernest. *Henry Adams, The Major Phase*. Cambridge: Belknap Press of Harvard University Press, 1964.

———. *Henry Adams, The Middle Years*. Cambridge: Belknap Press of Harvard University Press, 1958.

———. *The Young Henry Adams*. Cambridge: Harvard University Press, 1948.

Samuels, Peggy, and Harold Samuels. *Frederic Remington: A Biography*. Austin: University of Texas Press, 1985.

Sandweiss, Martha A. "Undecisive Moments: The Narrative Tradition in Western Photography." In *Photography in Nineteenth-Century America*. Ed. Martha A. Sandweiss. New York: Harry N. Abrams, 1991.

———. "Views and Reviews: Western Art and Western History." *Under an Open Sky: Rethinking America's Western Past*. Ed. William Cronon, George Miles, and Jay Gitlin. New York: Norton, 1992.

Sapir, Edward. Foreword to *Son of Old Man Hat*, by Walter Dyk. New York: Harcourt, Brace, 1938.

Schama, Simon. *Landscape and Memory*. New York: Knopf, 1995.

Scheyer, Ernst. *The Circle of Henry Adams: Art and Artists*. Detroit: Wayne State University Press, 1970.

Scott, Marjorie. "History: Knott's Berry Farm." Pamphlet. Buena Park CA: Knott's Public Relations Department, date unspecified.

Sedgwick, Eve Kosofsky. *Between Men: English Literature and Male Homosocial Desire*. New York: Columbia University Press, 1985.

Sergeant, Elizabeth Shepley. *Willa Cather: A Memoir*. 1953. Reprint, Athens: Ohio University Press, 1992.

Silko, Leslie. "Here's an Odd Artifact for the Fairy Tale Shelf." *Studies in American Indian Literatures* 10, no. 4 (1986): 177–84.

Slotkin, Richard. *Regeneration Through Violence: The Mythology of the American Frontier*. Middletown CT: Wesleyan University Press, 1973.

Slovic, Scott. "A Paint Brush in One Hand and a Bucket of Water in the Other: Nature Writing and the Politics of Wilderness. An Interview with Rick Bass." *Weber Studies* 11, no. 3 (fall 1994): 11–29.

Smith, Donald B. *Chief Buffalo Child Long Lance: The Glorious Imposter*. Red Deer AB: Red Deer Press, 1999.

———. *Long Lance: The True Story of an Imposter*. 1982. Reprint, Lincoln: University of Nebraska Press, 1983.

Snyder, Gary. *Turtle Island*. New York: New Directions, 1974.

Society of American Indians. *Report of the Executive Council on the Proceedings of the First Annual Conference of the Society of American Indians, 1912*. Washington DC, 1912.

347

Soja, Edward W. *Thirdspace: Journeys to Los Angeles and Other Real-and-Imagined Places.* Cambridge: Blackwell, 1996.

Sone, Monica. *Nisei Daughter.* Seattle: University of Washington Press, 1953.

Sontag, Susan. *On Photography.* New York: Delta, 1977.

Sorkin, Michael. "See You in Disneyland." *Variations on a Theme Park.* Ed. Michael Sorkin. New York: Farrar, Straus & Giroux, 1992. 205–32.

Splete, Allen P., and Marilyn D. Splete. *Frederic Remington—Selected Letters.* New York: Abbeville Press, 1988.

Stafford, Barbara Maria. *Good Looking: Essays on the Virtue of Images.* Cambridge: MIT Press, 1996.

———. *Visual Analogy: Consciousness as the Art of Connecting.* Cambridge: MIT Press, 1999.

Standing Bear, Luther. *My People the Sioux.* Lincoln: University of Nebraska Press, 1975.

Stegner, Wallace. *Beyond the Hundredth Meridian: John Wesley Powell and the Second Opening of the West.* New York: Viking Penguin, 1992.

———. "Conservation Equals Survival." *Crossroads.* Ed. Tom E. Kakonis and James C. Wilcox. Lexington MA: D. C. Heath, 1972.

———. *One Way to Spell Man.* Garden City NJ: Doubleday, 1982.

———. *The Sound of Mountain Water.* Lincoln: University of Nebraska Press, 1985.

———. *This Is Dinosaur: Echo Park and Its Magic Rivers.* New York: Knopf, 1955.

———. *Where the Bluebird Sings to the Lemonade Springs: Living and Writing in the West.* New York: Penguin, 1992.

Stegner, Wallace, and Page Stegner. *American Places.* Moscow ID: University of Idaho Press, 1983.

Stewart, George R. *Names on the Land: A Historical Account of Place-Naming in the United States.* New York: Random House, 1945.

Stocking, George W. *Race, Culture and Evolution: Essays in the History of Anthropology.* New York: Free Press, 1968.

Stout, David. "No Place for John Wayne at Indian Bureau." *New York Times,* 22 Sept. 2000.

Stout, Janis P. *Strategies of Reticence: Silence and Meaning in the Works of Jane Austen, Willa Cather, Katherine Anne Porter, and Joan Didion.* Charlottesville: University Press of Virginia, 1990.

Szasz, Margaret Connell. *Between Indian and White Worlds: The Cultural Broker.* Norman: University of Oklahoma Press, 1994.

Tagg, John. *The Burden of Representation: Essays on Photographies and Histories.* 1988. Reprint, Minneapolis: University of Minnesota Press, 1993.

Tehan, Arline Boucher. *Henry Adams in Love: The Pursuit of Elizabeth Sherman Cameron.* New York: Universe Books, 1983.

Thacker, Robert. "Erasing the Forty-Ninth Parallel: Nationalism, Prairie Criticism, and the Case of Wallace Stegner." *Essays on Canadian Writing* 61 (1997): 179–202.

———. *The Great Prairie Fact and Literary Imagination.* Albuquerque: University of New Mexico Press, 1989.

Thoreau, Henry David. *Walden.* New York: Time Inc. Book Division, 1962.

———. *Walden; or, Life in the Woods.* New York: Library of America, 1985.

Tilton, Robert S. *Pocahontas: The Evolution of an American Narrative.* New York: Cambridge University Press, 1994.

Tompkins, Jane. *West of Everything: The Inner Life of Westerns.* New York: Oxford University Press, 1992.

Townsend, Kim. *Manhood at Harvard: William James and Others.* New York: W. W. Norton, 1996.

Trachtenberg, Alan. *Reading American Photographs.* New York: Hill and Wang, 1989.

Turner, Frederick Jackson. *Rereading Frederick Jackson Turner: "The Significance of the Frontier in American History" and Other Essays.* Commentary by John Mack Faragher. New York: Henry Holt, 1994.

———. *The Significance of the Frontier in American History.* Ed. Harold P. Simonson. New York: Ungar, 1963.

———. "The Significance of the Frontier in American History." In *The Frontier in American History.* Tucson: University of Arizona Press, 1986. 1–38.

Twain, Mark. *The Adventures of Tom Sawyer.* New York: Oxford University Press, 1996.

Uchida, Yoshiko. *Desert Exile: The Uprooting of a Japanese-American Family.* Seattle: University of Washington Press, 1982.

———. *The Invisible Thread.* Englewood Cliffs NJ: Julian Messner, 1991.

Van den Abbeele, Georges. "Sightseers: The Tourist as Theorist." *diacritics* 10, no. 4 (winter 1980): 3–14.

Vanderhaeghe, Guy. *The Englishman's Boy.* Toronto: McClelland and Stewart, 1996.

Van Doren, Mark, ed. *Travels of William Bartram.* New York: Dover, 1928.

Van Herk, Aritha. "A Gentle Circumcision." In *A Frozen Tongue.* Sydney: Dangaroo, 1992. 90–99.

Vizenor, Gerald. *Fugitive Poses: Native American Indian Scenes of Absence and Presence*. Lincoln: University of Nebraska Press, 1998.

——. *Manifest Manners: Postindian Warriors of Survivance*. Hanover: University Press of New England, 1994.

——. "On Thin Ice, You Might as Well Dance." In *Some Other Frequency: Interviews with Innovative American Authors*. Ed. Larry McCaffery. Philadelphia: University of Pennsylvania Press, 1996.

Vorpahl, Ben Merchant. *My Dear Wister: The Frederic Remington–Owen Wister Letters*. Palo Alto: American West, 1972.

Wagner, Vern. *The Suspension of Henry Adams: A Study of Manner and Matter*. Detroit: Wayne State University Press, 1969.

Wald, Gayle. *Crossing the Line: Racial Passing in Twentieth-Century U.S. Literature and Culture*. Durham: Duke University Press, 2000.

Walker, Don D. "Can the Western Tell What Happens?" In *Interpretive Approaches to Western American Literature*. Ed. Daniel Alkofer et al. Pocatello: Idaho State University Press, 1972. 33–47.

Ward, Geoffrey C. *The West*. Boston: Little, Brown, 1996.

Wardhaugh, Robert, ed. *Toward Defining the Prairies*. Winnipeg: University of Manitoba Press, 2001.

Waterman, Bryan. "'Awaiting Translation': Timothy Liu, Identity Politics, and the Question of Religious Authenticity." *Dialogue: A Journal of Mormon Thought* 30, no. 1 (spring 1997): 159–76.

Weglyn, Michi Nishiru. *Years of Infamy: The Untold Story of America's Concentration Camps*. Seattle: University of Washington Press, 1976.

Wexler, Laura. *Tender Violence: Domestic Visions in an Age of U.S. Imperialism*. Chapel Hill: University of North Carolina Press, 2000.

White, G. Edward. *The Eastern Establishment and the Western Experience: The West of Frederick Remington, Theodore Roosevelt, and Owen Wister*. New Haven: Yale University Press, 1968.

White, Lynn, Jr. "The Historical Roots of Our Ecologic Crisis." Address to the American Association for the Advancement of Science, 26 December 1966.

Wiebe, Rudy. "Passage By Land." In *The Narrative Voice: Short Stories and Reflections by Canadian Authors*. Ed. John Metcalf. Toronto: McGraw-Hill Ryerson, 1972. 257–60.

Wilkinson, Charles F. *The Eagle Bird: Mapping a New West*. New York: Pantheon, 1992.

Will, Barbara. "The Nervous Origins of the Western." *American Literature* 70 (June 1998): 293–316.

Williams, Terry Tempest. "Bloodlines." In *Testimony: Writers of the West Speak on Behalf of Utah Wilderness.* Ed. Stephen Trimble and Terry Tempest Williams. Minneapolis: Milkweed Editions, 1996.

———. "A Man of Questions: A Tribute to Wallace Stegner, April 12, 1996." *Journal of Land, Resources, and Environmental Law* 17, no. 1 (1997): 1–7.

———. *Pieces of White Shell: A Journey to Navajoland.* New York: Scribner's, 1984.

———. *Refuge: An Unnatural History of Family and Place.* New York: Vintage, 1991.

Williams, William Carlos. *In the American Grain.* Norfolk CT: New Directions, 1940.

Wilson, Michael. "Speaking of Home: The Idea of the Center in Some Contemporary American Indian Writing." *Wicazo Sa Review* 12, no. 1 (spring 1997): 129–47.

Wilson, Raymond. *Ohiyesa: Charles Eastman, Santee Sioux.* Urbana: University of Illinois Press, 1983.

Wind, Wabun. *Woman of the Dawn: A Spiritual Odyssey.* New York: Prentice Hall, 1989.

Wister, Owen. *The Virginian: A Horseman of the Plains.* 1902. Reprint, New York: Macmillan, 1955.

Wolf, Bryan Jay. *Romantic Re-Vision: Culture and Consciousness in Nineteenth-Century American Painting.* Chicago: University of Chicago Press, 1982.

Womack, Craig S. *Red on Red: Native American Literary Separatism.* Minneapolis: University of Minnesota Press, 1999.

Wong, Hertha Dawn. *Sending My Heart Back Across the Years: Tradition and Innovation in Native American Autobiography.* New York: Oxford University Press, 1992.

Woodmansee, Martha. "On the Author Effect: Recovering Collectivity." In *The Construction of Authorship: Textual Appropriation in Law and Literature.* Ed. Martha Woodmansee and Peter Jaszi. Durham NC: Duke University Press, 1994. 15–28.

Woodress, James. *Willa Cather: A Literary Life.* Lincoln: University of Nebraska Press, 1987.

Wyckoff, William. *Creating Colorado: The Making of a Western American Landscape, 1860–1940.* New Haven: Yale University Press, 1999.

Wyile, Herb. "Regionalism, Postcolonialism, and (Canadian) Writing: A Comparative Approach for Postnational Times." *Essays on Canadian Writing* 63 (1998): 139–61.

Yamada, Mitsuye. *Camp Notes and Other Poems.* 1976. Reprint, Latham NY: Kitchen Table/Women of Color Press, 1992.

Zeki, Semir. *Inner Vision: An Exploration of Art and the Brain.* New York: Oxford University Press, 1999.

Ziff, Bruce, and Pratima V. Rao, eds. *Borrowed Power: Essays on Cultural Appropriation.* New Brunswick NJ: Rutgers University Press, 1997.

Žižek, Slavoj. *The Plague of Fantasies.* London: Verso, 1997.

———. *The Sublime Object of Ideology.* London: Verso, 1989.

CONTRIBUTORS

Christine Edwards Allred earned her Ph.D. in English at UCLA. Currently Preceptor of Expository Writing at Harvard University, she is at work on a book investigating the representation of American Indian cultures in popular magazines at the turn of the twentieth century.

Susan Bernardin is Assistant Professor of English at SUNY College at Oneonta, where she teaches American Indian, American, and postcolonial literatures. Her publications include articles on foundational and contemporary Native writers as well as book projects focusing on narrative and visual accounts of cross-cultural encounters in northwestern California. She is a co-author of *Trading Gazes: Euro-American Women Photographers and Native North Americans, 1880–1940* (Rutgers University Press, 2003). Currently, she is restoring the complete text of *In the Land of the Grasshopper Song: Two Women in Klamath River Indian Country, 1908–09*, in collaboration with regional and tribal historians and with the University of Nebraska Press.

Joanna Brooks is Assistant Professor of English at the University of Texas at Austin. She is co-editor with John Saillant of *Face Zion Forward: First Writers of the Black Atlantic, 1785–1797* (Northeastern University Press, 2002) and author of *American Lazarus: Religion and the Rise of African-American and Native American Literatures* (Oxford University Press, 2003).

Alison Calder is Assistant Professor of English at the University of Manitoba, where she teaches Canadian literature and creative writing. She has been a Social Sciences and Humanities Research Council of Canada postdoctoral fellow at the University of Calgary and a distinguished junior scholar in residence at the Peter Wall Institute for Advanced Studies at the University of British Columbia. In addition to articles on Guy Vanderhaeghe, Sharon Butala, and Sky Lee, she has published essays on environmental determinism in the criticism of Canadian prairie writing, prairie realism, regionalism, and prairie self-representations in popular culture.

Nancy Cook is Associate Professor of English at the University of Rhode Island and has taught at the University of Montana. Her publications include essays on the Great Plains, Thomas McGuane, Josiah Gregg, Mark Twain, and on Long Lance's role in the 1930 film *Silent Enemy*. She is at work on a book, *The American West and the Politics of Inscription*.

353

Melody Graulich is Professor of English and American Studies at Utah State University and Editor of *Western American Literature*. She is the editor of *Exploring Lost Borders: Critical Essays on Mary Austin* (1999) and of *Yellow Woman* (a collection of essays on Leslie Silko's "Yellow Woman"), and she has also edited editions of Austin's *Cactus Thorn* and *Earth Horizon*. Graulich has published widely, including numerous essays on such topics as western women writers, Wallace Stegner, Leslie Silko, and feminism.

William R. Handley is Associate Professor of English at the University of Southern California and has also taught at Harvard University. He has published articles on Zane Grey, Virginia Woolf, and Toni Morrison, among other topics. His first book is *Marriage, Violence, and the Nation in the American Literary West* (Cambridge University Press, 2002), a study of how novelists retrospectively imagine western significance in the twentieth century through scenes of alienated domesticity.

Hsuan L. Hsu is a Ph.D. candidate at the University of California at Berkeley, where he studies geography and nineteenth-century U.S. literature. His writing has appeared in *Nineteenth-Century Studies*, *Early American Literature*, *American Quarterly*, and *Arizona Quarterly*. He is also coediting an essay collection on geography and American literature before 1888.

Nathaniel Lewis is Associate Professor of English and Co-Director of the American Studies program at Saint Michael's College in Vermont. A past member of the Western Literature Association's executive council, he is the author of numerous publications on western American literature, including *Unsettling the Literary West* (University of Nebraska Press, 2003).

Bonney MacDonald is Associate Professor of English at Union College in Schenectady, New York, where she teaches American literature. The author of *Henry James's Italian Hours: Revelatory and Resistant Impressions*, she has also written numerous articles on Hamlin Garland and western literature, which have appeared in journals such as *Western American Literature* and in the anthology *Updating the Literary West*.

Lisa MacFarlane is Professor of English and Coordinator of the American Studies program at the University of New Hampshire. Her publications include *Trading Gazes: Euro-American Women Photographers, 1880–1940* (Rutgers

University Press, 2003), coauthored with Susan Bernardin, Melody Graulich, and Nicole Tonkovich, the Penguin Classics edition of Henry Adams's *Esther*, and essays and collections on nineteenth-century American writers, race, and religion. She is the lead editor of the University Press of New England's Revisiting New England series.

Scott Slovic, who served as the founding president of the Association for the Study of Literature and Environment (ASLE) from 1992 to 1995, has written, edited, or co-edited nine books, including *Seeking Awareness in American Nature Writing* and, most recently, *Getting Over the Color Green: Contemporary Environmental Literature of the Southwest* and *The ISLE Reader: Ecocriticism, 1993–2003*. He is Professor of Literature and Environment at the University of Nevada, Reno, where he also currently directs the English department's graduate program in literature and environment. He edits the journal *ISLE: Interdisciplinary Studies in Literature and Environment*, Milkweed Editions's Credo series, and the University of Nevada Press's Environmental Arts and Humanities series.

Stephen Tatum teaches American literature and culture courses in the English department at the University of Utah. His recent publications include *Cormac McCarthy's All the Pretty Horses: A Reader's Guide* (2002) and the co-edited (with Melody Graulich) volume of essays *Reading "The Virginian" in the New West* (University of Nebraska Press, 2003). "Animal Calling/Calling Animal" is part of a book manuscript in progress with the working title "Dwelling in the Remington Moment."

Gerald Vizenor is a novelist, essayist, and Professor of Native American literature and American Studies at the University of California, Berkeley. The recipient of numerous prizes and honors, he is the author and editor of more than twenty books. His works include *Shadow Distance: A Gerald Vizenor Reader*, *Bearheart: The Heirship Chronicles*, and *Narrative Chance: Postmodern Discourse on Native American Literatures*. His most recent publications are *Fugitive Poses: Native American Scenes of Absence and Presence*, *Manifest Manners: Narratives on Postindian Survivance*, *Chancers*, and *Postindian Conversations* (with A. Robert Lee).

Drucilla Mims Wall is a poet, essayist, lecturer, and Ph.D. candidate in English at the University of Nebraska–Lincoln. Her poetry has appeared in

355

Cream City Review, Kalliope, Red River Review, and in the anthologies *Who Stayed Behind: Southeastern Indian Writing after Removal* and *Times of Sorrow/Times of Grace: Writing by Women of the Great Plains/High Plains*. Her essays have appeared in *Eighteenth-Century Life* and elsewhere. Recipient of numerous fellowships and awards, Wall has also presented papers and performed creative readings exploring Native American and Irish writing and identity. She is of Alabama Creek (Muscogee) descent.

INDEX

Page references in **bold** indicate a drawing or photograph.

In the POSTWESTERN HORIZONS series

True West:
Authenticity and the American West
Edited by William R. Handley and Nathaniel Lewis

Unsettling the Literary West:
Authenticity and Authorship
By Nathaniel Lewis